The Network Experience

Peter H.M. Vervest • Diederik W. van Liere
Li Zheng

The Network Experience

New Value from Smart Business Networks

 Springer

Prof. Dr. Peter H.M. Vervest
Rotterdam School of Management
Erasmus University Rotterdam
Burgemeester Oudlaan 50
3000 DR Rotterdam
T9-03
The Netherlands
e-mail: vervest@d-age.com

Dr. Diederik W. van Liere
Rotterdam School of Management
Erasmus University Rotterdam
Burgemeester Oudlaan 50
3000 DR Rotterdam
T9-14
The Netherlands
e-mail: dliere@rsm.nl

Prof. Dr. Li Zheng
Tsinghua University
Dept. of Industrial Engineering
100084 Beijing
China
e-mail: lzheng@mail.tsinghua.edu.cn

ISBN: 978-3-540-85580-4   e-ISBN: 978-3-540-85582-8
DOI: 10.1007/978-3-540-85582-8

Library of Congress Control Number: 2008933366

Cover design: WMX Design GmbH, Heidelberg, Germany

Printed on acid-free paper

9 8 7 6 5 4 3 2 1

springer.com

Preface: The Process Challenge

To lead in this business environment is to embrace change. The modern firm must be highly flexible and able to change its business strategy very quickly. Traditionally it has taken enterprises up to 2 years to change their strategy, while the human structural organization of the enterprise traditionally changes every 3 to 6 months. But now enterprises must be able to change faster to meet this required speed of strategic and organizational change. However, the back-end information and communications systems that are needed to facilitate and enable such change are not readily available to the business. Underlying enterprise legacy software has proved to be difficult to integrate. It is a nightmare to change the infrastructure built on such complex integrations. Traditionally it has taken between 6 and 10 years to modernize such infrastructure. To resolve this gap between lagging infrastructure and the required rapid strategic change, as well as to speed the time for business to take action on this strategy, a business process layer is required between the current crop of planning tools used by the business and their existing related back-end communications systems. At Cordys we call this business process layer the Cordys Business Operations Platform, a platform that facilitates instant deployment of strategic business change.

A key question of this book is why organizations should, and how they can, build such a Business Operations Platform, thereby enabling true business agility. Implementing the Business Operations Platform allows the business leaders of the enterprise to design, build, and rapidly deploy executable business processes directly from those designs. In the early 1990s most business leaders did not appreciate or even understand the rapidly emerging communications revolution driven by the Internet and the wireless mobile world. The impact of the Internet has been, and will continue to be, profound. We now know that the successful organization must operate in a world of the Internet, quickly find business partners and rapidly link business processes across that network. The company must provide customized services for use in its market place from generic components in ever-changing business setups with business partners. How should companies work together in networks – and what should they do particularly well, or differently? This is the intriguing challenge for today's business success: It is no longer about business process reengineering; it is about business *network* (re)engineering, which is the main thrust of this book.

From my viewpoint as a provider of one of the leading technologies for the modern networked world, this meeting of scholars and business professionals was pleasant and fascinating. It was particularly rewarding. I have learned that most of an organization's processes are generic and commonly found in almost all businesses, so there is little to gain from doing-it-yourself: There is much more to gain from outsourcing shared services in a dynamic business network, allowing the company to dedicate its resources to those business processes that make it stand out, that differentiate it from its competitors, and provide its partners with easy interfaces for doing business together with the enterprise. This will be the great transition for the coming decade: Networked organizations that, through sharing of business processes, become highly efficient and agile, thereby facilitating a combination of a multitude of business and social networks to mutual advantage. In this book you will find the critical ideas for what you should do particularly well to win as a networked company.

Jan Baan
Founder and Chief Executive Officer
Cordys

Preface: The Business Challenge

Zurich Financial Services must take advantage of the increasing challenges its fast moving business environment presents. For some the insurance industry may seem a fairly traditional business sector, which adheres to strict governance and compliance rules to protect its competitive insurance knowledge. The reality is that the communication patterns within society are having a significant impact on our business. In recent times we have experienced a strong trend towards social and business networks: Our customers are highly influenced by the networking trend, with individuals in both personal and professional capacities connecting with one another, becoming more self-aware and forming active interest groups. For us it means that we must continue to change our mindsets. We must keep moving forward and not just hold on to the old ways of doing things.

The network approach enables us to open up our silos of knowledge and leverage the intelligence of the network to the benefit of our customers and ourselves. This sounds like a daunting prospect but, if you aim to be excellent in execution, it becomes a competitive advantage. For example, consider our sales and customer service operations: An increasing number of customers want and are capable of self-service; they are not prepared to pay extra for administration or claims notification if they do not need or want to use it. Our future customers want to pick what they need from our product offerings and compose their own insurance products. Our value chain must enable this: A future direction for the networked insurance business is that modular products are offered in a global web as a new way to create value.

At the SBN2008 meeting in Beijing, it was impressive to see that this networking trend is developing even faster in an emerging market like China. Network thinking seems deeply embedded in the behavior of Chinese companies: This might give them interesting commercial opportunities as they enter the Western business world.

The Smart Business Networks Initiative (SBNi) supports us in determining our journey from an integrated institution to a flexible network orchestrator. Academic research on business networking tools, methods and practice is giving us essential insights to effect this transformation. As we operate on a global scale, SBNi as orchestrator of the best-in-class network of academics from top universities from around the world is uniquely placed to assist us.

Theo Bouts
Chief Executive Officer
Direct and Partnership Europe General Insurance
Zurich Financial Services Group

Preface: The Academic Challenge

As a leading business school it is our duty at Rotterdam School of Management to continually look out for new developments and try to identify the beginnings of business and managerial innovation. We must connect with many different academic disciplines and uncover the gems for new business practice and theory. For this reason I applaud the Smart Business Networks Initiative for bringing academics together with business practitioners to identify new directions for managerial study.

The organizers of SBN 2008 Beijing chose the right theme: Business networks! It deserves an impact at least equal to that of business process reengineering (BPR). In 1993 Michael Hammer and James Champy[1] in their book "*Reengineering the Corporation*" claimed: "For two hundred years people have founded and built companies around Adam Smith's brilliant discovery that industrial work should be broken down into the simplest and most basic *tasks*. In the post-industrial business age we are now entering, corporations will be founded and built around the idea of reunifying those tasks into coherent business *processes*".

Let me build on that: For the past twenty years very capable managers have founded and built corporations around the information industry's discovery that information work should be broken down into the simplest and most basic processes. In the post-information business age that we are now entering, corporations will be founded and built on the idea of unifying those processes into coherent business networks.

The organizers chose the right venue: Beijing, the exciting capital of China, combines past and future as it undergoes substantial change and enormous development. This was manifest in the Beijing Olympics, 2008. Similarly, business schools should aim to bring together academic athletes from different disciplines: An academic Olympics where business leaders can learn of the important new ideas from research. Innovation emerges from such confrontation and questioning: Smart networks of knowledge!

Prof. Dr. George Yip
Dean
Rotterdam School of Management
Erasmus University Rotterdam

---

[1] Hammer, M., Champy, J. (1993), *Reengineering the Corporation - a Manifesto for Business Revolution*, Harper Collins, New York

Table of Contents

Setting the Scene

1. The Network Experience – New Value from Smart Business Networks

Peter H.M. Vervest[1] and Li Zheng[2]

[1] Rotterdam School of Management, Erasmus University Rotterdam, The Netherlands,
pvervest@rsm.nl

[2] Department of Industrial Engineering, Tsinghua University, Beijing, China,
lzheng@mail.tsinghua.edu.cn

Introduction: Beijing, 18–23 May 2008

This introduction gives an overview of the Discovery Event *"The Network Experience – New Value from Smart Business Networks"*, Beijing, 18–23 May 2008, it presents the background, the objectives, the programme organisation, the structure of the book and a readers guide. In addition, we pay tribute to the many people who helped to make the event an unforgettable experience for all who could join.

The Starting Points

Business networks rather than individual companies are now determining competitive advantage. Organisations and companies combining in agile and dynamic networks are able to generate exceptional or "smart" results. Smart business networks (SBNs) enable new ways for organisations to derive value from the combination of many individual organisations which, grouped as a network, are able to compete more effectively and respond with more agility to a changing world. The rapid advances of digital networks are creating and demanding new organics – the ways in which organisations combine and act to generate sustainable growth and profit.

In the industrial times of Marx and Taylor, the main source of growth and profit was provided by production facilities with coordinated processes in a single location (a factory or department store). Then, with improvements in communication, the coordination of processes within and between linked organisations in the supply chain provided the better margins.

We are now witnessing the emergence of smart business networks enabling dynamic and agile relationships between companies. Acting as nodes in the network, suppliers, customers, business partners and competitors combine to generate "smart" results enabled by "smart" technologies. Companies are beginning

P.H.M. Vervest et al. (eds.) *The Network Experience*
© Springer-Verlag Berlin Heidelberg 2009

to understand that skills in managing dynamic networks can provide more profit and greater competitive advantage than a single facility or supply chain can.

The Challenge

The individual company will no longer lie at the hub of its business network. It must participate in many technology-enabled business and social networks. Rather than acting in near-to-static value chains, dynamic process paths will connect the business network participants. To achieve this the business processes of each participant must connect quickly and effectively. To be able to participate, the business processes of all network players will need to be compatible and information needs to be portable. This is a formidable challenge!

For instance, how does one define atomic modules of processes that plug and play seamlessly within and between companies? How does one develop and implement them? How can consensus be attained? How does one manage a network of processes effectively as well as efficiently?

Companies recognise these issues but lack the benefit of a body of research and experience to underpin their actions. Academic researchers are now beginning to define relevant research topics and to provide answers and guidelines.

Taking this challenge, this book presents the results of an intense gathering of academics and business people, in Beijing, discussing and interacting to try to find answers.

Background: The Smart Business Network Initiative

On invitation of Cordys and Rotterdam School of Management, a group of international academics met for the first time in 2004 at the castle The Vanenburg, The Netherlands.[1] Cordys is a prime provider of Business Process Management software. Based on its founder's longstanding and highly respectable experience in enterprise software, in particular enterprise resource planning software (ERP), Cordys believes that the future organisation will become "process centric" and will operate in a flexible network of business partners that co-operate and execute parts of the processes among themselves. A business operating platform is required that enables the flexibility needed in tomorrow's agile world.

---

[1] See the results published in: Vervest, van Heck, Preiss and Pau (2005) and Vervest, van Heck, Preiss and Pau (2004).

The key question discussed in 2004 was the shape of the future organization that is increasingly "being networked": What would be really different and what must companies do particularly well, or differently, in this new world of networks?

The Vision for Smart Business Networks

The new competitive business model will be founded on delivering smart outcomes by rapidly configuring effective capabilities from a network of organisations and people.
Smart networks will cooperate and compete to fulfil customer needs in a more effective and efficient way: competitive advantage will be created by the network rather than by the individual organisation. Smartness will be enabled by accelerating the network's ability to combine and act.

Intelligence will be embedded in the smart business network – captured in a *business operating system* which coordinates the processes among the networked organisations.
Winning organisations will grasp and act on the immediate and growing possibilities of smart business networking by identifying the real business opportunities with a thorough understanding of the science.

We continued to work on the issues across the globe; we met many new scholars and shared our views. We also discussed many business peoples' views: How they saw this new world of networks and what they felt was important. We asked if they want to join a co-operative research programme. We met as a group for the second time in June 2006. At that meeting we laid down the foundations of what subsequently developed as the Smart Business Network Initiative ("SBNi") (www.sbniweb.org) founded in 2006.[2]

The Smart Business Network Initiative (SBNi) Mission

SBNi is the not-for-profit catalyst and coordinator of a collaborative network of enterprises, governmental organisations and universities committed to identifying, researching, sharing and acting on the concepts and capabilities of smart business networks.

The third gathering took place in Beijing, from 18 to 23 May 2008. The event was hosted excellently by Tsinghua University, Beijing, ranked as a leading university in China. Taking place in the year of the Beijing Olympics the meeting gave the participants the opportunity to be involved in the excitement and dynamics of a rapidly developing China.

---

[2] The second event was published in Vervest, van Heck and Preiss (2008).

The Programme: The Network Experience

The Objectives and Programme Design

The overriding objective of the Beijing meeting was to extend the frontiers of knowledge in this essential and challenging field of smart business networks. As a result we described the meeting as a "discovery event" rather than a conference, seminar or workshop. We invited qualified senior "SBNi scholars" with one or two of their PhD students coming from different fields such as information systems, telecommunications engineering, social network analysis, complex systems theory, management strategy and organisational development.

We also invited people from practice: Business executives and organisational leaders such as chief information officers, marketing, organisation, business development and strategy executives and other business and organisational professionals.

We asked the academics to prepare a paper which was formally peer-reviewed prior to the event. Only the best or most original contributions, selected by the Programme Committee, were invited to present in Beijing. These papers have been assessed publicly during the event by a dedicated reviewer. They were presented and discussed in focused sessions. Rapporteurs recorded each session and presented the results to the plenary convention.

We asked business participants to prepare and present a brief position paper on selected themes. Business people presented a range of topics. Cordys gave two very interesting presentations on Business Process Management. Zurich Financial Services presented business development challenges in the insurance world. Electronic business development in China was presented by Tsinghua School of Economics and Management and Tsinghua University's Head of Department of Automation. Thebigword explained how their massive international network of individual professionals provides translation services to large customers. The BT Group presented the development and implication of their next generation IP networks replacing their current telecommunication infrastructures. Alibaba described the success and challenges of a Chinese e-business platform; Elsevier China gave the experiences and challenges of managing science and technology publishing in China. The challenges and issues in managing the logistics network for the Beijing Olympics 2008 were presented by one of Tsinghua's professors who is a member of the Olympics organising committee.

Each presentation was assessed on relevance for the development of our understanding of smart business networks: What is new, what is different and what can we learn? Is this a new approach; does this deserve special tools and methods to do the research? What can academic research contribute? What can be the impact on business?

Developing the programme has been a challenge: We brought academics and business people together, from many different parts of the world, with clearly different objectives. The academics would put the "why" question: The rigour of the methodology, the contribution to theory. The business audience asked the "how" question: The relevance of the topic and the contribution to tomorrow's success. Academic presentations would not always live up to the expectations of the business person and at times they would be disappointed if an academic presentation was not instantly understandable, or applicable, to their world of today. Some had to be reminded that the networked world has been underpinned by the achievements of academics who designed the Internet protocols and the browser programmes of the World Wide Web.

Business Meets Science

The programme was divided into two parts: The first part focused on the academic contribution: *Business meets Science*. This was the academic part including the academic presentations, reviews and evaluations. In this book, selected papers have been grouped in four tracks:

- *Network Essentials*: Papers essential for understanding methodology development and theory building in smart business networks.
- *Networks in Action*: Leading examples and practical cases of smart business networks with sound analysis methods and implications for empirical research.
- *Networks Enablers*: Tools and techniques available or under development that enable smartness in business networks. Network enablers include software tools and process languages as well as standards and protocols.
- *Network Orchestration*: The orchestration of cooperation in business networks – governance, conflict resolution and the allocation of risks and rewards. Many papers dealt with this important topic which is not always straightforward, in non-hierarchical networks.

We invited keynote speeches on specific topics:

- Dr. Yuhong Li, Director of Tsinghua University Office of International Affairs, and Mr. Siebe Schuur, the Dutch Economic Consul in China opened the event and introduced the basics of networks and business in China.
- Prof. Guoqing Chen, Executive Associate Dean of Tsinghua University's School of Economics and Management and Chair Professor of Information Systems, introduced Tsinghua's School of Economics and Management and presented his views on the development of e-business in China, in particular from an information systems viewpoint.
- Jon Pyke, Chief Strategy Officer, Cordys Company, a well-known specialist and industry leader in business process management, spoke about the process challenges in the end-to-end management of business processes with execution taking place across a network of business partners.

- Theo Bouts, Chief Executive Officer, Direct & Partnership Business, Zürich Financial Services, presented the challenges of "networked insurance" and the cooperative research – the "Being Networked" programme – with the universities combined in the Smart Business Network Initiative.
- Prof. Yueting Chai, Professor of Automation, Tsinghua University, Head of the Chinese Government National eBusiness Research Center. On his behalf, Dr. Hao Sun spoke on the experiences with e-business in China showing the specific approaches and different solutions.
- Gerrit Schipper, Chief Executive Officer, RDC, The Netherlands, presented his business experience in developing a smart business network and his views for future directions.
- Nicola Carmyllie, General Manager of *thebigword* translation services company, China – a key example of a smart business network – hosted one of the dinners and challenged our understanding of the business issues around operating a network of thousands of linguists working together to deliver professional services to demanding customers.

The Experience Tour

The second part of the programme was called the *Experience Tour*. We visited a number of companies; others joined us to give presentations. We had intense discussions on what our smart business networking thinking could contribute to real-life business issues. It was a learning expedition for all concerned. It has given some very valuable insights in the networked world and the new ways of generating value. It helped to initiate the development of a common framework for research and the SBN business agenda. Experience Tour speakers included:

- Curtis Eubanks, General Manager, BT Group, Dalian, China, who spoke about the development of networks in practice, experiences in China, and the BT view on how business can use networking technologies as well as networking methodologies in a smart way.
- Dr. Liang Lu, Senior Director Research and Development, Alibaba, who made us understand not only the enormous success of the Alibaba Group, but more precisely how it is done and how it is different from the commonly known American equivalent, eBay.
- Sharon Ruwart, Managing Director Elsevier Publishers, China, presented Elsevier's experiences in China in respect of science and technology publishing and gave her views on how networks impact their business.
- Tsinghua University has delegated a number of its professors and experts to the committee for the preparation and organisation of the Beijing Olympics. Dr. Adrian Guo, Asset Management Manager, Beijing Olympic Logistics Center, presented the logistical network and his view on "networks and organising".

- Jan Baan, founder and Chief Executive Officer, Cordys Company, summed up the week brilliantly and put the development of process management and business networks in an industrial historical context.
- Nico Barito, Senior Fellow and Director of the United Nations Institute for Training and Research, spoke on training and research issues in a global world; and specifically what UNITAR's views are on assisting the research into networks and SBNs.

We were also introduced to some of the latest technologies that help organisational networks becoming smart at IBM's Beijing Innovation Centre and Tsinghua University Science Park (Tuspark).

Readers Guide

For academics this book should provide a challenging view and innovative ways to understand the pervasive impact of networks on business and organisations at large. Business and organisational professionals should gain from the latest insights in essential, new developments, and their application in real life. The executive level may benefit from understanding the SBN guidelines and management implications applying these for a successful development of their organisation in a "being networked" world: A future where everything a manager tries to manage is directly impacted by the network effect.

The first part of the book, Setting the Scene, summarizes the development, organisation and structure of SBN 2008 for the Beijing meeting. The next chapter, *The Network Factor – How to Remain Competitive*, sets the scene for the development of smart business networks. We present our conclusions, the insights and the indicators from the presentations and discussions at the meeting. We propose four guidelines for business attention and academic research. We conclude with a plea for a unified theory of business networks and an exploration of the manager's challenges.

In Chap. 3, *Process Management in Business Networks*, Jon Pyke of Cordys sums up his views on smartness in business networks arguing that organisations require a business operating platform to capture and manage processes within and between themselves. Jon emphasizes the need to manage and control process execution in real time. In Chap. 4, *Next Generation Agility – Smart Business and Smart Communities*, Professor Roger Nagel of Lehigh University gives an intriguing contribution on "next generation agility" discussing how value is created in global communities. While this is work in progress we felt it too important not to be included. Roger stresses the role of people as connectors in a networked world and makes us understand that there are networks within networks; and that social networks are embedded in business networks and vice versa (see also Janneck et al., 2008). The next part of the book brings together the selected academic papers in four sections: *Network Essentials, Networks in Action, Network Enablers,* and *Network Orchestration*. These papers were selected by the Programme Committee being the most relevant for the future directions in SBNs. Each section has a brief introduction of its content. Where applicable we have included the reviewer's report of specific papers.

We aim to create and contribute to a new way of thinking on the management issues of business networks specifically and interorganisational networks in a broader sense. As such the book is intended for:

- Academics from such fields as information systems and strategy, telecommunications, engineering, social network analysis, complex systems theory, management strategy and organisational development;
- Business and organisational professionals in information systems and information strategy, marketing, organisational development and change management, and management strategy;
- Senior business executives and organisational leaders such as chief information officers, marketing and human resources officers and business strategists.

The Actors

When we were challenged, back in 2006, to organise this event, it seemed a very good idea: The exciting combination of China, Beijing, Olympics, Tsinghua University, networks, a new economy, an international programme committee, speakers from all over the world, academics and people from practice mixing and mingling to generate new questions and ideas. It turned out to be that and much more. What began as a loosely-coupled network of individuals became a web of strong nodes. As organising, programme and executive committees we all searched for our role, we all carefully watched what the others were doing before we did it ourselves.

It worked – and the result has been magnificent. The event was impressive. Beijing, the environment, the receptions, the hotel and Tsinghua University, watching the Olympics at the new stadium – the "Bird's Nest"; even the coaches that transported us back and forth, have given us indelible memories. With the Chinese we shared the pain of the aftermath of the Sichuan earthquake during the three days of national mourning. We understood the enormous size of the disaster and the daunting task for the area's recovery. It made us appreciate China even more.

The result is a strong network of senior and young academics and business executives that have shared their work and views and, in so doing, have created enthusiasm and friendships. Weak ties became strong ties, non-connectors became connected. This book is the immediate result. We hope and anticipate that it has further impacts: The meeting, the book and the follow-up is intended to create a community of people to carry the Smart Business Network Initiative into the research community and into business execution.

Some people deserve special mention. We would like to thank our project manager, Mrs. Ria Visser, Rotterdam School of Management, who was with us throughout the whole eighteen month journey. Her continual support and infectious optimism really made this event take place. Professor Ming Yu from Tsinghua University and his wife, Betty, were always there to organise the many practical details that are required for such an event. Mrs. Ting Li, our Chinese PhD student at Rotterdam School of Management understood the fine art of translating not only the language but also culture. Dr. Diederik van Liere after receiving the prestigious Rubicon grant from The Netherlands Organisation for Scientific Research (NWO) took on the enormous task to manage the whole process from call for papers to review, selection, instructing authors, preparing the proceedings, reviewing again, informing everyone, and making some final choices on the papers. Arnoud van de Laak provided technical support and Tsinghua's local student team ensured great local support!

We also respect and thank our business sponsors and their CEO's for their support: Jan Baan of Cordys and Larry Gould of thebigword. David Fung of Cordys Greater China and his team brought Chinese business people to make the closing dinner a truly unforgettable event. Theo Bouts of Zurich Financial Services has always been a keen supporter of SBNi and his presence has been both inspiring and joyful. We thank the Erasmus University Trust Fund whose contribution made it possible for many to attend. We are also grateful to the Erasmus Research in Mamagement School (ERIM) and Tsinghua University for their contributions.

Active participation makes for a good event: This is what the participants of SBN 2008 Beijing have achieved. We compliment them. Their roles are captured in this book for the future to see.

The Next Steps

One and a half years ago, as we planned for this event we chose the title *The Networked Experience – New Value from Smart Business Networks*. We believe we chose right – even though the discoveries may differ in many ways from our expectation. From our Chinese colleagues we learned in practice that Western-style planning is not always a good idea: If you plan too early it takes too much time to make all the changes and keep everyone informed. "Do not plan if you can improvise" is an expression that remains with us.

We learned also that the gap between business and science is wider than we expected. It does not have to be! And for management scientists it should not be! Rigour and relevance are two sides of the same coin. Academics should be clearer in respect of the business and societal impact of what they do and the practitioners should articulate what they need and expect more clearly. Everyone agreed on one fundamental: Networks matter – and new management tools and methods are needed to master the rapid change spurred by technological as well as social innovation.

During the event the Programme Committee awarded the Best Paper Award to the author(s) who made the most innovative contribution for smart business network research and was best able to present and explain his or her research to the business and academic audiences. Dr. Wolfgang Ketter and his co-authors John Collins and Maria Gini were announced as the winners for their contribution *Flexible Decision Support in a Dynamic Business Network*. This Award is sponsored by the Network Foundation and was presented at the launch of this book. Let the spirit of our experiences in Beijing spill into the academic and business communities to generate new ideas, new business and new discoveries.

Prof. Dr. Peter H. M. Vervest
Prof. Dr. Li Zheng
(General chairs)

References

Janneck, C. D., Nagel, R. N., Schmid, P. D., Raim, J. D., Connolly, M. L., & Moll, M. A. (2008). Smart business networks – core concepts and characteristics. In P. H. M. Vervest, E. van Heck, & K. Preiss (Eds.), *Smart business networks: A new business paradigm*. Rotterdam School of Management, Erasmus University Rotterdam, The Netherlands: Smart Business Network Initiative (SBNi).

Vervest, P. H. M., van Heck, E., & Preiss, K. (Eds.). (2008). *Smart business networks: A new business paradigm*. The Netherlands: Rotterdam School of Management, Erasmus University.

Vervest, P. H. M., van Heck, E., Preiss, K., & Pau, L. F. (2004). Special issue on smart business networks. *Journal of Information Technology, 19*(4).

Vervest, P. H. M., van Heck, E., Preiss, K., & Pau, L. F. (Eds.). (2005). *Smart business networks*. Berlin – Heidelberg, Germany: Springer Verlag.

The Programme Committees SBN 2008

General Chairs

Peter Vervest, Erasmus University Rotterdam, The Netherlands
Li Zheng, Tsinghua University, China

Executive Programme Committee

Al Dunn, The Network Foundation, UK
Eric van Heck, Erasmus University Rotterdam, The Netherlands
Chris Holland, Manchester Business School, UK
Benn Konsynski, Emory University, USA
Kenneth Preiss, Ben Gurion University, Israel

Business Committee

Jan Baan, Founder and CEO, Cordys, The Netherlands
Theo Bouts, CEO, Direct and Partnership. Europe General Insurance Zurich Financial Services Group, Switzerland
Sinclair Stockman, former CIO BT Group and CTO BT Global Services, UK

Programme Committee

Amit Basu, Southern Methodist University, USA
Dan Braha, New England Complex System Institute & UMass, USA
Xavier Busquets, Esade, Spain
Guoqing Chen, Tsinghua Business School, China
Eero Eloranta, Helsinki University of Technology, Finland
Wolf Ketter, Erasmus University Rotterdam, The Netherlands
Helmut Krcmar, Technical University Munich, Germany
Roger Nagel, Lehigh University, USA
Rajesh Pillania, Management Development Institute, India
Louis Pau, Erasmus University Rotterdam, The Netherlands
Piotr Ploszajski, Warsaw School of Economics, Poland
Piet Ribbers, Tilburg University, The Netherlands
Jens Riis, University of Aalborg, Denmark

Jorge Sanz, IBM Almaden Research Centre, USA
Bhusnan Saxena, Gurgaon Management Development Institute, India
Arjan van Weele, Technical University Eindhoven, The Netherlands
Hannes Werthner, Technical University Vienna, Austria

Organising Committee

Ting Li, Erasmus University Rotterdam, The Netherlands
Diederik van Liere, Erasmus University Rotterdam, The Netherlands
Ria Visser, Erasmus University Rotterdam, The Netherlands
Ming Yu, Tsinghua University, China

2. The Network Factor – How to Remain Competitive

Peter H.M. Vervest,[1] Diederik W. van Liere[2] and Al Dunn[3]

[1]Rotterdam School of Management, Erasmus University Rotterdam, The Netherlands, pvervest@rsm.nl

[2]Rotterdam School of Management, Erasmus University Rotterdam, The Netherlands, dliere@rsm.nl

[3]The Network Foundation & D-Age Management Limited, United Kingdom, dunn@d-age.com

Abstract

The network rather than the individual firm is becoming the focal point of economic development and business success. What should executives and managers do particularly well, or different, to thrive in the networked world? Based on the Discovery Event "The Networked Experience", Beijing 18–23 May 2008, hosted by Tsinghua University (see www.sbniweb.org), we develop a number of propositions, or guidelines to understanding the network factor in today's competitive business arena. Building on the work of the Smart Business Network Initiative established in 2004 (Vervest, van Heck, Preiss, & Pau, 2005) we call for action to develop a unified theory of business networks.

The Network as Focal Point

The key question posed in 2004: What is the relationship between the intelligence of networks and the "smartness" of the companies that use these networks? We introduced the term "smartness" as a novel and different behaviour indicating the ability to generate "better than usual" results. We assessed that companies working together in a network using the intelligence of advanced communication technologies would be able to generate smarter results than competitors that were not using that intelligence. Even though smartness would be relative to others, time-bound or short-lived and situation-dependent, it would pay for companies to invest in smart business networking to create the future competitive edge.[1] Did it happen? Did companies apply smart business networking techniques? The answer: Yes, and no!

---

[1] The concept of smart business, or smart organisational, networks can also be applied to not-for-profit, or governmental organisations. Smartness refers to the way in which the result is being achieved, not as much as to the goal itself, be it monetary profit or societal welfare.

P.H.M. Vervest et al. (eds.) *The Network Experience* © Springer-Verlag Berlin Heidelberg 2009

15

Over the past four years we have witnessed the success of networked businesses such as eBay, Amazon, Google (van Heck & Vervest, 2007): These companies usually create a platform that radically lowers the cost of doing global business. We have seen the spur of social network sites such as LinkedIn, Youtube, Facebook together with the emergence of a multitude of blogsites on the Internet. The music industry demonstrates how an industry is radically changed as direct result of network platforms. In this case, Apple with iTunes, who followed in the footsteps of peer-to-peer music sharing created new digital music distribution channels while the incumbent companies did not take advantage of this significant new way of doing business.

Signals from the edge: the music industry

The music industry is the most visible victim of digital networks. The digitisation of content and the ability of rapid distribution and sharing has had a dramatic impact on the major incumbents. The major labels are struggling to reinvent their business models. For some they be too late! The (record) labels have wonderful assets – they just can't make money out of them. "Here we have a business that is dying...the record companies have created this situation themselves" says Simon Wright, CEO of the Virgin Entertainment Group".
Drawn from Brian Hiatt and Evan Serpick, Rolling Stone, 28 June 2008)

What is happening in the industry is a signal to many industries: The network will erode and destroy business. It spreads to movies, to publishing, to financial services and beyond.

"My question is: What is the future role for publishers in this digital world? Our industry will change from being a 'knowledge factory' between authors and readers to being one of the networks of knowledge. Digital networks bring new challenges and new competitors. Will we have the same role tomorrow in providing 'content experiences'? Will users be willing to *pay* publishers for their contributions, or will they insist on managing their own experiences directly for free (using blogs, wikis, etc.). Do publishers have a future?"
Sharon Ruwart, Managing Director China, Elsevier Science & Technology; 21 May 2008, Beijing, China.

"I see amazing amazing opportunities in the networked world: I see some 50 million networked individuals who will buy insurance services. But I also see the threats: The digital aggregation platforms coming between us and our customers; new 'insurance' companies who will steal our business. I also see the challenges: Discovering the 50 million; creating compelling 'networked insurance products'; organising in new ways to act in new worlds".
Theo Bouts, CEO, Direct and Partnership. Europe General Insurance Zurich, Financial Services Group; 19 May 2008, Beijing, China.

In past years, there seemed to be a focus on creating a proprietary network platform, loosely defined as telecommunications-based access to a computing environment allowing the user to perform pre-determined platform-controlled and supported actions to attract as many actors as possible on to that platform.

A networked platform has some compelling advantages. Most importantly, the users have access to a more or less complete suite of business processes (from search and selection, to ordering, delivery, payment and administration). Since the platform owner controls who is given access and their access rights, the linking of the business partners and the end-to-end management of business processes is not a significant issue. However, this creates user over-dependence on the network platform. If you are on Amazon you cannot access Bol. Skype does not give access to its competitors. This traditional lock-in resembles the islands of computer-based messaging systems in those early days of the 1970s. These disadvantages are not a problem as long as the price and quality are acceptable and the users are not enslaved. But networks have an interesting effect on size: The marginal cost of serving each additional user drops disproportionally. This means that at a certain point in time the integral cost of the market leader for adding the next user will be less than the marginal cost of its next-in-line competitor. Then natural monopolies develop and the winner takes all. That is when markets typically go wrong and outside regulation steps in.

So smart business networking may not always have happened. Outsourcing is an intriguing example of the development of not-so-smart business networks. Using today's telecommunication capabilities, a company can outsource specific tasks to other companies located in remote parts of their previously constrained world. This can be done easily and swiftly at lower transaction costs than ever before. Friedman (2005) revealed the power of the Internet to flatten the world. The idea is simple: Any (part of the) production process can be performed by picking the right – low cost – partners from all over the globe; contracting them for the execution of those tasks thereby reducing overall costs while maintaining ultimate control over the market place. So large companies outsource IT systems to India and manufacturing to China expecting that they will continue to control who makes the profit from the customer. Complicated outsourcing webs have developed as a result.

Practitioners have felt the pain of transferring tasks that are being outsourced. When outsourcing, the company not only transfers the execution of a certain task but it also transfers the logic that goes with the task. Tasks are combined in processes and processes are linked together to deliver the required customer performance: If that chain breaks, you need to know. In fact, you need to know before it breaks. You need alternatives ready. You must be able to make switches in the supply chain, to link to alternative resources to overcome the failure. But you cannot. The outsourcing company has lost the logic, the detailed understanding of management and control of specific tasks, and the skill to manage the process integration of discrete tasks.

It was not smart to outsource both execution and logic of the business processes. The outsourcer gets poor execution and no logic in return. This may be an exaggeration. However, business process management has become more critical for corporate success than ever before. In this "flat world" (Friedman, 2005) the future company must find ever-newer ways to obtain the best position in a network of interlinked companies. Without modern tools for process management and network positioning it will fail. The outsourcer no longer controls, or even understands, the execution of its basic business processes. In addition, it no longer masters the search and selection of trustworthy business patners. The company gets lost in an intricate web of thousands of business partners and is no longer able to claim a favourable position.

Making Smart Business Networks Happen

The key idea behind "smart business networking" is that organisations deliver new value by smart positioning of their capabilities in global networks of interconnected organisations and individuals. One strategy, as mentioned above, is to form the platform of choice, to be the cheerleader and club manager (Stabell & Fjeldstad, 1998), to attract as many actors as possible into your "own" network. The platform operator aims to define and create the "ecosystem" (Moore, 1993) for the platform users, dominating their ways of interacting and doing business.

Another strategy is becoming the "capability hub": Try to have as many actors as possible that outsource their capability to you as the cost leader and the performer with the greatest operational excellence.

Are these strategies sustainable? These strategies are successful because they create over-dependency of the user on the platform or of the outsourced service. The essence of today's technology-enabled networks is different: They lower the cost of interaction (Butler et al., 1997) while greatly increasing its value. At the same time, the utility of the community increases disproportionally with size (the more the better). Smart business networking should not aim to create closed environments such as is the case in many platforms, rather it should "open" environments.

Only few companies will be able to become a networked platform that compels other actors to use their platform and comply with their prescribed environment. Only few will be able to become dominating capability hubs. What, then, should the remaining companies do? We propose they have a role as "orchestrators" (Hinterhuber, 2002). Directing actors in the business network, these companies orchestrate the combining of various capabilities for specific results aimed at the customer.

In the mid 1990s, at the highpoint of business process reengineering (BPR), Treacy and Wiersema (1995) introduced three strategies ("value disciplines") for market leaders: Operational excellence, product leadership, and customer intimacy. Let us use these strategies to clarify the basic business networking strategies discussed above:

- Capability hubs deliver a combination of quality, price and ease of purchase that no one else in their market can match, they pursue operational excellence in networking terms.

- Platform providers focus on the constant use of and interaction on their platform, continually finding new ways and value to increase their size. This is the product leadership strategy that aims at providing the best product offering and "continually push their product into the realms of the unknown, the untried or the highly desirable".
- Network orchestrators understand the needs of the customer, access the network and select the nodes or capabilities that are required to fulfil the customer need building bonds with customers "like good neighbours": A company executing the customer intimacy strategy does not deliver what the market wants but what the customer wants.

Each of these strategies has a different operating model in terms of operating processes, business structures, management systems and culture (Treacy & Wiersema, 1995). The same will apply to the different business network strategies:

- Operating processes must function in a network setting. Accessing network resources demands process control across and between the different network actors: Guideline one – network resources need process control.
- Business network structures concern both position in and awareness of the network. On the one hand, an actor's position in the network will be critical for its performance. On the other hand, there is a trade-off between network knowledge and actor performance: Guideline two – Network position drives actor performance.
- Management systems measure between-actor performance, incentivise cooperation and ensure better-than-individual-results. This is a key to generating smart, better-than-usual results based on smart (use of) information and communication technologies: Guideline three – Network openness unlocks smartness.
- Culture (in Treacy & Wiersema's view, 1995) centres on core values and change. Business networks typically mix different cultures and have no single point of authority with change through voluntary leaders: Guideline four: Network leaders are orchestrators.

The above-mentioned guidelines are fundamentals for a successful business networking strategy. They trigger a call for action addressed at the business research community to investigate: What is the unified theory of business networks? The guidelines should help business people in developing their own successful networking strategy.

Guidelines for Smart Business Networks

Network Resources Need Process Control

Access to capabilities of other companies is one of the key benefits of being positioned in a network. Gulati (2007) speaks of "network resources": Resources that accrue to a company from its ties with key external constituents including, but not limited to, partners, suppliers, and customers. In his seminal study Gulati is particularly interested in networks as conduits of information.

Van Liere (2007) assesses that increased specialization drives the search for network resources. When specialized, the company can focus on fewer capabilities while network resources enable access to complementary capabilities that collectively are required to deliver the desired result (such as "fulfil a customer order"). The traditional value chain is dissected in discrete components or modules. Each module needs to be put in a process chain (in its simplest form a sequence of events). The execution of the process chain needs to be managed. As each actor in the chain develops choices to elect other actors to link to and do business with, the chain becomes a network (with selection points and iterations).

Saxena (2008) sums up the key characteristic of a SBN being the ability to dynamically combine different capabilities, sourced from various members, to create new capability as one of the major factors for its competitive success (Stalk, Evans, & Shulman, 1992). The building blocks of a SBN's competitive strategy are not the products and markets but its business processes. Saxena continues: "Consequently an important function of a SBN's "smartness" is its "smart" business process management (BPM); that is, its ability to inherit *dynamic adaptation* and *continuous experiential learning*".

Managers must understand the vital importance of network resources and process management for their company. This requires:

1. Understanding the essence of "capability" from a network perspective;
2. Process control: Mastering the linking of capabilities in a network of different actors, i.e., how to manage, end-to-end, discrete processes distributed in a network of business partners.

A capability can be defined as a company's capacity to deploy resources, usually in combination, using organisational processes to realize a desired end (Amit & Schoemaker, 1993). Prahalad and Hamel (1990) spoke of the core competence of the company as "consolidating corporate-wide technologies and skills into competencies that empower individual businesses to adapt quickly to changing opportunities". The essence of a capability is to combine and transform resources for a specific goal such as creating, producing, and/or offering products to a market. The competence concerns the way of doing it, i.e., how and how well the resources are being used. Burt (2005) refers to the competence – capability gap focusing, in particular, on the increased coordination capabilities of today's communications technologies and the failing incompetence of many organisations to use them properly. Social capital develops if people are better connected than others and are able to develop advantage over others. The compliment to this is that network capital develops if a company can mobilize capabilities across different network actors.

In a network environment the company must continually assess which capabilities it will perform itself and which capabilities to source. As capabilities become more short-lived this decision resembles the traditional make-or-buy decision. However, the capability choice is more strategic than a mere cost consideration. It requires a conscious assessment of the imitability and uniqueness of a capability; the complexity and inter-connectedness of the capability; and the experience of the company in performing that capability (Koppius & van Fenema, 2006).

Beimborn, Martin, and Homann (2005) propose the development of "capability maps" linked to process flow models. Saxena (2008) proposes a process management architecture that decomposes capabilities into functionalities: Each function is related to a dedicated process and allocated to members of the network. It is important to understand that business process (out- or in-) sourcing is not only a matter of business process management. The linking of capabilities and the management of this linking is an important but often overseen aspect in the BPM literature (see for instance the BPM and Workflow Handbook 2008; Fischer, 2008). Figure 2.1 illustrates the development from traditional outsourcing of entire functions to outsource modular business processes which results in a company pursuing a capability hub strategy (step 4).

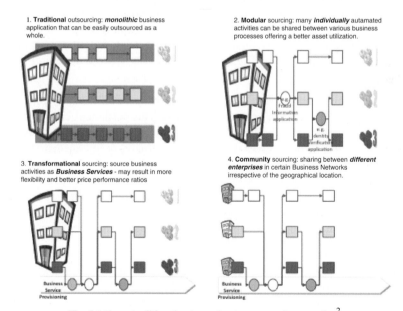

Fig. 2.1 From traditional outsourcing to community sourcing[2]

---

[2] Business Service Provisioning is not traditional outsourcing. It is a fundamentally new way for customers to source business activities. (Courtesy: Gerrit Schipper, CEO, RDC, The Netherlands).

Process control has become a key challenge, if not a stumbling block, in developing SBNs. This is why Pyke (2008) argues in favour of a business operating platform as the glue between different organisational information systems: In 2004 we spoke of the Business Operating System (Vervest, van Heck, Preiss, & Pau, 2005). Today's business process management technologies enable processes to be contained in human-understandable logic (defined as discrete process steps, the relationship diagrams between these steps, and the business rules that govern the execution of the process steps) and the execution of these processes on different information systems or computer platforms. There is a gradual shift from hardware oriented architecture to software oriented architecture. The real challenge is still to come: Process management that follows a business-oriented architecture i.e., that gives the full flexibility to design and execute business processes irrespective of the operational environment.

Network Position Drives Actor Performance

The network structure can be defined as the collection of network actors and their relationships, or links, at any given point in time (van Liere, 2007). The structure of a business network does often not follow clear or predefined design rules (e.g. the division of tasks and responsibilities, the functional and business grouping of subunits, the assignment of authority and power) as is mostly the case for the internal organisation of companies. The individual actor must try to discover the structure of its business network from its *ego* position. This is important as the network position of an actor will impact performance. Some network positions (defined as the pattern of relations to and from an actor within a network structure) can be very favourable:

- In the bridging position (Burt, 1992) the firm spans a structural hole, i.e., there are no direct links between its business partners. This position offers information and control benefits. The bridge gets the information sooner and can control who gets what information. It gives the potential to broker, or intermediate between the business partners.
- The closed, or embedded position develops when firms have direct links between themselves. Closed positions facilitate shared understanding and reputation which builds as information flows more freely among actors. It also enables effective sanctioning mechanisms since information on deviant behaviour will quickly spread.

The bridging and closed positions can be extremes on a scale. Just like a star-configured network and a complete grid network in telecommunications design.

The effect of network position on individual actor performance is fiercely debated among social network analysts (Baum & Rowley, 2008; Burt, 1992). Some argue that the better position results in better performance. Others claim better performance gives you a better position. It is important to define performance: Does it mean profit, market share, authority or status? We propose that the more companies get bound in networks, the bigger the network gets, therefore the more important the impact of network position on the performance of the individual actor. The impact of network size on actor performance is an important area for research: Is network position the dominating driver for firm performance? We need a clearer view on how past performance gives a better network position and therefore better performance in the future.

In today's world of advanced communications, business networks are not static but are highly dynamic as firms pursue beneficial network positions to compete. Focusing on the bridging position van Liere (2007) investigated why the network position of a firm changes and found three important drivers:

1. Resource similarity – similarity of resources between partner firms lowers the likelihood for bridging as firms will seek new positions where they can differentiate their capabilities better.
2. Resource dependency – if partner firms are dependent on each other because of scarce or specific resources they are less likely to move their network position and this will strengthen a bridging position as the bridge, or broker, holds the information on who has what capability.
3. The amount of information which a firm holds on the structure of its interfirm network at a given point in time or "network horizon".

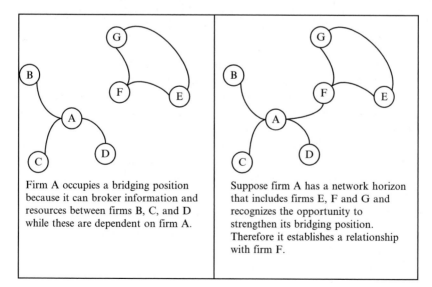

Firm A occupies a bridging position because it can broker information and resources between firms B, C, and D while these are dependent on firm A.

Suppose firm A has a network horizon that includes firms E, F and G and recognizes the opportunity to strengthen its bridging position. Therefore it establishes a relationship with firm F.

Fig. 2.2 Illustration of network horizon

Figure 2.2 gives an illustrative example of the effect of a firm's network horizon Using tools specifically developed to study interfirm networks (the Business Network Engine and LINKS) van Liere (2007) shows that the size of a firm's network horizon is a critical determinant of a firm s ability to strengthen and keep its bridging position. This does not mean that a firm should always try to expand its network horizon as the study indicates a threshold: Expanding the network horizon beyond this point gives rapidly diminishing returns.

Extensive simulation revealed that a key factor for sustainable network positions is the way in which network horizon is distributed across the different firms (the amount of *network horizon heterogeneity*). The results were striking. In the traditional supply chain where all firms have a low network horizon (that is, the firms know their upstream and downstream partners but little of the other actors) a competitive advantage can be sustained for some time (van Liere, Koppius, & Vervest, 2008). However, when the network horizon becomes more heterogeneous, firms change their network positions faster until all firms in the network have a high degree of network horizon and the network becomes homogenous again: "Any opportunity can be spotted by many firms and any competitive advantage is therefore short-lived". Network horizon heterogeneity is found to be an important predictor of competition for network positions.

As business networks expand it will be more important for companies to have a map of their network. This network map visualizes, at minimum, who is connected to whom, what types of transactions are conducted and the volumes traded through these relationships. These kinds of maps have often been made to visualize the structure of the Internet, Internet sites, business partnerships and social networks. One of the key challenges is the automatic discovery of the network structure and network position which a firm occupies starting from the ego network of the firm and searching for the nodes and links of its alters, alters' alters, and so on. With more accurate network maps of individual actors it should be possible to analyze changes over time and perhaps make predictions on short term and longer term developments of the network. Reggiani, Nijkamp, and Cento (2008) and Braha and Bar-Yam (2004) demonstrate the use of mapping of business networks and the analysis of the structural properties of such networks. Managers need tools to identify which networks are relevant for their business; and tools that help them manoeuvre their companies to the correct network position.

Network Openness Unlocks Smartness

Network openness describes how various groups and organisations interact. Open interaction between such organisations is typified by communal or shared management and open access to the resources needed to meet shared objectives, the result being deliverd by contributions from a diverse range of participants: Both users and producers. These open groups are typically flat hierarchies with fluid organisational structures.

As digital business and mass-collaboration networks evolve, an understanding of "network openness" becomes important. Goldman, Nagel, Davison, and Schmid (2008) propose "community openness" in which participants can join, contribute, engage and leave according to a basic set of rules. Such openness can create the collaborative economy and enable collaborative production.

Participative Economy: new forms of collaboration enabled by digital networks allowing almost any individual to combine to create new products and/or services at extremely low cost.

Collaborative Production: networking skill sets to support innovation and enable production.

One can conclude that surprising "smartness" emerges from such open networks. Smartness has not been predetermined: It is not a deterministic result that can be achieved by following a set of prescribed rules. It emerges only when the specific knowledge and skills of individual actors are captured and, in some cases, synthesised.

We suggest that there are two key forms of openness exhibited by business and social networks:

1. Capability openness: capabilities are made available to network participants to allow them to combine the chosen capabilities to create or reconfigure new products or services.
2. Process openness: business processes are made available across the network to allow network participants to operate together.

Capability openness underpins the growth of Amazon's and Google's businesses. By providing their capabilities to their wider networks of individuals and companies, these in turn create new capabilities which add value to the business network. In this way, rather than the network platform prescribing a multitude of services to meet numerous available revenue opportunities and markets, network partners create new capability clusters for themselves or their own customers and/or network partners.

Capability openness can form the basis of emerging networked sourcing: Rather than process and execution being handed over to the hub, the hub makes services available (for example Software as a Service) that can be exploited by customers. In doing so, these hubs can migrate towards network orchestration.

Process openness enables the participants in the network to combine and act together: Participants can cooperate and are synchronised to deliver the required result. The differing processes of the collaborating participants must be managed to connect, act and disconnect rapidly (Koppius & van de Laak, 2008).

Business networks can exhibit multiple forms of openness. The platform strategy centres on capability openness with a limited need for process openness. They require that participants conform to the platform processes as the platform dictates who, when and how can use their network platform. In contrast, the capability hub strategy focuses on process openness allowing the outsourcer to access, monitor and manage the outsourced processes. Network orchestration can be enacted through capability or process openness: Network orchestrators access the network and select the nodes or capabilities that are required to fulfil the customer need. Without process orchestration one can argue that the orchestrator returns to the platform strategy. Orchestrators become "smart" when they combine both forms of openness: This may be the truly smart business network.

Smart business network strategies will emphasise one or more of these forms of openness. Indeed, if one considers the ecosystem in which these networks participate, one can discover that all forms may exist somewhere within it.

Where, then, is this "smartness" that can be unlocked? Smartness can be embedded in the network itself or emerge from the behaviour of the network: Engineered smartness or emergent smartness. Preiss (2005) stated that smartness is engineered in the network when it is located within the nodes, on a single link between nodes, on a chain of links, or in the whole network. It can be embedded in the technology: For example, BT embeds the smartness in its 21CN; in retail or logistics networks smartness can be embedded in RFID chips; Skype embeds it in its users' computers; thebigword embeds it in their translation engine ("Language Director").

"Our next generation network – 21CN – allows BT to combine the core network asset with virtualized capabilities delivered from the network. Taken individually, these technical components facilitate products and services that the customer can choose to utilize either as part of a broader service (billing in conjunction with voice or data services for instance) or as a stand alone capability (simple billing for instance) to complement or augment their existing products and services".

Curtis Eubank, General Manager, BT China: 21 May 2008, Beijing, China.

Emergent smartness is created when the network is configured – orchestrated – to meet a specific requirement. The smartness does not exist within the latent network; it exists only when the network is in action. Emergent smartness can be transient, the rapid formation of a network to meet unexpected challenges. Consider hastily formed networks (Denning, 2006) to meet emergencies. Van Baalen and van Fenema (2008) define this as: A network that did not exist previously forms and acts rapidly. The business network becomes smart when it is able to enact hastily-formed networks to continually meet the rapidly-changing demands of its participants and customers: The smart business wins the race every time!

Smartness results in generating better-than-usual results: Network openness enables the smartness. To achieve this, firms must open up their knowledge of the network. To ensure the smart linking of those participating in the network, a company must have detailed knowledge of their networks, their network position, and the activities in the network, in particularly between participants. Collins, Ketter, and Gini (2008) have designed a decision support system which can gather activity information from the different nodes of the business network and, with a dashboard architecture present the data to give organisational decision-makers deeper understanding of the network structure and facilitate decision-making. They are developing an interactive network dashboard to allow the manager to make appropriate structural changes to the network.

Such observation, measurement and decision tools will greatly enhance the firm's ability to optimize their network position, determine risk and reward models based on participant performance and contribution. When combined with data made available from business operations platform, such near-to-complete and near real-time information on the business networks will strengthen the company's operational and strategic decision making.

Network Leaders are Orchestrators

As the firm becomes intrinsically networked, its power base becomes a derivative of its access to network resources: Whatever network capital it develops, it is shared ownership. The outcomes of network cooperation for each participating actor may be unclear, or at best, uncertain. There is not necessarily a single point of control or authority to resolve conflicts. This is an intimidating prospect for so many executives and upwardly mobile managers who are trained in and accustomed to hierarchical decision making and preset spans of control. As business networks expand to a universal scale different cultures mix. No single one may be able to dominate. A new culture may develop: Network culture, inherently more flexible but difficult to define clearly since it changes as new actors enter and others leave the network group.

> The human factor in business network is underrated. Human-centric Business Process Management is essential for successful business networks. People need to link prior to a business process. This requires levelling, linking and engaging people. The personal win is critical for networks to emerge.

So how are business networks governed? Networks typically do not have one single authority that regulates actor behaviour: Podolny and Page (1998) see the lack of a legitimate organisational authority to arbitrate and resolve disputes as one of the distinguishing factors of business networks. Networks are in between hierarchies and markets. The key feature of a hierarchy, says Thompson (2003), is that it requires some form of overt rule-driven design and direction, broadly speaking an "administration" or "management". Conversely, the market is self-coordinating without any conscious organising centre that directs it.

Gulati (2007) takes the contract as the prime form to communicate the governance (between alliances): The contract is the mechanism by which firms protect themselves from partner's opportunistic behaviour. Trust – the expectation that alleviates the fear that one's exchange partner may act opportunistically (Gulati, 2007) – may develop over time. Burt (2005) defines trust as "a relationship with someone (or something if the object of trust is a group, organisation, or social category) in which the contractual terms are incompletely specified. The more unspecified, taken-for-granted, the terms, the more that trust is involved." Repeated interactions develop trust. Ties between actors become stronger. As word gets around, this gives an actor a "trustworthy reputation". Burt (2005: 109) makes an important case that reputation requires network closure. Citing Coleman he claims: "Reputation cannot arise in an open structure, and collective sanctions that would ensure trustworthiness cannot be applied". Burt continues: "Network closure is social capital, closed networks are more likely to create trust and reputation and therefore can be capitalized." In this way a firm's brand identity constitutes social capital.

This traditionalists' view on governance boils down to two alternative routes: One is the creation of legally binding, multi-party contracts prior to the actual exchange. The second is the joint acceptance of the binding authority of a reputable and trusted third party. In 2004 (Vervest, van Heck, Preiss, & Pau, 2005: 38–43) we came up with different notions. We wrote:

- The governance of SBNs will not be based on cooperation: Rather it will be based on finding an agreed equilibrium in the conflicting goals of the individual actors and the network goal which must be transparently communicated to all actors.
- At the heart of this is the notion of network awareness of network states and network processes: It will be both reactive awareness (responding to changes) and proactive awareness (monitoring and anticipatory actions). Adaptiveness and learning are essential features for network coordination and governance.

These internal network properties such as adaptability and learning are different ways to create network governance. Senge (1990) wrote on "the illusion of being in control" citing a retired CEO of a large American firm: "Just because no one is 'in control' does not mean there is 'no control'...the essence is to maintain internal balances critical to stability and growth". Senge compares this to the homeostasis in the human body and sees adaption and learning as the critical enablers: "Today's problems come from yesterday solutions". Managers fail to adapt and learn new ways in time before the wall hits them.

> "In moving from the traditional authoritarian, hierarchical organization to a locally controlled organization, the single greatest issue is control. Beyond money, beyond fame, what drives most executives of traditional organizations is power, the desire to be in control. Most would rather give up anything than control". (Senge, 1990: 290)

In *Out of Control* Kelly (1994: 419) quotes control research by Jon Bates in his fabricated world called *Oz* where the narrative is defined by characters and automatons in a physical environment. Without a script:

- How do you organise a narrative to allow deviations yet keep it centered on its intended destination?
- How do you construct an environment that can generate surprise events?
- How do you create creatures that have autonomy, but not too much?

This is what now happens in blogs and "twittering" on the Internet: The bloggers define the play and the narrative. Their blog presents the environment. They are in control, yet no one is in control. This happens in social networks. It will happen in business networks. Using the tools of Internet and mobile telephones consumers become "prosumers" (Toffler, 1980): They act as counsellors for one other in electronic commerce sites, write product reviews, share experiences, answer unsolicited questions, join slamming, blaming and faming sites, date, engage in politics and social action groups, populate blogs and prove powerful creators and distributors of content in whatever form, whatever the quality and despite the quantity.

Goldman et al. (2008) sees community-mobilizing strategies as a critical enabler for future agility imposed on successful companies. Companies must understand how to create and become mediators of a community: Not as leaders, not working as teams, but as orchestrators and collaborators; as synthesizers and integrators, as explainers making complex things easy to understand, as leveragers and systems thinkers, problem solvers, adapters of new ideas. These community aggregators act as the connectors of different community networks and they link different domains together.

Becoming a community orchestrator...

One of the largest financial services groups wants to link millions of people together to form a new, cooperative insurance network: Not insurance in the traditional sense of selling packaged products for assumed risks, rather insurance services embedded in everyday processes: You buy a television; they know and it is insured. You drive the car; they know and it is insured. Your TV is stolen, the car is broken; they know and settle the damage. They want an "eBay" model for auctioning risks and managing repair. With social networks to control and manage risks.

Busquets (2008) proposes an innovative concept for orchestration of SBNs as a process of regulating network boundaries. Acknowledging both centripetal forces (forces for actors to join the network) and centrifugal forces (forces to leave the network) successful orchestration is the new talent to deploy network resources, open opportunities and organize "forward" in the process.

Shaw and Holland (2008) analyze the role of technology platforms to facilitate complex coordination tasks (in their case for the translation industry): Orchestration can actually be embedded into the business operating platform shared between network actors.

> "Technology is now becoming so entwined with translation that their relationship is about to become virtually indistinguishable. Translation services speed was constrained by communication speeds: The end-to-end process of translating was obviously much lengthier, with buyers greatly reliant on the postal service for turnaround times".
>
> "We have embedded the translation process as software in our translation network: our LanguageDirector™ This not only speeds the process, it captures intelligence on our clients – the translation memory – and gives our clients more control over the translation process. The embedded translation memory reduces the words to translate from the original numbers of words received by 70%".
>
> *Nicola Carmyllie, General Manager, thebigword China: The Summer Palace, Beijing, 22 May 2008.*

Research on governance in networks has placed much emphasis on concepts like trust and contracts: We need to understand better how voluntary networks develop homeostasis while adapting to changing environmental conditions. We are challenged to grasp the culture of a SBN as an operating model. We must understand if the notion of "culture" does apply to networks. How can there be leadership without powerbase; without reputation or trust? How can the swarm of network actors still develop to the intended destination? One strategy is to mobilize communities; another is to embed coordination mechanisms inside the business operating systems. The human factor, however, is critical in understanding the future development of SBNs.

Towards a Unified Theory of Business Networks

Preiss (2005) told us that "practice precedes theory": The business "networks are being constructed, and the practical construction is followed by the development of suitable theories. Eventually the theory should promote improved business efficiency of such networks and should enable the expansion of business networks to much larger sizes".

Over the past years we have created a body of knowledge, composed of practical cases, examples, and some rigorous scientific studies (e.g. van Liere, 2007). It is now time to develop a composite theory to answer important questions that practitioners are beginning to ask: To try unify constructs from different fields such as organisational theory, information systems theory, (tele)communications theory, complexity theory, and social network theory, in a coherent and well defined frame. This unifying theory should provide as a minimum a common vocabulary that enables scientists from different disciplines to communicate without noise. This will also help to resolve the general Babylonic misuse of the term "network" in business and society at large.

The study of SBN needs a common vocabulary – of terms, constructs, methods, objectives, boundaries, and research challenges – that serves as the multi-disciplinary communications language.

"One wonders sometimes if science will not grind to a stop in an assemblage of walled-in hermits, each mumbling to himself words in a private language that only he can understand." (Boulding, 1956, one of the founders of General Systems Theory)

Our ambition should go beyond a common vocabulary. We should strive for a theory that answers questions such as:

- How does the structure of a business network impact network performance?
- Where and when do we see smart business networks emerge?
- How and which network strategies improve firm performance?
- How can the network horizon help organisational decision-makers in shifting their firm's network position?

We should develop algorithms and tools to help practitioners apply this network knowledge. For example, we need algorithms to help uncover and map business networks, or algorithms that assess the strength of network positions of competitors and we need tools to visualize and analyze network structures to facilitate organisational decision-makers in managing their networks.

Eminent scholars such as Boulding (1956) and Von Bertalanffy (1968) faced the enormous challenge in creating General Systems Theory in the 1950s. The resulting "Systems Thinking" (Emery, 1969) impacted deeply organisational research and the education of the then young people that now populate the management echelons. There are intrinsic differences between networks and systems. In a provocative way one can say that systems have predetermined boundaries; networks do not. Systems have deterministic entity-to-entity relationships; networks do not. Systems have control boxes; networks do not. Systems are simple representations of reality; networks are complex. Networks can uncover hidden systems' properties (Preiss, 2005).

The real understanding of networks – in their multifaceted appearances – deserves a serious academic effort to create a unifying networking theory, at the very minimum for the business world, with an accepted set of methods and tools: To develop "Network Thinking" for a future generation of managers.

The Manager's Challenge

We distinguished three network strategies: the capability hub, the platform provider and the network orchestrator. These network strategies determine the actor and network capabilities and this will determine how a firm will position itself in its business network and consequently determine the performance both at the individual and network level. As Treacy and Wiersema (1995) noted, in practice these strategies are mixed. However, a company should be very clear on its choice of the dominating strategy and build its operating model accordingly. Thus a platform provider needs to be capable and an orchestrator needs the platforms. As managers build their operating models for the networked world they must ask:

- What network resources are critical, how should I develop valuable network resources and how should network processes be managed? What are my critical capabilities and how are these linked to processes?
- What is the appropriate mix of network strategies at the actor level (how many and which firms should pursue a capability hub, platform provider and network orchestrator strategy) that will improve the performance of the network?
- What is my position in the network, what do I know about the network(s) in which I am active? How does this impact my performance?
- Is the network open and am I open? Am I using networking technologies in the appropriate way and am I able to manage network processes smartly?
- Do I, as network leader, and my company act and behave as orchestrators of the band: Continually adapting and learning, engaging my community and developing networked ways of embedded coordination?

What should the Chief Executive Officer do in the networked world?

- Networks equal networth – build your networks deliberately and for real business goals.
- Think networks, act networks – forget command and control, lead by values, networks are the organisational DNA.
- Networking is people empowered by technology – bond people via networks, make them engage themselves, create their own vision, set their own common goals, give complete transparency.
- People only connect if leveled – you must break down the hierarchy and find a network way to make people want to share, or leave the network.
- Networks make you highly visible and 'always on' – choose carefully which networks to enter and ensure you can leave if you wish.
- Where you are in the network is what you are – identify network structures and work on your network position.
- Connect to the customer – use networks widely to link with customers and communities and be their network enchanter.
- Befriend the supplier – use supplier networks sparsely to be efficient and economical.
- Partner choice on volume – every network partner should do no less than 30% and no more than 70% of its business with us (30/70 rule from Li & Fung).

Inspired by the Executives' Elevator Pitch Discussion, Beijing 20 May 2008.

The network strategies that we have witnessed so far may be early and naive forms of much more advanced business models. As smart technologies develop and a new, networking-adept generation matures, the ways to create value in business and society will be very different. To remain competitive managers must take the networking challenge very serious.

Acknowledgments

Diederik van Liere would like to thank The Netherlands Organisation for Scientific Research (NWO) to enable him to conduct this research as part of his Rubicon Grant.

References

Amit, R., & Schoemaker, P. J. H. (1993). Strategic assets and organizational rent. *Strategic Management Journal, 14*(1), 33–46.

Baum, J. A. C., & Rowley, T. J. (Eds.). (2008). *Network strategy*. Bingley, UK: Emerald Group Publishing Ltd.

Beimborn, D., Martin, S. F., & Homann, U. (2005). *Capability-oriented Modeling of the Company*. IPSI 2005 Conference, Amalfi, Italy.

Boulding, K. E. (1956). *General systems theory – The skeleton of science*. General Systems I.

Braha, D., & Bar-Yam, Y. (2004). Information flow structure in large-scale product development organizational networks. *Journal of Information Technology, 19*(4), 244–253.

Burt, R. S. (1992). *Structural holes – The social structure of competition*. Cambridge, MA: Harvard University Press.

Burt, R. S. (2005). *Brokerage and closure: An introduction to social capital*. Oxford, UK: Oxford University Press.

Busquets, X. (2008). Orchestrating smart business networks. In P. H. M. Vervest, D. W. van Liere, & L. Zheng (Eds.), *The network experience – New value from smart business networks*. Berlin, Germany: Springer.

Butler, P., Hall, T. W., Hanna, A. M., Mendonca, L., Auguste, B., & Sahay, A. (1997). A revolution in interaction. *The McKinsey Quarterly, 1*, 4–23.

Collins, J., Ketter, W., & Gini, M. (2008). Flexible decision support in a dynamic business network. In P. H. M. Vervest, D. W. van Liere, & L. Zheng (Eds.), *The network experience – New value from smart business networks*. Berlin, Germany: Springer.

Denning, P. J. (2006). Hastily formed networks. *Communications of the ACM, 49*(4), 15–20.

Emery, F. R. (1969). *Systems thinking*. Harmondsworth, UK: Penguin Books Ltd.

Fischer, L. (Ed.). (2008). *2008 Bpm and workflow handbook*. Lighthouse Point, USA: Future Strategies.

Friedman, T. L. (2005). *The world is flat*. New York, NY: Farrar, Straus and Giroux.

Goldman, S. L., Nagel, R. N., Davison, B. D., & Schmid, P. D. (2008). Next generation agility: smart business and smart communities. In P. H. M. Vervest, D. W. van Liere, & L. Zheng (Eds.), *The network experience – New value from smart business networks*. Berlin, Germany: Springer.

Gulati, R. (2007). *Managing network resources – Alliances, affiliations, and other relational assets.* Oxford, UK: Oxford University Press.

Hinterhuber, A. (2002). Value chain orchestration in action and the case of the global agro-chemical industry. *Long Range Planning, 35*(6), 615–635.

Kelly, K. (1994). *Out of control: The new biology of machines.* London, UK: Fourth Estate Ltd.

Koppius, O. R., & van de Laak, A. (2008). The quick-connect capability and its antecedents. In P. H. M. Vervest, D. W. van Liere, & L. Zheng (Eds.), *The network experience – New value from smart business networks.* Berlin, Germany: Springer.

Koppius, O. R., & van Fenema, P. C. (2006). *Efficacy, Effectiveness, and Efficiency of Organizational Capabilities: Implications for Learning.* Paper presented at Academy of Management 2006, Atlanta, GA.

Moore, J. F. (1993, May–June). Predators and prey: A new ecology of competition. *Harvard Business Review.*

Podolny, J. M., & Page, K. L. (1998). Network forms of organization. *Annual Review of Sociology, 24*, 57–76.

Prahalad, C. K., & Hamel, G. (1990). The core competence of the corporation. *Harvard Business Review, 68*(3), 79–91.

Preiss, K. (2005). Where are the smarts located in a smart business network. In P. H. M. Vervest, E. van Heck, K. Preiss, & L. F. Pau (Eds.), *Smart business networks.* Berlin, Heidelberg, Germany: Springer.

Pyke, J. (2008). The rise of the business operations platform. In P. H. M. Vervest, D. W. van Liere, & L. Zheng (Eds.), *The network experience – New value from smart business networks.* Berlin, Germany: Springer.

Reggiani, A., Nijkamp, P., & Cento, A. (2008). Connectivity and competition in airline networks – A study of lufthansa's network. In P. H. M. Vervest, D. W. van Liere, & L. Zheng (Eds.), *The network experience – New value from smart business networks.* Berlin, Germany: Springer.

Saxena, K. B. C. (2008). Business process management in a smart business network environment. In P. H. M. Vervest, D. W. van Liere, & L. Zheng (Eds.), *The network experience – New value from smart business networks.* Berlin, Germany: Springer.

Senge, P. (1990). *The fifth discipline: the art & practice of the learning organization.* New York, NY: Bantam DoubleDay Dell Publishing Group.

Shaw, D. R., & Holland, C. P. (2008). Strategy, networks and systems in the global translation services market. In P. H. M. Vervest, D. W. van Liere, & L. Zheng (Eds.), *The network experience – New value from smart business networks.* Berlin, Germany: Springer.

Stabell, C. B., & Fjeldstad, O. D. (1998). Configuring value for competitive advantage: On chains, shops, and networks. *Strategic Management Journal, 19*(5), 413–437.

Stalk, G., Evans, P., & Shulman, L. E. (1992, March–April). Competing on capabilities – The new rules of corporate strategy. *Harvard Business Review*, 57–68.

Thompson, G. F. (2003). *Between hierarchies and markets – The logic and limits of network forms of organization.* Oxford, UK: Oxford University Press.

Toffler, A. (1980). *The third wave.* New York, NY: Bantam Books.

Treacy, M., & Wiersema, F. (1995). *The Discipline of Market Leaders: Choose Your Customers, Narrow Your Focus, Dominate Your Market.* Reading, M: Addison-Wesley.

van Baalen, P. J., & van Fenema, P. C. (2008). Fighting sars with a hastiy formed network. In P. H. M. Vervest, D. W. van Liere, & L. Zheng (Eds.), *The network experience – New value from smart business networks.* Berlin, Germany: Springer.

van Heck, E., & Vervest, P. H. M. (2007). Smart business networks: How the network wins. *Communications of the ACM, 50*(6), 29–37.

van Liere, D. W. (2007). *Network horizon and the dynamics of network positions – A multi method multi-level longitudinal study of interfirm networks*. Rotterdam, The Netherlands: Rotterdam School of Management, Erasmus University Rotterdam.

van Liere, D. W., Koppius, O. R., & Vervest, P. H. M. (2008). Network horizon: an information-based view on the dynamics of bridging positions. In J. A. C. Baum, & T. J. Rowley (Eds.), *Network strategy* (Vol. 25). Bingley, UK: Emerald Group Publishing Ltd.

Vervest, P. H. M., Preiss, K., van Heck, E., & Pau, L. F. (2004). The emergence of smart business networks. *Journal of Information Technology, 19*(4), 228–233.

Vervest, P. H. M., van Heck, E., Preiss, K., & Pau, L. F. (Eds.). (2005). *Smart business networks*. Berlin, Heidelberg, Germany: Springer.

Von Bertalanffy, L. (1968). *General system theory – Foundations, development, applications*. New York, NY: George Braziller Inc.

3. Process Management in Business Networks

Jon Pyke

Cordys, Putten, The Netherlands, jpyke@cordys.com

The Role of BPM

The first vows sworn by two creatures of flesh and blood were made at the foot of a rock that was crumbling to dust; they called as witness to their constancy a heaven which never stays the same for one moment; everything within them and around them was changing...

Oeuvres Romanesques, Denis Diderot (1713–1784)

Much management thinking and writing is about entities – things – that are unmoving, unchanging and separate. The reality is that most of what you see around you, whether you can touch it or not, is part of some process or processes. It is on its way to being something else. As Diderot suggests, nothing in this world is unchanging.

The processes deployed in all organizations define the culture of that entity, they are what differentiate it from other, seemingly, similar entities – they define the corporate backbone and are, quite simply, the way things get done around here. Needless to say then, they are pretty important and need to be managed and exploited just like any other corporate asset.

The importance of managing business processes will only increase as we are entering the networked age. For organizations to be able to participate in networks it will be crucial that they have mastered their internal processes before they can start collaborating in networks and connecting business processes across the boundaries of their organization.

One of the most effective ways of exploiting these vital assets is to explore ways of managing them and this is where Business Process Management (BPM) comes into its own. But what exactly is BPM and is the technology hype or reality? A good deal of the technology that underpins Business Process Management concepts has its roots in the late 1980's and early 1990's and stems from the early efforts of the workflow community. So BPM is not new. Business software has long supported major business processes. What has changed is the realization that business managers need to understand and improve those processes. Getting a handle on the myriad processes that exists in all organizations is the easiest way to be more competitive, adaptable, responsive and manage costs.

P.H.M. Vervest et al. (eds.) *The Network Experience*
© Springer-Verlag Berlin Heidelberg 2009

Using process-based software delivers an improved ability to respond to or anticipate changing business demands. Also, the organization saves money whenever it changes computerised working methods – usually an expensive and protracted rigmarole. As a bonus, the organization becomes better fitted to exploit future business and computing opportunities, including business process outsourcing (BPO) and Web services. One of the significant changes to the organizational aspects stems from the fact that the processes can extend beyond the "four walls" of the company. The net result is a network of processes that require process enabled "Smart Networks". As a result, the company can quickly change the players and the structure of the process without losing ownership or compromising the single view of the business.

This means that tasks that were under the direct control of the business are now dynamically outsourced to other actors in the network enabling the process owner to flex the business dynamics one second before the transaction occurs. The big question is what kind of technology is required to make this happen – the answer is The Business Operations platform. But before discussing the BOP, let's first look at the technology that leads us up to this new way of thinking (Fig. 3.1).

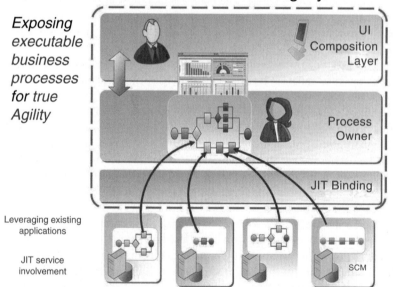

Fig. 3.1 The business operations platform as enabler for true agility

The History of BPM

BPM is not a new concept, and we're certainly not trying to solve any new problems with its introduction and use. However, we are solving them differently. The old way was to create isolated "stove pipe" solutions. These were rigid, difficult to maintain, costly to set up and, worst of all, obsolete by the time they arrived. We want to solve problems cheaply, quickly and effectively. How? By seeing those problems as a set of well-defined and integrated processes.

Carr (2003) argues that it is a mistake to assume that as IT's potency and ubiquity has increased, so too has its strategic value. What makes a resource truly strategic – what gives it the capacity to be the basis for a sustained competitive advantage – is not ubiquity but scarcity (Barney, 1991). You only gain an edge over rivals by having or doing something that they can't have or do. By now, the core functions of IT – data storage, data processing and data transport – have become available and affordable to all.

Carr's article spawned a "may-bug" industry of counter argument and rebuke – books were written, behemoths were angered – so this paper is not going to enter the fray except to say that what if Carr is right? Buying more IT simply keeps you in that game? What that means of course is that if an organization is only going to get to a "me too" position by spending vast sums on IT infrastructure then managers need to look at what it is that will give them the edge and apply technology to that aspect to gain a competitive advantage. The obvious candidate is business process – the way you do things – or the backbone of your organization.

Applying IT to process technology is going to give you that competitive advantage; it will show a return on the investment – it will keep you in front – and that is where the value will come from – and that is what I believe the Business Process Management revolution is all about. Setting all that aside for the moment let us briefly review the technologies and where better to start than at the core of it all, The Business Process Management System (BPMS). A well-defined BPMS has three major parts:

- An execution engine that executes process models;
- A series of tools that support the whole process life cycle (process specification, design and discovery tools, process configuration and deployment tools, process monitoring, analysis and optimization tools, as well as specific BPMS management tools); and
- Integration support that enable the BPMS to interact with the software programs required by the processes executed by the process engine.

In theory, a BPMS should act like a virtual machine that is executing process models rather than software code. Not all do, but despite what some purists might say, the majority of today's BPM products do work in this way. The best way to think of a BPMS is to draw an analogy with an application server or web server – a machine within a machine if you will. Furthermore, in the context of smart networks a BPMS can, and does become part of the network operating system. But why would it need to? The process defines the who, what, where, when and why of the organisation. In most private sector organisations, they can be broken down into the following four basic steps:

- Take an order/sell a product
- Source the product (buy it, build it, find it, create it)
- Fulfil the order
- Get paid.

Sounds simple enough. But this simple vision soon begins to branch off and multiply into a complex myriad of sub-divisions when you look more closely at each of the steps. Take step 2 for example. In order to source the product, lots of things need to have happened or will need to happen, such as:

- Buying in the raw components
- Manufacturing certain elements
- Maintaining and managing stock levels
- Providing packaging.

All of the resultant sub-processes are designed and implemented to support the high level vision. This approach involves technology, but it is not technology-led. The business need drives the process; the process drives the technology need. The "where" aspect no longer matters. What matters is having the flexibility to change processes on demand to meet demand. Being able to flex the process one second before the transaction takes place means that the process is totally flexible, yet still enables the owner to have a single view of the truth – a single view of the business.

Process-based solutions provide information to a user at a given point in a business process – not the other way round. There is also a need to understand that business processes exist at two levels: the systems and the people. Business processes almost always include people and this means that the technologies you need will be, fundamentally, collaborative applications. So the answer is not to try and develop a set of tools to deal with every anticipated business outcome or rule, but to build in flexibility, partly through the use of open communications standards and intelligent networks.

Key to Business Process Management – Analytics to Manage the Process

There is one key aspect the BPM does provide that Workflow did not; analytics – the ability to truly manage processes. This is the second key area of BPM technology (see below). We have established that the term workflow adequately covers the routing of work packets from one point in a process to another. The term may be "old-fashioned" but the technology, and tools that surround the technology, do a good job in enabling that to happen: But a lot more capability is needed to truly manage business processes – and unsurprisingly it's the market itself, what customers are buying, that is determining what BPM is. The key to delivering true Business Process Management, as opposed to services orchestration, process automation and workflow is the ability to get to the heart of the organization and extract the process analytics. This is what Gartner refer to as a Business Process Management Suite.

Analytics give business managers and executives the ability to track and measure performance based on real-time feedback of their processes giving them real insight into how the organization is operating. This enables end users to make informed decisions because they are presented with issues that need to be addressed so they can take the right action at the appropriate time. The solution being proposed by most process centric vendors is wrapped up in a technology labelled Business Activity Monitoring or BAM for short. The focus of most BAM tools is improving the efficacy of business decisions and facilitating fast and well-informed responses. The benefits derived are beneficial to all organizations regardless of industry. Despite offering myriad business benefits the majority of BAM solutions currently available do not go far enough.

Until now most BAM tools have been used by BPM solutions as simple reporting tools and feedback loops. What an organization needs is an offering that provides process simulation, real-time business intelligence and event monitoring of a BAM tool tightly coupled with a high performance BPM engine that is capable of process orchestration and sophisticated event handling and ad-hoc process management; in other words, business process optimization. Consider the following scenarios:

1. A process is contained in a number of applications and cannot be extracted from legacy applications without expensive re-write efforts.
2. A process can be easily defined, engineered and implemented as a BPM system – the environments where BPM comes into its own and provides fast development and implementation.
3. The combination of options one and two. Where neither approach will meet the customer need of a process centric solution based heavily on legacy environments – arguably most organizations operating today.

Scenario 1 – When the Process Cannot be Extracted

In this scenario the internal systems are part of a "business process" but they are silo legacy applications. Ordinarily, BPM vendors would argue that these applications would be better served if they were controlled by an independent process layer – a good idea – but not always feasible. The answer to this problem is to let the optimization tool monitor and manage the interaction of these systems and trigger exceptions and pass the exception processing to the BPMS. Once the exception is "caught" it can be passed to BPM tool for processing.

Scenario 2 – When the Process can be Extracted

In this particular scenario BPM users have recognized the need to re-engineer their systems and take a more process centric approach to implementation. This is the natural BPM vendor sweet spot and where a process suite solution fits best. Where the key differentiator comes in now is that this solution would offer a "real time" option rather than a "near" real time solution provided by reporting tools. The advantages of this are numerous and include:

- Real time process monitoring and managing – allowing for automated solutions and dynamic rerouting of work
- Easier integration into systems management systems such as Tivoli
- Extending the monitoring to sub flows (those triggered by EAI demands of process orchestration (web services)).

Scenario 3 – The Combination of the Above – The Composite Processes

There are situations where parts of an enterprise can be re-engineered (scenario 2) and where there are certain silo applications that cannot be touched (scenario 1) but need to be part of an overall BPM strategy. For example, Complex Order Management in telecommunication organizations comprises many back office systems which are an important part of the provisioning process yet they cannot be fully integrated into the process for a host of reasons – complexity being one of the main ones. Yet despite them being outside of the managed process they do run "micro" (think of them as sub) processes which need to be monitored. If a delay occurs in one of these systems, the impact on the automated process could be very significant – so being able to monitor and manage the interactions between the "external" applications the main process can be modelled and controlled far more easily. Doubts exist as to whether this could be done in products as they exist today – yet the solution is relatively simple.

This is what true process management is all about – being able to manage and monitor processes of every shape and hue and adjust the operation of the business accordingly. No single tool can achieve this in isolation – indeed a Business Process Management Suite includes tools to:

- Model the business process between workers, systems, and information to create shared understanding about how business results can be optimized. Also improve speed of deployment and reduce effort to change
- Simulate the business process to identify bottle necks, costs, areas for improvement
- Execute the business process; automate the execution of optimized processes providing consistency of execution. Use feedback loops and "round trip engineering to keep operations at their optimum.

Enter the World of the Business Operations Platform

So we see that Workflow and Business Activity Monitoring gives us the basic rudiments of first pass BPM. But there is a lot more needed to ensure that organizations can take full benefit of the technology and to do that we need a new way of thinking about processes and the shape of the technology needed to execute and support them.

This thinking is designed around the notion of the Business Operations Platform – a platform that supports the way business works, delivers shared services, flexible collaboration support, facilitates rapid innovation and change, and drives maximum value out of your existing IT investments. Enter the world of the Business Operations Platform (BOP) – A second-generation BPM technology that supports the demands of the globalization of business, an environment designed to deliver Total BPM. As mentioned previously, the importance of managing business processes will only increase as we are entering the networked age. For organizations to be able to participate in networks it will be crucial that they have mastered their internal processes before they can start collaborating in networks and connecting business processes across, and beyond, the boundaries of their organization.

The BOP provides a very different approach to managing the business operations and the delivery of shared services. What BOP delivers is very different from "traditional" BPM (and a million miles away from where all this started – workflow automation) since it is designed to ensure that the competitive organizations is more than just a performance centric entity – it is also able to see and manage value creation, provide process improvement and, more importantly, process innovation.

When coupled with a smart network, a network that is part of the operating system the BOP removes many of the issues normally associated with managing the typical supply chain. For example:

- Disparate applications with unique data formats and versions are readily accessible and normalized in a Just in Time environment.
- It enables the organization to work through the increasingly complex world of managing products and plants by ensuring that the process involves the right resources at the right time.
- Information and processes are instantly synchronized wherever they may be.
- Full process and functional interoperability are enabled right through the supply network.

As we have seen, BPM grew out of the world of workflow and became an amalgam of Workflow, Analytics and EAI. "Ok I got that, but what exactly is a Business Operations Platform and why is it different from the "traditional" way we view Process Management?" If we start from a business perspective we can see that the process is the point where the operations world meets the technology world. The process is where these two worlds collide, and is, therefore, where the two worlds can achieve the most in terms of collaborative development and common understanding.

The result is an improved ability to respond to, or anticipate, changing business demands. Also, the organization saves money whenever it changes computerised working methods – usually an expensive and protracted rigmarole. As a bonus, the business becomes better fitted to exploit future business and computing opportunities, including business process outsourcing (BPO) and Web services. The BOP goes a long way towards fixing the communications problem that has existed between the business and IT since computers were first deployed as business productivity tools. Now, if you imagine for a moment that an application is a process (or the process is an application, it doesn't make too much difference for this paper) then there is clear proposition that calls for developing applications from the business model up. The model driven organization, where what you model is what you execute. Some traditional BPM tools appear to do this but as you drill into them there are a lot of disconnects between the development of the process model and the deployment of the application.

One of the key aspects of the Business Operations Platform is that it is specifically designed to bridge the communications gap mentioned above. However, to date, most process modelling tools are often very far removed from the process implementation. Vendors either OEM or partner with modelling tool vendors and provide an import capability so that you can get the model in some form of "executable" mode. Others have very distinct products in their product portfolio which is almost as cumbersome as using a third party tool. So traditional BPM has not really delivered on its early promise and the issues are quite simple and straightforward:

When modelling business processes there is always a problem keeping the implementation model (the process definition) synchronized with the conceptual business models (what the business sees). This means that communication becomes a problem when the business user hands over his requirements to the implementation staff. Now that may not be an insurmountable issue but it does create a "moment of truth (MOT)" (the point at which things can break) in the development life cycle. This gets further complicated when the implementation staff attempt to keep the composite application components like business rules, web services, application UI's etc. synchronized with business models; another potentially damaging MOT. Finally, there is a problem keeping developers synchronized with the user so that they can collaborate easily in the development cycle to deliver exactly what the business asks for. Without the collaboration capabilities offered by this new breed of BPM, the problems of the past will be perpetuated and the business will never drive maximum value from its existing IT estate nor will it be agile, innovative or responsive enough to thrive in the global economy.

At the technology level, The Business Operations Platform allows us to create a process layer, which provides a level of process abstraction, and removes the processes from the control of applications. We decouple the process from the legacy in much the same way that middleware provided a data abstraction layer, Business Operations Platform provides a "process abstraction" layer that delivers business services when and where they are needed.

With the Business Operations Platform, instead of having each application being in charge of a set of processes, and trying to subjugate adjacent applications, to drive its processes, we take the control of the process away from the individual applications, and make them equal peers, subjugated to the Business Operations Platform layer that controls the execution of the processes, the provision of services and delegates tasks or activities to the individual applications according to their strengths. In order to do this well, the Business Operations Platform must support all the attributes of a business process, which we described above. For example, it needs to be able to:

- Manage applications in parallel as well as series
- It needs to manage people-intensive applications
- It needs to totally decouple the process from the application
- Inside and outside the organization
- Continuous and discrete, and allow processes to change over time
- Put the process into the hands of the business user.

This is a tall order, the Business Operations Platform delivers these needs like nothing that's gone before, at long last there is a new way of delivering the agility and flexibility needed to support today's rapidly changing business environment and the threat posed by globalization. The key benefits derived from a BOP are:

- Provides a platform that is totally decoupled from the tasks, resources a data used within the business operations.
- Ensures minimum risk due to the modular solution which can be implemented in "bite sized services".

- Ensures maximum flexibility at the operations level – this flexibility includes roles and processes.
- Ensures a single view of the business with easily maintainable KPI parameters.

How does the Business Operations Platform Differ from the Past?

One of the easiest ways to understand what a technology is to understand its capabilities. The capabilities of the Business Operations Platform are currently associated with a number of other technologies, such as: Web-Services, SOA, ESB, CAF, MDM, BI. As well as having the process-centric controlling layer, the Business Operations Platform will need the data-centric connectivity capabilities of EAI, to support the application-to-application integration, and the document-centric capabilities of workflow, to support the person-to-person interaction.

However, a true Business Operations Platform will be more than simply the sum of these parts – a true Business Operations Platform also functions as the Enterprise dashboard providing the business user with a single view of the business.

The real strength of the BOP arises when consider it as a platform that enables the user to assemble business processes using Lego-like business services. These business services are not just simple "get data, put data" constructs, they are real business services including KPIs, User Interface, business rules, metadata etc. that can be used throughout the organization and, when necessary, beyond – they can be shared with business partners or bought and sold as commodities. From what we have discovered we can quickly see that the BOP is a key enabler of process enabled networks and that one of the main benefits from this approach is to be able to provide a platform that is totally decoupled from the tasks, resources a data used within the business operations. Figure 3.2 illustrates the Business Operations Platform (This is the strategic vision and not technically correct).

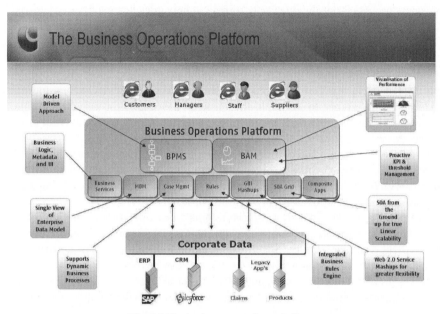

Fig. 3.2 The business operations platform

The impact this has on how processes are developed is quite profound. The fact that the key components of a process are totally de-coupled provides a high degree of flexibility, not only at design and development time, but at the point of execution. This means that the transaction can be changed one second before it is executed – so instead of building rigid inflexible solutions such as those found in ERP type solutions, we are able to deliver agile, dynamic solutions that can be flexed to support the changing needs of the business. The flexibility of this approach goes far beyond the ability to change transactions. Being able to use different actors in a network that execute different parts of a process and being able to optimize the process network using different parameters such as:

- Throughput time
- Margin
- Quality
- Occupancy rate.

Also changes the business dynamics in ways that were unimaginable until now. For example, one of the key objectives of BPM is to put existing and new processes under the direct control of business managers. While this notion has a lot of technology underpinning it, it's not a technology solution per se, and is far too an important concept to be left entirely in the hands of IT. The business need drives the process; the process drives the technology need. You need Process based IT solutions because you want to provide information to a user at a given point in a business process – not the other way round. So how does this need for end-to-end control square up with the dynamics of the process outsourcing market (BPO). Clearly it doesn't since you have no control over the outsourced process.

By decoupling the process from the various technologies and resources the business is able to regain the upper hand and manage and monitor the processes as needed, ensuring that the proposed benefits from Process Outsourcing are achieved. This ability to decouple the resources, the data, the services and the business rules enable the BOP to radically change the way you execute your processes. As was said earlier, the importance of managing business processes will only increase as we are entering the networked age. For organizations to be able to participate in networks it will be crucial that they have mastered their internal processes before they can start collaborating in networks and connecting business processes across the boundaries of their organization.

The BOP enables you to radically rethink your operations. The ability to turn your business into a plug and play business is easier than reengineering (Merrifield, Calhoun, & Stevens, 2008) since it enables projects to be of much smaller scope, shorter duration and less risk, yet can be more challenging since it requires profound technology changes. The Business Operations Platform delivers the profound required to support the process enabled global economy and rethink the way you do business forever.

References

Barney, J. B. (1991). Firm resources and sustained competitive advantage. *Journal of Management, 17*(1), 99–120.

Carr, N. G. (2003, May). It doesn't matter. *Harvard Business Review*, 11.

Diderot, D. (1962). *Oeuvres romanesques*. New York, NY: French & European Publications Inc.

Merrifield, R., Calhoun, J., & Stevens, D. (2008, June). The next revolution in productivity. *Harvard Business Review*, 11.

4. Next Generation Agility: Smart Business and Smart Communities

Steven L. Goldman, Roger N. Nagel, Brian D. Davison and Patrick D. Schmid

Lehigh University, Bethlehem, PA, USA, slg2@lehigh.edu, rnagel@lehigh.edu, bdd3@lehigh.edu, pds2@lehigh.edu

Abstract

In February 2008 a group of Lehigh University faculty and graduate and under-graduate students, led by Roger Nagel and drawn from all four of Lehigh's Colleges, launched a study of how organizations could derive value from communities analogous to those mobilized by popular social networking and virtual environment applications, and how those organizations would have to change to realize that value. The article that follows is an account of a work in progress with the goal of helping companies understand how the agile business paradigm is evolving and how to remain competitive.

First Generation Agility

The globalization of commerce, driven by ever more powerful information, production and communication technologies, is rapidly dissolving the organizational walls that marked the boundaries of traditional integrated enterprises. These integrated firms with neatly bounded organizational structures dominated commerce from the late 19th to the late 20th centuries, but this started to unravel in the 1980s. Competition arose first from centrally coordinated webs of interdependent companies – among them, Japanese *keiretsu* and Korean *chaebols*. Offshore outsourcing to cut costs was the initial response of many traditional firms, a strategy popular with management because it preserved the organizational status quo, but highly unpopular with the newly unemployed. In the 1990s, recognition slowly grew that a new structural status quo was possible, keyed to the promise of computer-based technologies to integrate total business capabilities out of personnel, physical resources, and business processes that are geographically and organizationally fully distributed.

First generation agility (Goldman, Nagel, & Preiss, 1995) comprised business strategies that leveraged cooperation internally and collaboration externally. These strategies exploited information and knowledge to gain competitive advantage from rapidly changing market conditions and new market opportunities. Virtual organization and networked enterprise models were adopted as extensions of, and in some cases as alternatives to, the integrated enterprise. They offered the promise of greater flexibility, greater speed, reduced transaction costs, and a greatly enhanced pool of knowledge and information to be applied to innovation.

Smart business networks (Janneck et al., 2008; Nagel, Walters, Gurevich, & Schmid, 2005) are the mature form of early attempts at creating value from agile business strategies based on inter-enterprise collaboration. The Internet was simultaneously the critical enabler of these networks and its greatest driver, as growing numbers of companies exploited the Internet to reorganize product development, manufacturing, supply chains, marketing, sales, and customer relations. Today, the evolution of Internet resources, especially social networking and virtual environment technologies, is again both enabling and driving the evolution of agile business strategies as well as of smart business networks. This evolution, in turn, is driving the further dissolution of organizational boundaries as companies strive to create value out of globally distributed information and knowledge (Friedman, 2006). In the process, new challenges are emerging to leadership, organizational structure, business processes, metrics and rewards, and workforce mindset or culture.

First generation agile business strategies required loosening the hierarchical control structures and control policies of traditional enterprises in order to enable cooperation and collaboration. Next generation agility strategies will require much more loosening of control. Executives will have to move from agile, top down motivational leadership to nurturing bottom up leadership and to opening even top down vision and executive decision making not only to bottom up input, but to input from outside the enterprise (Li & Bernoff, 2008; Tapscott & Williams, 2006).

Next Generation Agility

After little more than a decade, it is once again necessary to rethink organizational structures in order to support dynamic collaboration across ever more porous enterprise boundaries. It is necessary to rethink as well the fluid execution of globally distributed business processes, operational metrics, personnel incentives, and workforce culture that companies must master to continually form and reform value creating "agile communities" within and among enterprises (Chesbrough, 2006a, 2006b; Raymond, 1999):

The first generation agile business paradigm puts a premium on cross-functional teams as expressions of a commitment to a truly collaborative intra- and inter-enterprise work ethic. Networking among enterprises was a natural extension of the team concept, given the recognized value, at least in principle, of forming teams whose members possessed relevant knowledge and access to relevant resources, regardless of their physical or organizational location. The networked enterprise was a revolutionary, agile, business strategy in the 1990s, but it was then, and remains today, a top down-driven strategy (Preiss, Nagel, & Goldman, 1996). The value proposition for inter-enterprise networks, and thus the constitution of the network, its goals, terms of operation and evaluation metrics, are established in advance. This will not be the case in the emerging next generation agile enterprise.

Social networking and virtual environment (SNVE) technologies have added a new dimension to creating and operating competitive businesses. SNVE applications such as Facebook, MySpace, Second Life, World of Warcraft, and such SNVE tools as blogging, wikis and mashups are characterized by the self-organization of globally distributed communities of people and by the creation of new interaction "spaces", opportunities for new kinds of interactions, among people within and among these communities. The obvious question is: Can the systematic mobilization of open communities – analogous to those enabled by existing applications of SNVE technologies – create significant new value for businesses? There is a growing body of evidence that the answer to this question is "Yes". The recent and continuing experiences of companies such as Goldcorp, Navteq, InnoCentive and Procter and Gamble with open innovation models; IBM and Cisco with Second Life as a recruiting, training and meeting resource; dozens of companies from auto manufacturers like Toyota and Peugeot to software developers like SAP and Sugar-CRM using SNVEs for engaging customers in the product development process; Eli Lilly, Hewlett-Packard, and GE with prediction markets; and hundreds of companies, most notably Google and Amazon, using current SNVE communities as platforms for creating and selling goods and services, all testify that behind the inevitable hype there is real value to be earned.

These examples support the value proposition for mobilizing what we are calling agile communities. The next step is to understand *when* a company should implement a social community-mobilizing strategy and *how* to do so: What needs to change inside the company, from its leadership to its culture, what new capabilities need to be acquired, what infrastructure needs to be put in place? The question of which software technologies to use arises only after we know what we want to use them for and what the value of that use is. Figure 1 illustrates next generation agility.

We are beginning to identify, at least in broad terms, the core characteristics of next generation networked enterprises, that is, of companies that are capable of mobilizing social communities on behalf of new business strategies.

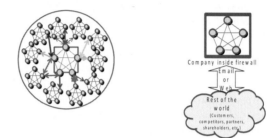

Fig. 4.1 Next generation agility

Community Mobilizing Strategies

In the most general sense, the goal of agile community-mobilizing strategies is to create synergies that generate real value. This value may lie in solving problems faster and more cheaply than before, or in solving problems that had been intractable using standard resources. Synergies emergent from communities are already generating ideas for new kinds of products and services, for new development pathways for existing products and services, and for alternatives to existing business processes. Social communities can generate "value surprises" by providing access to knowledge you need that is already possessed by people you do not know. Or the value surprise can come from emergent outcomes of unanticipated interactions among people largely unknown to you and among disparate communities not antecedently identified as relevant that enter into opportunistic interactions.

The agility-promoted strategy of moving from stand-alone companies to networking now appears to be the opening stage of an evolving process: Moving from networks of companies to clusters of independent, interdependent or overlapping communities of people who are consciously operating in evolving ecosystems defined by brand name companies that harvest the value created by communities. Communities are networks on adrenalin, so to speak, networks liberated from central control yet coupled to business objectives, and implemented and facilitated in ways that encourage serendipitous outcomes.

Trust is a critical enabler of collaborative relationships. Within social communities trust means transparency, honesty, and integrity. It also means competence in social skills that make a dynamically interactive, geographically distributed community work effectively; the ability to function in multiple communities; reliable and predictable community-related decision-making behavior; and loyalty to the community, which will surely require a broader definition of company loyalty than is the case today. Self-interest and self-promotion manifestly are drivers of existing SNVE-mediated communities, but so is a remarkable degree of selflessness, of a willingness to give assistance to otherwise unknown members of the community. Companies need to channel this combination of selfishness and selflessness on behalf of new business strategies.

Information integration is a central concept of agility and of the networked enterprise and of smart business networks. It becomes still more central in a communities environment. Sharing information at all levels of an enterprise and with members of a community independent of enterprise boundaries is a fundamental characteristic of a community environment. It is the sharing of information that knits individuals into a community, enabling emergent behaviors that generate values and accomplish goals. This implies a far greater degree of ceding control of products, of product development, of at least some hitherto proprietary information, and even of business processes, to the influence of "outsiders". Sharing information selectively with controlled networks of suppliers, customers and collaborators, including competitors, was central to agility. This ceding of control is ratcheted up dramatically with the adoption of business strategies keyed to open innovation, open sourcing, "crowdsourcing", and participatory marketing (Li & Bernoff, 2008; Tapscott & Williams, 2006).

The transition from networks to communities is a kind of phase transition, (Gladwell, 2002) characterized by qualitative as well as quantitative changes, and the emergence of new properties. To make the transition, companies need to identify the value in networking relationships that typically is "hidden" in weak links, intangible contributions, and informal connections. There is a distinctive though difficult to quantify value in a loosely structured yet focused relationship that stimulates interactive sharing, serendipitous experiences, a "we" ethos, and a consciousness of functioning within an evolving ecosystem of people, resources and markets (Libert & Spector, 2007).

Guidelines for Managers

A set of guidelines is beginning to crystallize for assessing the benefits that a company can gain from moving from networking strategies to agile community mobilization strategies, and also the dangers and vulnerabilities that come with those benefits. There is a need for taxonomy of communities and of internal and external community-enabled strategies. There is a need as well for an efficient means of assessing the value of these strategies and for identifying their implications for a company's leadership, organizational structure, business processes, metrics and incentives, and company culture, and the interdependencies among these.

What role do CEOs play in companies committed to pursuing value by mobilizing communities? How can bottom up communities be empowered with such typically top down tasks as vision, values, motivation, initiative, and tactics without creating managerial anarchy? What mix of personality characteristics and skills is necessary for business outcome-focused communities to work effectively? Can training alter personality characteristics or teach required skills? How much facilitation will such communities require to channel their interactions into valuable outcomes and what new facilitation skills might be required?

The rationale for our work in progress on next generation agility is the reality of how companies are using the evolving Internet via SNVE applications to do business better and to create new businesses in an unstable, information- and knowledge-driven, global competitive environment. Over a billion people are today connected to the Internet and they are becoming interconnected in ways that generate enormous possibilities for new kinds of individual and collective experiences (Friedman, 2006). Out of these experiences will come new forms of social, political, cultural and economic relationships, among them new kinds of markets and business opportunities. It is not a question of whether this will happen; it is happening, irreversibly. It is not a question of *whether* companies should be exploring the implications of what's happening for their futures; it's question of *how* to do so effectively. To the urgency of responding to this challenge must be added the pressure of meeting the expectations of the incoming "millennial" generation of employees, for whom social communities are as natural as oxygen, while retaining the knowledge locked up in retiring baby boomers. After a status quo of 100 years, we are witnessing in just twenty years the transition from the integrated firms to disintegrated "fuzzily"-bounded ecosystem enterprises leveraging evolving clusters of quasi-self organizing, dynamically interactive communities.

References

Chesbrough, H. (2006a). *Open business models: How to thrive in the new innovation landscape*. Cambridge, MA: Harvard Business School.

Chesbrough, H. (2006b). *Open innovation: The new imperative for creating and profiting from technology*. Cambridge, MA: Harvard Business School.

Friedman, T. L. (2006). *The world is flat*. Farrar, New York: Strauss and Giroux.

Gladwell, M. (2002). *The tipping point: How little things can make a big difference*. Boston: Backbay.

Goldman, S. L., Nagel, R. N., & Preiss, K. P. (1995). *Agile competitors and virtual organizations*. New York: Van Nostrand Reinhardt.

Janneck, C. D., Nagel, R. N., Schmid, P. D., Raim, J. D., Connolly, M. L., & Moll, M. A. (2008). Smart business networks: Core concepts and characteristics. In P. Vervest, E. van Heck, & K. Preiss (Eds.). *Smart business networks: A new business paradigm* (pp. 501–523). Rotterdam, the Netherlands: Smart Business Network Initiative (SBNi), Rotterdam School of Management, Erasmus University.

Li, C., & Bernoff J. (2008). *Groundswell: Winning in a world transformed by social technologies*. Cambridge, MA: Harvard Business School.

Libert, B., & Spector, J. (2007). *We are smarter than me: How to unleash the power of crowds in your business*. Philadelphia: Wharton School Publishing.

McMillan, J. (2002). *Reinventing the bazaar*. New York: Norton.

Nagel, R. N., Walters J. P., Gurevich G., & Schmid, P. D. (2005). Smart business networks enable strategic opportunities not found in traditional business networking. In P. Vervest, E. van Heck, K. Preiss, L.-F. Pau (Eds.). *Smart business networks* (pp. 127–143). Berlin, Heidelberg, Germany: Springer.

Preiss, K. P., Nagel, R. N., & Goldman S. L. (1996). *Cooperate to compete*. New York: John Wiley.

Raymond, E. S. (1999). *The cathedral and the bazaar*. Cambride: O'Reilly.

Tapscott, D., & Williams, A. D. (2006). *Wikinomics: How mass collaboration changes everything*. New York: Penguin.

5. The Actors

Jan Stentoft Arlbjørn
Professor at University
of Southern Denmark,
Denmark

Roel van den Berg
Director of Strategic
Projects & Alliances,
RSM Erasmus
University,
The Netherlands

Jan Baan
Founder and Chief
Executive Officer
at Cordys Group,
The Netherlands

Hans Borgman
Professor in Business
Administration
and Information
Management,
Leiden University,
The Netherlands

Nico Barito
Senior Fellow,
United Nations
Institute for Training
& Research

Theo Bouts
COO at Zurich
Financial Services,
Switzerland

Jan van den Berg
Associate Professor
Information and
Communication
Technology
at TU Delft,
The Netherlands

David A. Bray
Post-Doctoral
Research Associate, MIT's
Center for Collective
Intelligence & Harvard's
Leadership for a
Networked World,
USA

Xavier Busquets
Senior Lecturer
and Director Depart-
ment of Management
of Information
Systems at ESADE,
Spain

Hongbo Chen
Tsinghua Science
Park, Beijing, China

Nicola Carmyllie
Operations Manager
thebigword China,
UK

Weichao Chen (Vera)
Student at Tsinghua
University, China

Yueting Chai
Professor at Tsinghua
University,
China

Torben Damgaard
Associate Professor
at University of
Southern Denmark,
Denmark

Kalpana Chauhan
PhD student at Delhi
University, India

Yossi Dashti
PhD student
at Ben Gurion
University,
Israel

Guoqing Chen
Professor, Information
Systems and Executive
Associate Dean
at Tsinghua
University, School
of Economics and
Management

Dominique Delporte
Professor, Strategic
Management at
University Antwerp
Management School,
Belgium

Jing Dong
IBM Innovation
Center, Beijing,
China

Mark Greeven
PhD student at RSM
Erasmus University,
The Netherlands

Jürgen Dorn
Professor Information
Systems at the
Vienna University
of Technology,
Austria

Longyan Guo
Beijing Organizing
Committee for the Games
of the XXiX Olympiad

Al Dunn
Partner at D-Age
Management,
UK

Anders Haug
Assistant Professor
at University
of Southern Denmark,
Denmark

Curtis Eubanks
Curtis heads British
Telecom's offshore IT
development office in
Dalian,
China

Eric van Heck
Professor of Information
Management
and Markets at RSM
Erasmus University,
Rotterdam,
The Netherlands

David Fung
Managing Director
at Cordys Greater
China,
China

Christopher Herzog
Researcher for the
E-Commerce
Competence Center
in Vienna,
Austria

Robert Hexspoor
Senior Consultant
Organization &
Change, Meeting More
Minds,
The Netherlands

Barbara Krug
Professor Economics
of Governance,
RSM Erasmus
University,
The Netherlands

Christopher Holland
Professor of Infor-
mation Systems,
Manchester Business
School,
UK

Arnoud van de Laak
Junior Consultant
Greenwich Consulting
Benelux,
The Netherlands

Ton Jorg
Affiliated Educational
Scientist at the
University of Utrecht,
The Netherlands

Otto Koppius
Assistant Professor
at RSM Erasmus
University,
The Netherlands

Wolf Ketter
Assistant Professor
at RSM Erasmus
University,
The Netherlands

Ting Li
PhD student at RSM
Erasmus University,
The Netherlands

Benn R. Konsynski
George S. Craft
Professor of Informa-
tion Systems & Opera-
tions Management
at Emory University,
USA

Diederik van Liere
Post-doctoral
Researcher at RSM
Erasmus University,
The Netherlands

Kelly Bowles Lyman
Services Researcher,
IBM Almaden
Research Center,
USA

Jurriaan Meyer
Senior Consultant
at Dutch Railways,
The Netherlands

Liang Lu
Sr. Director Taobao,
Alibaba Group,
China

Sanneke Mulderink
Independent
Consultant,
The Netherlands

Fang Lu
Student at Tsinghua
University,
China

Roger Nagel
Senior Fellow
and Wagner Professor
at Lehigh University,
USA

Shuai Luo
Student at Tsinghua
University,
China

Marcel van Oosterhout
Scientific Researcher
at RSM Erasmus
University,
The Netherlands

Johannes Meuer
PhD Student
at RSM Erasmus
University,
The Netherlands

Kenneth Preiss
The Sir Leon Bagrit
Professor: Technology
and Global Competi-
tiveness at Ben Gurion
University,
Israel

Jon Pyke
Chief Strategy
Officer at Cordys,
The Netherlands

Sharon Ruwart
Managing Director
of Elsevier Science
and Technology,
China

Shalini Rahul
PhD Student
at Management
Development Institute,
India

Gavriel Salvendy
Professor and Head
of Department
of Industrial Engineering,
Tsinghua University,
China

Aura Reggiani
Professor in Economic
Policy at Bologna
University,
Italy

Jorge Sanz
Manager Services
Modeling Group,
IBM Almaden
Research Center,
USA

Jens Ove Riis
Professor of Industrial
Management Systems
at Aalborg University,
Denmark

**Kul Bhushan
Chandra Saxena**
Professor of Informa-
tion Management,
Management Devel-
opment Institute,
India

Paul Rooijmans
Consultant Purple
Orange Company,
The Netherlands

Gerrit Schipper
President & CEO
of RDC,
The Netherlands

Siebe Schuur
Dutch Economic
Council, China

Fernando Vega
Professor of Economics
at European University
Institute,
Italy

Duncan Shaw
Lecturer in Informa-
tion Systems
at Nottingham
University Business
School,
UK

Albert Veenstra
Assistant Professor
at RSM Erasmus
University, Rotterdam,
The Netherlands

Hao Sun
PhD, Tsinghua
University, China

Peter Vervest
Professor of Business
Telecommunications,
RSM Erasmus
University,
The Netherlands

Zoran Trifkovic
Co-Owner at ZMG
Zurich Management
Group

Ria Visser
Project Manager
at RSM Erasmus
University,
The Netherlands

Sascha Turck
Strategic Assistant
at Zurich Financial
Services,
Switzerland

Lei Wang
PhD Student
at University of Lugano,
Switzerland

Chengbo Wang
Academic
Director/Deputy
Director
LEAD-China/IED

Xiaobo Wu
Vice Dean, School
of Management; Director,
National Institute for
Innovation Management,
Zhejiang University,
Hangzhou,
China

Wei Wei
Master Student
at Tsinghua
University,
China

**Sheng Yun Yang
(Annie)**
PhD Student
at RSM Erasmus
University,
The Netherlands

Wendy Wen
Master Student
at Tsinghua
University,
China

Ming Yu
Associate Professor
at Tsinghua
University,
China

Hannes Werthner
Professor
E-Commerce
at the Vienna
University
of Technology,
Austria

Li Zheng
Professor at Tsinghua
University,
China

Martin Wong
PhD Student
at Harbin Institute
of Technology,
China

Fang Zhong (Vivian)
Assistant Professor
at RSM Erasmus
University,
The Netherlands

Network Essentials

Network Essentials

Network Essentials refer to a set of theories, concepts and ideas that are essential to understanding how networks are built, managed and changed. We have chosen four papers each addressing a different aspect of smart business networks. Our aim with these papers is to initiate a common vocabulary that will be shared by both academics and practitioners.

To begin, Bhushan Saxena formalizes concepts about Business Process Management. In previous chapters of this book (Pyke, 2008; Vervest, van Liere, & Dunn, 2008) it has been stressed that Business Process Management and the Business Operating System are crucial enablers of building digital-enabled interfirm networks: Network resources need process control. This paper is particularly important because it clarifies the difference between organizational capabilities, organizational functionalities and functionality delivery through business processes. By offering a clear hierarchy of these three concepts, Bhushan Saxena gives us a number of core concepts that should be part of our network vocabulary.

David Bray and Benn Konsynski offer a new approach on smartness in business networks. Previously, smart business networks were defined as (Vervest, Preiss, van Heck, & Pau, 2004):

- A group of participating businesses – organizational entities or "actors" – that form the nodes
- Linked together via one or more communication networks forming the links between the nodes
- With compatible goals
- Interacting in novel ways
- Perceived by each participant as increasing its own value
- Sustainable over time as a network.

David Bray and Benn Konsynski offer an additional perspective. The previous definition focuses on smartness *in* the network (i.e. the smart actors) while David and Benn speak of smartness *of* the network. In their view, smartness of the network is an property emergent that cannot be attributed to a single actor. According to them we can speak of 'smartness' when a digital network itself is capable of doing the following three things: (1) self-organizing, (2) externally communicating on its own behalf (we will return to this in the Network Enablers theme) and (3) internally creating new tools. They apply this thinking to possible future versions of the Internet.

Duncan Shaw and Chris Holland focus on the importance of loose coupling, uncoupling and modularity. Modularity is not only important at the process and product level, but it will be increasingly important at the firm level. As organizational decision makers increasingly view their firm as a "bundle of capabilities" it will become increasingly important to be able to plug-in a capability on an as-needed basis. This required capability may be located within the traditional firm boundaries or it might be offered by one of the network partners. Duncan Shaw and Chris Holland apply their modularity theories to thebigword, a UK based international company that offers networked translation services to global customers.

Finally, Kelly Bowles Lyman, Nathan Caswell and Alain Biem offer a methodology to model how value is created in business networks, or extended enterprises, as they understand them. Such a methodology is valuable because it facilitates communication between network partners (we return to this topic in *Network Orchestration* theme) and allows for the redesign of business processes that cut across the boundaries of an individual organization. Furthermore, they show the potential of using complex network analysis in analyzing these business networks to address such issues as network stability, network robustness and network cohesion. Complex network analysis is an important methodology for analyzing business networks. In the first chapter of Networks in Action, Aura Regianni, Peter Nijkamp and Alessandro Cento demonstrate its application to mapping and understanding Lufthansa's airline network.

Network Essentials moves towards our goal of building on a set of theories, concepts and methods that allow both practitioners and academics to increase their understanding of how smart business networks are developed and operated and to facilitate the development of tools to analyze them.

References

Pyke, J. (2008). The rise of the business operations platform. In P. H. M. Vervest, D. W. van Liere, & L. Zheng (Eds.). *The network experience – New value from smart business networks*. Berlin, Germany: Springer.

Vervest, P. H. M., Preiss, K., van Heck, E., & Pau, L. F. (2004). The emergence of smart business networks. *Journal of Information Technology, 19*(4), 228–233.

Vervest, P. H. M., van Liere, D. W., & Dunn, A. (2008). The network factor – How to remain competitive. In P. H. M. Vervest, D. W. van Liere, & L. Zheng (Eds.). *The network experience – New value from smart business networks*. Berlin, Germany: Springer.

6. Business Process Management in a Smart Business Network Environment

Kul Bhushan C. Saxena

Management Development Institute, Gurgaon, India, bsaxena@mdi.ac.in

Abstract

The current business environment is undergoing a dramatic change, increasingly being characterized by competition from a variety of players, emergence of a multitude of delivery channels and demand for more flexibility and agility leading to an increasing demand for innovation, flexibility and shorter time-to-market for new products/services. This paper proposes a Smart Business Network environment as an organizational design paradigm to fulfil these demands successfully. It evaluates the operational implications of adopting a SBN design for organizational flexibility in terms of the business process management (BPM) dimension and proposes a conceptual architecture for meeting the process management requirements for the SBN environment. Finally, the paper makes an assessment of the proposed architecture and suggests future direction for research.

Changing Business Environment and Need for Business Flexibility

The current business environment is undergoing a dramatic change, increasingly being characterized by competition from a variety of players, emergence of a multitude of delivery channels, a plethora of regulatory and governmental compliance requirements, and demands for more flexibility and agility. The influence of these issues has led to an increasing demand for innovation, flexibility,[1] and shorter time-to-market for new products/services. Consequently businesses are increasingly beginning to focus on their core competencies and their traditional corporate resources are getting deconstructed to emerge as "collaborating ecosystems". This concept called *componentisation*, involves an enterprise to deconstruct, analyse, and then reconstruct into *value nets*, in which partnerships with customers and

---

[1] Flexibility, in the interpretive model of strategic management, is defined as an imaginative capacity for creating strategic schemas broad enough to encourage strategic initiatives (Volberda, 1998).

suppliers operate in a network supported by real-time information flows and integrated IT systems (Cherbakov, Galambos, Harishanker, Kalyana, & Rackham, 2005). However, componentisation by itself is not sufficient. Interaction among business components need to be seamlessly and tightly integrated across the value net. The need for flexibility across the value net requires that the enterprise can "in-source" an outsourced component and vice-versa; replace on demand a current partner with a different partner; change the terms of the contract between the two components, and so on. Thus a Smart Business Network (SBN) environment is an ideal choice for enterprise componentisation.

The paper is organized as follows. The next section presents Smart Business Networks as a strategy for organisational design and focuses on a SBN facilitating different capabilities from different network adapters. The section following it identifies the requirements of business processes in a SBN environment. The section following this proposes a conceptual architecture for process management in SBN environments, and describes the four building blocks of this architecture. The last section evaluates the proposed architecture and suggests how this process-oriented thinking about SBNs could lead to wider adoption of the concept as an organizational design paradigm.

Smart Business Networks as Organisational Design Strategy

According to Vervest, van Heck, Preiss, and Pau (2005: 31), a SBN is a network of organizations coordinating their business processes in a manner that exhibits adaptive, agile and robust behaviour that is generated or reproduced when a robust and necessary set of networked structures and networking processes are established. According to this definition, the smart behaviour of a business network is shaped by its structure, processes and technology. Structurally (Fig. 6.1) a SBN combines "shapers" (one or more organisations which initiate and/or orchestrate the network) as well as "adapters" (organisations which comply with the requirements set by the shapers) (Vervest, van Heck, & Preiss, 2008: 36). Furthermore, there could be certain positions called *bridging positions* in the SBN layout which are more attractive to SBN adapters because the adapters link through these positions and the adapter holding the bridging position (called the *Bridger*) holds the network *bridge* (Vervest et al., 2008: 20). The bridge structure not only brings information and control benefits to the Bridger but also encourages the dependent adapters to find alternative routes, i.e. to disintermediate the Bridger. The shapers of a SBN also create a *business operating support system* (BOSS) which coordinates the processes among the networked businesses and its logic is embedded in the systems used by these businesses (Vervest et al., 2005: 5).

Conceptual Layout of a SBN

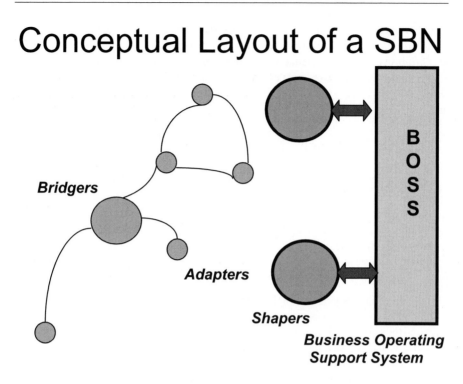

Fig. 6.1 Conceptual layout of a smart business network

Our perception of an SBN is that of an organisational design strategy of building a *networked business* enabled through information technology (IT) (Möller & Rajala, 2007; Möller, Rajala, & Svahn, 2005). Consequently we define an SBN as an IT-enabled platform for dynamically linking different businesses having different *capabilities* to build a "networked business enterprise" with innovative business strategies for competing in the changing markets and environmental conditions.

Smart business networks are enabled when organisations combine to amplify their cooperative abilities to deliver a specific value to a specific customer (Vervest et al., 2005: 37). SBNs leverage a network of relationships to add value to their products or services and enable collections of smaller organisations to compete for business with larger ones – a feat that can be highly unsuccessful if attempted by small organisations acting alone. This particular network effect – the power of many over one or a few – is sometimes called the *swarm effect* (Janneck et al., 2008). An SBN environment is characterised by the following features (Basu, 2005):

- Value systems that have more complex topologies than linear chains or tree-structured hierarchies

- Coordination mechanisms that can effectively manage the necessary interactions among component firms and their processes
- The ability to adapt to changing markets and environmental conditions
- The ability to learn from past performance.

SBN environments have been studied from a variety of perspectives: collaboration and governance, execution, design, etc. (Vervest et al., 2005). The focus in this paper, however, is organizational. That is, how organizations combined as a swarm, networked businesses (SBN) can produce exceptional or "smart" results they were not previously capable of generating (van Heck & Vervest, 2007). These SBN businesses make different linkages, combine different capabilities from many different network members to adapt to changing markets and environmental conditions, are more agile, and move positions faster. Specifically the paper focuses on the SBN's characteristic of dynamically combining different capabilities (sourced from various members) to create new capability as one of the major factor for its competitive success (Stalk, Evans, & Shulman, 1992). In this context, competing on capabilities involves two basic principles (Stalk et al.,1992):

1. The building blocks of a SBN's competitive strategy are not the products and markets but its business processes.
2. An SBN's competitive success depends on transforming its key processes into its strategic capabilities that consistently provide superior value to the customers. This may also involve building new capabilities by deve-loping new processes.

Thus, a capability of a SBN is a set of its business processes strategically understood. In this context, a business process is not merely limited to work processes based on organizational workflows, but include both the work processes as well as the behavioural processes, which involve widely shared patterns of behaviour and ways of acting/interacting (Garvin, 1998). An SBN is smart in identifying its key business processes, manage them centrally, and invest in them heavily, looking for a long-term payback. Consequently an important function of a SBN's "smartness" is its "smart" business process management (BPM); that is, its ability to inherit *dynamic adaptation* and *continuous experiential learning*. It is not that these two characteristics are not exhibited in the existing BPM environments,[2] but the challenge in an SBN is to embed these activities/processes such that they could be operational in real-time. This paper identifies the issues which need to be addressed for dynamic adaptation and continuous experiential learning and proposes a BPM functional architecture to realize this objective in a SBN environment. The

---

[2] For example, implementation of ERP system in a new industry/business sector almost always involves designing and building new "to-be" processes through dynamic adaptation of old "as-is" processes and experiential learning from earlier ERP implementations.

proposed BPM architecture is conceptual and based on the existing ongoing BPM research.

The paper is organized as follows. The next section identifies the requirements of business processes in a SBN environment. The section following this proposes a conceptual architecture for process management in SBN environments, and describes the four building blocks of this architecture. The last section evaluates the proposed architecture and suggests how this process-oriented thinking about SBNs could lead to wider adoption of the concept as an organizational design paradigm.

Requirements of Business Processes in a SBN Environment

The business processes in a SBN should be dynamic and be capable of building composite processes. Business processes in a traditional enterprise are in addition to being sequential, are also synchronous – that is, processing each of the process activity depends on and waits for the results of the previous activity. However, the business processes in a SBN must be *dynamic*; that is, the choice of subsequent activity for execution may be based on the full or even partial results of previous activities rather than on a pre-defined static sequence.

In the traditional value-chain oriented business environment, every major process/sub-process adds value to the output of the previous activity. These activities assembled in a production-line style, with or without some iterative or parallel streams, delivered cumulative results in a largely sequential workflow (Cherbakov et al., 2005). However, as a SBN-oriented business, the enterprise needs to have the option of assembling its processes by using activities provided by other network partners. In addition, the business processes can also be created by using a composition of existing activities in a new enhanced business process or a *meta-process* (Crawford, Bate, Cherbakov, Holley, & Tsocanos, 2005). This composite process can be viewed as similar to combining "products" of parallel production lines. This concept of "process composition" in a SBN is a powerful concept, because the "composite process" may be recursively combined to produce even more processes, offering new *functionality* and satisfying diverse non-functional requirements of potential customers. However, in order to offer these new functionalities as new services, they need to be combined according to certain business logic to deliver specific functionality and quality of service.

Furthermore, the creation of a new functionality may not just be a combination of several existing functionalities. It may involve modification or enhancement of existing functionalities, and these may include activities involving human intervention. For example, human intervention might be required when an unexpected exception occurs and a decision that could not be pre-programmed must be made.

Moreover, the processes to be used for composing new functionalities could be distributed across the entire set of SBN partners; therefore dynamic process composition will also require a search for processes that could provide the required capabilities being searched for.

The other requirement of a BPM in a SBN environment is their ability to learn from their past performance. People in knowledge-intensive processes must continually learn and adapt their activities to evolving process goals (Grant, 1996). However, integrating learning into business processes requires ways to go beyond current standard practice of standard learning modules into more personalized systems that address knowledge gaps on a just-in-time basis as they are discovered during process execution (Hawryszkiewycz, 2005).

These changes in process design required for a SBN environment also requires new approaches to process modelling. New models need to be able to support more than just process decomposition. One such process modelling approach is goal-based business process modelling (Kueng & Kawalek, 1997). According to this approach, goals are statements which declare what has to be achieved or avoided by a business process. This approach involves capturing different kind of goals from process participants, assess the captured goals for compatibility, manage inconsistencies, if any, and then create business processes which fulfil "all" goals. Thus goals of a process are used to structure the process design, to evaluate the design, to evaluate the operating process, and also to comprehend organizational changes that must accompany a process redesign. Nurcan, Etien, Kaabi, Zoukar, and Rolland (2005) describe a map representation system which conforms to a goal-oriented process modelling. Since one of the requirements of process modelling is to support process composition for supporting new functionalities, the modelling method should support building and using/re-using business process patterns. Andersson, Johannesson, and Perjons (2005) describe how goal-oriented business process patterns can be created which may be used for process composition. Also, in goal-oriented process design, it may be necessary to evaluate the implications of a process design on process performance even before it is implemented. Balasubramanian and Gupta (2005) describe structural metrics – both functional and performance-based, which could be used for process design and evaluation.

Process Management Architecture for a SBN Environment

In order to meet the business process requirements given above, we propose a conceptual architecture for process management. The architecture is based on one assumption – that business capabilities[3] can be related to functionalities provided by one or more processes as a means of realizing them by a given SBN. Thus a

---

[3] A business capability is described always in business terms – what the business will be able to accomplish, but a process functionality description is always in operational terms – what the process operation will do.

capability can be exhibited by a SBN through application of one or more functionalities:

Capability C   ==>   Functionalities (F1, F2)

As for instance, the capability of a business like 1-800-FLOWERS.com to "promise delivery of a given type of flowers at a remote place like Gurgaon in India in real-time" can be acquired when it has processes to provide the functionality of "locating a delivery agent in Gurgaon, India" and "availability of the given type of flowers with that delivery agent" concurrently. If for another business similar to 1-800-FLOWERS.com, these functionalities are not available, but it has alternative functionalities of "search availability of delivery agent in Gurgaon, India" and "query availability of given flowers with the delivery agent", it can still do the business which 1-800-FLOWERS.com conducts, selling flowers on the Internet, but may require much more order fulfilment time because of the missing capability of "promising delivery in real-time".

In this context we are not merely trying to introduce yet another level of organizational mapping – from business capabilities to process functionalities. The implications of this mapping are much deeper than it may appear initially. This is because "organisational capabilities" in a way facilitate or improvise competitive strategy of an organization.

Similarly, the functionalities of business processes of the organization determine the extent to which a competitive strategy can be implemented successfully.

Linking Business Strategy to Business Processes

Business Strategy Formulation

Required Organizational Capabilities

Required Organizational Functionalities

Functionality Delivery through Processes

Fig. 6.2 Linking business strategy to business processes

Thus, mapping of capabilities to process functionalities helps in determining the extent to which a formulated competitive strategy can in fact be implemented in the organization. Thus this mapping gives a strategic focus to the SBN's business process management (Fig. 6.2). In addition, there is also a need for a good methodology for the "capability-to-functionality" mapping. During the business process-reengineering era (1990–1995), a number of methodologies were developed for reengineering of business processes. However, many of these methodologies only provided innovative substitution of one or more process functionality with others rather than decomposing a capability into constituent functionalities. Out of these various methodologies, the language-action perspective based methodologies such as DEMO have some promise in terms of modifying/extending them for the "capability-to-functionality" decomposition purpose (Dietz, 2006).

Furthermore, the functionalities required for a capability could be provided by processes or sub-processes belonging to any of the SBN members for dynamically composing a SBN process. Therefore, we call them process-components and the composed process as a SBN process, to avoid confusion. Thus, a SBN process-component can be a process or a sub-process of any of the network members, which is used for composing a SBN process. A SBN process is constituted either by directly acquiring a process-component if it has the desired functionality, or can be composed through combining more than one process-component if that provides the required combination of functionalities.

Thus, Capability C   ==>   SBN Process P
      SBN Process P   ==>   Process-components P1 + P2

At present, the commercially available existing Business Process Management Systems (BPMS) and Enterprise Resource Planning (ERP) systems relate only the functionalities but *do not* relate business capabilities to functionalities (which will help in choosing appropriate processes for building a specific business capability). There has been an interesting effort to document process functionalities of all the processes of an organization in the Process Handbook Project at the MIT Sloan School of Management through an electronic repository of information (Carr, 1999; Davenport, 2005; Malone, Crowston, & Herman, 2003) but it has not yet gone beyond that. Establishing the relationship of business capabilities to process functionalities is still left to the experience of business domain experts and business analysts, but for an SSBN environment it is essential that this relationship should be included.[4]

The proposed architecture consists of four major building blocks: Process Builder (PB), Process Performance Manager (PPM), Process Execution Manager (PEM), and Process Learning Manager (PLM) (Fig. 6.3). The Process Builder is the most critical block as it helps through the process of relating capabilities to the

---

[4] IBM is researching on this aspect of capability to functionality association in their research on implementing "business-on-demand" philosophy (Cherbakov et al., 2005).

specific functionalities, and through them to process-components having those functionalities. Since these process-components are distributed across different network members, it must have a process-component directory showing various process-components, their functionalities and their location and ownership (i.e. which SBN member owns them). The second element of the PB block is capability links, which show the capabilities and their linkage to various functionalities required to build that capability. This can also reveal if there is a functionality gap, i.e. a required functionality but not provided by any of the existing process-components. In addition, the capability links also provide capability metrics, which are measurable indicators of successful capability achievement in SBN operations.

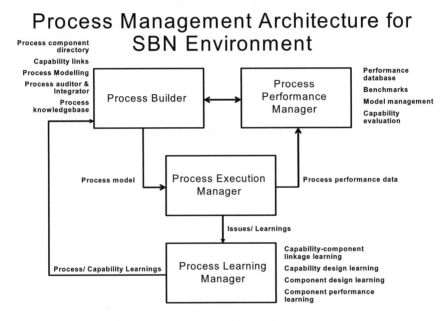

Fig. 6.3 Process management architecture for SBN environment

The next component in the Process Builder is the process modelling tool which supports goal-based process modelling, process goals specified both in terms of functionality goals as well as performance goals. Functionality goals coupled with capability links enable the process building team to compose a SBN process for a given capability, and the performance goals give some indication of the performance acceptance of the SBN process thus composed. The modelling tool also has a simulation function which can be used to simulate the composed process for an initial assurance of its functional and performance feasibility. Thus the process modelling tool is similar to many commercially available process mapping/design tools except for the fact that the mapping used in this tool should be goal-based.

The process modelling tool, however, is only a composite process design tool. In order to build an executable process, the design is to be implemented by integrating the various process-components using a process integrator tool. A number of process-integration tools are available commercially, and this tool could be similar to any of these tools. However, there is one important distinction in terms of process-integration in a SBN environment. Since the integration could involve process-components belonging to several SBN members, there is a possibility that some of these members may allow use of their process-components for functionality delivery but may like to keep the internal logic of their process-components confidential. To address this issue, the SBN members need to adapt a "public-private process partnership" approach in sharing the use of their process-components. In this approach a part of the process-component is declared "public" and is accessible to all members, but the other parts of the process-components are kept "private" (Punia & Saxena, 2004). After the integration of the executable process, it has to go through a process audit (Hammer, 2007) to ensure that the people-related aspects of the process are also designed and relevant roles and knowledge is available. In particular, the process audit decides the process role performers – people who will execute the process, particularly in terms of their skills and knowledge; process-owner – a senior person who has the responsibility for the process and its results; IT infrastructure that will support the process execution, and the performance metrics which will be used to track the process performance. In a composite SBN process, the decision about the process owner may be a difficult one when the process-components used come from several SBN members, and it may require specific process-governance guide lines to address this issue.

There is one more component in the Process Builder block, which is the process knowledgebase. It is a repository of all the learning – the do's and don'ts, the best practices, issues which are as yet unresolved, etc. The process knowledgebase is constructed from the inputs received from the Process Learning Manager block in the proposed architecture. The learning from the knowledgebase is applied while carrying out all the earlier functions of the Process Builder: creating/modifying capability links, modelling the process, integrating and auditing it.

Once the executable process is completed by the Process Builder block, the process model is passed on to the next block of the architecture – the Process Execution Manager (PEM). The PEM block acts like the process driver and executes the process as and when required by the Business Operating System (BOS) of the SBN. The PEM also monitors the process performance while executing it, and sends the process performance data to the next block – the Process Performance Manager (PPM).

The PPM is the next most critical block of the architecture after the Process Builder. It creates and manages a performance database for all the SBN processes, and monitors if the performance of a process is sub-optimal. In such a case it informs the Process Builder block. It also manages the executable process models of all the SBN processes, and makes them available to Process Builder in case the process requires a change in the process model for performance or other business reasons. It also maintains the performance benchmarks for all the processes and in case the performance differs from the benchmarks on a routine basis, it informs the Process Builder. Also, it routinely evaluates capability achievement successes using the capability achievement metrics (defined along with the capability linkage component in Process Builder), and informs Process Builder if any capabilities are failing, i.e. are not achieved, during SBN operations.

The fourth building block of the architecture is the Process Learning Manager (PLM), which extracts all the learning related to process design, process execution, process performance as well as capabilities achievements. It also accepts any unresolved design/execution issues related to process-components, network processes and capabilities of SBN. The learning could be classified as learning related to capability-process component linkage, capabilities design, process component design, and process-component performance. Any open issues are kept open to be resolved by SBN process owners and SBN management.

Assessment of the Proposed BPM Architecture

SBN is a powerful concept as demonstrated by various successful case studies (Vervest et al., 2005). However, design of a SBN is a complex issue and some of these issues are being addressed through ongoing SBN research. From an organizational design perspective, the SBN is a very promising structure as it addresses the flexibility dimension of organizational design, which is so critical in many of the industry sectors. However, this organizational dimension of the SBN concept also raises some fundamental questions such as "when there is a strategic need for businesses to form a SBN?", and a related question, "what it means organizationally for these businesses to function as a SBN?" Examples like Amazon are examples of a single organization building a SBN and others joining it. But what if many organizations selling books in niche areas want to decide how they go about building and competing as a SBN. This paper addresses this question by focusing on the business process management aspect in an SBN environment. The proposed BPM architecture serves two purposes. Organizationally it shows the nature and extent of the collaboration, coordination, and communication that would be necessary for the businesses intending to compete as a SBN business. Functionally the architecture provides an exposure to various functional issues which need to be addressed while building designing a SBN-based business. Technically the paper also attempts to identify which SBN process functions are likely to be supported by commercially off-the-shelf (COTS) available technologies and which still need to be researched and/or improvised at present. Last but not the least; the BPM architecture extends the operational aspect of SBN (its processes) to the strategic aspect of SBN (its capabilities). It is hoped that such a link between the strategic and operational dimensions of organizational design will facilitate better communication among the strategic management and operational management of networked businesses.

References

Andersson, B., Johannesson, P., & Perjons, E. (2005). Towards a formal definition of goal-oriented business process patterns. *Business Process Management Journal, 11*(6), 650–662.

Balasubramanian, S., & Gupta, M. (2005). Structural metrics for goal based business process design and evaluation. *Business Process Management Journal, 11*(6), 680–694.

Basu, A. (2005). Sharing Process Knowledge in Business Networks. In P. Vervest, E. van Heck, & L. F. Pau (Eds.), *Smart Business Networks*, (pp. 323–337), Heidelberg, Germany, Springer.

Carr, N. G. (1999, September–October). A new way to manage process knowledge. *Harvard Business Review*.

Cherbakov, L., Galambos, G., Harishanker, R., Kalyana, S., & Rackham, G. (2005). Impact of service orientation at the business level. *IBM Systems Journal, 44*(4), 653–668.

Crawford, C. H., Bate, G. P., Cherbakov, L., Holley, K., & Tsocanos, C. (2005). Toward an on demand service-oriented architecture. *IBM Systems Journal, 44*(1), 81–108.

Davenport, T. H. (2005, June). The coming commoditization of processes. *Harvard Business Review*.

Dietz, J. L. (2006). The deep structure of business processes. *Communications of ACM, 49*(5), 59–64.

Garvin, D. A. (1998). The processes of organization and management. *Sloan Management Review, 39*(4), 33–50.

Grant, R. M. (1996). Prospering in dynamically competitive environments: Organizational capability as knowledge integration. *Organization Science, 7*(4), 375–387.

Hammer, M. (2007, April). The process audit. *Harvard Business Review*, 1–15.

Hawryszkiewycz, I. T. (2005). *A framework for integrating learning into business processes*. Paper presented at the Proceedings of the South East Asia Regional Computer Confederation (SEARCC) 2005: ICT: Building Bridges Conference, Sydney, Australia.

Janneck, C. D., Nagel, R. N., Schmid, P. D., Raim, J. D., Connolly, M. L., & Moll, M. A. (2008). Smart business networks: Core concepts and characteristics. In P. Vervest, E. van Heck, & K. Preiss (Eds.), *Smart business networks: A new business paradigm* (pp. 501–523). Rotterdam, The Netherlands: Smart Business Network Initiative (SBNi), Rotterdam School of Management, Erasmus University.

Kueng, P., & Kawalek, P. (1997). Goal-based business process models: Creation and evaluation. *Business Process Management Journal, 3*(1), 17–38.

Malone, T. W., Crowston, K., & Herman, G. A. (2003). The MIT process handbook. In T.W. Malone, & K. Crowston (Eds.), *Organizing business knowledge*. USA: MIT Press.

Möller, K., & Rajala, A. (2007). Rise of strategic nets – New modes of value creation. *Industrial Marketing Management, 36*, 895–908.

Möller, K., Rajala, A., & Svahn, S. (2005). Strategic business nets – Their type and management. *Journal of Business Research, 58*, 1274–1284.

Nurcan, S., Etien, A., Kaabi, R., Zoukar, I., & Rolland, C. (2005). A strategy driven business process modelling approach. *Business Process Management Journal, 11*(6), 628–649.

Punia, D. K., & Saxena, K. B. C. (2004). *Managing inter-organisational workflows in eGovernment services*. Paper presented at the Proceeding of the Sixth International Conference on Electronic Commerce, ICEC'04, ACM, New York, 500–505.

Stalk, G., Evans, P., & Shulman, L. E. (1992, March–April). Competing on capabilities: The new rules of corporate strategy. *Harvard Business Review*, 57–68.

van Heck, E., & Vervest, P. (2007). Smart business networks: How the network wins. *Communications of ACM, 50*(6), 29–37.

Vervest, P., van Heck, E., & Preiss, K. (Eds.). (2008). *Smart business networks: A new business paradigm*. Rotterdam, The Netherlands: Smart Business Network Initiative (SBNi), Rotterdam School of Management, Erasmus University.

Vervest, P., van Heck, E., Preiss, E., & Pau, L. F. (Eds.). (2005). *Smart business networks*. Heidelberg, Germany: Springer.

Volberda, H. W. (1998). *Building the flexible firm: How to remain competitive*. Oxford, UK: Oxford University Press.

7. Towards Self-Organizing Smart Business Networks – Let's Create "Life" from Inert Information

David A. Bray and Benn R. Konsynski

Goizueta Business School, Emory University, Atlanta, GA, USA, dbray@bus.emory.edu, benn_konsynski@bus.emory.edu

Abstract

In this chapter, we review three different theories that can inform how researchers determine the performance of smart business networks, to include: (1) the Theory of Evolution, (2) the Knowledge-Based Theory of the Firm, and (3) research insights into computers and cognition. We suggest that each of these theories demonstrate that to be perceived as smart, an organism needs to be self-organizing, communicative, and tool-making. Consequently, to determine the performance of a smart business network, we suggest that researchers need to determine the degree to which it is self-organizing, communicative, and tool-making. We then relate these findings to the Internet and the idea of smart business networks.

Introduction

Isn't it amazing how many pieces of ourselves we leave scattered on the Internet, like photos or items from our wallet scattered along a winding street? Emails are sent and saved, blogs composed and posted, electronic searches, chats, credit card charges, and other transactions happen daily. It is easy to forget the Internet is not only vast in size and scale, but equally vast in the dimension of time. As authors, we have both left many moments ourselves on this networked web since its start, though (fortunately) some pieces have been lost to the ether.

Yet what isn't on the web now (because it has been forgotten) still can be found in one of the Internet archives. What was once a newly-born and somewhat confused Internet of information in the past, successively contributes to an increasingly more complex web of information and computer-mediated human interactions now. With the Internet, we humans access a relatively "unsmart" network, entangled both in terms of its present prolific growth and in the changing linkages to new data and information (as forward, time marches). We humans must either access distinct websites for information or subscribe to information feeds (such as RSS or Atom) because right now the web isn't alive, information cannot find us, only either pull us to it or be pushed by someone else to us.

The Internet that we currently access is not self-organizing; instead, it's relatively limited in its intelligent abilities and exists as a wonderful example as to how the processes of creation can quickly become cluttered and entropic. Human beings create and remix information streams, adding to the web. The promise with Web 2.0 was that human beings would organize all the clutter of the web; that human beings would provide the missing intelligence of networks. Alas, human beings have limited cognitive capabilities and the ever-growing amounts of information on the web probably will exceed our abilities to organize it. Additionally, human beings have flaws, creating divisions and perceived information "turf" that individuals own or have created (vs. someone else has created).

Whereas information is analyzed data; knowledge represents insights gleaned from viewing the patterns associated with information and consequentally arriving at "justified true belief" (March, 1994). The amount of information and the possible knowledge that can be generated from this information has been increasing exponentially since the start of the 20th century (Hawking, 2001). Cumulatively this creates a growing information complexity that can create problems of knowledge overload for individuals and intra- and inter-organizational tensions for firms, information "silos", and general disconnects among varying amounts of information available on both public and private networks.

Yet, at the most basic level, life does find form and does organize itself, both in terms of the lifestages associated with an individual life form and the variations and natural selection within the legacy of a species. Perhaps to be self-organizing is to be alive? We suggest, as demonstrated by the Internet, there are iterative causalities (i.e., links) to its data, information, and knowledge. This gives hope that one day the Internet, and other "smart" business networks, will become capable of self-organizing itself without human intervention. Would such smart business networks then not become alive? The Internet that we access (and are a social part of) is already nearly genetic in its programmed code, memetic in its exchanges, but as a whole not yet part of a larger, living system. As such, our chapter considers possible paths to enable the Internet and other digital networks to self-organize themselves (and the information they contain) independently into wholly new, more beneficial forms – thereby allowing us to measure the extent to which such forms as self-organizing, communicative, and tool-making, i.e., truly smart business networks.

The Internet and other digital networks cannot self-organize themselves (and the information they contain) into wholly new, more beneficial forms independently – yet.

Drawing from Academic Theory

We now review three different theories that can inform smart business networks, to include: (1) the Theory of Evolution, (2) the Knowledge-Based Theory of the Firm, and (3) research insights into computers and cognition. We suggest that each of these theories demonstrate that to be generally perceived as smart, an organism needs to be self-organizing, communicative, and tool-making.

From the Theory of Evolution

Why should some life forms be smart? Before answering that question, it probably is helpful to answer what it means to be smart. Merrier-Webster's Online Dictionary (www.m-w.com) defines the noun form of "smart" as slang for either intelligence or know-how. The adjective form of smart suggests mentally alert, bright, knowledgeable, shrewd, and intelligent. From this, it appears that to be smart has something to do with a high degree of mental ability, reflecting good judgment, and exercising superior cognitive thought.

So why should some life forms be smart? What is the "value-added" principle of being smart that makes it a good trait to have? For this, we suggest it is worthwhile to examine the Theory of Evolution and general Darwinian principles. Evolutionary biologists posit that, several million years ago, as the most basic of organisms competed for limited resources and changing environmental conditions, those organisms with higher levels of mental ability compared to others were more "fit" when confronted with selection pressures. Thus, "smartness" represented some random mutation that environmental pressures selected for within and across species. Those species that possessed a higher degree of smartness thrived and spread their genetic material more optimally than their less smart counterparts (Dawkins, 1979).

The Theory of Evolution also posits that no conscious hand designed "smartness" within a species. Smartness was initially a random mutation that environmental pressures later selected. If our world had experienced different environmental pressures, smartness may have either have not been selected or some other trait may have been selected instead (e.g., lethargy).

Side-note: the figurative jury is still out on the long-term adaptedness of a species possessing the trait of being (generally) smart. It could be that humans, in their glorified intelligence, leverage such smarts to create weapons of mass destruction that eventually destroy their species, leaving the cockroaches and bacteria to carry-on long after we're gone.

Humans may presume that smartness represents a desirable trait, but the lesson of the hermit crab provides a warning worth considering. Female hermit crabs are predisposed to choose a mate based on the size of the male's claw. Males with larger claws are more likely to be chosen by females (an evolutionary biologist might argue that the offspring of such males will also have larger claws and thus more likely to defend themselves from small predators compared to smaller-clawed peers – representing a better game theoretic choice for females who want to maximize the spread and longevity of their genetic material carried by their off-spring). Alas, one consequence of environmental pressures selecting for this trait is that, over thousands of years, male hermit crabs now exhibit much larger claws that are actually suboptimal – the supernormal-sized claws slow down crabs who attempt to run away from large predators! (Dawkins, 1979).

Such an example demonstrates that evolutionary biology is "blind" in its intentionality. The traits that environmental pressures select for may be fit for one environmental circumstance, but later, when confronted with a different environmental circumstance, be sub-optimal or even terminal for a species. But, more importantly, through experimentation, what can the lessons of evolutionary biology mean for "smart" business networks? Future research should examine what Darwinian principles can tell us about enabling smart networks?

From the Knowledge-Based Theory of the Firm

Playing the history of evolutionary biology on our planet forward several million years from single-celled organisms to multi-celled organisms, an interesting phenolmena emerges: first, cells began to communicate with each other (via chemical and physical triggers and receptors), and then the organisms themselves began to communicate with each other (also chemical, physical, visual, auditory, and other methods). Communication, from historical evidence, also seems to be a trait that environmental pressures selected for within and across species. Anthropological evidence of human skull sizes suggests a strong link between the development of human communication abilities and human skull sizes. Our brains grew roughly in parallel with our ability to communicate with each other (Wilson, 2001).

Stepping back for a moment from biology and considering the Knowledge-Based Theory of the Firm, this theory posits that knowledge represents the most strategically significant resource of an organization (Alavi & Leidner, 2001). Capturing and sharing knowledge of expert and innovative employees provides a strategic advantage influencing performance outcomes (Nonaka, 1994). For organisms with cognitive capabilities, we suggest that communication represents the ability to re-create knowledge across the minds of individuals. We communicate to share and receive knowledge.

With the modern world of business, in order for distributed, heterogeneous knowledge bases to be leveraged as a strategic asset within an organization, organizational decision-makers not only need to identify what its employees know (and do not know) so the leaders can appropriately target the transfer of knowledge, but also discern when such knowledge will be valuable both now and in the future. To perform these feats with any certainty, an organization has to predict both future events and future "new" knowledge needs (i.e., where best to focus research and development activities).

Thus, there is a temporal dimension to knowledge (i.e., an individual needs to know when particular knowledge is relevant and applicable and should be shared with others). Knowledge can be time-sensitive, potentially losing its relevance as environments change. Relaying information facilitates the exchange of tacitly stored knowledge (Galbraith, 1982). Such exchanges allow humans to relay thoughts, to relay perceptions of the environment, and to adapt. Knowledge exchanges allow inter-individual awareness of reality, opportunities, environmental changes, and trends. Ultimately, knowledge exchanges allow humans to become more "fit" to their environment (Clippinger, 1999).

From Research into Computers and Cognition

But sharing and reusing knowledge is only part of the picture. Fast-forward the history of evolutionary biology on our planet to the most recent developments of a certain species known as *Homo sapiens* and we see communication moving beyond just physical, visual, and auditory methods between two organisms occupying the same place and time. This species develops methods of communicating information (thereby attempting to re-create knowledge) across organisms that are either geographically or temporally dispersed. With uniform and subsequent technological advances, an ability known as writing and literacy occurred within this curious species, which also developed tools such as clay tablets and blunt reed stylus to store these asynchronous communication attempts. Several hundred years later and humans launched the next wave of tool-making: writing 2.0 technologies, to include papyrus, wedged quills, and a chemical known as ink.

We suggest that tool-making is the third hallmark of an intelligence organism or a "smart" species (Wilson, 2001) *en masse*. Broadly, *Homo sapiens* began to make and employ tools not only for physically reshaping the environment to better suit their species-specific needs, but also to relay cognitive thoughts, feelings, and perceptions. A revolution later occurs for *Homo sapiens* when one in particular, by the name of Johannes Gutenberg, develops a technology capable of transcribing asynchronous communications quickly and allowing multiple copies from a master. Subsequent versions of this technology include mimeographs and xerography. In parallel, the telegraph, phonograph, and telephone are added to these suites of communication technologies.

With these advances, it is worth considering what was "lost" in the tool-making move from chemical and physical, to subsequent visual and auditory, and later to asynchronous visual and auditory communication. With writing 1.0 and subsequent revisions, absent were either the chemical or physical cues present in human communication. While humans employ tools for inter-individual cognition (with the goal of sharing information in attempts to re-create knowledge), each of these tools has strengths and weaknesses in achieving this goal. Each tool may limit or enhance the information sent when compared to a single human communicating with another human face-to-face.

Such a view of human cognition and communications is not new and does have a strong bearing on information systems. Winograd and Flores (1987) discuss the opportunities posed by computers and human cognition. Their book centers on how best to design computers to complement and extend human cognitive abilities, discussing the rationalistic orientation toward language, decision-making, and problem solving while also recognizing cognition as a biological phenomenon.

The events that followed Winograd and Flores demonstrate the complementarities between information systems and human cognition. Having developed television 1.0 (representing a bundled offering of telephone and film technologies), *Homo sapiens* then further pressed its "smartness" as a tool-making species and developed a technology known as the Internet. Brief side-note, the early origins of Internet technologies are directly linked to fears that humans might leverage their smarts to create weapons of mass destruction that eventually destroy their species.

When a layer of Internet technologies commonly referred to as "the web" were first employed by academics, these cognitive tools were seen as an extension of Johannes Gutenberg' printing press technology. The web was text that could be navigated through links. Yet the goal of the web was the same, to share and reuse information. Later audio and video entered the Internet, representing extensions of television 1.0, and then the concept of massive multiplayer online games (MMOGs) and virtual worlds, representing computer-mediated extensions of human interactions with other humans (or dragons, trolls, or furries for that matter). With the ever-increasing immersive nature of the Internet, more and more dimensions of communication were added to this technology (Clippinger, 1999).

A View of "Webntropy" and Potential Solutions

At the same time, a figurative explosion of information occurred. In the human year 1900 A.D., there were 9,000 scientific articles published that year. Fifty years later, there were 90,000 and by 2000 A.D. there were 900,000 scientific articles published in that year (Hawking, 2001). The general empowerment of individuals to create, remix, and distribute information increased as well, with TIME Magazine recognizing every human individual (i.e., "you") as the 2006 Person of the

Year and embodying an accelerating trend where anyone can find, analyze, produce, and remix various media on the Internet.

This also created entropy (i.e., a trend to disorder characterized by a loss of uniqueness and a rise in uniformity) on the Internet. With the rise of digital tools to communicate in various fashions, so too emerged the volumes of digital clutter, chatter, and confusion on the web where the unique value of information becomes disaggregated and lost as noise.

If life, at the most basic level, defies entropy insomuch that life is self-organizing and maintains a relatively ordered pattern of structure and behaviors that embody a living life form – then Internet, so far, is not alive. Instead, we suggest that information, on either public or private networks, represents "non-living" and (for the most part) non-ordered structures. We would call this "webntropy". Yes, XML allows some structure to data and UML some structure to design, but all of these do little to enable information to organize itself. We still depend on human beings to expend energy to create order from the entropy of information on networks, and as the Second Law of Thermodynamics informs us, expending energy to remedy entropy actually creates more entropy elsewhere within a closed system (Hawking, 2001).

Fast-forwarding ten to fifteen years from now, we suggest we will confront an era where simply too much information will exist on networks for us to rely on human participants to filter, organize, and sort through this information via the Web 2.0 more, even if everyone on the planet played a role. Moreover, human beings have inherent cognitive biases. As of 2008, Wikipedia lists more than 30 cognitive biases to humans at http://en.wikipedia.org/wiki/List_of_cognitive_ biases. We note that some may object to Wikipedia as a reference of human biases, but we find a certain amount of poetic beauty in using a perceived biased source of information to detail human bases as an example within an example or mise-en-scène. Those also wanting an academic treatise regarding human decision-making and biases are referred to March (1994). Humans make decision-making and behavioral biases, biases in probability and belief, social biases, and memory errors. Imagine: even if we had a million humans viewing data, barring a random mutation we might all be subject to the same problems inherent in human decision-making, cognitive properties selected for as a result of natural selection pressures present in our evolutionary history. Yes, instances do exist where more people do make better decisions, but there are clearly other time where more people only magnify biases. As such, we cannot rely solely on a Web 2.0 model of humans providing "intelligence" to our relatively unsmart networks. To make improvements beyond human biases, we suggest that the world will need something better – something self-organizing outside of human input.

As such, we suggest that a "smart" network, at its most basic level, should be self-organizing. Our conjectures echo similar conjectures by Brown and Duguid (1991). Specifically: the content of a smart network should be self-organizing. Linked data, information, and knowledge, embodied by the web, will need to know what it is and be able to learn more about what it is both internally andexternally in relation to other data and information elements, through interaction with other elements. This is how we, as humans, live and learn as individuals (and as societies) through iterative, interactive experiences. Current information systems are limited, as they cannot rapidly adapt to turbulent situations or new environments. To organize itself more efficiently, the web will need to be self-organizing and self-improving (i.e., alive).

Yes, on one level, Internet packets do organize themselves to a degree. Yet they still are following rules written by humans and we would suggest we need to go much further in allowing packets to decide for themselves not only how to route and arrive at their destination, but enable information to achieve some degree of "knowing itself" and perceiving its environment, particularly unfamiliar environment and unfamiliar other selves outside of itself. That said, we harbor hope that the small degree of indeterminism we have been able to achieve with routing Internet packets can be carried over toward future, more advanced pursuits of self-organization. Currently, no one can tell you the specific route any packet will take on a mesh network until it has taken it, nor can anyone be sure it will repeat the same path again under different environmental traffic conditions – in the future, we envision information as being able to find related information, interested human consumers, as well as remix itself to assemble wholly new structures and designs.

So how do we do this? To explore our conjectures, we propose exploring several scenarios where the ability of networks to self-organize themselves, and thus be "smart", may prove beneficial. Unfortunately, we humans in our limited abilities do not know what specific event first triggered either life at the most basic level or what random mutations led to the emergence of generally accepted smart species, from fish to amphibians, amphibians to reptiles, reptiles to birds, and that small side track (during the era of the dinosaurs) called mammals, which seem to dominate the planet currently (though it is worth noting there are exponentially more insects and bacteria than humans). Thus, our proposed research aims to create conditions where self-organization might occur within the proverbial primordial soup, and from there assess the dimensions of such self-organization (i.e., smartness).

Empirical Analysis – Let's Create "Life" from Inert Information

Given our earlier conjectures, how can we humans create life from inert information? From the theories presented, we suggest that a life form needs to be self-organizing, communicative, and tool-making. We need to enable information to know what it is and be able to learn more about what it is both internally and externally in relation to other data and information elements, through interaction with other elements. We need to be enable information to "converse" with other information elements independent of any human activity. Finally, we need to enable information to test, try, (fail, and try again), and improve its own attempts at building tools or artifacts to help information interface with other information elements as well as its environment – embodied by the network and systems on which the information lives as well as the human users and their information needs. If the reader has not already realized, this chapter provides academic value as a conceptual thought piece, and the results that follow represent only hypothetical speculations.

If we let the environment be represented as both the network and systems on which the information lives as well as the human users and their information needs, what types of experiments can we perform to see if we can create life that is self-organizing, communicative, and tool-making? We suggest we might have to perform successive steps, where we iteratively "wean away" human intervention on information as we attempt to make information increasingly, independently smart.

Experiment One: A Cognitive Delivery Approach for Smart Business Networks

In this experiment, design efforts would be made to see if information systems can improve the smart delivery of information, thus representing "smart" business networks comprising both human and technology nodes. Most IS literature examines the use of a single system or technology artifact. While this approach allows for greater depth in analyses, this approach also ignores the reality that knowledge workers now use multiple technologies throughout their day at the office, during their commute, and during their personal time. Consider for a moment the consequences of diffusion, adoption, and ultimately use of multiple IS innovations:

(1)   The volume of increased information available through an IS innovation usually INCREASES as more humans adopt such a technology
(2)   Humans have FINITE memories and processing capabilities
(3)   More information does NOT always make for better decisions.

Ergo, widespread adoptions of multiple IS innovations concurrently can result in information pollution, manifested by an overload of redundant, excessive, noisy, or unhelpful information. These phenomena would include inefficient communications, time lost due to multi-tasking, spam, junk emails, trivial messages, multiple passwords, duplication of efforts, lost productivity, etc. Three corollaries flow from this:

- *First*: We need IS solutions that strive to REPLACE (not add) existing available information with BETTER information, specifically because of human cognitive load limitations
- *Second*: We should try to AVOID technologies that create constant SHIFTS of attention or frequent task-related interruptions where at all possible
- *Third*: We should treat human attention spans as a SCARCE resource; new IT solutions need to CONSERVE this resource, as it is exhaustible.

Such considerations logically follow from the points raised above and, on a deeper level, resonate intuitively with similar efforts to conserve the limited resources of our planet. Thus, an experiment investigating this approach to "smart" business networks would consider design elements of the IT artifact and their larger implications on individuals and group cognition, ultimately influencing individual and group performance.

As for design, multiple quasifield experiments could be performed which assess the state of individuals and groups prior to an IS "treatment" (or intervention), status during the treatment, and subsequent performance outcomes. The challenges with doing this include controlling for additional confounding influences. An alternative method would be for controlled laboratory experiments, but these might remove several salient elements crucial to exploring the coupling of the design elements of IT with design elements of individual and group cognitive activities, thus limiting the generalizability of results.

Data would include elements of an IS design (what interfaces to different users, different user roles, different user actions allowed, what information provided) and organization design (hierarchy, participatory, matrixed, etc.), as well as outcomes (efficiency, responsiveness or agility, profitability). Analyses would include structural equation modeling as well as qualitative assessments, either in the form of case studies or ethnographies.

Experiment Two: A Market-Based Mechanism for Smart Business Networks

For this experiment, complex adaptive systems would be coupled with free market dynamics. Curiously, free market economies and Darwinian evolution are quite similar, both featuring an "invisible hand" vs. conscious, directed actions.

This experiment would see if information arbitrage, where information asymmetry participants, could allow information to become "alive" through a series of transactions (buying and selling), such that the right information reaches the right individuals with better efficiency that consciously directed activities. Prediction markets (such to the 1988 Iowa Presidential Prediction Market, as well as prediction markets run internally to HP and Google and a start-up company called Sermo.com) have had some success in this area.

Specifically, we suggest altering design elements of the IS employed by participants in the market within a social dilemmas situation. Social dilemmas involve situations were individuals confront a shared situation where each receives a higher personal payoff for defecting rather than cooperating as a group, but cumulatively all individuals would be better off if they cooperated vs. defected (Ostrom, Gardner, & Walker, 1994). Thus, in such an environment, there will be human cognitive biases that may preclude efficient distribution of information either from information hoarding, deception, defection, or other detrimental activities. What we, as researchers, would want to see in this experiment is whether elements of IS design can overcome these biases and detrimental activities, thus enabling "smart" business networks – despite human participants (who may try and deceive the market to their own selfish ends).

Additionally, we submit that deciding whether to exchange information is akin to social dilemmas: (1) should an individual contribute knowledge to the group, with a future possible return, or (2) or should an individual opt not to contribute and free ride? Each individual in a situation may potentially receive a higher personal payoff for defecting rather than cooperating and exchanging knowledge, but cumulatively all group members would be better off if they cooperated vs. defected. However in markets, other mechanisms are available, to include price and buying/selling activities, thus allowing further dimensions of incentives (financial, reputational, personal, etc.) to see if incentives coupled with IS design elements can overcome human biases. Additionally, different communication forms can be employed as treatments in this experiment, since communication has been shown to ameliorate defections in social dilemmas (Ostrom, Gardner, & Walker, 1994).

As before, data from this experiment would include elements of an IS design (what interfaces to different users, different user roles, different user actions allowed, what information provided) and "market" or social dilemma design (what rules are given, what goals are encouraged, what rewards and punishments, etc.), as well as outcomes of the market (efficiency, responsiveness or agility, effective or ineffective information distribution). Analyses would include structural equation modeling of the outcomes observed.

Experiment Three: Files as Biological Units as Smart Business Networks

For this last experiment, information is given two simple rules for "files as biological units". The rules are (1), attempt to self-propagate to as many hospitable environments as possible, and (2) make friends with files of similar attributes (e.g., content, previous editors, use patterns). Then a networked environment

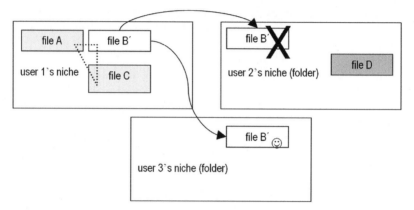

Fig. 7.1 Files as biological units, using evolutionary biology to inform IS mechanics

consisting of different environmental niches is created, per the example in Fig. 7.1. These individual niches can represent the virtual workspace of unique users with unique preferences in the type of information they would like to find them. In niche 1, File B has attributes similar to files A and C, forming a neighborhood of files belonging to user 1. Humans define the hospitable environments, as determined by their information needs and wants.

Following the two simple rules, File B attempts to send a copy of itself to niche 2. However, user 2 does not want File B and "kills" (i.e., deletes) this copy in niche 2, which triggers File B and its neighbors to favor niche 2 less. This action and response represents a changing environment becoming more hostile to files of certain characteristics. File B also attempts to send a copy of itself to niche 3. In this case, user 3 does want File B and appreciates its arrival. By using the file, user 3 triggers File B and its neighbors to favor niche 3 more. Files A and C, which are neighbors of File B in niche 1, will then try and send copies to niche 3. User 3 may find none, one, or both of the files useful, which will produce different environmental pressures for niche 3.

Analysis of these results would include quantitative assessments as to how well the users found (when surveyed) the information that "sought them out" was relevant to their needs and interests. Equally, behind the scenes, quantitative assessments of the efficiency within the network at distributing information could be performed – coupled with performance outcomes associated with individuals or the organization in which they operate. Specifically, did employing files as biological units increase the cognitive abilities of individuals, their efficiency, the overall revenue for the organization, the responsiveness of the organization, (etc.)?

Implications and Conclusions

Clearly, the three experiments we propose earlier represent conceptual thought-experiments that might one day, with sufficient resources, actually be done. In the meanwhile, there is still value in considering what results these thought-experiments might produce (Simon, 1969). We might even find, as a result of our (proposed) third experiment, that information could become "alive", self-organizing, self-communicative, and (as embodied by efforts by "smart" humans to embrace writing 1.0, writing 2.0, and the internet) tool-making. Files could organize communities, communicate with each other, and build improvements to their protocols and structure independent of *Homo sapiens*.

This chapter provides academic value as a conceptual thought piece, with an emphasis on considering theory and what may be possible in the future regarding smart networks; the results above and the conclusions below represent only hypothetical speculations. As our propositions show, if information gains "smartness", it could transform human society. Organizations could allow their information to self-organize into optimal configurations for profitability, performance, responsiveness, or other outcomes of interest. Individuals could let files "find them" in terms of their interests or tastes. Should information be able to self-organize itself, this would be a critical step forward toward artificial intelligence. If biological life is able to self-organize itself, why shouldn't digital life?

Of course, we should remember that biological life forms (assuming no predators, nor accidents) do have a finite period of time before eventually the self-organization ability ceases and death of the individual life form occurs. Entropy, embodied in the Second Law of Thermodynamics, always seems to win in the end. Yet even with individual deaths, genetic material still is passed along, so there are possibilities for digital information akin to genetic material to experience successive generations with environmental selection pressures present. In attempting to make smart business networks, would we need to consider information death and information predation? Are these required for environmental pressures to select for qualities of "smartness"? Additionally, would information begin to form species and sub-species, and within information species form dominance hierarchies and group identities and possible conflicts? For networks to be "smart" do we need to have competition?

Additionally, consider the implications if we are able to have information communicate with itself, beyond just XML and other messaging standards. The ability for information to know elements of itself and its perceived environment, and then communicate these perceptions with other information units (who also communicate) would represent a tremendous leap forward in terms of "smart" networks, databases, and applications. This would help address the information explosion that human beings, with our limited cognitive abilities, might not be able to address in fifteen years.

Lastly, the ability for information to test, try, (fail, and try again), and improve its own attempts at building tools or artifacts to help information interface with other information elements as well as its environment would help information structure itself. Human beings, with their needs and preferences, could supply environmental pressures which "select" for which information tools thrive. In terms of business applications, optimal algorithms could select for themselves either by human use or other performance criteria (such as financial return, lives saved, etc.) Superior code passes its qualities to successive generations, while inferior code withers away.

One last thought to tie-in the emergence of computer-mediated virtual worlds to the theoretical contributions of this research. Darwinism in our "real-world" has led to the emergence of species, including different smart species (dolphins, elephants, chimpanzees, etc.) with varying degrees of communication and tool-making. With virtual worlds, humans are recreating elements of their real environment, complete with environmental settings (which do not have to obey laws of physics) and actors (be they human or otherwise).

Consequentially, if we, as humans, can construct virtual worlds (i.e., environments that provide rewards for certain outcomes, randomly mutating autonomous agents, and an accelerated element of time) in which similar Darwinist principles of environmental selection can play out within digital reality, what will we eventually see emerge from these environments? Why should biological material be any different from digital material? We suggest that smart networks of the future will be able to self-organize themselves (and the information they contain) into wholly new, more beneficial forms – stay tuned.

Acknowledgments

The authors acknowledge both the support of the Claus M. Halle Institute for Global Learning at Emory University and the foresight of pioneers such as Herbert Simon, James March, Lawrence Lessig, Jay Galbraith, and John Seely Brown. As e.e. cummings wrote: "always the beautiful answer/who asks a more beautiful question", so too is there benefit in considering what possible future experiments might reveal to us as present-day researchers.

References

Alavi, M., & Leidner, D. (2001). Review: Knowledge management and knowledge management systems: Conceptual foundations and research issues. *MIS Quarterly, 25*(1), 107–136.

Brown, J., & Duguid, P. (1991). Organizational learning and communities-of-practice: Toward a unified view of working, learning, and innovation. *Organization Science, 2*(1), 40–57.

Clippinger, J. (Ed.). (1999). *The biology of business: Decoding the natural laws of enterprise*. San Francisco, CA: Jossey-Bass.

Dawkins, R. (1979). *The selfish gene*. Oxford, UK: Oxford University Press.

Galbraith, J. (1982). Designing the innovating organization. *Organizational Dynamics*, *10*(3), 4–25.

Hawking, S. (2001). *The universe in a nutshell*. New York, NY: Bantam Books.

March, J. (1994). *A primer on decision making: How decisions happen*. New York, NY: Free Press.

Nonaka, I. (1994). A dynamic theory of organizational knowledge creation. *Organization Science*, *5*(1), 14–37.

Ostrom, E., Gardner, R., & Walker, J. (Eds.). (1994). *Rules, games and common pool resources*. Ann-Arbor, MI: University of Michigan Press.

Simon, H. (1969). *The sciences of the artificial*. Cambridge, MA: MIT Press.

Wilson, E. (2001). *Sociobiology: The new synthesis: 25th anniversary edition*. Cambridge, MA: Harvard University Press.

Winograd, T., & Flores, F. (1987). *Understanding computers and cognition: A new foundation for design*. Boston, MA: Addison-Wesley Longman Publishing.

8. Strategy, Networks and Systems in the Global Translation Services Market

Duncan R. Shaw[1] and Christopher P. Holland[2]

[1]Nottingham University Business School, Nottingham, UK, duncan.shaw@nottingham.ac.uk

[2]Manchester Business School, University of Manchester, Manchester, UK, chris.holland@mbs.ac.uk

Abstract

The globalisation of markets has led to an increased demand for language translation services that support and enable all forms of communication between economic partners operating in an international environment. For example, technical documents, software systems, business documents and web sites all need to be translated into multiple languages for individual national markets, and the information changes periodically; for web sites, daily and even hourly changes are common. This paper sets out a theoretical framework that describes and encapsulates the business architectures of processes within and between separate firms used to support the delivery and management of language translation services by dynamically optimising the fit between externally generated problem complexity, from customers, and the internally generated complexity of different network configuration solutions. A case study of one of the major international translation companies is presented (thebigword) which illustrates how the framework is applied in practice. The focus of the case study is on how thebigword implement an IT-based system that acts as a platform or e-market to bring together the different participants and stakeholders including translators, translation services companies and clients in a global, smart business network.

Introduction

The globalisation of markets has presented firms with many challenges and communicating with their network of customers and suppliers is a significant one. International firms need to communicate with customers in any market that they

P.H.M. Vervest et al. (eds.) *The Network Experience*
© Springer-Verlag Berlin Heidelberg 2009

target and any firm with a web site has the potential to do business internationally. Similarly, firms that take advantage of differences in the international supply of resources, e.g. materials, knowledge or offshored process capacity are presented with complex communication challenges in the supply-side of their network as well as the demand side.

A specific communication challenge for firms comes from the different languages of customers and business partners. It is extremely difficult for companies to manage all of their language translation requirements using internal experts and most large firms use a combination of external translation services and in-house expertise. Another specific communication challenge for firms is in brand marketing. The cultural complexities that are part of communication convey much more information that a core message such as a product's functionality and price or a service level agreement. In brand marketing the 'look and feel', the context and other cultural associations are extremely important for avoiding misunderstandings with suppliers as well as for influencing customer buying decisions.

The language translation and brand marketing translation needs of international firms constitute a US$ 30 billion per year global market in translations services (LISA, 2007a). The language translation services market is fragmented and the top 20 firms account for revenues of US$ 2,139m in 2006 (Beninatto & DePalma, 2007, see Table 8.1). Translation services firms translate the language content of products and services from a source language to one or more target market languages (Holland, Shaw, & Westwood, 2004). This applies to software, web sites, and media services, as well as to traditional business communication related to standard commercial business processes. For example, British Airways operates in 93 countries, uses ten operating languages and aims to standardise brand messages on all of its multi-language web sites; these contain several hundred pages of frequently changing content. BA's customers come from a wide range of cultures and to make itself more attractive to each customer segment BA endeavours to present itself as a global organisation rather than as a purely British company (ibid). This requires the 'localisation' of content, i.e. the translation of concepts into the *local* language and cultural references. This also requires the maintenance of localisation through any product updates or changes. When content changes on one country or market's web site, it has to change on all other customer-facing web sites. Firms that have a presence in global markets apply this localisation process on a global level where it is called 'globalisation'. Firms that develop products for global markets may also use the expertise of translation services companies to 'internationalise' aspects of new product design.

Table 8.1 Top 20 language service providers worldwide for calendar year 2006 (Beninatto & DePalma, 2007)

Company	Revenue in US$ millions
L-3 Communications	622.0
Lionbridge Technologies	419.0
SDL International	174.5
Language Line Holdings	163.3
TransPerfect/Translations	112.8
SDI Media Group	95.0
RWS Group	73.4 (estimate)
Xerox Global Services	68.0 (estimate)
euroscript International S.A.	62.8
Moravia Worldwide	43.5
Logos Group	43.3
CLS Communication	40.7
Honyaku Centre	32.6 (estimate)
LCJ EEIG	32.1
Semantix	31.2
Merrill Brink International	29.8 (estimate)
Welocalize, Inc.	28.2
Skrivanek Group	23.6
Hewlett-Packard ACG	22.0
thebigword Group	21.0

As in most industries translation services firms compete by attempting to differentiate themselves via the innovative use of information technology and by their business processes. In this paper, we ask to what extent can Information and Communications Technology (ICT) be exploited to differentiate and deliver competitive advantages in these firms' activities. We also ask if such uses of ICT can be sold as a service in its own right to competitors and customers and, at the network level, what is the effect of such technologies on market structure and competition?

To explore these questions we assemble a theoretical framework from the literature that links market structure, Business to business (B2B) integration and coordination mechanisms, business activities and industry standards. First we use the concepts from investigations of organisational and market structure that is based on recent work on complex systems theory to assemble an architectural model of the translation services market. We then use this to analyse the relationship between ICT and market structure in this industry in order to investigate the network's Smartness embodied in its architectural form.

Background Literature

Organisational Architectures

Simon's (1969) concept of near decomposability and Weick's (1976) related concept of loose coupling (Orton & Weick, 1990) have long been used to analyse organisation problems. Near decomposability and loose coupling are concepts that describe the non-linearity in the intensity of relationships between different entities. This enables managers and researchers to use composition and decomposition in dealing with complex organisational problems (Ethiraj & Levinthal, 2004). The variation in the intensity of relations between different parts of a problem makes it possible to split the problem into smaller pieces and it also enables similar components of the problem to be clustered. The decomposition of complex problems is required because managers and researchers are boundedly rational and so there are upper limits on their ability to deal with complexity (Simon, 1997). Thus problem decomposition enables more complex problems to be tacked. The clustering of similar problem components helps the management of complex problems by allowing standardisation (Kindleberger, 1983; Langlois & Savage, 2001) and by allowing organisational complexity to be bounded into a discrete area. For example, Dell's product offer includes a bewildering number of variants of PC configuration and peripheral combination. But from Dell's perspective there is a standard menu of components and the configuration complexity is very much a 'problem', actually an advantage, for the customer.

However, in splitting up organisational design problems into smaller pieces managers also need to preserve a holistic view of the problem since the problem components are only *nearly* decomposed not completely decomposed. The danger here is that there are inter-relations between problem areas that whilst relatively weak still have the ability to produce unexpected consequences for managers. For example, in Hamilton's description of when Intel's engineers designed the Itanium chip (Ethiraj & Levinthal, 2004) a change to one module of the chip would affect many other modules in a manner that that was not possible to forecast. Boundedly rational managers can still coordinate complex organisations if they use Simon's (1962) concept of *hierarchy*. In a hierarchical solution to a complex problem, managers abstract away *non-salient* information from the problem. This why higher level managers deal with more abstract issues than shop floor supervisors and together with other management levels they are able to manage very complex organisations and environments.

The concepts of hierarchy, near-decomposability and loose coupling have been used to develop strategies based upon modular architectures as solutions to the complex problems generated by complex product or organisational systems (Baldwin and Clark 1997; Langlois, 2002; Parnas, 1972; Simon, 1962). Strategies that are based upon modular architectures enable problem components, design issues or system characteristics that have commonalities to be clustered together in modules. The intensity of relationships *inside* modules in relatively high and the intensity of relationships *between* modules is relatively low. The architecture of such a modular system is a model of the inter-relations between the modules. This is less complex than a model of the whole system because it is an *abstraction* of the whole. Intra-module information is *hidden* (Baldwin & Clark, 1997; Langlois, 2002). Another benefit of a modular strategy is that work on different modules can progress in parallel which also speeds production, design and any other problem resolution processes.

Market, Supply Chain and Firm Network Architectures

On a higher level of analysis the concept of modular architecture has also been used to study market structures, firm networks and supply chains (Galunic & Eisenhardt, 2001; Garud, Kumaraswamy, & Langlois, 2003; Henderson & Clark, 1990; Richard & Devinney, 2005; Schilling & Steensma, 2001). In these studies the modules are the whole firms themselves and the architectural relations between them are the products and services that they exchange. These are incorporated by the customer firm into its own production system as raw materials, component parts, sub-assemblies or enabling services. Each supplier firm-module produces these outputs via its own internal business processes and the ability to enact and change these processes is conceptualised as a *dynamic capability*, the sum of the processes which transform resources into firm assets and deal with external change. In a firm network these dynamic capabilities are constantly changing and new configurations of firms and their contributions constantly emerge (Galunic & Eisenhardt, 2001; Winter, 2003). Our proposed model of B2B interaction between a customer and a supplier is shown in Fig. 8.1, based on Kalakota and Robinson (2003).

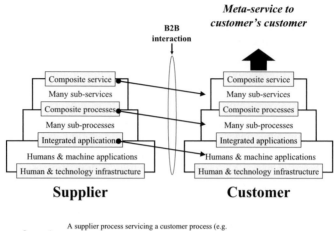

Fig. 8.1 Multi-level structural view of multi-stage processes composing supplier outputs into customer processes which produce a service for the customer's customer (based upon Kalakota and Robinson, 2003)

Inter-Organisational Architectures

The architecture of products and markets, or other environmental drivers, will typically determine the appropriate organisation and inter-firm architectural design. In this way, complex organisational and network systems can be divided into sub-systems whilst preserving important system level characteristics. Modular architectures divide systems into two levels, the modular or subsystem level and the architectural or system level. However, modules can contain sub-modules and architectures themselves can be part of modules. The hierarchy of levels is never limited to a stack of just two. In business process and information systems architectures there can be many levels.

Figure 8.1 shows this hierarchy of levels exists *structurally* as well as *processually*. The service/process/infrastructure structures of the supplier and the customer firms have several levels and each the level of the two firms are joined by business processes. The business processes that join the structural levels of the two firms have a *temporal* hierarchy of *stages*. The structural levels of the information system is generally known as the 'solution stack': the computer hardware (e.g. a PC) runs the operating system software (e.g. MS Windows) which in turn runs application software (e.g. MS Word). Another example of a hierarchical solution stack is 'LAMP': a Linux operating system running an Apache Web server which runs MySQL a database management system which can be use via a web page scripting language such as Perl.

Both the process stages and the structural levels are hierarchical, i.e. they are have some form of relational asymmetry. Process stages are asymmetrical in that their causal link is only in one direction and structural levels are asymmetrical in that higher levels emerge from a lower level, e.g. operating systems are a dynamic configuration of computer hardware, business processes are the emergent characteristics of the behaviour of humans and computers and software application are the emergent configurations of operating systems. Process stages are also emergent phenomena but their emergence is due to multiple option choices. Structural level emergence is due to different levels of natural frequency. Higher structural levels have lower natural frequencies and their phenomena are abstractions of lower level phenomena. *Top-down* design abstraction is especially valuable for boundedly rational managers. In later process stages choices have been made between multiple options. This is why design strategies that start with customer needs and work *backwards* are popular with practising managers.

In descriptions of product architectures the *platform* concept is used to label the structural level whose behaviour supports some higher level phenomena, e.g. MS Windows runs MS Word (Robertson & Ulrich, 1998). If the product is used for inter-organisational purposes then there needs to some sharing of the platform, i.e. in order for two or more firms to share the use of a product then the need to have a sub-system or platform in common. Thus, some level or sub-system of their information system has to be the same or else they are unconnected, i.e. there is no commonality.

Markets and inter-organisational networks depend upon the architectures of the multi-level systems that connect them. One example of the different levels that join organisations is the mixed mode form of inter-firm organisation which displays characteristics of a market and a hierarchy (Holland & Lockett, 1997). Other examples of architectural dimensions and their affect upon market structure are interoperability standards and the process of agreeing them (Rodon, Ramis-Pujol, & Christiaanse, 2007) and open standards (Christiaanse & Rodon, 2005). These inter-firm modular architectures have two enabling characteristics: (i) they decouple aspects of the market structure to allow information hiding (Parnas, 1972) and (ii) they couple the information systems market entities to allow easier business-to-business working. These two characteristics are simultaneously evident in platforms (Robertson & Ulrich, 1998). Platforms produce services for their users who can then focus on specific network roles and at the same time they act as a common medium for working together. The strategic role and significance of language services translation platforms will be discussed in more detail in the case study of thebigword.

Research Method

This study focuses upon how information and communications technologies affect the structure of a market and how they can be exploited to differentiate and deliver competitive advantages. To explore these issues we assemble a theoretical framework that is concerned with the modular architectures of inter-firm relationships and the technology that mediates these relationships. We use the framework to analyse a case study from the translations services industry. The translations services industry is a rich source of data and concepts regarding market complexity, evolving market structures, innovative use of technology and global business relationships.

The investigation is concerned with initial questions of 'how' and 'why' rather than of 'how many' which points to a qualitative approach. This is a multi-level study so it takes an interpretive stance, because of the subjective nature of human interaction, and iterates around a hermeneutic circle, between network, process and service level perspectives so as to consider an interdependent whole (Klein & Myers, 1999). Following Yin's (2003) recommendations our investigation uses a case study approach because it is concerned with contemporary phenomena, which we have no control over, and of business relationships between a large number of different firms from a range of sectors. The use of just one case study has external validity implications, that is, generalisation implications (Lee, 1989), but this is justified at the outset of theory generation (Benbasat, Goldstein, & Mead, 1987) and although sample size may limit statistical generalisation it does not degrade analytic or theoretical generalisation (Lee & Baskerville 2003; Yin, 2003).

We are concerned with dynamic phenomena so we have used different data collection methods and different sources (Eisenhardt, 1989). Overall, we used triangulation to converge evidence, analysis and synthesis upon the same process, service and market structure phenomena. A good relationship with the case firm over four years has also helped to reduce validity reactivity and increase trust as well as disclosure. Data sources included meeting notes, telephone conversations, archival data, organisation reports and the web site content of the different organisations involved. Preliminary case study findings were validated by senior management of the case organisation.

Case Analysis: The Architectures of the Translation Services Market

Introduction

The translation services market is made up clients that require translation services, translators, translation technology providers and translation services firms. Clients are organisations of all sizes that require translations services in order to have some form of presence in one or more global markets (Holland, Shaw, & Westwood,

2004). These services include the translation of very diverse sources of recorded and live language such as documents, technical writing translation, software, graphics, proofreading, editing, telephone interpretation, whole web site localisation, conference interpretation and escort interpretation. They also include 'internationalisation' which involves designing or translating products for localisation. For example, software, graphics and screen shots may contain text that requires translation and phone numbers or other country-centric information may need changing (Otter, 2008; LISA, 2007a). Translation in the context of global markets is concerned with much more than the translation of text. For example when internationalising software products East Asian languages can require thousands of characters; Arabic and Hebrew are read and written from right to left, which may require a more flexible user interface design; and there are different conventions for numerical separators and date formats (LISA, 2007a). In addition to the complexity of the *types* of translation objects and the diversity of source and target languages the *frequency* of change to the source text, and so the need for retranslation, is highly variable. This is especially true for web site content that often needs frequent updating, and for portfolios of short life cycle products.

The bulk of the translation is carried out by external contractors that work from home and on behalf of a range of clients which requires a high level of co-ordination that is managed by the translation services company. Translation services companies will also employ specialist in-house translators for quality control purposes and also to contribute to project management on behalf of clients. Translators typically operate within a narrow range of languages, and there are further specialisations into industry categories of content translation, e.g. for pharmaceuticals or engineering where the translators need to have specialist knowledge of technical and industry terminology.

Translation technology providers produce the various technologies that firms and individual translators use to support translation projects. Translation Memory (TM) reduces the work required for retranslation by storing and comparing source texts with past work. This also helps to reduce increases consistency with previous translations, e.g. in terms of style, and aides productivity Translation Management Systems (TMS) are used for project management, resource management and purchase order and invoice generation (DePlama, 2007). Terminology Management is a sub process of a TMS. Machine Translation (MT) is an automated translation process that uses linguistic or statistical analysis rules and is of a lower quality than human translation. However, it can be used in conjunction with manual translation (Sargent & DePlama, 2007; LISA, 2007c). MI is used most commonly with manual post editing, e.g. corrections if translations are factually wrong or for changing a machine translation into a style equal to that of a manual translation. The different uses of a machine translation output depend upon the purpose of the translated document itself, e.g. whether it is for an internal memo, for internal legal communications or for external customers.

Translation Management Systems are also known as Globalisation Management Systems (GMS) and these technologies contain separate tools used by translators.

Tools, e.g. SDL's Trados, run on the translator's PC as an editor that can also integrate with word processors and spreadsheets. GMS can integrate with other systems such as content management systems (CMS). CMS are used by large organisations to manage the flow of content creation and publishing. Linking a GMS into that process ensures that the translations stay in sink and allow the organisations to focus on the purpose of the document. CMS automatically detect changes to source documents which causes them to send 'child' documents in other languages, and instructions, to a GMS for translation. A GMS manages dynamic workflows that would be too complex to be managed manually such as for global web site content synchronisation and updating. GMS are used in-house by clients or by translation services companies to manage complexity in network structure and process complexity in activities.

Translation services companies are organisations that integrate and manage the translators' activities with each client's requirements. They accomplish these both organisationally, by hiring and then project managing the translators. There are a few large global firms but most specialise geographically or industrially. Beninatto and DePalma (2007) report that the top 20 firms accounted for only 18% (2.1 \$ billion) of the total globalisation market in 2006.

The Complexity of Large-Scale Translation Projects

Translation services companies and some of the larger user organisations commonly use GMS to project manage complex translation projects on behalf of their equally complex clients. Specifically, GMS and computer-aided translation and localisation tools manage the different files that pass between the client, the translators and any translation services company. A GMS typically contains:

- The XML source file that contains the text or source language to be translated
- The translation memory file that contains past translations of this source object
- The terminology file that contains special terminology, instances of terminology use and other information to support consistency
- The configuration file that tells the translation tool or the GMS which parts of the source file are to be translated and which parts of the XML schema requires translation
- The instructions file which tells each individual translator what to do
- Any reference files
- The style guide which helps maintain style consistency.

GMS files have a range of different file formats, for example Translation Memory eXchange (TMX) an open XML standard for translation memory data; Term-Base eXchange (TBX) a terminology data standard; Global information management Metrics eXchange (GMX) a future standard that will convey information about the complexity of localisation projects like word or character count; xml:tm a standard for embedding text memory such as translation memory within XML documents; and Segmentation Rules eXchange (SRX) a standard for defining how texts is segmented by computer-aided translation and localisation tools or a GMS. These open standards are developed and maintained by the OSCAR (Open Standards for Container/Content Allowing Re-use) standards body of LISA, the Localisation Industry Standards Association (LISA, 2007b).

The segmentation of text is particularly important. For example it is used for dividing up work between translators in projects with large source files to translate in order to reduce the elapsed time taken to translate a document by sharing it out amongst several translators, and/or to enable the document to be translated to multiple languages. The important capability of segmentation is not that you can divide up the text, it is that you can divide up and then later you can also *reintegrate* the translated work.

By standardising the way that the source text is divided up between translators and it can be decomposed and recomposed by workflow systems like a GMS. By standardising the architectural rules for dividing up and recombining source text it can be distributed for translation between the many different structural configurations of a supplier, i.e. the translator. Some network configurations are possible in this industry are shown in Fig. 8.2. More importantly, these architectural rules cover process as well as structural rules so the translated text can be recombined and partially automated in a GMS. LanguageDirector^{TM} is the proprietary platform of thebigword for managing the workflow between clients, thebigword, translators and competitor translation services companies.

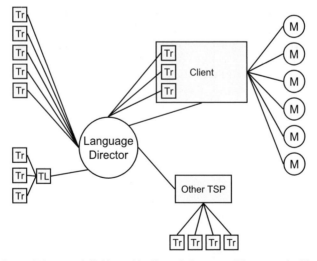

Fig. 8.2 Translators (Tr) network linking with client via LanguageDirector and with possible in-house translators and another Language Services Provider (TSP) to translate multiple media (M). Some translator networks are partially self-managed by a lead translator (TL)

Translator networks are networks of freelance translators that form around specific language pairs and specific sectors, e.g. automotive or mechanical engineering. Language pairs, e.g. English and German, are specific to each translator and therefore to the networks that they form. In some translator networks one of the translators, the lead translator, takes on an additional management role for an additional fee. The lead translator is initially sent the translation job and can either translate it themselves or assign it to another translator in the network. The lead translator can also see the translated file after it has been reviewed and act as a moderator. Essentially, the lead translator manages the workflow at a more detailed and specific level than the project manager does before and after the content is actually translated.

The challenge for the Translations Services Industry

The challenge for the translations services industry is in managing the complexity of stakeholders, processes, data structures, timescales and content types that are the key components of modern translations projects. From a demand perspective, as clients globalise their products and associated systems for product and service support, their distribution, maintenance, marketing and sales activities are also globalised. This structural complexity is multiplied by the increased process complexity that is caused by shortened product and service lifecycles. Process complexity is also amplified by the large increase in the different configurations of stakeholders, data structures that we have described and the different content types that clients use on their web sites, in their internal and external documentation and in conjunction with selling and supporting their products. Potentially, all these stakeholders can exchange all these data objects in all these formats in many different orders and iterations. But only some process configurations are the most efficient and effective use of the different stakeholders' resources.

From a supply perspective, translators mostly work as individual contractors. They may use a translation tool such as Trados and download the associated job files to work on their part of a project. The translator must be able to manage the different files and file formats that are associated with a particular project and client. When they are finished translating their segments they email the result to the translation services company or directly to the client for projects that are managed by the client. These translation segments then need to be checked, integrated and corrected. The separate translations must fit structurally within the client's content object but they must also fit in terms of style, terminology and timing. A single document project may require four translators to complete the work quickly. In a large, long-term project, many documents and content objects may be included which increases the overall complexity and amount of effort required to manage the work. Translation technology providers are developing technologies to meet this challenge.

The Next Stage of GMS Design: thebigword's LanguageDirector™

Thebigword's LanguageDirector software meets the challenge of the complex translations services market by using web services to connect and co-ordinate the various actors, files and systems involved in a translation project (Fig. 8.3).

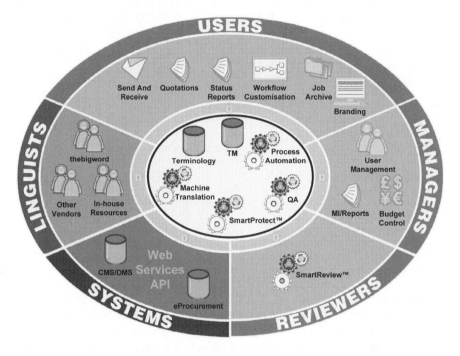

Fig. 8.3 thebigword's LanguageDirector platform. Key: TM (translation memory), QA (quality assurance), CMS/DMS (content document and management systems) (Otter, 2008)

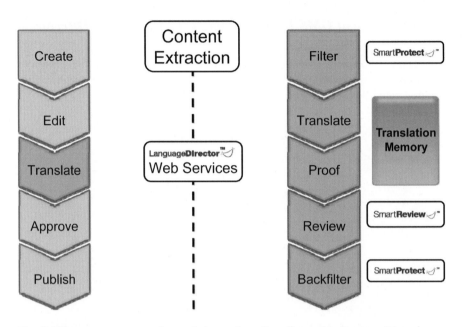

Fig. 8.4 The processes stages of a translation project. SmartProtect is a LanguageDirector component that divides up the projects many different files, according to what each activity and actor requires, but still preserves their structure. SmartReview is LanguageDirector's review management component (Otter, 2008; thebigword, 2008)

LanguageDirector extends the client's internal business processes via a web service application programming interface API for translation. The API allows any customer's system, whether bespoke or off the shelf, to be configured to use thebigword's translation service. The API allows the customer organisation to use the same translation workflow regardless of where their the content resides, e.g. one of the world's leading technology vendors uses this model to link up its fragmented content repositories to the agreed common workflow (Otter, 2008). From the client's perspective the edited content is sent off and then translated content is sent back for approval (Fig. 8.4). The complexity of filtering the specific content and associated files for each different translation team, team member or specialist is hidden from the client by web services and hidden from the translation network by LanguageDirector's process automation. A component called SmartProtect divides up and then organises the different pieces of the content, data and metadata that are required for subsequent stages of the translation process such as parallel translation, proofing, reviewing and reassembly.

Discussion

Dimensions of the Architecture of the Translation Services Market

Standards, standardisation processes and aggregators are architecture characteristics of a market. They are potential couplers or decouplers between aspects of the market that together are the 'glue' that binds the market's suppliers, products, services, customers and technology together. Standards agree commonality, i.e. they couple, but they also agree diversity, i.e. they decouple or preserve a decoupled relationship between aspects of the market. Design choices in the standardisation process that chose one option over another act to simultaneously 'freeze' or join some relationships whilst simultaneously 'thawing' or cutting others. For example, choosing the elements in an XML schema simultaneously divides the aspects of the market that are represented by the *different* categories and aggregates all other aspects of the market. An XML schema is a description of an XML document that is made up of constraints on what its structure and content could be. The design process agrees semantic constraints on the XML elements because when you define what anything is you simultaneously define what it is not. Essentially this is the equivalent to drawing a line between categories and the sum of such line form a pattern which we here we refer to an architecture. The objective is to design an architecture of XML elements that fits the architecture of the user's needs, which in turn should be strongly influenced by the architecture of the customers' needs, i.e. the segmentation of the market. The dimensions, or degrees of freedom, of the architecture of the translations services market are:

- Fee model – monthly fee versus user licences
- Location – on line or behind the customer's fire wall
- Modular or monolithic – Service Orientated Architecture (SOA) or non-SOA
- Service level – embedded versus set up, install, consult as necessary
- File management – automatic versus manual
- Organisational levels – multi level (translator level, lead translator, special translator networks) versus just the translator level
- Project management information – real time versus asynchronous/delayed
- Quality assurance – integral translator checks and sign offs versus project managers have to chase translators because checking is a separate stage.

These dimensions decompose into separate dimensions when two things happen. First, service and the technological options that are available to actors split into finer grain options. E.g. project managers may be able to organise their projects into more organisational levels by using lead translators and special translator networks, which reduces the management overhead of that part of the project.

Another example is that the technology uses an SOA which increases the technological flexibility of the service. Second, the decision-making burden on actors is relieved by the hiding or removal of some options. For example, the automation of processes like file management means that translators and project managers are relieved of a complex task that does not directly support the objectives of the project but has to be done manually when business rules are not set out in a common standard.

In order for the architecture of the market to change the increase in dimension of choice must be matched by a decrease in other choice dimensions because boundedly rational actors have a fixed capacity to make choices. However, there may be a lag between this restructuring of options where the market is just 'waiting for the second shoe to fall'.

Platforms also act to couple and decouple aspects of the market structure by providing new options for the various actors and by hiding the complexity of too many options via automation or service bundling.

The Role of a Platform in a Market's Architecture

The smartness of thebigword's network is embodied in the 'LanguageDirector' platform that links their shifting suppliers and customer networks or the networks of clients who use the LanguageDirector platform. Like any platform, or standard, LanguageDirector does this by managing the options that individual or corporate users are exposed to at any given time. LanguageDirector hides the complexity of managing many different translators, files, formats and processual arrangements by automating their relationships according to standard or negotiated business rules. This decoupling of the customer from the complexity of the supplier network is accomplished by an increase in the coupling between the technology and the supplier network by using web services delivered in a Software-as-a-Service (SaaS) mode.

Web services provide the ability to reconfigure service combinations because of their Service Orientated Architecture (SOA). The SOA allows any configuration of file transfer between stakeholders, the files standards that LanguageDirector supports allow integration between stakeholders and together the use of SOA and industry standards enable automatic workflow management between users. E.g. there is no lost time between a translator completing their translation and it being sent for review because LanguageDirector automatically sends the translation to the next stage in its workflow. The SaaS mode of service deliver enables all files to be held centrally by LanguageDirector which in turn enables groupware benefits. These benefits include automatic integration since files are not actually split between translators. Instead, metadata is just used to divide up the focus of each translator. Projects managers have real-time visibility of progress since the work is not off-line on a translator's PC so translator resource can be reconfigured in real-time if a project's progress deviates from plan.

Also, the real-time automation of workflows enables the addition of a new hierarchical level in the supplier network. Selected translators are paid an extra fee based upon a percentage of each job to lead a small team of other translators. The team will start with a face-to-face meeting and then continue work that is mediated by LanguageDirector's on-line environment. The advantage here is not just that the team's work is linked in real-time but that the team leader, who is a translator first and a manager second, is provided with a very strong workflow support. Lastly by working within this on-line environment all stakeholders automatically generate management information for real-time monitoring by project managers for client reporting and billing, and to support operational strategies such as continuous improvement. In this way, clients may get a monthly invoice but some client managers may require a real time total of money spent on their project or even an alarm when a pre-specified cumulative cost has been reached. The meta-data that enables this real-time management information includes 'sender id', which can identify individuals, systems, areas of systems, product groups or other data needed for cost analysis. Other meta-data includes key workflow information that is specific to the *translation* process, e.g. reviewer id, in addition to information specific to the *client* processes, e.g. non size-limited extensible fields or XML fields designed by the client or others. This meta-data can support many different client services, e.g. real-time calculations of translation memory savings, i.e. the extra cost to the project if translation memory were not used. The elements of the architecture of data, process, team structure and firm structure loosely coupled because they are connected in an SOA. This loose coupling enables the dynamic and low cost reconfiguration of people networks, processes and systems on a project specific basis.

Conclusions

The use of an SOA, web services and SaaS has the potential to change the market structure of the translation services industry. By simultaneously hiding complexity and increasing the complexity of possible structure and process configurations this technology is very attractive to translators, clients and translations service providers. The technology's smartness is in its ability to be a platform for managing complex networks that may only last as long as the project. Knowledge is preserved for reuse and error reduction purposes in the form of translation memory, terminology and style guides. But it is also preserved in the form of the translators' performance, competencies, contact and payment details as well as client preferences and any other data needed to model, improve and even rebuild any particular project network. This enables automation in a project and learning between projects.

The technology enables stakeholders to do more with fewer resources, and in less time, to meet the challenge of clients with increasingly global requirements. The complex translation problems that are generated by clients that span international markets, with more complex products and under greater time pressures can only be answered by increasing the smartness of the networks of translators that work on them. This changes the market structure of this industry from an off-line flat supplier structure with a slower cycle-time and distributed data structure to an on-line, multi-level hierarchy with a faster cycle-time and centralised data structure. The faster cycle-time that is enabled by removing data-transfer delays between translator and project manager enables the extra level of translator team leader. The addition of a team leader reduces the managerial load on the project manager. The project manager can then choose to focus on manage more complex projects or manage individual projects faster. The coordination cost of adding a new hierarchical level is minimised because of the automated workflow functions of the technology. This enables extra process stages, for a more refined output, or reductions in the total project cycle-time. The technology also makes it easier to integrate in-house and outsourced translator networks as well as speciality and ad hoc translators. This implies that the structural flexibility of the market will also increase.

The implications for researchers are that technological platforms can be designed to selectively couple and decouple the structural and processual relationships between the stakeholders in a network, and also the process stages that they enact, to increase the organisational capability of the network. This smart reconfiguration of a network can then produce increased benefits for the customers of the network by supporting them in dealing with more complex markets.

The implications for managers of complex project networks are that technological platforms can be used to hide complexity which allows their users to focus on other areas. Specifically, platforms manage the internally generated complexities that form the inter-relations between stakeholders so that users can focus upon the externally generated complexity from client problems.

Acknowledgements

We would like to thank thebigword and especially Simon Otter, the Group Technology Manager, for the research access that has been provided. As always, any errors in the paper are the sole responsibility of the authors.

References

Baldwin C. Y., & Clark K. B. (1997). Managing in an age of modulatory, *Harvard Business Review*, Sep-Oct, *75*(5), 84–93.

Benbasat, I., Goldstein, D. K., & Mead, M. (1987). The case research strategy in studies of information systems. *MIS Quarterly*, *11*(3), 369–386.

Beninatto, R., & DePalma, D. A. (2007). *Ranking of top 20 translation companies*. Retrieved March 7, 2008, from Common Sense Advisory, Inc. Web site: http://www.commonsenseadvisory.com/members/res_cgi.php/070502_Q_Top_20.php#Tab02

Christiaanse, E., & Rodon, J. (2005). A multilevel analysis of ehub adoption and consequences. *Electronic Markets*, *15*(4), 355–364.

DePalma, D. A. (2007). *Managing translation for global applications*. Retrieved March 10, 2008, from Common Sense Advisory Web site: http://www.gala-global.org/GALAxy-article-managing_translation_for_global_applications-7474.html

Eisenhardt, K. M. (1989). Building theories from case study research, *Academy of management review*, *14*(4), 532–550.

Ethiraj, S. K., & Levinthal, D. (2004). Bounded rationality and the search for organizational architecture: An evolutionary perspective on the design of organizations and their evolvability. *Management Science*, *49*, 404–437.

Galunic, D. C., & Eisenhardt, K. M. (2001). Architectural innovation and modular corporate forms. *The Academy of Management Journal*, *44*(6), 1229–1249.

Garud, R., Kumaraswamy, A., & Langlois, R. (2003). *Managing in the modular age: Architectures, networks and organizations*. London: Blackwell.

Henderson, R. M., & Clark, K. B. (1990). Architectural innovation: The reconfiguration of existing product technologies and the failure of established firms. *Administrative Science Quarterly*, *35*, 9–30.

Holland, C. P., Shaw, D. R., & Westwood, J. B. (2004). Marketing translation services internationally: Exploiting IT to achieve a smart network. *Journal of Information Technology*, *19*(4).

Holland, C. P., & Lockett, A. G. (1997). Mixed mode network structures: The strategic use of electronic communication by organizations. *Organization Science*, *8*(5), 475–488.

Kalakota, K., & Robinson, M. (2003) Service Blueprint: Roadmap for Execution, Addison-Wesly.

Kindleberger, C. P. (1983). Standards as public, collective and private goods. *Kyklos*, *36*(3).

Klein, H. K., & Myers, M. D. (1999). A set of principles for conducting and evaluating interpetive field studies in information systems. *MIS Quarterly*, *23*(1), 67–93.

Langlois, R. N., & Savage, D. A. (2001). Standards, modularity, and innovation: The case of medical practice. In R. Garud, & P. Karnøe (Eds.). *Path dependence and path creation* (149–168). Hillsdale: Lawrence Erlbaum.

Langlois, R. N., (2002). Modularity in technology and organization, *Journal of economic Behaviour & Organization*, *49*, 19–37.

Lee, A. S. (1989). A scientific methodology for MIS case studies. *MIS Quarterly*, *13*(1), 33–50.

Lee, A. S., & Baskerville, R. L. (2003). Generalizing generalizability. *Information Systems Research*, *14*(3), 221–243.

LISA. (2007a). *Globalization industry primer*. Switzerland: Localization Industry Standards Association.

LISA. (2007b). *OSCAR, LISA's standards committee*, Retrieved March 10, 2008, from Localization Industry Standards Association Web site: http://www.lisa.org/OSCAR-LISA-s-Standa. 79.0.html?&no_cache=1&sword_list[]=oscar

LISA. (2007c). *Globalization technologies*. Retrieved March 10, 2008, from Localization Industry Standards Association Web site: http://www.lisa.org/Globalization-Techno.63.0.html

Otter, S. (2008). Interview with Simon Otter thebigword's Group Technology Manager.

Orton, J. D., & Weick, K.E. (1990). Loosely coupled systems: A reconceptualization, *Academy of Management Review*, *15*(2), 203–223.

Parnas, L. (1972). On the criteria to be used in decomposing systems into modules. *Communications of the ACM*, *15*, 1053–1058.

Richard, P., & Devinney, T. M. (2005). Modular strategies: B2B technology and architectural knowledge. *California Management Review*, *47*(4).

Robertson, D., & Ulrich, K. (1998). Planning for product platforms. *Sloan Management Review*, *39*(4), 19–31.

Rodon, J., Ramis-Pujol, J., & Christiaanse, E. (2007). A process-stakeholder analysis of B2B industry standardisation. *Journal of Enterprise Information Management*, *20*(1), 83–95.

Sargent, B. B., & DePalma, D.A. (2007). *How TMS developers pitch their wares to LSPs*. Retrieved March 10, 2008, from Common Sense Advisory, Inc. Web site: http://www.gala-global.org/GALAxy-article-how_tms_developers_pitch_their_wares_to_lsps-7850.html

Schilling, M. A., & Steensma, H. K. (2001). The use of modular organizational forms: An industry-level analysis. *The Academy of Management Journal*, *44*(6), 1149. From http://thesaurus.reference.com/browse/height1168

Simon, H. A. (1997). *Administrative behavior. A study of decision-making processes in administrative organizations* (4th ed.). New York: The Free Press, Simon & Schuster.

Simon, H. A. (1969). *The sciences of the artificial*. Cambridge, MA: MIT Press.

Simon, H. A. (1962). The architecture of complexity. *Proceedings of the American Philosophical Society*, 467–482.

thebigword. (2008). *SmartProtect*, Retrieved April 23, 2008, from company Web site: http:// www.thebigword.com/SmartProtect.aspx

Weick, K. E. (1976). Educational organizations as loosely coupled systems. *Administrative Science Quarterly, 21*(3), 1–19.

Winter, S. G. (2003). Understanding dynamic capabilities. *Strategic Management Journal*, *24*, 991–995.

Yin, R. K. (2003). *Case study research: Design and methods* (3rd ed.). Applied Social Research Series (Vol. 5). Newbury Park: Sage.

9. Business Value Network Concepts for the Extended Enterprise

Kelly Bowles Lyman,[1] **Nathan Caswell,**[2] **and Alain Biem**[1]

[1]IBM Research, USA, kellylyman@us.ibm.com, biem@us.ibm.com

[2]Janus Consulting, USA, nathan@myjanus.com

Abstract

In this paper, we address how business value is produced in networked economic systems with a focus on representation and analysis of the transfer of value between enterprises through resources. These enterprises, termed *service units*, "[provide] a resource for the benefit of another", following the Service Dominant Logic of Vargo and Lusch (2004, 2006) with the definition of a service in a context of use value as opposed to exchange value. Analyses based on this representation provide insight into the strategic positioning of individual firms by accounting for all of the resources needed to satisfy a customer value proposition. The analysis also provides insight into the value structure of *extended enterprises* comprised of resources obtained outside their ownership boundaries through outsourcing and partnership arrangements.

Introduction

The revolution in information and communication technology is reaching a maturity point where high bandwidth availability now enables large-scale communication, with global access to a large amount of information on demand. This phenomenon has opened up new opportunities in enterprise restructuring (Palmisano, 2006), market efficiency and value creation. Customers have many channels for accessing relevant information and are able to make sound judgments based on information such as price regularities or item availability.

Today's geographic dispersal and commensurate organization has called for a more connected and global model of business value network emphasizing the need for detailed coordination among actors, processes, and resources. Now organizational resources need not be replicated at each location, but instead can be globally co-owned. The ability to process large volumes of information and access them from any geographic location means that the co-location of highly coordinated functions is no longer necessary.

P.H.M. Vervest et al. (eds.) *The Network Experience*
© Springer-Verlag Berlin Heidelberg 2009

Today's business reality sees companies moving towards globalization and specialization, and needing to manage and analyze more relationships with partners, suppliers, competitors, and other organizations. Business decision makers need to describe, measure, understand, and transform these business value networks in new ways not common in the days of the integrated vertical enterprise.

In this paper, we describe a business structure analysis to address issues of globally integrated enterprise and specialization. We focus on the extended enterprise, which is a subset of the overall business network. Sample decision problems addressed include but are not limited to: identification of business partners, roles, dependencies, and contributions; assessing balance between competitive and partner relationships; assessing network health, risk, and transformational opportunity.

We start by an introduction to several business value network analysis concepts important to the current evolution of business structure: the concept of the *value network* itself, the entwined concepts of *service* and *resource*, the concept of *value* provided by a service and its extension to a *value network*, and the view of an *extended enterprise* where multiple firms own and manage parts of a global pool of resources. We then follow by outlining a set of techniques that could be used to analyze the extended enterprise.

Related Work

Various modeling concepts and techniques have been utilized to analyze the fundamental structures of the modern enterprise. Theories have been put forth that span various disciplines including organization theory, economics, and strategy as seen through work on Transaction Costs Economics (Coase, 1937; Williamson, 1975), the resource-based theories of the firm (Barney, 1991) that posit the need for scarce resources as a reason for firms to enter into exchange relationships, and Porter's (1980) value chain analysis as one of the pioneering works in providing a macro view of firms' analysis.

Exchange Relationships

Networks of independent entities involved in economic exchanges have been examined from many perspectives. Resource and capability-based perspectives (Das & Tseng, 2000; March, 1991; Teece, Pisano, & Shuen, 1997) focus on the internal source of value while social networking (Uzzi, 1996), structural holes (Burt, 1992), and transaction cost perspectives (Coase, 1937) focus on the external (Williamson, 1975).

The Actor, Resources, and Activities (ARA) model (Hakanson & Johanson, 1992) provides a conceptual representation model for describing interactions in an industrial network. Industrial Network theory views the industrial market as complex networks of inter-organization relationships, position and processes (Easton, 1992), specifically tying firm performance to its position in the network (Burt, 1992). Actors are companies, firms, or individuals that perform activities using a set of resources. Interactions are governed by three networks where Actors are connected by bonds, Activities by links, and Resources by ties.

The e3-value analysis (Gordijn, Akkermans, & Vliet, 2000), based on the ARA model, provides an exchange transaction view of actors and activities. A *value object* is defined as a service, good or money that has an economic value. Exchange of value objects is the defining interaction between actors. Actors internally perform *value activities* to obtain a profit. A *Market Segment* is a clustering of actors that assign economic value to objects equally, typically used to model a group end-consumer with similar interest. While the approach has been used in wide array of modeling engagements and provides insight into the operation of business models, it provides little explicit guidance on the strategic questions of how those networks came to be and how they might change.

The c3-value modeling scheme (Weigand et al., 2007) extends the e3-value to allow for competitive analysis by including competition, customer and capability analysis. Starting from the resources-based view of the firm (RBV), with its claim that sustained competitive advantage is gained by owning valuable, rare, inimitable, and non-substitutable (VRIN) (Barney, 1991) resources, with a particular emphasis on competition as a means to realize the VRIN characteristics.

Indeed the c3-model explicitly takes into account the value proposition that is conveyed by the e3-value's value objects and proposes a dichotomy of the transferred value: a primary value object that conveys the intended businesses of an actor and the secondary value object that enhances the value delivered by the primary value object. The c3-value modeling approach is a powerful strategic technique but lacks the network view because of its focus on the direct competitor and direct customer, thus neglecting the potential given by the network perspective.

Non-Transactional Relationships

The idea that partnerships and relationships are strategic resources was exposed by Dyer and Singh (1998), as are specific roles played in the network when viewed as an ecosystem of competencies (Iansiti & Levien, 2004).

Coopetition was proposed as the conceptual model of these views and suggests a method and technique for analyzing partnerships and roles within a network (Brandenburg, 1997). The model, however, is limited as it focuses on dyadic relationships and overlooks the n-tier dynamics that are important in the connected economy. Gulati (1998) asserts that networks are manageable. They provide a rich overview of the literature regarding the use of organizational alliances as deliberate strategic moves. He identifies several patterns of strategic moves including flexibility in management, trust, patterns of information exchange, and conflict management.

Moving beyond the exchange of goods and services is a focus on value transfer. *Value Networks* have been an object of interest in academia and consulting practice (Allee, 2002; Brandenburg, 1997; Normann & Ramirez, 1993; Parolini, 1999). However, the term evokes conflicting views, and proposed studies lack rigorous and comprehensive models that could allow for descriptive and prescriptive analysis of business design, value creation, and strategic insight.

Parolini (1999), extending the value constellation concept of Normann and Ramirez (1993) conceptualizes the Value Network as "*a set of activities linked together to deliver a value proposition at the end consumer.*" Parolini's core entities are the activities within the network. The Value Network has a *purpose*, which is satisfying the value proposition for the end consumer. This purpose also implicitly sets the boundaries of the network. This is a strategic view of the network that allows for a more prescriptive model.

Allee, deriving from the knowledge view of the firm (Allee, 2002), views a Value Network as "*a complex sets of social and technical resources that work together via relationships to create economic value in the form of knowledge, intelligence, a product (business), services or social good.*" Allee's Value Network is differentiated through representation of the intangible exchanges, and is less inclined to allow for strategic analysis. A more comprehensive strategic intangible-oriented value network model was proposed along with a comprehensive framework of analysis (Biem, Zadrozny, & Rose, 2007).

The Extended Enterprise as a Value Network

The model proposes a taxonomy of exchanges through the notion of *offering* and the clear analysis of how value is created and captured, viewing an economic agent through three perspectives: the actor perspective, the capability perspective, and the asset perspective. Each perspective provides a different dimension of analysis of the network and associated set of metrics (Caswell, Feldman, Nikolaou, Sairamesh, & Bitsaki, 2006).

Since required work can now be done regardless of the geographic location, this has led to silos of specialized resources, which can be tapped from anywhere and for varying purposes. Silos of competencies are thus areas of potential *resources* that be combined into a form. A business value network can be described as a collection of firms or business units that coordinate to deliver interdependent elements of an overall value proposition (Biem & Caswell, 2008; Caswell et al., 2006).

Four concepts underlie the representation and analysis of the business network:

- *Resource* defined as any mixture of competencies and set of assets to used in conjunction (Barney, 1991; Hamel & Prahalad, 1994)
- *Service* defined as "the provision of *resources* for the benefit of another" (Sampson & Foehle, 2002; Vargo & Lusch, 2006)

- *Value* defined as the "use value" of resources provided by a service and its extension to a *value network*
- *Extended enterprise* where multiple firms own and manage parts of an integrated enterprise.

Current thought on business structures uses these concepts to understand the decomposition of enterprises into specialized units through outsourcing and the need for structured composition at a global scale. The concept of *ecosystem* plays a peripheral role here. The value network formed by service units in an extended enterprise is composed of individuals and our analysis will focus on the interactions between individuals. The concept of ecosystems refers to the interactions between populations. Population dynamics is a powerful technique for examining economic systems on a large scale.

Service as Provision of Resource

Service seen as "the provision of resources for the benefit of another" generalizes the typical distinction between goods and services. Deciding whether to classify a particular business interaction as involving "goods" or "services" is problematic. For example, a retail sale involves the transfer of goods, but the value added is customer service. A car wash may be a service (Sampson & Foehle, 2002) but involves the provision of soap, water, and other material goods for the benefit of the customer. Information services can be particularly problematic. Is a printed set of customized driving directions a good or a service? Contracts often display a strong Goods-Dominant (Vargo & Lusch, 2006) bias by defining the deliverable for a service engagement as a physical entity such as a CD ROM or paper document. This even occurs for "time & materials" contracts where the resource provided is clearly the skilled labor. The definition of service as "provision of resource" would make an opposite assumption and focus on measurable utilization of the resource that produced the content on the incidental CD ROM or paper document.

Resources are broadly defined to include material goods, money, people, tools, information, structured compositions of resources as in a process, and intangible assets as brand or reputation. Providing a service involves some change in the resources of the parties involved. The transfer of goods from one party, with or without the reciprocal transfer of money, is such a change. This simple service also includes providing the resources that perform the transfer, such as a store and sales clerks. For instance, in retail exchange transactions the clerk resource transforms ownership of the goods involved (Caswell et al., 2006; Vargo & Lusch, 2004).

Service Units are described as service centers that provide multiple services; these are the nodes in the network of business that can represent business units as controlled by focal firm, suppliers, or partners. From the definition of service used in this paper, Service Units have a set of resources they make available to other Service Units. *Offerings* define the resources available that are to be provided as services.

Value

Two notions of *value* exist in the economics literature. Both are useful for the analysis of value networks.

Exchange value is an attribute of a resource measured by its equilibrium market price. As an attribute of the resource, the exchange value leads directly financial accounting perspectives based on individual assets. As pointed out by Vargo and Lusch, a whole Goods-Dominant Logic emerges which creates difficulties when applied to a predominantly service oriented economy (Caswell et al., 2006; Vargo & Lusch, 2004, 2006).

Use value is an attribute of the user of a resource, measured by a subjective judgment to rank potential "states-of-affairs." The definition of service as the provision of resources provided embodies the notion of "use value." This conception of value informs the analysis and structure of networks of Service Unit parts interacting to satisfy the goals of the enterprise as a whole. This is not a new idea, as Smith (1976) recognized the concept of use value. Also, the notion of value as a subjective rank ordering is a fundamental premise of von Mises (1949) economic theory. The term *state-of-affairs* refers directly to some set of resources and their composition.

A use value approach amounts to a practical practice of the intuitive notions of "win-win" and "customer focus." Creation of a commodity or performance of an action has no intrinsic value. Value is created when that commodity is combined with other resources, resulting in a state-of-affairs more highly ranked by the customer. Service interactions provide resources for "co-creation" of value so that both the provider and consumer "win" with a more highly ranked state-of-affairs.

Goods based exchange is obviously included as a simple case: One party has money, wishes to write, but lacks a pencil. Another party has pencils and needs the freely exchangeable resource of money to satisfy other needs. An exchange leaves both with a more highly ranked state-of-affairs. This co-creation of value is the concrete meaning of win-win. In this case the change in state-of-affairs reflected by possession of pencil and monetary resource is complimentary. Such a close relation is not generally the case.

The asymmetric source of value for service provider and consumer is a source of insight and clarity into the structure of service relations. Value for the provider of a resource through a service agreement focuses on the specific resource. The change may be either an increase of money, a change in the resource itself, or some other impact of the resource on the provider's state-of-affairs. The customer value proposition can be defined as the intended interaction of a coordinated set of resources, including those provided through a service agreement to achieve a state-of-affairs. Clarity comes from recognition that the service provider is not delivering customer value in a goods-dominant sense. The service provider delivers a specific subset of the necessary resources for a customer value proposition.

Value Network as Network of Service Units

A service provider may also be a service consumer. Starting from any service provider of some resource, it is possible to connect both downstream to consumers of the resource and upstream to providers of the resource, and then apply the same procedure to those consumers and suppliers. What emerges is a network of entities that provide resources, consume resources, possess resources, and create value by the transformation state-of-affairs with respect to resources. Through dependencies, the measure of value shifts from providing the resource to the customer judgment on the use of the resource. The customer value judgment may in turn depend on the creation of value at the customer's customer and so on. Furthermore, multiple paths and loops in the network may drive complex dynamic behavior.

As service centers, Service Units form a value network, interacting through service agreements with other Service Units that can utilize the provided resource with other resources to create value. Each Service Unit also contains resources of its own that it either uses or provides directly to other service units. At a minimum, a Service Unit must have the resources that it can provide to other Service Unit.

Extended Enterprise

An extended enterprise is a restriction on the span of the value network described in the previous section. Without focus the network scope can expand to encompass the entire economy. This is too much for practical use. The notions of an enterprise and an extended enterprise bound a portion of the value network.

Historically the description of an enterprise focuses on a single firm with a business model defining a set of products, an intended market for those products, and a means for producing the products (Sloan, 1964). However, the expansion of upstream resource provision and downstream participation in value creation stops abruptly at the boundaries of the enterprise.

An *extended enterprise* extends the value network to include downstream customers, who realize the value of the resources provided by the enterprise, and the upstream providers, who provide necessary resources. Because both the suppliers and customers are outside the scope of the enterprise, they encapsulate their resources so there is no further dependence. The lack of further visible dependency bounds the extended enterprise.

The extended enterprise also includes "service providers" that depend on resources provided from within the extended enterprise. These typically provide operant resources, but many structures are possible. As service providers, they are Service Units in the extended enterprise. Unlike Service Units from the focal firm, they encapsulate all resources requirements and contained resources. The only Provided Resources listed are those from other extended enterprise Service Units. Like suppliers and customers, service providers simplify and bound the size and complexity of the value network.

The original firm that defined the extended enterprise remains. It is referred to as the focal firm in the larger ecosystem of suppliers, service providers, channel participants, and customers. The focal firm, at a minimum, must define the set of Service Units and determine that they form a value network. Consistent with the notion of a firm as a nexus of contracts, there is a need to distinguish and to treat service units not owned by the focal firm differently from governance, measurement, and financial accounting.

Modeling the Extended Enterprise

Given the concepts outlined above, this section describes the coordinating model that unfolds. The model is presented in UML diagram form and is ready for analysis and simulation.

Internal Structure of Service Units

Figure 9.1 shows the composition of a Service Unit. For the purposes of the analysis here, the offering is defined by the set of Offered Services which in turn are comprised of a set of Deliverable Resources. The capacity of Deliverable Resources is shared across Offered Services. Also note that the Offered Service may involve internal use of resources that are not provided to the customer.

The Required Resource is the list of the resources that the Service Unit uses in order to create the Deliverable Resources and deliver them through Service Offerings. Required Resources are either Own Resources, where the Service Unit has ownership rights over the resource, or Provided Resources.

Network Structure of Service Units Linked by Service Agreements

Service Agreements link Service Units and trace actual resources used in order to enable network analysis. Specifically, the Service Agreement connects an Offering in one Service Unit and a Required Resource in another. It is possible that a Service Unit utilizes its own Offerings.

The Service Agreement is anonymous. It may contain a description of any unique features of the agreement and serves as an extension point for metrics, governance, and other information about the specific relation between Service

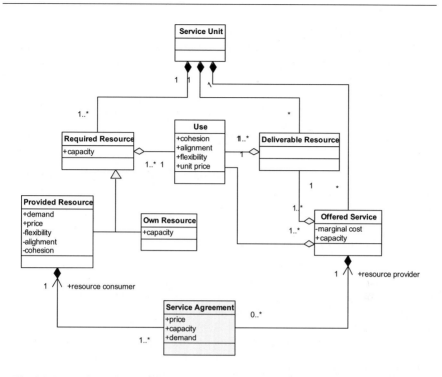

Fig. 9.1 Composition of a Service Unit as the core unit of analysis in the Extended Enterprise

Units. If different Firms are associated with the linked Service Units, the Service Agreement may contain or refer to the contract between the firms.

Extended Enterprise Framework

Service Units are a resource owned by one of the firms that comprise an *extended enterprise* where not all Service Units are part of a single firm. In an extended enterprise, the owning firm coordinates a collection of Service Units from multiple firms to produce the enterprise Offerings. A firm, for present purposes, is a legal entity capable of exercising property rights and entering into contracts. It has the attributes necessary to identify the firm such as the legal name, headquarters address, and the names of principal officers. The notion of a firm responsible for the - overall coordination (the "nexus of contracts") retains a unified set of overall business.

All Service Units are described from the perspective of the extended enterprise. Individual Service Units provided by external firms do not represent the entire providing and may not even match a Service Unit of the external firm. An external firm may provide the Service Offerings for any number of Service Units in the extended enterprise.

The explicit inclusion of provider and customer firms is a very natural extension, allowing the enterprise to encompass the entire system from source to sink for both resources and revenue. For customers and suppliers, such as retail or spot markets, there is no particular Firm responsible for the Service Unit. Associating one or more Firms with Suppliers or Customers allows analysis that is more specific.

Analysis Techniques for the Extended Enterprise

The model presented above enables various analyses of the extended enterprise. In this section, we outline some these analyses.

Network Connectivity Analysis

Basic network connectivity analysis provides common capabilities for other network analysis features (Reggianni, Nijkamp, & Cento, 2008). Basic analysis of the Service Unit value network within an enterprise provides a first check of the ability to deliver Offerings to external customers.

The network analysis feature also provides the algorithmic basis for the analysis features described below. We envisioned it as an extendable feature depending on various business objects, links, and their attributes. In particular, the several value network analysis features (Service Units + Service Agreements) and key performance indicator value tree analysis can utilize the same graph level functions. In this section the graph is described by the standard terms "node" (for Service Unit) and "link" (for Service Agreement). Graph theory describes the properties of the abstract nodes and links structure. The analysis described here depends on attributes of both the nodes and the links beyond the graph theory foundation for its real world utility.

The basic analytical approach starts with reduction of the network to a dependency tree, breaking loops and representing multiple paths by node replication[1]. Links are defined by a Service Agreement, which are taken to be directed from Required Resource to Offering. The dependency tree then extends from a selected Service Unit, called the "root node", through the Service Units that provide direct or indirect resources. Each Service Unit has a dependency tree.

Two types of analysis are supported based on this tree:

- Network structure based analyses such as connectivity, number of multiple paths, disjoint subsets, etc.

---

[1] In implementation, the dependency tree need not be explicitly constructed. Standard recursive path enumeration algorithms generate this tree dynamically.

- Analysis based on link attributes which may be aggregated, have network determined values, or be used to prune the network into sub-networks correlated in some way

Basic Service Unit Network Validation

The Service Unit value network has two criteria:

1. Each Required Resource must be connected to an Offering that provides a matching Offered Resource
2. Each Offering should be connected to at least one Required Resource.

The user receives an error for each failure of the first criterion and a warning for each failure of the second criterion. Validation starts at a Service Unit that delivers an Offering to another Firm.[2] Each Provided Resource of the Service Unit is verified as being connected by a Service Agreement to an Offering that provides that resource. Validation proceeds by performing the same verification on each connected Service Unit, traversing the dependency tree. Leaves of the tree are Service Units that either:

1. Have no Provided Resources;
2. Are an already validated Service Unit (i.e. a loop) or;
3. Have Provided Resources with no associated Service Agreement.

A successful validation for the external offering terminates with all leaves satisfying condition 1 or 2. A "complete map" is one where every customer Offering results in a successful traversal. This is a validation that the overall composition of the extended enterprise is sound.

Basic network analysis provides opportunities for improvement. Trivially, it may simply uncover errors in the Service Unit representation. This is a useful internal check. More significant is discovery of Provided Resources with no supply, or with an unrecognized/unmanaged Own Resource.

A more sophisticated version of dependency analysis employs the Design Structure Matrix (DSM) approach (Baldwin & Clark, 2000). DSM maps Service Unit dependencies in such a way that the larger interconnected structures of the enterprise are visible. Significant structures are clusters of service units with a high degree of internal dependence and relatively sparse dependence between clusters. Matching these dependency structures to organizational and physical business structures is diagnostic and a source of improvement opportunity. As an

---

[2] An Offered Service intended to support Service Agreements with other Firms is called an "external offering". The present model does not define a separate type for this situation.

example, different product lines might show up as different clusters, all supported by an administrative cluster interacting with each of them. In an extreme case, a disjoint set of service units that essentially forms an independent business may be discovered.

Identification of dependency clusters is an important diagnostic in the identification and analysis of outsourcing opportunities. Since the cost of Governance and transactions depends on the number of service connections involved in between sets of service units, it is advantageous to outsource situations where tightly coupled clusters exist as a whole.

Resource Capacity Analysis

The purpose of capacity analysis is to validate that a sufficient quantity of resources is available throughout the network.

Resource Capacity refers to the maximum amount of the resource a Service Unit can deliver. Assessment of capacity depends on adding *capacity* attributes to Offering and a *demand* attribute to Required Resource. Both the capacity and demand perspective analysis are generated from these attributes. This analysis is also useful for "what if" exploration in addition to immediate "balance" diagnostics.

The enterprise impact of fluctuations in customer demand or provider capacity is a major concern. An interesting visualization of this would be showing one of the analyses above while continuously varying one or more external demand or capacity parameters. The impact could be explored of changing the kind and capacity of *own resources*, and alternate providers of resources. The unique value is visibility of the ripple effect, whereby increasing a capacity in one Service Unit depends on an increased capacity in another.

Note that *capacity* is a dimensional quantity. This means that a resource may have several *capacity* measures. A sophisticated extension to this requirement would allow for detailed tracing of measurements and key performance indicators through the resource utilization in the service units. Also note that because the capacities will generally be defined as rates (how much or how many per unit time), this requirement provides the structure needed for detailed dynamic simulation of the business at the Service Unit level.

Financial (Cost) Analysis

The purpose of value network financial analysis is to compute the cost associated with Service Units from standard internal costs and the transfer price of services. Computing costs through the value network ensures that dependencies are included, avoiding local optimization problems.

Several aspects of financial analysis are enabled by adding cost information to the resource, capacity information, and estimated of demand for external offerings. Depreciation and operational costs are associated with Own Resources and Transfer Price is associated with Service. The Transfer Price includes both the marginal cost of a delivery unit and a markup. Opportunity cost may be added to account for the gain in favoring one service agreement over another.

Cost (of satisfying *Provided Resources*) and revenue (sum of transfer prices over demand) analysis on the model of the capacity and demand provide information on the internal distribution of value add.

The obvious difference between a financial and a resource analysis is that monetary units are freely exchangeable. This means simple measures over the extended enterprise can be computed. The sum of transfer prices along the resource dependency tree should be less than the transfer, price to a customer and the net of all customer transfer prices should exceed the net costs.

The simple financial analysis here contributes to construction of business cases. With suitable future extensions in the sophistication of the financial attributes of resources and their transfers, preliminary business case generation would be possible.

Perform Environmental Change Response (Flexibility) Analysis

The purpose of environmental change response analysis is to assess the impact of environmental changes on the cost and ability to deliver to customers. Environmental response can be assessed by combining capacity and cost analysis to measure the flexibility of an extended enterprise. A simple measure of flexibility is to ask if the system can respond to a given environmental change. Environmental changes, such as changes in the market or industry, manifest as a changes in the *Provided Resources* of customer service units or *Offerings* of supplier or service provider service units.

The simplest change is in *demand*. A factor added for the flexibility analysis is the extra cost incurred. The clear threshold is that the increase results in a net financial loss. This analysis and associated analyses can be automatically generated. The implications, however, are a matter of judgment.

A more interesting change is a change in the details of the *Required Resource*. For example, a programming resource changes from COBOL to Java skills. In this case, the dependency tree must be manually updated based on the details of the enterprise. It may or may not be the case that the existing labor pool contains capacity in both in Java and COBOL programming skills. If it is the case, then the question moves down through the ecosystem to ask if the capacity is sufficient. If the end of the ecosystem is reached, then the extended enterprise is flexible enough to accommodate this change.

Perform Core Cluster (Cohesion) Analysis

The purpose of core cluster analysis is to identify groups of tightly integrated Service Units where the Offered Resources are specific to the interacting Service Units.

Core cluster analysis looks for subsets of the Service Unit ecosystem with strong internal dependencies. It contributes to core and non-core analysis but extends it to discovery of alternate "core" centers and inclusion of strong dependencies. The strength of a dependency is measured by the notion of resource "cohesion." The notion of "cohesion" between service units represents the degree of specificity of the resource provided in the Offering to the Service Unit Required Resource. *Cohesion* is an attribute of the connecting Service Agreement. Highly specific resources imply a dependency on a narrow, specific set of sources and are more cohesive than commodity resources. Service units may also be cohesive because the Offering and Service Unit Required Resource require matching Own Resources. This often occurs in technical systems where infrastructures must match.

Reducing cohesiveness is a source of improvement opportunities. Such opportunities generally involve restructuring *own resources*. As an example, injection molded plastic parts are very specific resources. Providing the parts requires an injection molding machine and the mold for the specific part. If the *Required Resource* is the part, then the *Offering* is highly cohesive. Recall that a service, as defined by a *service agreement*, is the provision of a resource for a co-creation of value with the combined set of resources. If the mold is provided by the Service Unit that requires the part, the *Offering* becomes production using a standard machine. This is a much less cohesive service agreement. Lower cohesiveness means more flexibility in alternate sources of *required resource* or ability to utilize alternate *Provided Resources*.

Useful visualizations are extensions of the dependency visualizations where the dependency is weighted by the cohesion. Analysis of the cohesion of a single Service Unit relative to other service units may reveal local clusters of highly cohesive service units. This is important in assessing outsourcing opportunities, as highly cohesive inter-firm *service agreements* may increase risk and cost.

The user shall be able to indicate whether or not a Service Agreement is cohesive. A Service Agreement is qualitatively assessed as being cohesive by the degree of specificity of the Provided Resources needs.

Perform Direct Value Contribution (Alignment) Analysis

The purpose of direct value contribution analysis is to select a subset of service units and resources that have a one to one relationship between the Offered Resource and the content of the Offering delivered to an external customer.

Direct value contribution analysis provides another view of important clusters of service units in the Service Unit ecosystem. It is similar to value chain analysis, but provides a more nuanced view by incorporating all resources. In this case, the weighting is on the internal connection between *Provided Resources* and their utilization in *Offerings*. Alignment is a measure of the relative utilization.

The notion of "alignment" between a resource and an Offering is a measure of how well a unit of the resource matches a unit of the Offering. In the limit, this reduces to a simple distinction between supply and "means of production," where supply is consumed and the means of production is not. *Alignment* is a property of the *utilization* connection between *Provided Resources* and *Offerings*. It is 1 if one unit of the resource is consumed for one Offering unit. For example, if the *service agreement* is to drill a well, three drill bits may be consumed and drill bits are highly aligned with the service. On the other hand, the drilling rig may have a useful life of 10,000 wells. It's alignment with a particular well is correspondingly smaller.

The key implications of alignment are that highly aligned service units will have the biggest impact on the marginal cost of Offerings, chains of aligned service units will represent the "value chain" of the Offering, and highly aligned service units will need to have similar response time characteristics.

The last implication suggests that the dynamic response of service units is an important consideration, with highly aligned service units being required to respond coherently. This extends the flexibility analysis.

Illustrative Examples

The following business scenarios speak to the overall utility of value network analysis and motivate software requirements rather than illustrate specific uses of the analysis.

Major Reengineering Effort Produces New Issues

A client's reengineering effort strongly focused on optimization of core internal processes, yet informal information flows became broken, one of which detrimentally affected the communication and coordination between the firm and a key customer. Through representation of the customer as part of the extended enterprise, and analyses such as ecosystem completeness, core cluster (cohesion), and direct value contribution (alignment), the issues were brought to light. Some informal information exchanges about future expected order demand (occurring by phone after order placement) were overlooked as part of the process redesign and therefore, were no longer being shared in the new web form for order placement.

Changes in resources and an additional newly designed *offered service* around future order volume projection solved this business problem.

Extended Enterprise Evaluation of Outsourcing

A client requested assistance in formulating a strategy for outsourcing that supported their core competencies. They had been intuitively reluctant to outsource, but were feeling pressure since some of their competitors were increasing profits by reducing operating costs though outsourcing. A representation of their firms' ecosystem helped them understand the tight cohesion between what they considered their core business capabilities and what their competitors considered an unimportant support area. By not following their competitors, they discovered they would retain flexibility that would be advantageous to them in the next few years. They lowered costs instead by creating a network of highly cohesive service units. In this way, they still reduced costs while also utilizing a unique strategy for addressing outsourcing in their industry that took into consideration the complex ecosystem they were operating in.

Conclusion

In this paper, we have introduced concepts and models that are the basis for analyzing and describing the extended enterprise. The model is based on the concept of services and resources as provided in the network of Service Units. This model can be used to estimate the validity of a business network for strategic insight and better design.

Acknowledgments

The authors would like to thank Jorge Sanz of IBM Research for his support and advice.

References

Allee, V. (2002). *The future of knowledge: Increasing prosperity through value networks*. Boston, MA: Butterworth-Heinemann.

Baldwin, C. Y., Clark, K. B. (2000). Managing in an age of modularity. In *Harvard Business Review on managing the value chain*. Boston, MA: Harvard Business School Press.

Barney, J. B. (1991). Firm resources and sustained competitive advantage. *Journal of Management, 17*, 99–120.

Biem, A., & Caswell, N., (2008). *A value network model for strategic analysis*. Paper presented at HICSS 2008, Hawaii, International Conference on System Sciences.

Biem, A., Zadrozny, W., & Rose, R. (2007, October). *A value network approach for leveraging intangible assets*. Paper presented at the 3rd Workshop on Visualizing, Measuring and Managing Intangibles & Intellectual Capital, Ferrara, Italy.

Brandenburg, N. (1997). *Co-opetition*. New York, NY: Doubleday Book.

Burt, R. (1992). *Structural holes: The social structure of competition*. Cambridge, MA: Harvard University Press.

Caswell, N., Feldman, S., Nikolaou, C., Sairamesh, J., & Bitsaki, M. (2006). *Estimating value in value networks* (IBM Research Report).

Coase, R. (1937). The nature of the firm. In R. Coase (Ed.), *The firm, the market, and the law*. Chicago, IL: University of Chicago Press.

Das, T. K., & Tseng, B. (2000). A resource-based theory of strategic alliances. *Journal of Management, 26*(1), 31–61.

Dyer, J. H., & Singh, H. (1998). The relational view: Cooperative strategy and sources of interorganizational competitive advantage. *Academy of Management Review, 23*(4), 660–679.

Easton, G. (1992). Industrial network: A review. In B. Axelsson, & G. Easton (Eds.), *Industrial networks: A new view of reality* (pp. 3–34). London: Routledge.

Gordijn, J., Akkermans J. M., & Vliet J. C. van (2000). Business modeling is not process modeling. In *Conceptual Modeling for E-Business and the Web, LNCS 1921* (pp. 40–51). Berlin: Springer.

Gulati, R. (1998). Alliances and networks. *Strategic Management Journal, 19*(4), 293–317.

Hakanson, H., & Johanson, J. (1992). A model of industrial network: A review. In B. Axelsson, & G. Easton (Eds.), *Industrial networks: A new view of reality* (pp. 28–34). London: Routledge.

Hamel, G., & Prahalad, C. K. (1994). *Competing for the future*. Boston, MA: Harvard Business School Press.

Iansiti, M., & Levien, R. (2004). *The keystone advantage: What the new dynamics of business ecosystems mean for strategy, innovation and sustainability*. Boston, MA: Harvard University School Press.

March, J. G. (1991). Exploration and exploitation in organizational learning. *Organizational Science, 2*(1), 71–87.

Mises, L. von. (1949). *Human action: A treatise on economics*. Irvington-on-Hudson, NY: The Foundation for Economic Education, Inc.

Normann, R., & Ramirez, R. (1993, July–August). From value chain to value constellation: Designing interactive strategy. *Harvard Business Review*, 65–77.

Palmisano, S. (2006, May/June). The globally integrated enterprise. *Foreign Affairs*.

Parolini, C. (1999). The value net: a tool for competitive strategy. England: Wiley.

Porter, M. (1980). Competitive strategy. New York, NY: Free Press.

Reggianni, A., Nijkamp, P., & Cento, A. (2008). Connectivity and competition in airline networks – A case study of Lufthansa. In P. H. M. Vervest, D. W. van Liere, & L. Zheng (Eds.). *The network experience – New value from smart business networks*. Berlin, Germany: Springer.

Sampson, S. E., & Foehle, C. M. (2002). Foundation and implication of a proposed services. *Production and Operation Management, 15*(2), 329–343.

Sloan, A. P. (1964). *My years at general motors*. New York: Doubleday.

Smith, A. (1976). In E. Cannan (Ed.), *An inquiry into the nature and causes of the wealth of nations*. London: Methuen and Co.

Teece, D. J., Pisano, G., & Shuen, A. (1997). Dynamic capabilities and strategic management. *Strategic Management Journal, 18*(7), 509–533.

Uzzi, B. (1996). The sources and consequences of embeddedness and economic performance of organizations: The network effect. *ASR, 61*, 674–698.

Vargo, S. L., & Lusch, R. F. (2004, January). Evolving to a new dominant logic for marketing. *Journal of Marketing, 68*, 1–17.

Vargo, S. L., & Lusch, R. F. (2006). Service-dominant logic: What it is, what it is not, what it might be. In R. F. Lusch, & S. L. Vargo (Eds.). *The service-dominant logic of marketing: Dialog, debate, and directions* (pp. 43–56). Armonk, NY: M.E. Sharpe.

Williamson, O. E. (1975). *Markets and hierarchies, analysis and antitrust implications: A study in the economics of internal organization.* New York, NY: Free Press.

Weigand, H., Johannesson, P., Andersson, B., Bergholtz, M., Edirisuriya, A., Llayperuma, T. (2007). *Strategic analysis using value modelling – A c3 approach.* Paper present at the Proceedings of the 40th Hawaii International Conference on System Sciences, 175c.

Networks in Action

Networks in Action

Networks in Action presents a collection of case studies that illustrate how business networks operate in a diverse range of empirical contexts. *Network Essential* focused on creating a common body of knowledge and a shared vocabulary. This chapter demonstrates the importance of business networks in practice. In particular, there are studies that focus on business networks in China. China represents a fascinating empirical context with different institutions, customs and state of technology (for example very few legacy issues) that warrant a closer inspection and interpretation.

Aura Reggiani, Peter Nijkamp and Alessandro Cento present a complex network analysis of Lufthansa's airline network. Lufthansa, the German airline carrier, is partner in the StarAlliance. Resource pooling motivates the use of these alliance networks in the airline industry as individual airline carriers are unable to offer the diversity of destinations mandated by customers. Sharing resources (airplanes, frequent flyer programs) and the integration of flight reservation systems allowing code sharing are characteristic of airline travel networks. They use complex network analysis techniques, an extension of graph theory, to measure network robustness and network stability to identify the most important nodes; the airports, in this case. Their study suggests that Lufthansa's airline network can be characterized as a hub-and-spoke network using multi-criteria analysis (MCA).

Peter van Baalen and Paul van Fenema present a detailed case study of forming a business network to meet unforeseen circumstances: the organizational response of health authorities to the outbreak of SARS. This paper makes two important contributions. First, it introduces the notion of network performance defined as outcomes generated by the network that are not attainable by individual actors. The second contribution is that organizational preparedness is crucial when an organization has to quickly connect to other organizations with whom they do not have prior experience. This lack of preparedness can have devastating consequences, especially when there is little time to react. This is true for many organizations in addition to those responding to natural disasters.

Barbara Krug and Hans Hendrischke focus on the Chinese institutional environment and how networks are devices to manage uncertainty, the pooling of resources and the monitoring and identification of valuable resources and assets. Their study is particularly important as it describes the importance of institutional competence. Institutional competence refers to the capability of a network to align the interests of the greater environment with those of the network, the activation and de-activation of network members for economic purposes and the pooling and mobilization of valuable resources in order to pursue the creation of innovative products and services. For practitioners, the implication of their study is that foreign companies should become a little bit Chinese if they want to succeed in China: one way is to develop this institutional competence.

Mark Greeven presents a detailed field study of the software development industry in the province of Hangzhou distilling five competences that contribute to the success rate of recently founded Chinese software companies. His study shows that Chinese companies had to develop the following five competences: 1) the ability to integrate resources through firm-specific learning, 2) the ability to access and secure financing of the firm, 3) the ability to locate, access and absorb external knowledge, 4) the ability to create a reputation for being innovative thereby creating innovation prominence to overcome liabilities of newness and attract new talent, finance and information, and 5) the ability to continuously change as circumstances dictate (also referred to as strategic flexibility). While Barbara Krug and Hans Hendrischke depicted the conditions under which a network of people coalesces to start a company in China, Mark Greeven shows the circumstances under which an entrepreneurial Chinese company might become successful.

Johannes Meuer gives a detailed field study about the Chinese biopharmaceutical industry in the Shanghai area. While we have been stressing the importance of modularity and loose coupling (Shaw & Holland, 2008), Johannes Meuer demonstrates that not all industries are suited to modular organization. The opposite of modularity is integrality. Johannes Meuer demonstrates how integrality significantly reduces the ability of actors to reconfigure a system, in this case an industry, to changing requirements. The results of the study might be seen as a call for modularity as interdependencies create barriers to change.

References

Shaw, D. R. and Holland, C. P. 2008. Strategy, Networks and Systems in the Global Translation Services Market. In P. H. M. Vervest, D. W. van Liere & L. Zheng (Eds.), *The Network Experience – New Value from Smart Business Networks*. Berlin, Germany: Springer.

10. Connectivity and Competition in Airline Networks

A Study of Lufthansa's Network

Aura Reggiani[1], Peter Nijkamp[2] and Alessandro Cento[3]

[1]Department of Economics, University of Bologna, Italy, aura.reggiani@unibo.it

[2]Department of Spatial Economics, VU University Amsterdam, The Netherlands, pnijkamp@feweb.vu.nl

[3]KLM Royal Dutch Airlines, Milan, Italy, alessandro.cento@klm.com

Abstract

Air transport networks have exhibited a trend towards complex dynamics in recent years. Using Lufthansa's networks as an example, this paper aims to illustrate the relevance of various network indicators – such as connectivity and concentration – for the empirical analysis of airline network configurations. The results highlight the actual strategic choices made by Lufthansa for its own network, as well in combination with its partners in Star Alliance.

Towards Connected and Competitive Airline Networks

The airline industry has moved from a patchwork of individual and protected companies to a liberalized system of globally interconnected corporate organizations (see Martin & Voltes-Dorta, 2008 and Nijkamp, 2008). The aviation sector has traditionally been a publicly controlled industry, with a high degree of government intervention, for both strategic and economic reasons. Already in 1919, the Paris Convention stipulated that states have sovereign rights in the airspace above their territory. Consequently, a series of bilateral agreements was established between countries that the airlines wished to fly over. The Chicago Convention (1944) made a distinction between various forms of freedom for using the airspace, ranging from the 1st freedom (the right to fly over the territory of a contracting state without landing) to the 8th freedom (the right to transport passengers and cargo within another state between the airports in that state). The airline sector ultimately became an overregulated – and thus inefficiently operating – industrial sector in the post-war period all.

The US Airline Deregulation Act (1978) set the tone for a clear market orientation of the aviation sector in the USA, where US-based airlines were allowed to autonomously determine their routes, destinations, frequencies and airfares on their domestic flights, while new firms that were fit, willing and able to properly perform air transportation were free to enter the market. The resulting competition led to a rise in efficiency and innovative strategies in the airline industry and resulted in lower airfares, the entry of many new companies, and a significant increase in demand.

The airline deregulation in Europe has taken a much slower pace, due to the heterogeneity among European countries, the diversity of air traffic control systems and nationalistic motives for promoting a national carrier. Since the year 1988, Europe has gradually introduced a series of steps (so-called packages) to ensure a full deregulation of the European airline sector by the end of the last century, based on an integrated airline market characterized by fair competition and sound economic growth.

The next step in this deregulation process has been the Open Skies Agreement between the USA and Europe, which has opened up many more opportunities for carriers on both sides of the Atlantic to increase their financial viability and their market shares in a free competition across the Atlantic.

The changes in regulatory regimes in the European airline sector have prompted various new actions and strategies of European carriers in the past decade, such as mergers, take-overs and alliances. But the fierce competition has also led to bankruptcy of several existing carriers (such as Swissair and Sabena). More competition in a free market in Europe has largely had the same effects as in the USA, except for the fact that flag carriers still kept a large share of the market. But there are striking similarities in developments, in particular:

- A trend towards the development of hub-and-spokes networks of the existing major airlines in Europe (though less pronounced than in the USA, because of the greater diversity in Europe);
- The trend towards advanced computer reservation systems and electronic booking systems, in order to reduce transaction costs;
- The emerge of a wide variety of – often less transparent – airfare systems, which can even fluctuate daily, depending on demand and capacity (yield management systems);
- The growth in loyalty programmes in order to create bonds with various groups of frequent-flyer passengers;
- The development of various forms of airline alliances, not only within Europe, but also worldwide (such as Sky Team and Star Alliance), allowing also for efficient forms of code-sharing among participating companies as well;
- The emergence of low cost carriers which have taken a significant market share in the European aviation industry, next to charter companies, based on an aggressive pricing policy.

The above mentioned trends are largely similar to those in the USA, but there are a few marked differences:

- Europe is still strongly influenced by nationally oriented carriers (although flag carriers are rapidly loosing their influence);
- Most European flights are international, but cover only relatively small distances, so that a competition with the railway system (especially the fast trains) is also emerging;
- The European air traffic control system is still made up of a patchwork of various systems, and this hampers an efficient management of the air control system in Europe;
- The charter market in Europe is well-developed, and has become a serious competitor to the scheduled airline sector (in contrast to the USA);
- Airports in Europe are often still largely in the hands of national or regional governments or authorities, and, as a consequence, their operation often does not meet the highest efficiency standards.

It is clear that the European airline sector has witnessed rapid changes and challenges in recent years, in particular (1) disruptions caused by external conditions (for example, September 11 2001, the Iraq war, the SARS virus), (2) the emergence of low cost carriers (LCCs) with a rapidly rising market share, and (3) the need to comply with environmental standards. Nevertheless, there has been a general trend towards more competition, more passengers, more mergers, more entries of new firms, a decline in airfares, and more variability in forces in most markets.

In Europe, we currently observe – as a result of the deregulation packages – three airline business models: (1) full-service carriers (offering a variety of services and network linkages); (2) LCCs (offering a limited number of services on specific segments of the network (for example, regional airports) at low prices; (3) charter companies (offering various services to specific holiday destinations). The changing scene in competition in response to the deregulation has prompted a variety of network strategies (ranging from hub-and-spoke systems to point-to-point systems) and yield management practices (for example, through market segmentation, product differentiation, booking classes, price setting and distribution channels). Various alliances have also occurred, but less mergers, to strike a balance between scale advantages and national identity/visibility.

Among the above recent developments, it should be noted that one of the most striking facts in Europe has been the rapid emergence of LCCs (for example, Ryanair, easy Jet). Despite the relatively low fares, most LCCs manage to be profitable and to conquer a significant part of the (rising) passenger demand. In most cases, they offer elementary services and fly uniform – but often modern – aircraft. A major challenge for the near future will be the question whether – and to which extent – LCCs will be able to benefit from the Open Skies Agreement on transatlantic routes.

In conclusion, deregulation policy has had a deep impact on the airline industry in Europe, in terms of airfares, number of passengers, market coverage and product variability. A new major question will now be how the sector will respond to tighter environmental policy constraints (for example, noise, CO_2 emission). This will be decisive for the future of the aviation industry in Europe.

The above described for field has had far-reaching implications for the network strategies of airline companies. In the present paper we will investigate the structure and evolution of the airline network of Lufthansa, both individually and in association with its international partners (for example, Star Alliance). The paper is organized as follows. After this introduction on airline networks from an organizational and policy viewpoint, section "Network Analysis "will illustrate the principal elements of network analysis useful to characterise our case study, that is, four Lufthansa networks, by focussing on the critical indicators concerning the network topology, viz. concentration and connectivity. These indicators will then be applied to the four Lufthansa's network configurations under analysis, and subsequently employed in a final experiment (carried out by means of multicriteria analysis) aiming to classify these four network configurations according to the above indicators/criteria (section "Application to Airline Networks: the case of Lufthansa"). The final section "Retrospect and Prospect" will offer some concluding logical reflections, in the light of future policy and research strategies.

Network Analysis

Boolean algebra in combination with digital information form the constituents of network analysis, as exemplified for instance by traditional graph theory. Network analysis has become an established tool in, for example, operations research, telecommunication systems analysis and transportation science, while in more recent years it has also become an important analytical tool in industrial organization, sociology, social psychology, and economics and business administration (Barthélemy, 2003; Gorman & Kulkarni, 2004; Gorman, 2005; Schintler, Gorman, Reggiani, Patuelli, & Nijkamp, 2005; Schintler, Gorman, Reggiani, Patuelli, Gillespie, et al., 2005; Reggiani & Nijkamp, 2006; Patuelli, 2007). Air transport is a prominent example of modern network constellations and will be addressed in this paper from a connectivity perspective. Air transport shows indeed clear network features, which impact on the way single airline carriers operate (Button & Stough, 2000). The abundant scientific literature on airline networks has addressed this topic in terms of theoretical modelling and empirical measurements on different typologies of airline network configurations.

In this context, interesting research has emerged that mainly addressed the issue of describing and classifying networks by means of geographical concentration indices of traffic or flight frequency (Caves, Christensen, & Tretheway, 1984; Toh & Higgins, 1985; McShan, 1986; Reynolds-Feighan, 1994, 1998, 2001; Bowen, 2002; Lijesen, 2004; Cento, 2006). These measures, such as the Gini concentration index or the Theil index, provide a proper measure of frequency or traffic concentration of the main airports in a simple, well-organized network. However, if a real-world network structure is complex, including multi-hub or mixed point-to-point and hub-spokes connections, the concentration indices may record high values for all types of structure, but fail to clearly discriminate between different network shapes (Alderighi, Cento, Nijkamp, & Rietveld, 2007). There is a need for a more appropriate measurement of connectivity structures in complex networks.

Starting from the above considerations and research challenges, the present paper aims to investigate the scientific potential and applicability of a series of network connectivity/concentration indices, in order to properly typify and map out complex airline network configurations. The application of an analysis will address Lufthansa's network, both European and World-Wide, while making a distinction between Lufthansa as an individual firm and Lufthansa in combination with Star Alliance.

Modelling complex networks is also a great challenge: on the one side, the topology of the network is governing the complex connectivity dynamics (see, for instance, Barabási & Oltvai, 2004); on the other side, the functional-economic relationships in such networks might also depend on the type of connectivity structure. The understanding of these two interlinked network aspects may be instrumental for capturing and analysing airline network patterns.

In the last decades network theory has gained scientific interest and sophisticated network models have been used in different fields, including economics and geography (Waters, 2006). This trend faced also quite some difficulty, because existing models were not able to clearly describe the network properties of many real-world systems, whose complexity could not fully be understood (Barabási & Albert, 1999).

Spatial-economics systems – including air transport networks – are complex, because agents interact, obtaining significant benefits by means of a joint activity (Boschma, 2005). This interacting process may become a permanent feature thus leading to a new meso- or macro structure, for example, to the creation of clusters.

Air transport systems have over the past years been experiencing such clustering processes. An example is provided by airlines' alliances.[1] The main reason why airline carriers cooperate of aggregate stems from cost reductions they can thus obtain. Being a member of an alliance impacts on the carriers' strategy for a long time and also influences the network configuration they adopt. It is worth noteworthy that alliances play also an important role in determining market dynamics; in 2005, the three main alliances in air transport accounted for 80 per cent of the total capacity offer.[2] Therefore, we need to develop airline network models that can adequately take into account clustering and merger processes.

A further important trend many real networks show is the so-called 'Small-World (SW) effect'. This term indicates that the diameter[3] of a network is so short that it takes only a few movements along links in order to move between any two nodes of a network (Reggiani & Vinciguerra, 2007). In air transport systems, we

---

[1] The processes underlying the creation of an alliance can be clearly depicted by considering the integration of Lufthansa and Swiss, described in the Lufthansa Annual Report (2005); available on the website http://konzern.lufthansa.com/en/html/ueber_uns/swiss/index.html).

[2] See http://www.tourismfuturesintl.com/special%20reports/alliances.html.

[3] The concept of diameter is defined in Table 10.1.

can point out the SW effect by taking into consideration and comparing the network configuration of single carriers or of alliances; such systems exhibit a clear SW effect when it takes only a small number of flights to link the two most distant airports in the network.

Alongside the SW effect, the SW network model has been developed in order to take into account both the SW effect and the related clustering processes (Watts & Strogatz, 1998). The main features of this model are a short diameter and a high clustering coefficient.

A further elaboration of the SW model is the so called Scale-Free (SF) network introduced by Barabási and Albert (1999) in order to incorporate two mechanisms upon which many real networks have proven to be based: *growth* and *preferential attachment*. The former points to the dynamic character of networks, which grow by the addition of new nodes and new vertices; the latter explains how new nodes enter the network, namely by connecting themselves to the nodes having the highest number of links.

An important feature of SF networks is represented by their vertex degree distribution[4] $P(k)$ which is proportional to $k^{-\gamma}$ (with k being the number of links), that is, to a power law. The value of the degree exponent γ depends on the attributes of the single systems and is crucial to detect the exact network topology, in particular the existence of the hubs (highly connected nodes). As Barabási and Oltvai (2004) highlight, a SF network embeds the proper hub-and-spoke model only when $\gamma = 2$, while for $2 < \gamma \leq 3$ a hierarchy of hubs emerge. For $\gamma > 3$, the hub features are absent and the SF network behaves like a random one.

In air transport systems, we can point out SW networks by considering fullservice carriers. Without national or political impediments in a free market, these carriers typically organize their network into a hub-and-spoke system, where one or a few central airports called 'hubs' have a high number of links to the other airports called 'spokes'. Passengers travelling from a place of origin to a place of destination have to stop typically in one or a few hubs to change aircraft. Hubs are organised in order to allow flight connectivity by coordinating the scheduled timetable of the arriving and departing flights. Investigating the airline strategy in designing hub connectivity and timetable coordination has been the aim of several empirical network studies. Some examples of theoretical and empirical investigation of hub connectivity can be found in the works of Bootsma (1997), Dennis (1998), Rietveld and Brons (2001), Veldhuis and Kroes (2002), and Burghouwt and de Wit (2003). As a consequence, the hub has to manage normally a high volume of traffic at the same time, due to their central connecting role in the network.

---

[4] $P(k)$ is the probability that a chosen node has exactly k links (Barabási and Oltvai 2004). See also Equation (10.1).

In contrast to SF networks, we have to highlight also random networks (Erdös & Rényi, 1959), which display homogeneous, sparse patterns, without cluster characters. Their vertex degree distribution follows a Poisson distribution.[5]

In air transport, random networks are useful to map point-to-point connections, as it is the case for low-cost airlines (Cento, 2006). In the ideal point-to point network all airports are connected to each other, so that passengers can fly from one airport to any other directly without stopping in any hub to change aircrafts. These networks have a low diameter, as a consequence of the high number of direct links between airports. Reggiani and Vinciguerra (2007: 148) point out that a random network can be seen as '*a homogeneous system which gives accessibility to the majority of the nodes in the same way*'. Furthermore, as it is evident by looking at the plot of the exponential function, the probability to find highly connected nodes is equal to 0. Therefore, no clear hubs exist, and the network configuration appears to be random because no single airport displays a dominant role in a connected network.

The vertex degree distribution is one of the key tools we may use to point out the network configuration (Reggiani & Vinciguerra, 2007), since this function determines the way nodes are connected. It can be defined as the probability $P(k)$ of finding nodes with k links. In general, we can state that:

$$P(k) = N(k)/N, \qquad (10.1)$$

where $N(k)$ is the number of nodes with k links and N is the number of nodes of the network.

With regard to the network topologies developed in the framework of graph theory, complex systems tend to show two main degree distributions: the *Poisson* distribution (Erdös & Rényi, 1959) and the *power-law* function (Barabási & Bonabeau, 2003). The former is defined as:

$$P(k) \sim e^{<k>} \frac{<k>^k}{k!}, \qquad (10.2)$$

and describes networks – so-called random networks – where the majority of nodes have approximately the same number of links, close to the average $<k>$ (Barabási & Albert, 1999). Equation (10.2) is a distinctive feature of point-to-point networks, such as those adopted by low-cost airlines; this network topology is typical of equilibrated economic-geographical areas, where a high number of direct links can be profitably operated.

The power-law function is defined as:

$$P(k) \sim k^{-\gamma} \qquad (10.3)$$

and characterizes networks having a small number of nodes with a very high degree while the majority of nodes have a few links. Equation (10.3) has impor-

---

[5] For a review of random models, SW models and SF models, see Albert and Barabási (2002) and Jeong (2003).

tant economic implications: it characterizes SF networks, where the term SF refers to the fact that '*the power-law distribution does not change its form no matter what scale is used to observe it*' (Reggiani & Vinciguerra, 2007: 150), and that, in these networks, distances are irrelevant. Therefore, we expect to find SF networks in 'global networks', such as the Internet and air transport, and in general in those networks where relevant economic aggregation clusters (preferential attachments) attract flows from distant nodes.

Networks can be analyzed from the perspective of their geometry and their concentration. Various relevant indices are included in Tables 10.1 and 10.2, respectively.

Table 10.1 Network's topology indices

Index or measurement	Description	Formulation	Variables	Source
Degree	The degree of a node is given by the number of its links	$k(v)$	$k(v)$ is the number of links of node v	Barabási and Oltvai (2004)
Closeness	It indicates a node's proximity to the other nodes	$C(v) = \dfrac{1}{\sum_{t \in V} d_{vt}}$	d_{vt} is the shortest path (geodesic distance) between nodes v and t; n is the number of nodes in the network	Newman (2003)
Betweenness	It indicates a node's ability to stand between the others, and therefore, to control the flows among them	$B(v) = \sum_{s \neq t \neq v \in V} \dfrac{\sigma_{st}(v)}{\sigma_{st}}$	$\sigma_{st}(v)$ and σ_{st} are, respectively, the number of geodesic distances between s and t that pass through node v, and the overall number of geodesic distances between nodes s and t	Freeman (1977)
Diameter	It measures the maximum value of the geodesic distances between all nodes	$D = \max_{s,t \in V, s \neq t} d_{st}$	d_{st} is the geodesic distance between nodes s and t	Boccaletti, Latora, Moreno, Chavez, and Hwang (2006)
Clustering coefficient	It measures the cliquishness of a node	$Cl(v) = \dfrac{l_v}{\max l_v}$	l_v and $\max l_v$ are, respectively, the number of existing and maximum possible links between the nodes directly connected to node v (its neighbours)	Watts and Strogatz (1998)

Table 10.2 Network's concentration indices

Indicator	Formula	Use	Variables used	Sources
Gini concentration index	$G = \dfrac{\sum_{i=1}^{n}\sum_{j=1}^{n}\left|x_i - x_j\right|}{2n^2\mu}$	It is a measure of geographical concentration	x_i, x_j are the number of weekly flights from airports i and j, ranked in increasing order; n is the number of airports in the network; μ is $\sum_i x_i / n$	Cento (2006)
Freeman centrality index	$F_B = \dfrac{\sum_i\left[F_B(x^*) - F_B(x_i)\right]}{n^3 - 4n^2 + 5n - 2}$	It is a measure of similarity to a perfect star network	$F_B(x_i) = \sum\sum b_{jk}(x_i)$ is the $j < k\,j < k$ betweenness centrality of node x_i; $F_B(x^*)$ is the highest betweenness centrality value of the distribution	Cento (2006)
Entropy function	$E = -\sum_{ij} P_{ij}\ln P_{ij}$	It measures the degree of spatial organization and variety in a system	p_{ij} is the probability of a link between nodes i and j	Nijkamp and Reggiani (1992); Frenken and Nuvolari (2004)

All the indicators in Tables 10.1 and 10.2 will be utilized in the empirical analysis concerning the exploration of the Lufthansa network's topology and concentration (See the following section).

Application to Airline Networks: the Case of Lufthansa

Introduction

We will now address the geographical analysis of Lufthansa's aviation network in the year 2006. The airline network measurement is essential for exploring the airline behaviour and its implications for the supply, the traffic demand, the airports' infrastructure and aviation planning. The airline network can be subdivided into domestic, international or intercontinental configurations depending on whether the airports connected are located within a country, a continent or in different continents. Furthermore, an airline network can be interconnected or interlined to partner's networks within the alliance concerned. This classification is based on geographical, air transport-political and economic characteristics, such as airlines' degree of freedom from the Chicago Convention (see Cento, 2006) market liberalization, or costs and traffic demand. Therefore, the overall network configuration is the result of the integrated optimisation of the domestic, international, and intercontinental parts of the total network. These sub-network configurations may range from fully-connected or point-to-point to hub-and-spokes configurations to alliances (fully-contracted) or to a mix of these configurations. Within this conceptual framework, we will position our analysis of four sub-networks of Lufthansa. As summarized in Table 10.3, we coin networks A1 and A2, referring respectively to the flights operated by Lufthansa in Europe and in the whole world, while networks B1 and B2 take into consideration – respectively at a European and at a global level – the flights operated by all the carriers which are members of Star Alliance (to which Lufthansa belongs).[6]

Table 10.3 Lufthansa's network constellation (2006)

Network	Area under considera-tion	Carrier or alliance operating the flight	Nodes	Total number of links
A1	Europe	Lufthansa	111	522
A2	World	Lufthansa	188	692
B1	Europe	Star Alliance	111	3,230
B2	World	Star Alliance	188	6,084

The variable under analysis is represented by the number of direct connections of each airport in the summer season of the year 2006, measured on a weekly basis. In all four cases we only consider those airports where Lufthansa operates with its fleet and not by partner's airlines. When we consider A1 and A2 networks, we clearly see that the majority of Lufthansa's flights are operated at a continental level. On the contrary, nearly half of Star Alliance's flights are operated outside Europe. This finding is not surprising, if we consider that the carriers making up Star Alliance are mainly from non-European countries.

Network Geometry

In order to examine the nodes' location, we have computed the three centrality measures (degree, closeness and betweenness) described in Table 10.1. Concerning the investigation of the nodes' relations, we have examined the diameter and the clustering coefficient of the network (see again Table 10.1).

---

[6] The Star Alliance member carriers are currently: Air Canada; Air New Zealand; ANA; Asiana Airlines; Austrian; bmi; LOT Polish Airlines; Lufthansa; Scandinavian Airlines; Singapore Airlines; South African Airlines; Spanair; Swiss; TAP Portugal; THAI; United Airlines; US Airways; VARIG (the list was retrieved from www.staralliance.com).

The degree of a node (Table 10.1) can be seen as a measure of centrality if we assume – in the framework of our analysis – that the best connected airports have a greater power over the whole network, as they can control a considerable amount of all flights. In all networks we find that the airports of Frankfurt and Munich have always the highest degree (see Table 10.8 in Appendix A).

A further analysis of nodes' centrality focuses on their 'ease-of-access' to the other nodes.[7] In order to investigate this concept we have computed the closeness centrality[8] (Table 10.1). The values of this index for the networks under consideration (listed in Table 10.9 in Appendix A) show that the highest values usually correspond to the best connected nodes; therefore, closeness centrality is able to map out – in the framework of our study – the most important airports in terms of connectivity. A similar trend can be observed by considering betweenness centrality (Table 10.1; the values for networks A1, A2, B1 and B2 are listed in Table 10.10 in Appendix A). This finding is not surprising, since hubs – in the framework of the hub-and-spoke model – are chosen from those airports falling among the highest possible number of pairs of other airports (O'Kelly & Miller, 1994; Button & Stough, 2000).

The networks' topology can also be explored by examining how the various nodes relate and link, since this last attribute impacts the configuration of the whole structure. For this purpose we have computed the clustering coefficient (defined in Table 10.1; the ten highest values for the nodes of the four networks of our experiments are listed in Table 10.11 in Appendix A). The values indicate a significant difference between the networks A1 and A2 and the networks B1 and B2; in the former case the airports of Frankfurt and Munich dominate the chart; in the latter case, other airports appear to emerge, thus showing that flights are spread more equally on the whole network.

In addition, we will also consider the diameter of the above networks in order to investigate how the links' patterns influence the ability to move inside the network. Both A1 and A2 have a diameter of 4, while B1 and B2 have a diameter of 2. This can be justified only if there is no significant difference in the geographical configuration between A1 and A2, approximately a hub-and spoke, while B1 and B2 can be a mixture of hub-and-spoke and point-to-point networks. In other words, the integration of Lufthansa network in the Star Alliance reduces the travel distance, as the passengers can benefit from more connections and thus shorter paths to travel between the origin and the destination. This has important implications in the context of our study, because it entails that Lufthansa's networks shrink, when we consider the flights of all Star Alliance members.

---

[7] It can be assumed that access to the network is easier when nodes are closer (Freeman 1979).

[8] We compute the closeness centrality, as well as the subsequent betweenness centrality, using the Pajek software (http://vlado.fmf.uni-lj.si/pub/networks/pajek/).

Network Concentration

The study of the networks' degree of concentration – which is carried out in the present subsection – is crucial in order to detect the exact network topology, because the hub-and-spoke model is highly concentrated, while point-to-point networks do not show this feature.

First, Table 10.4 presents the normalized Gini index (see Table 10.1) for the four networks under consideration. Both Star Alliance networks are less concentrated than the Lufthansa counterparts, meaning that when we enlarge the measurement to a broader network including intercontinental destinations and partners' networks, the configuration will probably evolve into a mix of multi hub-and-spoke and point-to-point structures. In particular, network A2 appears to be the most concentrated.

The information provided by the Gini index refers to the degree of concentration existing in a network, without any evidence on how this concentration impacts on the network topology. For this last purpose the Freeman centrality index (Table 10.1) has been computed. Its normalized values are represented in Table 10.4. This index assumes the value 1 for a hub-and-spoke network, and the value 0 for a point-to-point network (Cento, 2006).

Table 10.4 Concentration indices

Network	Gini index	Freeman index	Entropy
A1	0.762	0.504	5.954
A2	0.813	0.757	6.194
B1	0.524	0.059	7.790
B2	0.699	0.056	8.389

According to the Freeman index, again networks A1 and A2 turn out to be the most concentrated ones. In particular, A2 network seems to be again the closest to the hub-and-spoke model; we may suppose that this network is characterized by a strong hierarchy among nodes.

Finally, concerning the last concentration index, that is, entropy (Table 10.1), Table 10.4 shows the related values for the networks A1, A2, B1 and B2. The results show that the entropy values are higher when we consider those flights operated by Lufthansa's partners (networks B1 and B2). A likely explanation for this increase is given by the process of construction of these networks, obtained by the addition of flights to the nodes of A1 and A2, respectively. Both B1 and B2 are therefore the 'sum' of the networks implemented by the different carriers that are members of Star Alliance, and hence they are not the result of a specific strategy, as is the case for A1 and A2. Clearly, the above values indicate that A1 and A2 networks are more concentrated and less dispersed than the B1 and B2 networks; more specifically, A1 appears to be the most concentrated network.

In conclusion, from the above three indicators, networks A1 and A2 appear to be the most concentrated. However, among these two networks, A2 seems the most concentrated with respect to two indicators (Gini and Freeman), while A1 seems the most concentrated with respect to the entropy index.

Network Configuration

Degree Distribution of the Lufthansa Networks

The vertex degree distribution function is important in order to detect the most plausible network configuration. In this section, we will explore whether the variable 'number of weekly connections' is rank-distributed – over A1, A2, B1 and B2 – according to either an exponential or a power function. The $R2$ values and the b coefficients of the two interpolating functions (exponential and power) concerning the four ranked distributions (in log terms) are listed in Table 10.5. The plots of both functions for the four networks under consideration are displayed in Appendix B (Figs. 10.1 and 10.2).

Table 10.5 Exponential and power fitting of rank distributions

Network →	A1		A2		B1		B2	
Network parameters →	R^2	b	R^2	b	R^2	b	R^2	b
Distribution function ↓ ↓								
Power	0.95	0.99	0.93	0.82	0.75	0.67	0.70	0.65
Exponential	0.75	0.03	0.67	0.01	0.66	0.02	0.48	0.01

Both Table 10.5 and Figs. 10.1 and 10.2 (in Appendix B) highlight that our data sets better fit a power function, as the higher $R2$ values indicate. It is worth noting that the b coefficient of the power function for the networks A1, A2, B1 and B2 is respectively equal to 0.99, 0.82, 0.67 and 0.65. If we carry out a transformation[9] of these coefficients, we observe that the A1 network displays a power-law exponent equal to 2, thus indicating a stronger tendency to a hub-and-spoke system according to Barabási and Oltvai (2004), while the other three networks A2, B1 and B2 display a power-law exponent between 2 and 3, thus indicating a tendency to a hierarchy of hub/agglomeration patterns.

A further issue concerns the fitting of the exponential function. Also in this case we obtain high $R2$ values, although inferior to the ones emerging in the power

---

[9] Adamic (2000) shows that the power-law exponent γ (emerging from the nodes' probability distribution (Equation (3))) is related to the power function coefficient b (emerging from the distribution relating the degree of the nodes to their rank (rank size rule) (see Figs. B1 and B2 in Annex B) as follows: $\gamma = 1 + (1/b)$.

case; however, the coefficient of the exponential function is always very low, ranging from 0.01 to 0.03 (Table 10.5). Therefore, if we look at the $R2$ indicators, all networks under consideration appear to be in a 'border-line' situation (that is, an ambiguity between a power and exponential fitting). Nevertheless, if we look at the coefficient values, the four networks seem to show a tendency toward an agglomeration structure of SF type, expressed by a clear power-law vertex degree distribution, with the degree exponent γ equal to 2 (network A1), or varying between 2 and 3 (networks A2, B1, B2).

A further consideration concerns the plots of networks B1 and B2 (Fig. 102 in Appendix B). We can clearly see that both identify a power function with a cut-off. Thus, if we eliminate – in both networks B1 and B2 – those nodes which have less than 10 links, we slightly improve the fitting of their power function, obtaining for networks B1 and B2 respectively $R2$ values of 0.84 and 0.75, but still lower than the $R2$ values regarding A1 and A2.

In conclusion, from our estimation results, the networks A1, A2 appear to show the strongest characteristics of concentration and preferential attachment. In particular, network A1 appears to be the closest to the hub-and-spoke model, from the perspective of Barabási and Oltvai's approach. Given these preliminary results, it is worth to examine these configurations, jointly with some indicators of network concentration and topology previously implemented. Consequently, a multidimensional method, such as Multicriteria Analysis (MCA), taking into account – by means of an integrative approach – all adopted indicators and related results, was next carried out and utilized for further analysis.

Classification of the Lufthansa Networks by means of Multicriteria Analysis

A multidimensional assessment approach, such as MCA, will now be applied[10] to the four Lufthansa networks in order to identify the 'best' system, according to the network indicators previously calculated.

Consequently, the alternatives are the four networks A1, A2, B1, B2 under consideration, while the criteria have been grouped according to three macro-criteria: network concentration, topology and connectivity (Table 10.6). It should be noted that, concerning the geometric criteria, we have considered the diameter and the clustering coefficient, since these two indices provide the network geometry's features. In particular, concerning the latter, the average clustering coefficient has been adopted (Barabási & Oltvai, 2004).

The first group of macro-criteria is related to the networks' concentration. It should be noted that in our MCA procedure, the entropy indicator needs to be transformed positively because the real values of the entropy function increase when networks are more heterogeneous, that is, less concentrated. The second group of macro-criteria refers to the networks' physical measurement. Here, the diameter needs to be converted in utility, because its value is higher when

---

[10] Here the Regime method and software has been used (Hinloopen & Nijkamp, 1990).

networks are less centralized. The third group of macro-criteria is related to connectivity. This property is investigated through the interpolation of the ranked degree distributions, where – in the power function – the highest exponent of 0.99 implies a value of the exponent degree[11] – in the associated power-law distribution – close to 2 (perfect hub-and-spoke). The $R2$ and the coefficient of the exponential function need to be converted to utility, since both values indicate random and homogeneous patterns.

Table 10.6 Alternatives and criteria

Alternatives	A1 (Lufthansa, Europe)
	A2 (Lufthansa, World)
	B1 (Star Alliance, Europe)
	B2 (Star Alliance, World)
'Concentration' criteria	Gini index
	Freeman index
	Entropy
'Topology' criteria	Diameter
	Average Clustering Coefficient
'Connectivity' criteria	R^2 of the fitted power function (ranked degree distribution)
	Coefficient of the power function
	R^2 of the fitted exponential function (ranked degree distribution)
	Coefficient of the exponential function

We have carried out five scenarios by considering: (a) all the criteria mentioned above; (b) each macro-criteria separately; (c) concentration and topology criteria together. In each scenario an equal weight, that is, unknown priority, has been given to the single criteria. The results are listed in Table 10.7.

Table 10.7 Findings of multi-criteria analyses

Criteria considered	All criteria combined	Concentration criteria	Topology criteria	Connectivity criteria	Concentration and topology criteria
Hierarchy of the alternatives	A1	A2	B1	A1	A1
	A2	A1	B2	B1	B1
	B2	B2	A1	A2	A2
	B1	B1	A2	B2	B2

These findings point out that network A1 prevails, however with two exceptions. The former is represented by network A2, which is the top-scorer when we consider the criteria related to the networks' concentration/geography: this finding comes from the higher centralization and concentration degree of network A2, as

---

[11] See Footnote 9.

demonstrated by the Freeman and Gini indices. The latter exception is represented by network B1, which prevails when we consider the criteria related to the physical measurement of networks.

It turns out that the Lufthansa network A1 is the most connected one; we can conjecture that A1 is close to a hub-and-spoke system, according to the values expressed by its exponent degree in the power-law distribution (see Table 10.5). This result confirms the dual-hubs network strategy advocated by the German carrier (Lufthansa, 2005). Frankfurt and Munich act as central hubs, where all intercontinental flights depart and arrive in conjunction with the European and domestic flights. This timetable coordination is designed to allow passengers to transfer from one flight to another for different national and international destinations.

Retrospect and Prospect

Network analysis turns out to be a powerful tool for analyzing the structure and evolution of transportation systems. Airline networks are fascinating examples of emerging complex and interacting structures, which may evolve in a competitive environment under liberalized market conditions. They may exhibit different configurations, especially if a given carrier has developed a flanking network framework together with partner airlines.

The present paper has investigated the network structure of four networks of Lufthansa by considering several indicators concerning the concentration, topology and connectivity (degree distribution) functions characteristics of this carrier. An integrated multidimensional approach, in particular multicriteria analysis has been adopted, in order to take into account all information obtained by the above indices, and thus extrapolate the most 'appropriate' network, according to these indicators.

The related results point out that all the four Lufthansa networks can be properly mapped into the SF model of the Barabási type. In particular, network A1 can be formally identified as a hub-and-spoke structure. In general, we can conjecture a 'tendency' towards a hubs' hierarchy or hub-and-spoke configuration in Lufthansa's European network (network A1), as also witnessed by the emergence of various nodes (Frankfurt, Munich and Dusseldorf) which are organized as hubs in the framework of Lufthansa's activities. All in all the four networks exhibit a hierarchical structure mainly dominated by German airports.

The results obtained thus far highlight various characteristic features of complex aviation networks, but need to be complemented with additional investigations, in particular, on the structure and driving forces of the demand side (types of customers, in particular). Furthermore, the market is decisive in a liberalized airline system, and hence also price responses of customers as well as competitive responses of main competitors would need to be studied in the future.

From a methodological viewpoint a refined weighted network analysis – taking into account the strength of each connecting link – might offer better insights into the topological structure of the airline network at hand (see, for example, Barrat, Barthélemy, Pastor-Satorras, & Vespignani, 2004).

Another, and perhaps more interesting type of new research on network topologies might be to identify the existence of 'structural holes', which refers to the strategic importance of a relationship of nonredunancy between two contacts or nodes (see Burt, 1992). Such analyses are particularly important to map out the individual gains or losses of being connected to other parts of a complex network. It is thus clear that modern network analysis offers a wealth of new and important research challenges to the scientific community.

Acknowledgments

The present chapter is a revised version of a previous paper "Network Measures in Civil Air Transport: A Case Study of Lufthansa", published in '*Networks, Topology and Dynamics*', Springer Series Lecture Notes in Economics an Mathematical Systems, 2008, Vol. 613 (A.K. Naimzada, S. Stefani, A. Torriero, eds). The authors wish to thanks Sara Signoretti (University of Bologna) for her assistance concerning the empirical application, as well as Roberto Patuelli (Institute for Economic Research, University of Lugano) for his comments on the present chapter, as well as for his cooperation in the editing process.

References

Adamic, L. A. (2000). Zipf, power-laws, and Pareto – A ranking tutorial. http://www.hpl.hp.com. Accessed 16 April 2007.

Albert, R., & Barabási, A. -L. (2002). Statistical mechanics of complex networks. *Reviews of Modern Physics, 74*, 47–97.

Alderighi, M., Cento, A., Nijkamp, P., & Rietveld, P. (2007). Assessment of new hub-and-spoke and point-to-point airline network configurations. *Transportation Reviews, 27*, 529–549.

Barabási, L. A., & Albert, R. (1999). Emerging of scaling in random networks. *Science, 286*, 509–512.

Barabasi, L. A., & Bonabeau, E. (2003). Scale-free networks. *Scientific American, 288*, 60–69.

Barabási, L. A., & Oltvai, Z. N. (2004). Network's biology: understanding the cell's functional organization. *Nature Reviews Genetics, 5*, 101–113.

Barrat, A., Barthélemy, M., Pastor-Satorras, R., & Vespignani, A. (2004).The architecture of complex weighted networks. *Proceedings of the National Academy of Science of the United States of America,* 8 March. http://www.pnas.org/cgi/doi//10.1073/pnas.0400087101.

Barthélemy, M. (2003). Crossover from scale-free to spatial networks. *Europhysics Letters, 63*, 915–921.

Boccaletti, S., Latora, V., Moreno, Y., Chavez, M., & Hwang, D. -U. (2006). Complex networks: structure and dynamics. *Physics Reports, 424*, 175–308.

Boschma, R. A. (2005). Proximity and innovation. A critical assessment. *Regional Studies, 39*, 61–74.

Bootsma, P. D. (1997). *Airline flight schedule development; analysis and design tools for European hinterland hubs*. Utrecht: University of Twente.

Bowen, J. (2002). Network change, deregulation, and access in the global airline industry. *Economic Geography 78*, 425–439.

Burghouwt, G., & de Wit, J. (2003). *The temporal configuration of European airline networks*. University of Montreal, Publication AJD-74.

Burt, R. S. (1992). *Structural holes*. Cambdridge, MA: Harvard University Press.

Button, K., & Stough, R. (2000). *Air transport networks: Theory and policy implications*. Cheltenham: Edward Elgar.

Caves, D. W., Christensen, L. R., & Tretheway, M. W. (1984). Economics of density versus economies of scale: why trunks and local service airline costs differ. *The Rand Journal of Economics 15*, 471–489.

Cento, A. (2006). Challenge to the airline industry: emergence of carriers and low cost carriers. PhD Thesis, VU University Amsterdam.

Dennis, N. P. S. (1998). Competition between hub airports in Europe and a methodology for forecasting connecting traffic. *8th World Conference on Transport Research*, Antwerp.

Erdös, P., & Rényi, A. (1959). On random graphs I. *Publications Mathematiques, 6*, 290–297.

Freeman, L. C. (1977). A set of measures of centrality based on betweenness. *Sociometry, 40*, 35–41.

Freeman, L. C. (1979). Centrality in social networks: a conceptual clarification. *Social Networks, 1*, 215–239.

Frenken, K., & Nuvolari, A. (2004). The early development of the steam engine: an evolutionary interpretation using complexity theory. *Industrial and Corporate Change, 13*, 419–450.

Gorman, S. P. (2005). *Networks, security and complexity*. Cheltenham, Edward Elgar.

Gorman, S.P., & Kulkarni, R. (2004). Spatial small worlds. *Environment and Planning B 31*, 273–296.

Hinloopen, E., & Nijkamp, P. (1990). Qualitative multiple criteria choice analysis: the dominant regime method. *Quality and Quantity, 24*, 37–56.

Jeong, H. (2003). Complex scale-free networks. *Physics A, 321*, 226–237.

Lijesen, M.G. (2004). Adjusting the Herfindahl index for close substitutes: an application to pricing in civil aviation. *Transportation Research E 40*, 123–134.

Lufthansa (2005). *Annual report*. http://konzern.lufthansa.com/en/html/ueber_uns/swiss/index.html (2005)

Martin, J. C., & Voltes-Dorta, A. (2008). Theoretical evidence of exciting pitfalls in measuring hubbing practices in airline networks. *Networks and Spatial Economics, 9*, 161–182.

McShan, W. S. (1986). An economic analysis of hub-and-spoke routing strategy in the airline industry. PhD Thesis, Northwestern University.

Newman, M. E. J. (2003). A measure of betweenness centrality based on random walks. arXiv:condmat/0309045 (2003)

Nijkamp, P. (2008). Policy developments in the airline industry. In: D. De Jong, B. Kaashoek, & W. J. Zondag (eds.) *Blue Skies or Storm Clouds: Essays on Public Policy and Air Transport.* Scienceguide, The Hague, pp. 20–25.

Nijkamp, P., & Reggiani, A. (1992). *Interaction, evolution and chaos in space*. Berlin: Springer.

O' Kelly, E. M., & Miller, H. J. (1994) The hub network design problem: an overview and synthesis. *Journal of Transport Geography, 2*, 31–40.

Patuelli, R. (2007). *Regional labour markets in Germany: statistical analysis of spatio-temporal disparities and network structures*. PhD Thesis, VU University Amsterdam, September.

Reggiani, A., & Nijkamp, P. (eds.). (2006). *Spatial dynamics, networks and modelling*. Cheltenham: Edward Elgar.

Reggiani, A., & Vinciguerra, S. (2007). Network connectivity models: an overview and empirical applications. In: T. Friesz (ed.), *Network Science, Nonlinear Science and Infrastructure Systems*. New York: Springer, 147–165.

Reynolds-Feighan, A. J. (1994). EC and US air freight markets: network organisation in a deregulated environment. *Transportation Reviews, 14*, 193–217.

Reynolds-Feighan, A. J. (1998). *The impact of US airline deregulation on airport traffic patterns. Geographical Analysis, 30*, 234–253.

Reynolds-Feighan, A. J. (2001). Traffic distribution in low-cost and full service carrier network in the US air transport market. *Journal of Air Transport Management, 7*, 265–275.

Rietveld, P., & Brons, M. (2001). Quality of hub-and-spoke networks; the effects of timetable coordination on waiting time and rescheduling time. *Journal of Air Transport Management, 7*, 241–249.

Schintler, L. A., Gorman, S. P., Reggiani, A., Patuelli, R., & Nijkamp, P. (2005). Small-world phenomena in communication networks: a cross-Atlantic comparison. In A. Reggiani, L. A. Schintler (eds.), *Methods and models in transport and telecommunications: cross Atlantic perspectives*. Berlin: Springer, 201–220.

Schintler, L. A., Gorman, S. P., Reggiani, A., Patuelli, R., Gillespie, A., Nijkamp, P., & Rutherford, J. (2005). Complex network phenomena in telecommunication systems. *Networks and Spatial Economics, 5*, 351–370.

Toh, R. S., & Higgins, R. G. (1985). The impact of hub-and-spoke network centralization and route monopoly on domestic airline profitability. *Transportation Journal*, 24, 16–27.

Veldhuis, J., & Kroes, E. (2002). Dynamics in relative network performance of the main European hub airports. *European Transport Conference*, Cambridge.

Waters, N. (2006). Network and nodal indices. Measures of complexity and redundancy: a review. In: A. Reggiani, P. Nijkamp (eds.), *Spatial dynamics, Networks and Modelling*. Cheltenham: Edward Elgar, 16–33.

Watts, D. J., & Strogatz, S. H. (1998) Collective dynamics of small world networks. *Nature, 393*, 440–442.

Appendix A Top-Ten Airports

In this Appendix, we will present the top ten scores of the airports – according to the main topological indices illustrated in Table 10.1 – belonging to the four airline networks A1, A2, B1 and B2 (see Tables 10.8–10.12).

Table 10.8 Top-ten scores of airports according to the degree index (corresponding values in brackets)

A1	A2	B1	B2
MUC (82)	FRA (138)	FRA (106)	FRA (183)
FRA (81)	MUC (100)	MUC (105)	MUC (179)
DUS (39)	DUS (41)	BRE (97)	HAM (172)
HAM (24)	HAM (24)	HAM (97)	DUS (171)
STR (18)	STR (18)	BSL (94)	STR (168)
TXL (10)	TXL (10)	DUS (94)	LEJ (166)
CDG (8)	CDG (8)	LEJ (92)	ZRH (165)
NUE (8)	NUE (8)	NUE (92)	TXL (164)
BRU (7)	BRU (7)	STR (92)	NUE (163)
LHR (6)	MXP (6)	CGN (89)	BRE (162)

Table 10.9 Top-ten scores of airports according to the closeness index (corresponding values in brackets)

A1	A2	B1	B2
MUC (0.78)	FRA (0.79)	FRA (0.96)	BRE (1)
FRA (0.76)	MUC (0.64)	MUC (0.95)	DUS (1)
DUS (0.60)	DUS (0.53)	HAM (0.89)	ZRH (1)
HAM (0.55)	HAM (0.51)	DUS (0.87)	FRA (0.98)
STR (0.54)	STR (0.50)	NUE (0.86)	MUC (0.95)
TXL (0.51)	CDG (0.49)	STR (0.86)	HAM (0.93)
CDG (0.51)	NUE (0.49)	LEJ (0.85)	STR (0.91)
NUE (0.51)	BRU (0.48)	CGN (0.84)	LEJ (0.89)
LHR (0.51)	LHR (0.48)	TXL (0.84)	NUE (0.89)
MXP (0.51)	MXP (0.48)	ZRH (0.84)	FMO (0.85)
	VIE (0.48)		

Table 10.10 Top-ten scores of airports according to the betweenness index (corresponding values in brackets)

A1	A2	B1	B2
MUC (0.51)	FRA (0.76)	MUC (0.06)	MUC (0.06)
FRA (0.50)	MUC (0.03)	FRA (0.06)	FRA (0.06)
DUS (0.06)	DUS (0.03)	DUS (0.05)	DUS (0.06)
KUF (0.05)	BKK (0.02)	HAM (0.05)	BRE (0.05)
HAM (0.03)	KUF (0.02)	STR (0.05)	CGN (0.05)
GOJ (0.02)	HAM (0.01)	BRE (0.04)	HAM (0.05)
STR (0.01)	CAI (0.01)	HAJ (0.04)	NUE (0.05)
CDG ($4.5e^{-4}$)	CAN (0.01)	NUE (0.04)	STR (0.05)
CGN ($9.5e^{-5}$)	GOJ (0.01)	TXL (0.04)	ZRH (0.05)
BRU ($1.9e^{-5}$)	GRU (0.01)	CGN (0.04)	CGN (0.05)
	JED (0.01)		DRS (0.05)
	KRT (0.01)		LEJ (0.05)
	LOS (0.01)		
	PHC (0.01)		

Table 10.11 Top-ten scores of airports according to the clustering coefficient (corresponding values in brackets)

A1	A2	B1	B2
MUC (0.82)	FRA (0.75)	FRA (0.96)	BRE (1)
FRA (0.80)	MUC (0.48)	MUC (0.89)	DUS (1)
DUS (0.24)	DUS (0.11)	LEJ (0.77)	ZRH (1)
HAM (0.10)	HAM (0.04)	ZRH (0.67)	FRA (0.96)
STR (0.06)	STR (0.02)	BSL (0.66)	MUC (0.88)
CDG (0.01)	TXL (6e−3)	STR (0.57)	LEJ (0.84)
TXL (0.01)	CDG (5e−6)	DUS (0.55)	BSL (0.81)
NUE (9e−3)	NUE (4e−3)	HAM (0.55)	GVA (0.67)
BRU (6e−3)	BRU (2e−3)	GVA (0.48)	HAM (0.63)
MXP (4e−4)	ZRH (2e−3)	TXL (0.47)	STR (0.60)
VIE (4e−4)			

Table 10.12. Nomenclature of airports under study

BKK	Bangkok	JED	Jedda
BRE	Bremen	KRT	Khartoum
BRU	Bruxelles	KUF	Samara
BSL	Basel	LEJ	Leipzig
CDG	Paris Charles de Gaulle	LHR	London-Heathrow
CGN	Koln	LOS	Laos
DRS	Dresden	MUC	Munich
DUS	Dusseldorf	MXP	Milano-Malpensa
FMO	Munster	NUE	Nuremberg
FRA	Frankfurt	PHC	Port Harcour
GOJ	Novgorod	STR	Stuttgart
GRU	Sao Paulo	TXL	Berlin-Tegel
GVA	Geneva	VIE	Wien
HAM	Hamburg	ZRH	Zurich

Appendix B Rank Distributions

In this appendix, we will present the rank distribution fitting for the networks A1, A2, B1 and B2, with reference to the following variables: y-axis = number of weekly connections; x-axis = airport (node) rank. The related fitting has been carried out by considering both an exponential and a power interpolation (see Table 10.5 for the synthesis of the results) (see Figs. 10.1 and 10.2) .

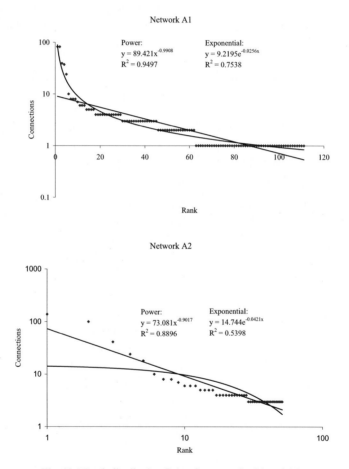

Fig. 10.1 Rank distribution fitting for networks A1 and A2

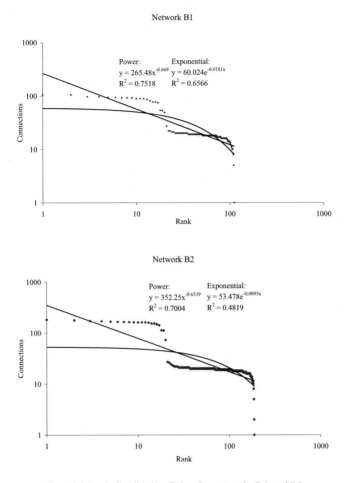

Fig. 10.2 Rank distribution fitting for networks B1 and B2

11. Fighting SARS with a Hastily Formed Network

Peter J. van Baalen[1] and Paul C. van Fenema[2]

[1]Rotterdam School of Management Erasmus University Rotterdam, The Netherlands,
pbaalen@rsm.nl

[2]Netherlands Defense Academy, Breda, The Netherlands, pfenema@gmail.com

Abstract

Globalization and advanced Information and Communication Technologies have enhanced the role of networking between organizations in business and public sectors. Examples of public networking are disaster relief (Stephenson, 2004), disease control management, military (coalition-based) campaigns (Alberts, Garstka, & Stein, 2000), and law enforcement. We discuss the SARS (Severe Acute Respiratory Syndrome) case to learn how global interorganizational networks can be successfully instantiated. The purpose of this study is to improve our understanding of interorganizational network instantiation and to examine some mechanisms leading to successful interorganizational network performance. The paper is structured as follows. First, we present briefly the SARS case. Next, we discuss the concept of hastily formed networks and some concepts that have been introduced by Hagel and Brown (2005). Finally, we analyze the SARS case with these concepts and draw some lessons from the case study.

Introduction

Globalization and advanced Information and Communication Technologies have enhanced the role of networking between organizations in business and public sectors. Business examples include networks in clothing, aviation, car and electronics industry (for instance the battle of standards for new generation electronics). Examples of public networking are disaster relief (Stephenson, 2004), disease control management, military (coalition-based) campaigns (Alberts et al., 2000), and law enforcement. Interorganizational networking rallies competencies (Katzy & Crownston,

2001–2007) and leads to coordinated performances. Potentially, networks out-perform organizations and dyads of organizations (Smith, Caroll, & Ashford, 1995) in terms of speed, flexibility, reliability, knowledge intensity, scale, and efficiency. Interorganizational networks have the potential to respond to urgent events or opportunities to create value.

At the same time, failures of interorganizational networking have become apparent. Those in the public sector tend to draw most attention in the media. The multi-agent US government response to the Katrina disaster was considered unsuccessful, as were many international relief efforts to a certain extent (Daly Hayes & Weatley, 1996). Other unexpected major disasters such as the Tsunami in the Indian Ocean in December 2004 and the devastating earthquake in Kashmir in October 2005 revealed the global need for a deeper understanding of network coordination in response to unexpected major disasters.

The purpose of this study is therefore to improve our understanding of interorganizational network instantiation and to examine some mechanisms leading to successful interorganizational network performance. By instantiation we mean an organized, concerted effort to configure re-sources into a means-end relationship within a short time span. In the process of instantiation interorganizational networks undergo a 'phase transition' from a defined state into another state in response to changing levels of urgency awareness (Johnson, 2004). Network performance refers to the collective achievements that could not be achieved by the network actors individually.

Network response to major disasters requires an enormous amount of coordinated activities at different levels and in different phases of the response. In this paper we confine ourselves to the instantiation of knowledge and information which, to a large extent, determines the quality of network response (Denning, 2006). We discuss the SARS (Severe Acute Respiratory Syndrome) case to learn how global interorganizational networks can be successfully instantiated. For analyzing the SARS network we use the recently coined concept Hastily Formed Networks (HFN) (Denning, 2006) and network dynamic as discussed by Hagel and Brown (2005). The SARS case is widely discussed in the academic and professional literature. However, few attempts have been made to understand the SARS response from an interorganizational network perspective. For the case material of SARS we rely mainly on abundantly available secondary data such reports and documents, academic papers and books, websites (especially of the World Health Organization, 2000).

The paper is structured as follows. First, we present briefly the SARS case. Next, we discuss the concepts of hastily formed networks and some concepts that have been introduced by Hagel and Brown's (2005). Finally, the SARS case is analyzed using these concepts and we draw some lessons from this case study.

The SARS Outbreak

The SARS outbreak commenced in Guangdong (China) on November 2002 and spread to other countries – such as Singapore, Hong Kong, Canada – following travel patterns of infected individuals. The SARS outbreak shocked health care systems worldwide. SARS was a new corona virus not previous identified in humans and animals. There was no knowledge about how to identify, diagnose and treat SARS. Once SARS reached Hong Kong it spreaded, within a few days internationally "with the speed of an airplane" (National Advisory Committee on SARS and Public Health, 2003). China (including Hong Kong) was severely attacked: more than 600 people died (Table 11.1). As of early June 2003, the World Health Organization (WHO) counted 8098 people that were infected, 774 died. Most countries in the western world were hardly hit by SARS. The exception was Canada (Toronto and Vancouver) where 251 people were infected and 43 of them died. In July 2003, WHO declared that SARS had been contained and was no longer viewed as a global threat. Considering the potentiality of the threat of SARS as a 'globalizing disease' the impact remained modest.

Table 11.1 SARS cases worldwide. November 1, 2002- July 31, 2003 – Source: adapted from Abraham, 2005

Areas	Female	Male	Total	Number of deaths	Case fatality ratio	Date onset first probable case	Date onset last probable cases
Australia	4	2	6	0	0	26-Feb-03	1-Apr-03
Canada	151	100	251	43	17	23-feb-03	12-Jun-03
China	2674	2607	5327	349	7	16-Nov-02	3-Jun-03
China, Hong Kong SAR	977	778	1755	299	17	15-Feb-03	31-May-03
China, Macao SAR	0	1	1	0	0	5-May-03	5-May-03
China, Taiwan	218	128	346	37	11	25-Feb-03	15-Jun-03
France	1	6	7	1	14	21-Mar-03	3-May-03
Germany	4	5	9	0	0	9-Mar-03	6-May-03
India	0	3	3	0	0	25-Apr-03	6-May-03
Indonesia	0	3	3	0	0	25-Apr-03	6-May-03
Italy	1	3	4	0	0	13-Mar-03	20-Apr-03
Kuwait	1	0	1	0	0	9-Apr-03	9-Apr-03
Malaysia	1	4	5	2	40	14-Mar-03	22-Apr-03
Mongolia	8	1	9	0	0	31-Mar-03	6-May-03
New Zealand	1	0	1	0	0	20-Apr-03	20-Apr-03
Philippines	8	6	14	2	14	25-Feb-03	5-May-03
Republic of Ireland	0	1	1	0	0	27-Feb-03	27-Feb-03
Republic of Korea	0	1	1	0	0	19-Mar-03	19-Mar-03
Russian federation	0	1	1	0	0	5-May-03	5-May-03

Singapore	161	77	238	33	14	25-Feb-03	5-May-03
South Africa	0	1	1	1	100	3-Apr-03	3-Apr-03
Spain	0	1	1	0	0	26-Mar-03	26-Mar-03
Sweden	3	2	5	0	0	28-Mar-03	23-Apr-03
Switzerland	0	1	1	0	0	9-Mar-03	9-Mar-03
Thailand	5	4	9	2	22	11-Mar-03	27-May-03
United Kingdom	2	2	4	0	0	1-Mar-03	1-Apr-03
United States	14	15	29	0	0	24-Feb-03	13-July-03
Vietnam	39	24	63	5	8	23-Feb-03	14-Apr-04
Total			8098	774	**9,6**		

Table 11.1 clearly shows that China (including Hong Kong and Taiwain) and Singapore were severely hit by SARS. In the western countries the spread of SARS remained limited to a few cases. A striking exception here is Canada where quite a number of SARS cases were identified. New was the fact that many (1707) health care workers were infected; 21 of them died.

GOARN: Spider in the Information Web

In March 2003, the WHO issued a global alert for the outbreak of SARS. With the advance of global traveling, disease outbreak has become a major concern for public health officials. The SARS alert was enabled by WHO's Global Outbreak Alert and Response (GOARN) system. Commenced in 2000, this system tracks outbreaks and spreading of SARS continually. GOARN consists of experts in various areas whose knowledge must be integrated to combat major diseases. Teams on the ground in relevant countries receive information from and provide information to WHO. These teams work together through video- and teleconferencing. In cooperation with other agencies, WHO orchestrates a global network for monitoring disease outbreaks and communicating about these, mainly through its website.

In March 2003, WHO commenced planning for addressing the risks of SARS in multiple areas. Their efforts included arranging for medical supplies, mobile teams of specialists traveling to sites with urgent situations, and organizing networks of experts trying to develop a better understanding of SARS diagnosis and treatment. WHO organized multiple networks: organizations involved in medical supply logistics; epidemiologists studying patterns of outbreaks; clinicians involved in specific SARS case were interconnected to share experiences; and laboratory staff across the world attempting to understand causes of the disease.

GOARN operates according to guiding principles to improve coordination. These principles include:

1. WHO ensures outbreaks of potential international importance are rapidly verified and information is quickly shared within the Network.

2. There is a rapid response coordinated by the Operational Support Team to requests for assistance from affected state(s).
3. The most appropriate experts reach the field in the least possible time to carry out coordinated and effective outbreak control activities.
4. The international team integrates and coordinates activities to support national efforts and existing public health infrastructure.
5. There is a fair and equitable process for the participation of Network partners in international responses.
6. There is strong technical leadership and coordination in the field.
7. Partners make every effort to ensure the effective coordination of their participation and support of outbreak response.
8. There is recognition of the unique role of national and international nongovernmental organizations (NGOs) in the area of health, including in the control of outbreaks. NGOs providing support that would not otherwise be available, particularly in reaching poor populations. While striving for effective collaboration and coordination, the Network will respect the independence and objectivity of all partners.
9. Responses will be used as a mechanism to build global capacity by the involvement of participants from field-based training programs in applied epidemiology and public health practice, e.g. Field Epidemiology Training Programs (FETPs).
10. There is commitment to national and regional capacity building as a follow up to international outbreak responses to improve preparedness and reduce future vulnerability to epidemic prone diseases.
11. All network responses will proceed with full respect for ethical standards, human rights, national and local laws, cultural sensitivities and traditions.

SARS showed the successful orchestration of globally distributed medical research laboratories in identifying the SARS virus by the WHO. This international scientific cooperation was unusual. International health treaties were dominated by state sovereignty; international intervention in another state's internal activity used to be unthinkable (Wallis, 2005). In 2000 the WHO launched a new vision on its role in coordinating global outbreak of infectious diseases. The WHO relied on its international mandate based on the International Health regulations, and unique country specific experiences and knowledge.

Code Orange

Apart from these successes, SARS revealed the failure of national health care systems (Canada) in fighting global infectious diseases. Underpinning this problem was the underinvestment in microbiological research and testing capacity at the laboratories in Canada. While researchers in Hong Kong were able to correlate clinical and laboratory features of SARS with epidemiological data, the Canadian researchers were not able to do so. The latter were too busy with patient care and did not find time to do the required research. From an operational perspective, the state of emergency (Code Orange) was declared in Canada in March 2003. This threatened the Canadian health care system. Code Orange is part of the Uniform Emergency Codes which has been adopted by the Ontario Hospital Association in 1993. It indicates an external disaster which alerts hospitals to prepare for a rapid influx of patients being brought to hospital by ambulances. The code is intended to be applied to a specific area and to be used for a limited period of time. However, it soon appeared that the Code Orange was not the appropriate response for an infectious disease outbreak such as SARS. The code paralyzed the health care system because there was in fact no extraordinary number of incoming patients, as would be the case during natural disasters. In fact, the challenge in controlling SARS was to significantly restrict access to healthcare facilities. Moreover, Code Orange was not meant for such a broad geographic area and for a sustained period of time. As a consequence, many hospitals unaffected by SARS were forced to reduce their service level significantly. They delayed current procedures and thereby put critical patients at risk. The SARS case illustrates that an organization (the Canadian health care system) might be well-prepared for responding quickly to risks that are induced by the external environment (calculated risks). But the same organization finds it difficult to respond adequately to the indirect and unintended consequences that threatened the system self. Furthermore, procedures and codes (such as Code Orange) may seem reasonable in the eyes of disaster planners. But their effectiveness remains unknown in case of a real disaster that may differ from the anticipated situation.

The purpose of this study is to improve understanding of interorganizational network coordination and to examine the drivers of successful inter-organizational network coordination. Before analyzing the SARS case with its mixture of successful and less successful operations, we introduce concepts for building a theory of interorganizational network instantiation.

Hastily Formed Networks

We define networks as exchange structures with their own governance structure and patterns of interaction in which flows of resources between independent units (or individuals) take place (Van Baalen, Bloemhof-Ruwward, & van Heck, 2005). Network governance refers to interorganizational coordination that differs from market- and hierarchical coordination because they employ a wider set of coordination mechanisms (Grandori, 1999). Most research focuses on existing networks with stable relationships, while we are interested in instantiating and emerging network relationships and coordination. In the case of emerging networks, social structure is conceived as an outcome and not as a starting point of repeated exchange relationships between participants of the network. For the SARS response network no existing social structure was available. Network structures had to be formed and instantiated in response to the threat of the highly infectious SARS virus.

Denning (2006) recently coined the concept of Hastily Formed Network (HFN) which refers to multiple network organizations that are instantiated in response to disasters like earthquakes, terrorist attacks, hurricanes, global infectious diseases. HFN's can be classified according to the kind of events to which they have to respond and for which and organization/country can be prepared. The categorization concerns the relationship between network capabilities and the type of event. Eventually, the type of response gravitates to the availability of information about the event that disrupts our social and economic worlds (Table 11.2).

Responding adequately to U-category events implies that a jump (ad hoc stretch) has to be made from an unprepared situation to tightly coordinated action in order to contain the rapid spreading of the SARS virus. Figure 11.1 shows that, in order to respond adequately, preparedness should be connected to the capability to act.

Table 11.2 Kinds of events requiring responses from HFN's – Source: adapted from Denning, 2006

Category of Events	Characteristics	Examples of Events
K-Events: *Situation and Network Factors Known*	Network is in control: – Network knows what to do, and uses existing network structures – Network may choose not to respond	Fast response team for time-critical business problem or opportunity (focused, contained task environment)
KU-Events: *Mixture of Known and Unknown Factors*	Normal response activation: – Network knows what to do, yet doesn't know time or place – Responding network structure known	Local fire, small earth quack, civil unrest, military campaigns (recurrent, small to medium scale events with limited disruption)
U-Events: *Situation and Network Factors Unknown*	Network overwhelmed or disrupted: – Network doesn't know what to do and doesn't know time or place – Responding network structure unknown	Terrorist attacks, large earth quacks, major natural disasters, SARS (unique, large-scale, disruptive task environment)

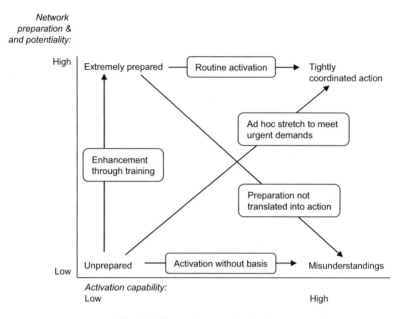

Fig. 11.1 Preparedness and activation

Relying on recent insights of Hagel and Brown (2005) about global process networks we argue that four elements are crucial for understanding SARS as an HFN's: dynamic specialization, connectivity and coordination, leveraged capability building, and network orchestration. In the next section we discuss these network elements, applied to the SARS case.

Dynamic Specialization

Hagel and Brown (2005) use the concept of dynamic specialization to refer to the commitment to eliminate resources and activities that do no differentiate firms and to concentrate on accelerating growth from capabilities that truly distinguish the firm in the marketplace. In the world of health care systems can mean something different. The SARS case has demonstrated the indisputable role of scientific research and the role of medical labs. The need to specialize in different activities like diagnoses of infections, characterization of micro-organisms, reference services, and support to epidemiological surveillance and epidemic investigation. Acquiring deep knowledge into these different most important knowledge domains requires large investments in basic and fundamental research. However at the beginning of the outbreak of the corona virus there was no knowledge how to identify, diagnose and treat SARS. David Heymann, a veteran epidemiologist at the WHO, stated that "we had no cause of the disease, we thought it was infectious, no vaccine, no drugs" (quoted in: Abraham, 2005: 84).

The urgency awareness put research labs under pressure and resulted in an unprecedented speed of scientific discovery and publication of research results (National Advisory Committee on SARS and Public Health, 2003). New knowledge had to be created and exchanged between globally distributed research labs in order to find proper diagnoses and treatments methods. The results of this global collaboration of the research labs were quite amazing. SARS was first identified in February 2003. The first scientific papers describing SARS were published already in March 2003 on the New England Journal of Medicine. They came from the research labs in Hong Kong and Canada. The following weeks, papers were published in high-ranked medical and scientific journals with traditionally long lead times like The Lancet, British Medical Journal, Science, New England Journal of Medicine, and JAMA – The Journal of the American Medical Association. In the period March – July 8 256 SARS papers were written by 38 countries (Chiu, Huang, & Ho, 2004). Interestingly, only 17% of SARS-related papers resulted from international collaboration. This indicates that specialization within research labs or research groups and fierce competition between those researchers still dominated but that through instant flexibilization of the publication system researchers were able to identify SARS cases and work on new treatments.

Connectivity and Coordination

Getting access and mobilizing resources of various specialized organizations appeared to be the most important success factor in the global attempt to control and contain the spreading of SARS. Perhaps more amazing than the speed of scientific discovery of the corona virus was 'the almost instantaneous communication and information exchange' about various aspects of the network response (Geberding, 2003). Hardly any modern communication tool was left unused to disseminate up to date information to health care workers, travelers, clinicians, health officials, researchers, etc. The first scientific papers were published online in order to get immediate access to the scientific findings about the corona virus. By setting up the Global Outbreak Alert and Response Network (GOARN) in March 2003, the WHO had a potent role as key coordinator and interpreter of epidemiological information. The WHO decided to set up a secure web-site where each research lab could post its findings. Daily teleconferences were organized to discuss the research results and to share information. Because of the firm competition between research labs, the WHO guaranteed that research data would be kept confidential and the labs and re-searchers were not allowed to use someone's finding without prior permission (Abraham, 2004). This "novel approach to science", as Abraham (2004) calls it required a lot of diplomacy and patience from the part of the WHO-coordinators. On one hand they had to ensure that knowledge and information sharing was optimized by connecting all relevant research labs to each other in order control and contain global epidemic as soon as possible. On the other hand they had to cherish the competitive environment in which international reputed researchers were used to work in. The WHO coordinators hoped to publish a single scientific article in the name of all participating laboratories. However it soon appeared that the research groups started to publish their research results individually Abrahams, 2004).

The central role of modern information and communication technology became apparent in the failure of the Canadian health care system to respond adequately to the SARS outbreak. Professor Johnson, responsible to set up a SARS surveillance system in Canada stated that Canada was un-able to provide optimal support for outbreak investigation and management. Because a sound database and new software tools to deal with tracking cases and contacts were missing at the moment of the breakout. This prevented researchers and health care workers tracking infectious disease and outbreaks because of "an archaic DOS platform used in the late eighties that could not be adapted for SARS" (quoted in: National Advisory Committee on SARS and Public Health, 2003: 29).

The website of GOARN provided up to date information, not only for scientists, public health officers, and policy makers but also started to communicate directly to citizens. This open information strategy was quite new for the WHO which was traditionally slow acting global organization in which decisions mostly took years of ponderous debate and in which individuals governments tend to obstruct decisions to defend their own interests (Abraham, 2004). SARS instantly transformed the WHO into rapid responding, and to a large extend independent, spider in the web of information processing.

Probably more important than connectivity provided by modern information and communication technologies was the social or political connectivity. While in November 2002 the first patient was identified with a mysterious respiratory disease in the Chinese Guangdong province, it was only in February 2003 that the Chinese government informed (still not complete) the world through a press conference about the disease outbreak. The SARS outbreak was no more under control. In April 2003 the Chinese press was allowed to publish about the SARS and only then a WHO team was allowed to visit the province of Guangdong. Until February 2003 the Chinese government was able to prevent scientists, healthcare workers, doctors, patients and media to disclose information about the mysterious disease to the outside world. In early February an anonymous SMS began circulating in Guangzhou about this new disease that in the end was caught up by people from the WHO global influenza surveillance network. From then on the WHO started to put the Chinese government under pressure to open up and to exchange information about SARS.

Leveraged Capability Building and Network Orchestration

Although the WHO orchestrated the network of scientific laboratories, no party dictated top down what different labs would do, what viruses or samples the researchers would work on, or how information would be exchanged (Surowiecki, 2004). The labs agreed that they would exchange research data, and figure out by themselves the most efficient way to divide up the work. The very fact that the labs were working independently appeared also a particular strength in their search for identifying the SARS virus.

However the success of the SARS-HFN cannot be fully explained by the international collaboration of research labs, facilitated by GOARN. The GOARN operated as what Hagel and Brown (2005) call a 'loosely coupled interface' between researchers, representatives of national health care systems, and the public. When the WHO, spurred on by the resolute leadership of director-general Gro Harlem Brundland, decided upon the open information strategy, rather independently from the continuously conflicting national governments, it invited scientists, public healthcare workers, policy makers, travelers, and citizens to collaboratively help to control and contain the spreading of SARS. This open information strategy helped to leverage untapped resources and allowed people to take responsibility. It sharply contrasts the closed information approach of the Chinese government during the first three months of the SARS outbreak.

The SARS case also illustrates the need for a high level of preparedness at country and organizational levels. Networks capabilities build on the availability of specialized knowledge and competencies to instantiate this knowledge way and to translate and use this knowledge in coordinated action. Canada, the country that was hardest hit by SARS outside Asia suffered from an outdated IT-infrastructure, unconnected information flows, unclear responsibilities, a failing alert system, a lack of coordination, a weak analytical capacity of the Ontario Public Health Branche, and a lack of involvement by the federal government (Zhan, 2004).

The quality of the response of HFN's therefore largely depends on the quality of information and information flow at the network and organizational/country level and within the network. Here it is important to distinguish between the network and the organizational (in this case country) level. In the end the alertness and response of the HFN depends on the quality of the information and information flow at the organization/country level. The SARS case included successful instances of coordinating specialized knowledge and translating this knowledge into swift, relevant, local action. Explaining the difference in performance requires attention for (the interplay between) two levels of analysis: organizations (hospitals, World Health Organization), and the network level. The SARS case suggests that individual organizations' research labs accumulate specialized knowledge. In addition, they participate in inter-organizational research networks in the area of disease control. We call the latter network transactive memory (NTM) (knowledge of who knows what at which organization), an extension of the traditional transactive memory concept (Moreland, 1999). NTM combined with specialized organization level knowledge drives a network's potential for coordination. This latent network capability must be activated at unexpected times. The actual SARS outbreak in 2003 made coordinated response urgent in order to contain the disease and avoid a global epidemic. The World Health Organization took on the role of network orchestrator. It coordinated specialized knowledge from globally distributed research labs, and it ensured translation of this knowledge into global and local response. Canada, the unsuccessful case, decided in the early 1990s to economize on research labs. This jeopardized long term development of local specialized knowledge and thereby participation in global knowledge networks. Resourcefulness of network nodes thus matters for network level performance.

Lessons from the SARS Case

As global cooperation between organizations will increase, it is important to understand the coordination dynamics of interorganizational networks. However, interorganizational networks are mostly understood in terms of rather stable network relationships. We think it is important to search for management and organizational concepts, like hastily formed networks, dynamic specialization, connectivity and coordination, network orchestration and leveraged capability building to understand new dynamics of inter-organizational globally operating and agile networks. In this paper we discussed the SARS case which can be viewed as a clear example of a non-stable, hastily formed network. We were primarily interested in the ways the SARS network was instantiated. The SARS case is interesting because contains very successful and very unsuccessful examples of network instantiation. Several interesting lessons can be drawn the SARS case.

1. The quality of the network response largely depends on the quality of the information and the information sharing within the network;
2. Providing a proper 'conversation space' (Denning, 2006), information rich and interactive websites and information systems, appears to be of crucial importance for publishing and sharing information;
3. Deep, specialized knowledge proves to be the core resource of interorganizational networks;
4. However the values of specialized knowledge only accrues only when it is dynamically connected to other specialized knowledge;
5. Open information strategies allow people with different acting roles to participate and to take responsible action.
6. Network performance depends to large extend on the level of preparedness of individual network contributors;
7. Independent network orchestration proves to be one of the main success factors for a high level network performance;

8. The SARS case showed that a high level of competition between knowledge providers can co-evolve with a high level of collaboration.

Future Research

The recent rise of globally Hastily Formed Networks like SARS, challenge our current understandings of networks as one of the dominant organizational forms. Networks, like any other organizational form, develop over time and can be instantiated towards coordinated actions. However in the case of SARS diagnosing and treatment expertise were lacking, (trust-) relationships at a global network level were often not yet established and network leadership was hardly developed. Although there is a vast network research literature, less attention has been paid to the consequences of the 'compression of time' for the emergence of networks in response to existential threats. Research into Hastily Formed Networks not only requires multilevel and multi-theory analyses like Monge and Contractor (2003) argue, but also reconsideration of our theoretical knowledge about networks. Of crucial importance here is to understand the impelling force of the urgency awareness that drives the 'phase transition'. Future research should address questions such as: Why did people start to collaborate without any antecedents? Why did the WHO receive legitimate leadership from national governments to orchestrate the SARS fighting campaign? How could the GOARN website play such a dominant role in the coordination of research activities and spreading of information about SARS to the wider public. And, how can global information systems play a role in the prevention and containment of unexpected major disasters?

References

Abraham, Th. (2005). *Twenty-first century plague. The story of SARS.* Baltimore: The John Hopkins Press.

Alberts, D. S., Garstka, J. J., & Stein, F. P. (2000). *Network centric warfare: Developing and leveraging information superiority.* Washington DC: CCRP Publication Series.

Chiu, W. -T., Huang, J. -S. & Ho, Y. -S. Bibliometric analysis of severe acute respiratory syndrome-related research in the beginning stage. *Scientometrics, 61*(1), 69–77

Daly Hayes, M., & Weatley, G. F. (1996). Interagency and political-military dimensions of peace operations: Haiti – A case study. Washington, DC: National Defense University.

Denning, P. J. (2006). Hastily formed networks. *Communications of the ACM, 49*(4), 15–20.

Grandori, A. (1999). Interfirm networks: organizational mechanisms and economic outcomes. In: A. Grandori (ed.), *Interfirm networks. Organizational and industrial competitiveness* (pp. 1–14). London: Routledge.

Hagel, J., & Brown, J. S. (2005). *The only sustainable edge: Why business strategy depends on productive friction and dynamic specialization.* Boston, MA: Harvard Business School Press.

Johnson, S. (2004). *Emergence. The connected lives of ants, brains, cities, and software.* New York: SCRIBNER.

Katzy, B. R., & Crowston, K. (2007). "Competency Rallying Processes in Virtual Organization," In Virtuality and Vitrualization, IFIP (ed.) Springer, Heidelberg, 2007.

National Advisory Committee on SARS and Public Health (2003). *Learning from SARS.* Ottowa, ON: Renewal of Public Health in Canada.

Smith, K. G., Caroll, S.J., & Ashford, S. J. (1995). Intra- and interorganizational cooperation: Toward a research agenda. *Academy of Management Journal, 38*, 7–23.

Stephenson, M., Jr., (2004). Making humanitarian relief networks more effective: Exploring the relationships among coordination, trust and sense making. *Paper prepared for Delivery at the National Conference of the Association for Research on Non-Profit Organizations and Voluntary Action (ARNOVA).* Los Angeles, California, 2004, pp. 48–62.

Surowiecki, J. (2004). *The wisdom of crowds.* New York: Doubleday.

Wallis, P. (2005). Review in focus: SARS.David P. Fidler, Governance and the Globalization of Disease, Basingstoke: Palgrave Macmillan, 2004. *Social History of Medicine, 18*(3), 496–498

World Health Organization (2000). Global outbreak alert and response. *Report of a WHO meeting.* Geneva

Zhan, X. (2004). Controlling SARS in Federal Systems: a comparative case study analysis of SARS control in Canada and the European Un-ion, Health Economics, Policy and Law, Erasmus University Rotterdam, MSc thesis

12. Smart Business Networks with Chinese Characteristics

Barbara Krug[1] and Hans Hendrischke[2]

[1]Rotterdam School of Management, Erasmus University Rotterdam, The Netherlands,
bkrug@rsm.nl

[2]University of New South Wales, Australia, h.hendrischke@unsw.edu.au

Abstract

This study contributes to the research on Chinese business networks which are a ubiquitous element of China's emerging private enterprise sector. The two standard features of the research literature on Chinese business networks are its sociological and cultural orientation and the representation of business networks as family networks. Analyzing Chinese business networks from an institutional and transition economics perspective, we find that business networks are better represented as public-private networks and economic actors. They form a crucial link between local entrepreneurs and local governments and participate in institution building. Their institutional competence is as important as their market and technological competence.

Introduction

In China as in all transition economies the emergence of a competitive business sector depends on the development of three competences. Market competence is the ability to explore new market opportunities and cope with competition; technical competence is the ability to develop and utilize new technology; and institutional competence is the ability to invent and organize business processes that facilitate the operation of a firm. While market and technical competence and their interplay are at the core of management studies (Dosi, Nelson, & Winter, 2000; Nelson & Winter, 1982), institutional competence remains an under-researched topic. Re-search on transition economies shows that institutional competence is crucial for the emergence, survival and expansion of firms, and ultimately, the emergence of a market economy (Frye, 2002). Without institutions that facilitate the emergence of market-conforming firms, organizations and behavior market reforms might get stuck in rent-seeking coalitions and accompanying non-productive investments (Meyer & Peng, 2005). Only the interplay between change at the micro-level of firms and the macro-level of political institutions crates the co-evolutionary process that shapes the institutional architecture of an emerging business system

China's economic success as a transition economy is obvious in terms of entrepreneurship and total factor productivity, integration into the international value chains, increasingly brokered by outward FDI, export performance and rapid usage of modern technology and R&D investment (OECD, 2006). Chinese entrepreneurs and firms were quick in developing market and technical competences. In fact, their commercial success has over-shadowed their institutional competence that enabled them to build an internationally competitive, private business sector within less than two decades. Our question is how Chinese firms generated such an institutional competence.

In our view, networking in China is neither a cultural institution as claimed by cultural approaches (e.g. Hofstede, 2007) nor a static, group-based form of corporatism (as claimed e.g. by Walder, 1995). We argue that in China the interplay between change at the micro-level of firms and the macro-level of political institutions happens through public-private networks in form of a co-evolutionary process that is specific to the institutional architecture of China's emerging business systems. From an individual (firm's) perspective networking is a strategic tool with three components: business management, i.e. searching for the best alignment with the changing market environment, innovation management, i.e. searching for incentives that facilitate organizational and technical innovation, and politics management, i.e. searching for the best alignment with local and national state agencies and their vested interests. Business networks therefore include private, corporate and public partners. From a macro perspective, the public-private networks are potentially able to mediate between private and public interests. We aim to show that in local Chinese business environments, networks play a crucial role as a means for institutional co-evolution and the generation of organizational capabilities and institutional competence.

The chapter proceeds as follows. We start with a short overview of the relevant literature on institutions and competence in ill-functioning markets. We then propose and elaborate our definition of institutional competence in terms of the interaction between networks and China's emerging business sector the links between institutional competence and institutional change, and relations between institutional competence and the development of a new institutional architecture in China. In the conclusion we sketch out how "Western" firms can make use of our findings. We are not proposing that networking is an undisputed solution; the coordinated institutional competence we observe is not without costs.

Analyzing Institutional Competence

The Comparative Business Systems literature and macro-economic comparative studies have shown that emerging markets and transition economies cannot be used as merely another data (sub-) set confirming conventional assumptions about firms and their behavior (Djankov, Glaeser, La Porta, Lopez de Silanes, & Shleifer, 2003; Hoskisson, Eden, Lau, & Wright, 2000). Different institutional frames such as emerging markets, transition economies or market economies lead to different organizational forms of firms and different strategic decisions (Crouch, 2005; Nelson, 1992). In China reforms did not start with the privatization of assets but with decentralization and devolution of decision making power to local state agencies and (private) entrepreneurs. Their response to the new opportunities offered by the reforms is not a given, but an open empirical question.

We therefore take firms not merely as the unit of analysis but as a crucial source for information when questioning entrepreneurs about formal and informal incentives and constraints in their direct business environment (Krug & Hendrischke, 2007). Our results support the findings in the International Business literature that the institutional context of entrepreneurship and competition merit detailed scrutiny (see also Grabher & Stark, 1997; Yamakawa, Peng, & Deeds, 2008). The concept of dynamic organizational capabilities, which endogenize external institutions (Dosi et al., 2000) is better suited to this approach than the resource based view with its focus on internal resources and learning. We draw support from strategic management literature which has shown that strategic political management creates firm-specific value (overview in Pearce et al., 2008) and that ownership forms of firms and location-decision (Chen & Chen, 1998) reflect changing political constraints.

Hence, analyzing institutional competence requires a dynamic perspective in order to identify the systemic factors in building up competences for aligning the firms' interests with political actors, business partners, competitors, or (foreign or domestic) investors (Krug & Polos, 2004). Such an analysis has to include informal institution building and therefore transcends the legalistic perspective which concentrates on formal (politically defined) institutions. Firms are not only subject to and recipients of institutional change. They actively create new institutions by setting local technical standards, defining business practices and routines, and by participating in local public governance. In this process firms create inter-firm capabilities and form alliances with political or administrative agents. Disregarding these informal aspects of institution building is tantamount to excluding a large part of China's economic dynamism from analysis (Li et al., 2006).

All in all, a definition of institutional competence that satisfies the three considerations above reads as follows: Institutional competence involves the ability to configure an organization so that it can identify and monitor volatile key resources and search for innovative organizational capabilities and routines in order to influence the external environment, including potential business partners or government agencies, in the interest of the organization. The organizational form which controls this competence is a network. A network is understood here as a group of people with flexible membership who crystallize around business ideas by drawing in people who control the required resources.

The Emergence of Institutional Competence

Institutional competence in its organizational form of networking is the response of firms to ill-functioning markets (Hoskisson et al., 2000). Networks serve as a 'surrogate' for formal institutions by achieving a better alignment with the market (Xin & Pearce, 1996). In transition economies, two other problems are connected to the 'liability of newness' of the whole private sector (Krug & Polos, 2004). In the absence of a regulated environment, firms cannot rely on existing business routines nor can they acquire expertise about best practices through the formal education system. Second, there is no 'template' for success or failure of private firms, as there is not (yet) a collective memory of what can go wrong. Individuals, firms or collectives, such as villages, respond to this situation by forming networks for pooling assets, information, privileges, knowledge and interests.

In other words, the institutional competence of networks precedes and is embedded in firms which are the outcome of pooling resources and strategic decisions on how to best exploit market opportunities (Peng, 2001). The pooling of resources is not limited to physical resources or capital. As shown by Boisot & Child (1996), "intangible assets", such as access to market information or prior knowledge about policy changes, are crucial components in the initial endowment of firms. Moreover, in an environment of rapidly increasing competition with fluctuating relative prices and ongoing political change, firms opt for a strategy which secures maximum flexibility in recombining productive forces (Grabher & Stark, 1997). Firm formation in China is thus an iterative process that involves changes in product, labor, financial or even political structures with the aim to find the best adaptation to and embeddedness in a dynamic local environment.

Institutional Competence and Networks

In contrast to popular clichés, Chinese business networks are not family based organizations (Hendrischke, 2007; Pistrui, Huang, Oksoy, Zhao, & Welsch, 2001). Neither are they merely transaction cost saving devices based on the ability to overcome constraints imposed by an adverse political environment. Not unlike diversified business groups (e.g. Hokisson et al., 2005) networks are rather a rational organizational response to an environment with limited constitutional and legal protection (Child, Lu, & Tsai, 2007) leaves many resources untapped. Economic actors in such an environment require the ability to mobilize resources across a range of local organizations and power holders.

First, networks centre on personal relations, which can be mobilized for political and economic purposes. Once the collaboration has outlived its productive usefulness, the business side of the relationships is de-activated, while the social side remains. It is this activating – de-activating mechanism, which allows economic actors to switch from political to economic links and to adapt quickly to changing economic situations at low cost, since the de-activation does not imply the end of a contract, let alone a break-up of the social relationship. The advantage of personalizing business relations lies in the fact that social sanctioning mechanisms can be hijacked for economic purposes.

Second, networks in China are fluid, non-structured organizational forms for co-coordinating resources and strategic decisions. Centered around a social or functional group (such as investors) they expand or shrink according to business opportunities and constraints. Networks are economic actors able to activate and de-activate their membership in line with commercial opportunities. The dynamic capabilities of networks include the ability to accumulate technical and organizational capabilities and to allocate property rights to firms, investors, stakeholders or managers. By the same token, property rights can be re-allocated or firms can be closed down in case of failure or reconfigured if a re-combination of assets promises higher returns. This fluid concept of property rights is akin to socially generated property privileges, but at the same time exploits the legal benefits of incorporation. It is in striking contrast to the legal concept of private property rights which are granted and protected independent of the (profitable) usage of resources.

Third, networks with their formal and informal information channels make it possible to convert informal ad hoc practices as employed between firms or between firms and local regulatory agencies into procedures or, by extension, into sectoral and formal local business standards. In this sense networks are institutional entrepreneurs and initiate entrepreneurial activity that precedes formation and strategic decisions of firms (see an interesting example in Child et al., 2007). At the same time, networks give voice to firms in the creation of local business procedures and thereby generate firm-specific value.

Fourth, networks function as repositories of productive slack. This includes un- or underused assets for which the network has not yet been able to calculate best employment. Productive slack refers further to the accumulation of knowledge, information as well as management skills learned by experience.

For these networks, the control of local politics is a core competence at par with the required market and technical competence. In general, networks aim to search for the most effective governance structure, including the organizational form of firms. Alignment with local politics promises access to prior information about further reform steps, protection of property rights and business agreements, if not participation in local political decision making. From a firm's perspective, the underlying role of networks is important in three main aspects.

Networks respond to market shifts when they search for organizational solutions that mitigate the effects of market fragmentation, lack of market information, and local embeddedness. Effective governance structures allow appropriating arbitrage, jurisdictional arbitrage, as well as generating enough leverage to limit local government intervention.

Networks align the interests of the firm with the interests of potential investors by designing incentives which secure (ongoing) private investment, exclusive access to shared or jointly produced knowledge, information or business routines; and commitments by investors and local authorities to limit moral hazard.

Finally, networks establish a political architecture when aligning the interests of political actors and other stakeholders with the interests of managers or entrepreneurs. Such alignment promises access to prior information about further re-form steps, protection of property rights and business agreements, if not participation in political decision making at the local level.

Institutional Competence and Institutional Change

As argued above networks establish firms by allocating property rights or delegating control rights to certain people and by doing so, determine the type of firm and its corporate governance. The empirical picture of China's business sectors shows that over the last two decades the organizational form of firms moved from collective enterprises with fuzzy ownership rights and non-professional management to those with registered capital and individual property rights and clear separation of managerial tasks. Each of the dominant forms of firms, such as Township and Village Enterprises (TVEs), privatized TVEs, Public/Private partnerships, and incorporated firms can be positioned within a continuum that runs from socialist firms to "market firms" with State-owned enterprises (SOEs) as the organizational form of socialist firms and foreign Multi-national corporations (MNCs) operating as market firms. Their hybrid character reflects the need to align the firms with the interest of local state agencies as well as the market and overall the willingness to 'innovate', as described in Fig. 12.1 below.

A descriptive analysis of the institutional competence of networks in aligning firms with markets, technology change and local politics over two decades or privatization, suggests the following framework:

Organizational choice	Alignment with markets	Innovation	Alignment with politics
Township-village enterprise	Negotiated access to local markets	Innovation through mobilizing local resources	Township and Village employment creation
Privatized TVE	Negotiated gradual expansion into other local markets, e.g. Joint ventures with other TVEs	Ownership rights in return for knowledge and technology	Local tax and non-tax revenue plus locally controlled real estate market
Public/private partnership	Integration of local markets, promotion of market – conforming institutions, multi market operations in different sectors	Access to non-tradable R&D and state controlled technologies, access to international know-how	Exploiting state investment in local infrastructure, market coordination in local economy, reducing local state taxation
Incorporated firm	inter-firm networking without government intervention, internal competition instead of external competition	Inter-firm synergies, rate of return driven innovation, trading equity for innovation	replacing cash flow access by formal taxation and informal subsidies

Fig. 12.1 Institutional competence of networks in China, 1988–2008

The descriptive framework helps to put specific properties of Chinese networks into a chronological and transitional perspective. Each column in Fig. 12.1 describes from top to bottom the accelerating trend towards privatization unleashed by corporate reforms in 1988. Before going into details a remark about the general validity of this trend seems to be appropriate. We do not want to give the impression that this is a homogenous and centrally coordinated development trend. On the contrary, we observe a great diversity with large parts of China lagging behind advanced provinces (Krug & Hendrischke, 2007). However, the centre of business activity and institutional innovation are generally shifting towards incorporated firms operating in an environment of market coordination, "state-free" inter-firm relations and return-driven innovation.

The right hand column illustrates how the organizational form of firms moved from collective enterprises with fuzzy ownership rights and unspecified management roles to firms with statuary and legally enforceable corporate governance. The change in organizational forms is accompanied by decreasing political constraints and increasing scale of economic incentives and risk diversification. As a result, management tasks (alignment with markets and innovation) become more professionalized and absorb more formal elements as they expand in scale.

The alignment with markets started with local market, rather than sectors and industries. The formation of a national market is still not complete. Firms started off from local markets where they could rely on local supply and protection of third property rights. The expansion of markets followed geographical-jurisdictional lines rather than sectoral markets. As a result, the decision where to produce or sell precedes the decision what to produce. The organizational response are multi-market firms aimed at aims at pooling risks across locations as well as industries. The integration of local market into an 'economic region' and access to new market-conforming organizations, such as banking, R&D facilities and foreign partners leads to the generation of inter-firm capabilities coordinated by networks in which the influence of state agencies looses out. These inter-firm capabilities allow trading goods and services 'internally', based on transfer prices thereby escaping both state intervention and (still) distorted market prices.

Innovation started with shop floor innovation based on first hand knowledge how productivity. From removing supply side constraints by tapping into private savings or capital accumulation within firms, collaboration with (foreign) companies or state research facilities, technical and organizational capabilities became located within inter-firm relations, such as supply chains or the networks in the background. Incorporation of firms and increasing competition set incentives to swap equity for innovation and to increase in-house R&D facilities.

Alignment with politics started from townships and counties which had a remarkable degree of local autonomy, including institutional autonomy, or example in the form of 'fiscal federalism.' This shows in the increasingly diversified revenue portfolio. Instead of depending on central budget transfers local government agencies appropriated the following revenue sources: share on national taxes, revenue from local taxes and fees plus income from local commercial activities such as public utility revenues, ownership on "non state" firms and real estate. The richer a locality in terms of (prices of) land and capital income, the stronger the autonomy for local government agencies and, in turn, the tendency to co-operate with economic networks.

Foreign Companies and Institutional Competence

The dynamic analysis above offers some insights why foreign companies in China's dynamic environment would move away from their state oriented position toward organizational forms that resembles more those of their private Chinese counterparts.

Like domestic firms, foreign firms too need to build up networks for generating institutional competence in order to find the best fitting strategy that allows aligning with (local) politics and markets while searching for innovation and an appropriate form of (corporate) governance.

Organizational choice in the Chinese context is not limited to ownership and agency considerations but includes decision about private-public partnerships, multi market firms, or supply chain contracts that ensure political support and innovative slack. In order to benefit from the institutional competence of their Chinese partner firms, foreign investors need to permanently reconfigure themselves by aligning and re-aligning to changing political and market environments.

The empirical analysis suggests further that there is not one strategy or organizational form that fits best the Chinese business environment. Instead, the best fitting combination will vary according to location, industry, age of firm and conformity in behavior of business partners. The more competitive the sector or location the less alignment with politics plays a role. Thus, for example in a location such as Hangzhou or in the standard software industry, firms can place their emphasis on market driven strategies. On the other hand, in provinces such as Shandong or the pharmaceutical sector, alignment with politics will have a significant influence on firms' performance. The newer the firm or sector in which the firm operates the more important it is to gain "social legitimization" via alliances with local government agencies. The stronger the prevailing conformity in business behavior the more firms are able to pursue business collaboration outside vertical integration or formal joint ventures.

Conclusion: Institutional Competence and Networking

The preceding analysis showed that institutional competence involves the ability to configure an organization so that it can identify and monitor volatile key resources while at the same time influence the behavior of potential business partners and government agencies. In the case of China such an organization is a network and not a firm, as general economic literature suggests. Firms are the outcome of the accumulated institutional competences of networks. Instead of firms engaging in networking activities, we find networks as economic actors engaging in the establishment of "open border" firms that have an optimum fit with the local institutional environment.

The need to cope with the external environment defines the search process and management tasks of networks in line with their competences. Networks respond to market shifts when they search for organizational solutions to avoid local protectionism and market fragmentation (market management). Networks align the interests of the firm with the interests of potential investors by securing access to shared or jointly produced knowledge, information or business routines (technical management). Networks influence the political environment by aligning the interests of political actors and other stakeholders with the interests of managers or entrepreneurs (institutional management).

Networks, in a dynamic institutional environment, are mobilized for economic purposes. They are fluid, non-structured organizational forms for co-coordinating resources and strategic decisions with the ability to flexibly activate and de-activate individual economic actors. Their openness and use of formal and informal information channels makes it possible to convert informal ad hoc practices as employed between firms or between firms and local regulatory agencies into procedures or, by extension, into sectoral and formal local business standards. In this way networks and their related firms synchronize changes at the micro level in their business sector or locality with institutional changes at the macro-level, i.e. politics (co-evolution).

The expansion of network control raises the issue of the costs of Chinese networks. In contrast to general literature on networks and our own detailed research which confirm the transaction cost savings role of networks in transition economies, the economic literature on rent-seeking and collective action also points to potential drawbacks. As these are frequently raised in Chinese public debates and the media, we take up jurisdictional competition and the future of networks.

Jurisdictional competition between localities may not be strong enough to ensure the integration of network driven local business system into national markets. Instead, segmentation of markets hardened by different local legislation and policy practices will become salient features of the institutional landscape. This risk is evident in China's domestic market barriers and local protectionism.

For the time being and pending further research, we find that China's institutional architecture will be characterized by the co-existence of different business systems in various stages of market transition and corporate transformation. The expansion of these local business systems into larger national and international markets is driven through institutional coevolution by growing institutional and professional competence of networks.

References

Boisot, M. H., & Child, J. (1996). From fiefs to clans: explaining China's emerging economic order. *Administrative Science Quarterly, 41*, 600–628.

Chen, H., & T. Chen (1998). Network linkages and location choice in foreign direct investment. *Journal of International Business Studies, 29*, 445–467.

Child, J., Lu, Y., & Tsai, T. (2007). Institutional entrepreneurship in building an environmental protection system for the People's Republic of China. *Organization Studies, 28*, 1013–1034.

Crouch, C. (2005). *Capitalist diversity and change. recombinant governance and institutional entrepreneurs*. Oxford: Oxford University Press.

Djankov, S., Glaeser, E., La Porta, T., Lopez de Silanes, F., & Shleifer, A. (2003). The new comparative economics. *Journal of Comparative Economics, 31*, 595–619.

Dosi, G. R., Nelson, R. R., & Winter, S. G. (2000). *The nature and dynamics of organizational capabilities*. Oxford: Oxford University Press.

Frye, T. (2002). Capture or exchange: business lobbying in Russia. *Europe Asia Studies, 54*, 1017–1036.

Grabher, G., & Stark, D. (1997). Organizing diversity: evolutionary theory, network analysis and post socialism. *Regional Studies, 31*, 533–544.

Hendrischke, H. (2007). Networks as business networks. In B. Krug & H. Hendrischke (Eds.), *China in the 21st century: economic and business behaviour* (pp. 227–248). Cheltenham: Edward Elgar.

Hofstede, G. (2007). Asian management in the 21st century. *Asia Pacific Journal of Management, 24*, 411–424.

Hoskisson, R., Eden, L., Lau, C. M., & Wright, M. (2000). Strategy in emerging markets. *Academy of Management Journal, 43*, 249–267.

Krug, B., Hendrischke, H. (2007). Framing China: Transformation and institutional change. Management and Organization Review, 4, 81-108.

Krug, B., & Polos, L. (2004). Emerging markets, entrepreneurship and uncertainty: the emergence of a private sector. In B. Krug (Ed.), *China's rational entrepreneurs. The development of the new private business sector* (pp. 72–96). London: Routledge.

Meyer, K. E., & Peng, M. W. (2005). Probing theoretically into Central and Eastern Europe: transactions, resources, and institutions. *Journal of International Business Strategy, 36*, 600–621.

Nelson, R. R. (1992). National innovation systems: A comparative analysis. New York, NY: Oxford University Press.

Nelson, R. R., & Winter, S. G. (1982). An evolutionary theory of economic change. Cambridge, MA: Harvard University Press.

OECD Science, Technology and Industry Outlook 2006. Paris: OECD.

Pistrui, D., Huang, W., Oksoy, D., Zhao, J., & Welsch, H. (2001). Entrepreneurship in China: characteristics, attributes, and family forces shaping the emerging private factors. *Family Business Review, XIV*, 141–158.

Walder, A. G. (1995). Local governments as industrial firms: an organizational analysis of China's transitional economy. *American Journal of Sociology, 101*, 263–301.

Xin, K. R., & Pearce, J. L. (1996). Guanxi: connections as substitutes for formal institutional support. *Academy of Management Journal, 39*, 1641–1658.

Yamakawa, Y., Peng, M.W., & Deeds, D.L. (2008). What drives new ventures to internationalize from emerging to developed economies? *Entrepreneurship, Theory and Practice, 32*, 59–82.

Review of "Smart Business Networks with Chinese Characteristics"

Focus on Institutional Competence

Jens Ove Riis

Center for Industrial Production, Aalborg University, Denmark, riis@production.aau.dk

A common perception of governance of China is that "The Country in the Middle" has a strong central government. However, as a connoisseur of the Chinese political situation once expressed the situation, we should view China in the same way as we look at Europe as a collection of rather inhomogeneous and independent states (provinces). And even further, as pointed out in the paper, the local institutions have gained economic strength and can exercise political power for instance over allocation of property rights to companies. The local authorities have gained significant influence because local decisions are detached from national and regional policies and are primarily governed by local political interests.

A foreign company or business network operating in China, or planning to start activities there, needs to devote much attention to dealing with institutions at various levels, not the least at the local level. The paper addresses this issue and argues that a company or business network operating in China needs to develop institutional competence in addition to technical and market competence.

The authors find that networking constitutes a key organizational form for developing institutional competence. Networks tied in with local governmental institutions are centered on personal relationships and are fluid, non-structured organizational forms with an "activating–de-activating" mechanism that allows economic actors to switch from political to economic links and to adapt quickly to changing economic situations at low cost.

Based on a comprehensive literature review, the paper provides an interesting overview of the development of China's business sectors over the last 25–30 years in which the organizational form of firms moved from collective enterprises with fuzzy ownership rights and non-professional management to those with registered capital and individual property rights and clear separation of managerial tasks.

Still, today there is a continuum of firms from state-own companies, via firms with joint public and private ownership to private companies. And the paper discusses interesting, recent developments in the composition of firms along this continuum.

The importance for a foreign company of the institutional competencies will vary from sector to sector and location in China. The more competitive the sector or location is, the less does alignment with politics play a role. On the other hand, the newer the firm or sector is, the more important it is to gain "social legitimization" via alliances with local government agencies. The authors anticipate that foreign firms need to build up networks for generating institutional competence.

It is impressive how a centralized socialist economy over a relatively short period of time has transformed itself to a rather open society with modern infrastructure and buildings that supports an internationally oriented business community experiencing a remarkable growth which seems to continue. This suggests a look into the future. The paper presents general projections of how foreign and national firms will interact with governmental institutions in years to come. But it would seem that also the role and practice of especially local institutions will need to adjust to a more open and international competitive market situation. It would seem fair to expect that the three institutional levels (national, regional, and local) will need to operate in a more coordinated way like in Western economies, and perhaps that the power balance will shift towards the national level, partly due to the need for expected transparent procedures and policies and compliance with WTO.

Hence, the theme of institutional competence is important for a single company as well as business networks in China and other transforming economies. And there is a need for further research in this area; for example to study the nature of networking practiced today and in the future, the needed transformation of governmental institutions, and how the notion of smart business networks could play a role seen from both a single business firm and a governmental agency.

13. Innovation, Competences and the Role of Knowledge Networks in Hangzhou's Software Industry

Mark Greeven[1] and Zhao Xiaodong[2]

[1] Rotterdam School of Management, Erasmus University Rotterdam, The Netherlands,
mgreeven@rsm.nl

[2] School of Business, Zhejiang University City College, China

Abstract

Why are Chinese private entrepreneurs able to develop innovations in China's transitional economy? This chapter tries to answer this question through a detailed comparative case study of 45 software enterprises in Hangzhou, Zhejiang Province. Combining resourse-based and institutional perspectives we argue that Chinese private enterprises in Hangzhou were able to develop unique innovative capabilities to overcome resourse constraints and manage technical – and marketing risks while respecting the location and sector-specific constraints.

Introduction

A significant private business sector has emerged in China since the mid-1990s (Asian Development Bank, 2003; Krug and Hendrischke, 2007; Tsui, Bian, & Cheng, 2004). In China as a transition economy the development of a private business sector depends on finding new ways for doing business, new ideas for re-combining productive factors, developing and producing new products or more efficient production technologies in order to not only compete with resource-richer state-owned enterprises (SOEs), and foreign firms, but also for coping with (in)direct political constraints (Batjargal, 2007; Krug, 2004; Tylecote & Visintin, 2008). To put it differently, *private entrepreneurs need to develop capabilities for indigenous innovation*, a problem that has drawn only little attention in the research on China's transition economy. This deficit is taken up when it is asked why and how entrepreneurs were able to develop such competences.

First, we combine the resource-based– and institutional perspectives for explaining the development of innovative competences of Chinese private enterprises. Such a combination promises valuable insights because it emphasizes the organizational nature of competitive advantages while considering institutional forces

P.H.M. Vervest et al. (eds.) *The Network Experience*
© Springer-Verlag Berlin Heidelberg 2009

which influence the way firms manage their resources and determine the value of their resources (Priem & Butler, 2001; Whitley, 2002; Lazonick, 2004). Second, we extend Lu's (2000) comprehensive work on indigenous innovation by studying Chinese private enterprises. Lu studied four major domestic computer enterprises that were neither state- nor privately-owned but had a special governance mode with a collective/public nature that allowed extensive managerial autonomy and access to state S&T resources. However, private enterprises that emerged since the 1990s without a strong connection to the state's socialist legacy face additional risks of low legitimacy (Krug & Polos, 2004), limited access to factors markets and no experience to build on, to name but a few (Xin & Pearce, 1996; Tylecote & Visintin, 2008).

The newly emerging software industry is a sector with such characteristics. First, it started to develop in the mid-1990s with few links to traditional industries and state developed technologies. Second, it is dominated by young and small private enterprises (SMEs). Third, the study of software development keeps an exceptional position in that it allows studying both disruptive as well as continuous, accumulative processes of innovation. In this chapter we present a detailed comparative case study of 45 software enterprises in Hangzhou. We propose that Chinese private enterprises in Hangzhou were able to develop unique innovative capabilities to overcome resource constraints and manage technical – and market risks while respecting the location and sector-specific constraints.

Conceptual Background

We argue that the development of innovative competences depends on the 1) resource base directly or indirectly accessible to entrepreneurs; 2) nature of the innovative activity pursued and 3) institutional arrangements in the business environment. The first point is put forward by the literature on (dynamic) capabilities and resources, that emphasizes idiosyncratic and valuable resources as factors explaining organizational form, behavior and performance, stressing the (dynamic) competence or capability to innovate (Teece, Pisano, & Shuen, 1997) and to learn (Fiol & Lyles, 1985). The second point is put forward by the recent literature on sectoral specialization and technological development (Malerba, 2004), that suggests that innovative activities in sectors with distinct technological and market characteristics affect the required competences necessary to innovate. The third point is put forward by comparative institutional approaches – see Hollingsworth and Boyer (1997), Whitley (1999), Hall and Soskice (2001) – that explain how institutional arrangements govern the development of organizational capabilities. In order to understand the development of innovative competence, three questions need to be answered: 1) What are innovative competences?; 2) How do characteristics of innovative activities affect the range of credibly developed innovative competences?; 3) How do institutional arrangements affect the range of credibly developed innovative competences?

Innovative Competences

A competence or capability, in its broadest interpretation, enables a firm to grow and take advantage of its opportunities (Penrose, 1995; Wernerfelt, 1984). Idiosyncrasies in resources, routines, identities and conceptions form the basis of specific capabilities of a firm (Buenstorf & Murmann, 2005). Teece et al. (1997) use 'dynamic capabilities' to stress the dynamics and organizational nature of competitive advantages: 'the firm's ability to integrate, build and reconfigure internal and external competences to address rapidly changing environment' (p. 516). We adopt most of this definition and apply it to our specific context by focusing on innovation and resources. Innovative competence is defined as *the firm's ability to integrate, build and reconfigure internal and external resources to develop and successfully commercialize new products and services.* An ability refers to the skills necessary to achieve a goal, in this case innovation. Innovative competences are firm-specific processes that manipulate the resource base of a firm, while being influenced by specific institutional arrangements (Lavie, 2006; Amit & Schoemaker, 1993; Teece et al., 1997; Whitley, 2003; Nooteboom, 2004; Priem & Butler, 2001).

Then, what types of innovation do we consider? Following Whitley (2000) we distinguish *incremental innovation* involving refining, improving, and exploiting an existing technological trajectory and *radical innovation* which implies a disruption of an existing technological trajectory. Another feature is the extent to which an innovation is *systemic, modular* or *stand-alone* (Nooteboom, 2004). A systemic innovation is one with tight constraints on interfaces (e.g. telecom industry, oil refinery) leading to high switching costs and limited exploration of new activities. In contrast a modular innovation has standards on interfaces yet allows flexibility and thus has lower switching costs. A stand-alone innovation is characterised by autonomy of elements and limited constraints on interfaces (e.g. consultancy, standard application based software) resulting in low switching costs and extensive exploration possibilities. In sum, we differentiate innovation types according to their characteristics and systemic features. Different types or trajectories of innovation require different kinds of competences.

Technological Regimes

Addressing the second question, the sectoral approaches to innovation show that sectors with distinct technologies can be differentiated according to their specific technical and market risks, or *technological regimes* (e.g. Malerba, Breschi, & Orsenigo, 2000; Malerba & Orsenigo, 1993; Dosi, 1988; Parker & Tamaschke, 2005). These regimes are comprised of opportunity and appropriability conditions in addition to characteristics of the knowledge base and degree of cumulativeness (Malerba, 2004). These characteristics of technological regimes and its knowledge base provide restrictions on firms' learning, competences and organization and coordination of innovative activities. Innovation in distinct sectors thus has relevant systemic features. However, innovation leads to economic change only to the extent that agents are successful in taking advantage of the opportunities (Carlsson & Stankiewicz, 1991). In other words, they need competences, which will thus differ strongly across technological regimes that characterize distinct innovative activities (Casper & Soskice, 2004). Beyond sectoral constraints, firms face locational constraints in the form of institutional regimes that shape and guide competences. How do institutional arrangements affect the range of credibly developed innovative competences (third question), a question to which we turn now.

Institutional Regimes

Institutions may either constrain or facilitate innovativeness (Hage & Hollingsworth, 2000; Edquist, 1997). For instance, studies on the market economies of the US and Europe has shown how distinct patterns of technological development can be explained by the different institutional arrangements of various kinds of economies (Hall & Soskice, 2001; Aoki, 2001; Whitley, 1999, 2002). In general the studies suggest that *institutional regimes* affect the dominant logic underlying decision making in organizations. Following Coriat and Weinstein (2002) and Whitley (2007) it is useful to distinguish two features of institutional regimes for our empirical study.

First, institutional regimes influence the provision of facilitative resources that are made available on a more or less non-market basis within the locality. For example: knowledge about new technologies and markets, availability of skilled workers of different kinds, access to capital, etc. The extent to which these are provided by national, local or sectoral institutions determines the embeddedness of organizations in the institutional context (Whitley, 2007). Second, institutional regimes specify, monitor and control the powers and responsibilities of private companies, especially their authority and discretion. For example: national and local state regulatory requirements, business association, labour unions, skill formation systems, etc. Institutional rules and constraints vary considerably across societies as for instance, state regulation, educational systems and extent of unionization vary considerably across societies and over time and influence competitive behaviour of firms (Whitley, 2007).

We cannot directly extend these studies developed for explanations of relatively stable, developed market economies to China's transitional economy. Institutional regimes in China's economy have two distinct features: institutional uncertainty and variety of local institutional systems. First of all, China's institutions originate both from the socialist era and market-oriented institutions, which presently co-exist (Krug & Polos, 2004). Institutions are incomplete and unpredictable in the sense that they do not provide a stable institutional frame (Qian,

2000), which would reduce the uncertainty emanating from innovation (Krug & Polos, 2004). Second, the heterogeneity of China's local business environment. On the one hand, this leads to vertical intergovernmental inconsistencies where local governments do not or only partly implement central policy. Meuer (2008) illustrates how far-reaching decentralization obstructed the coordination within China's biopharmaceutical industrial system. On the other hand, it leads to horizontal competition between local governments (cf Zhu & Krug, 2007). So, in contrast to most comparative institutional studies, which take the nation state as the boundaries of a unitary business system, China's economy is characterized by a *diversity* of business systems at the sub-national level asking for a local perspective.

In the remainder of the chapter we will explore what kinds of innovative competences are developed by Chinese private entrepreneurs. Considering the diversity of local business systems, we take one local institutional environment as our research setting: Hangzhou. Considering institutional uncertainty, we need to explore what kinds of competences can reduce institutional uncertainty in addition to technical and market uncertainties. Moreover, to be able to understand what kinds of innovation require what sorts of innovative competences we will compare distinct sectors with different types of innovations (and distinct technological regimes). In short, we will investigate innovative competence development while considering location – and sector specific constraints.

Empirical Study

Setting

Hangzhou city represents a local institutional regime within China. We take the institutional features as a given and will interpret the findings of this study within those institutional boundaries. We used two criteria to select Hangzhou: First, the presence of a significant software industry. The software industry in Hangzhou emerged successfully: 23,7 billion RMB in 2005 sales revenues of software products, 300 million dollars software product exports (Hangzhou Government Online, 2007; Hangzhou Statistics Online, 2007). Over 90% of the software business in Zhejiang province is located within the Hangzhou locality, making it the software centre of the province. According to the CSIA, Hangzhou's software industry is structured as follows: standard software (33%), enterprise software (32%), newly emerging middleware (18%), and hardware/software combinations (18%). Especially the middleware sector is growing fast last 2 years and many new firms are not included in CSIA yet[1]. Most firms are SMEs (87% less than 200 employees) and have on average 139 employees and average total asset value of 9.300.000

---

[1] Interview with president of Zhejiang Software Industry Association, September 26, 2007

RMB. Second, the private enterprise as a dominant form of economic coordination and organization. Hangzhou is one of the centres for China's booming private sector. The significant share (95%) of enterprises of other types of ownership, i.e. non-governmental enterprises and 90% contribution to gross industrial output of the city, illustrate this point (Hangzhou Statistics Online, 2007).

Sample

The selection criteria for enterprises were as follows: small or medium size (1–300 employees), non state-owned (at most a minority stake), and independent software developers, i.e. firms focused on software development rather than other businesses. The sample consists of 45 software enterprises in three distinct software sectors with an average age of 5,8 years (1995–2006), on average 75 employees (6–260) and, if making sales revenues, between 200.000 (Internet software) and 80 million RMB (large scale ERP project for government). Enterprise software is extensively customized software using platforms or modules. On average these firms are 6,6 years old (1995–2006) and employ 73 employees (6–200). Standard application based software is written for large homogenous markets. These firms are on average 5,6 years old (1996–2006) and employ 46 people (28–100). Middleware is a new sector focusing on interface technologies that link basic architecture of digital communication networks to standard application software, thereby coordinating various technologies. These firms are on average the youngest in the sample with 5,4 years (1995–2006) but employ the most people, 95 (8–260).

Method

Taking the institutional environment as a given, the goal is to identify innovative competences of Chinese private enterprises and their antecedents. We gathered qualitative data from a multiple-case study of 45 private enterprises. We used qualitative data from semi-structured interviews with either founders or senior managers. In addition we triangulated the qualitative data from the interviews with archival data, including company websites, industry news and industry publications. The interview covers the three broad topics of this study: innovative competences, technology and institutions. The main guide for developing questions was the analytical framework and preliminary conceptualization as developed in the previous section. We developed the Chinese semi-structured interview protocol in cooperation with a team of Chinese graduate students from Zhejiang University.

The questionnaire development started with a survey of competences and potential antecedents of innovation from the literature. This survey resulted in a set of categories of innovative competences and potential antecedents. The questions were designed accordingly and then organized according to the following categories: strategy, finance, innovation, external partners, organization of work, customers, competitors, technology & knowledge base, legal and administrative environment, new industry, challenges.

In the period from February to June 2006 the authors and a research team of Chinese graduate students interviewed software entrepreneurs in Hangzhou. The graduate students were all trained by the first author and sat-in at least one interview to get familiar with the procedure. The interviews were done in Chinese. The first author – with basic Chinese language skills – was always present and the interviews were done in tandem. The interviews were not allowed to be recorded. Therefore, both interviewers took detailed notes, discussed the notes directly after the interview. The interviews on average took 1 hour and 15 minutes. After the first round of interviews we started analyzing and drafting our first ideas, conferring with colleagues and industry experts and presenting our initial ideas. After having drafted our first ideas we went back to the field from September to November 2007. This allowed us to present and communicate some of our initial ideas and gather additional data to strengthen and refine our emerging ideas.

Data Analysis

The aim of the data analysis is to build on and move beyond our informants' descriptions. We began our analysis by building individual case studies of the firms, synthesizing the interview data with archival, news and website data (Eisenhardt, 1989). We focused on organizational processes and activities that manipulate the firm's resource base in order to innovate. Most important was cross-case analysis which allows to identify systematic features and the confrontation of those with existing knowledge on innovative competences (cf. Krug & Hendrischke, 2007).

We used the examples identified in previous conceptual and empirical research to guide our search for innovative competences. We looked at processes, activities and structural features in all parts of the innovation process. This resulted in a list of antecedents related to successful innovation per firm and the identification of several core abilities, or competences, based on these antecedents. Subsequently, we looked for similar processes and antecedents across multiple cases. As evidence amassed we went back to the literature to refine our ideas. Our last step focused on gaining construct validity by conferring with several successful software entrepreneurs. These discussions revealed few recording errors and supported most of the ideas we develop below.

Findings

Innovative Activities

We start with showing what kinds of innovative activities firms in the three sub sectors pursue. In the enterprise software sector, innovation takes the form of incremental improvement of products and processes (i.e. organization and coordination of software development), upgrading service to customers and introducing more products in the same production line. In contrast, standard software firms strive to be the technological leader and to that end innovate radically in product technology and opening up of new markets. The innovative activities of middleware software firms can be summarized as non-customized work for a mass market. Innovation takes the form of new business models, new product line or opening up a new market. These firms strive to be the technological leader and to that end undertake radically innovative activities.

Table 13.1 summarizes the type and dominant pattern of innovation per sector. Besides supporting the idea that the three sectors have distinct innovative activities, there are several other interesting results: it appears that more than half of the innovations in these sectors are not in new products or services, which are traditionally seen as 'real' innovation (Fagerberg, 2007). On the contrary, firms appear to be innovative in the way they organize their business both in terms of processes and business models, not unlike Western countries where successful catching-up historically also involved innovation, 'particularly of the organizational kind, and with inroads into nascent industries' (Fagerberg & Godinho, 2007: 515).

Table 13.1 Types of innovation in the sample

	Enterprise software	Middleware	Standard software
Opening new market	7%	20%	25%
Process innovation	29%	0%	8%
New product/service	57%	27%	59%
New business model	7%	53%	8%
Radical/incremental	Incremental	Radical	Radical
Stand-alone/modular/systemic	Systemic	Modular	Stand-alone

Innovative Competences

The analysis suggests five innovative competences of Chinese private software entrepreneurs in Hangzhou's institutional environment: financial commitment, strategic flexibility, external knowledge transformation, reputation development and organizational integration. These innovative competences reflect firm-specific abilities to integrate, build and reconfigure internal and external resources. These five competences are important for all three sectors but vary in degree of importance, see Table 13.2. How these five competences enable firm's to innovative will be discussed in what follows.

Table 13.2 Innovative competences across sectors

Innovative competence	Overall importance	Standard software	Middleware	Enterprise software
Financial committent	14%	21%	12%	12%
Organizational integration	14%	6%	9%	22%
External knowledge transformation	36%	39%	28%	41%
Reputation development	17%	18%	22%	12%
Strategic flexibility	15%	9%	24%	5%

Financial commitment refers to the ability of a firm to commit internal and/or external sources of financial capital for a long-term investment as to assure the collective learning necessary for innovation. The results show that:

– Commitment refers to *long-term* commitment of internal and/or external sources
– The main sources of capital are the government and private investors instead of capital markets
– Financial commitment is a firm specific competence: liability of 'smallness' (need for capital) and capital is not (yet) available on a capital market basis
– There are two noteworthy features of financial commitment: source and use.

The patterns in the data indicate the crucial role of diverse financial sources in different types of innovative ventures. In total 14% of all antecedents are related to access to financial capital; but especially important for standard software sector: 21% of all antecedents mentioned in that sector, compared to 12% in both other sectors. Unsurprisingly the standard software sector, characterized by radical, standalone innovations are in most need of capital. Enterprise software firms need less investments and can often draw on resources from the customer, whereas middleware firms have limited capital needs altogether.

Attracting capital becomes a firm specific competence because firms are small, require capital and capital is not (yet) available on a capital market basis, as our interviews suggest. Therefore, it is an important competence for these firms to be able to access capital. It is useful to distinguish two aspects of financial commitment: source and use: 1) most government subsidies flow to enterprise software firms, which pursue less radical innovations, carrying less risks; 2) the more risky type of investments – VC and founder capital – are found in middleware firms, firms prone to invest in more risky ventures. The availability of the former hinges on the local government policies, whereas the latter depends on the availability of own resources and/or personal networks that can mobilise financial resources. Summarizing, access to financial capital is a key competences where access to government and personal capital sources is sought instead of capital market based finance.

Strategic flexibility refers to the ability that allows firms to change strategic directions quickly to adapt to changing economic and institutional changes. The results show that:

- Strategic flexibility refers to changing strategic directions and goals quickly to enhance innovativeness, i.e. to respond to changes and opportunities in the enterprise's business environment
- Strategic flexibility is about finding the right business model; a *long-term* strategy instead of short-term opportunistic behavior
- Strategic flexibility enables to quickly establish a customer base and develop and learn complicated new technologies; either via local industry peers or imitation of foreign examples.

In total 15% of all antecedents are related to strategic flexibility, but especially important for middleware firms (24%) as compared to standard (9%) and enterprise software (5%). The patterns in our data show how business models reflect different strategic orientations for different technical fields or market considerations. Especially middleware firms appear to be flexible in their strategic choices, aiming to capture a part of the market as quickly as possible and learning skills from every source possible, which reflects long-term goals. Enterprise firms, on the other hand, focus mostly on learning from local customers and are flexible to the extent that they want to meet (changing) customer requirements. Standard software firms pursue more general flexible strategies that allow them to 'jump' into opportunity windows whenever they present themselves, reflecting short-term goals.

This result is not surprising for two reasons: First of all, middleware firms are the youngest, least experienced and most volatile among the three sectors. This sector did not quite yet develop and the firms are still searching for the right model. The interviews suggest that there are high rates of founding and failure – even though we cannot check this with official statistics because there is no recorded data on these vital rates – and moreover, that the key challenge for most middleware firms is to define their core business model. Furthermore, previous research on Chinese ventures suggested that private firms behave opportunistically and short-term focused (e.g. Tan, 2005; Peng & Luo, 2000). However, our interviews suggest that these firms are merely experimenting to find the right model and in that sense have a long-term focus on strategy. This strategy has to be flexible to quickly establish a customer base and develop and learn complicated new technologies, either via local industry peers or imitation of foreign examples. Generally, short term flexible – opportunistic – strategies are found in standard – and enterprise software sectors, whereas the middleware firms have a more long term goal but still flexible in mind.

External knowledge transformation refers to the ability that allows the firm to develop, acquire, transform and share knowledge across firm boundaries. The results show that:

- External knowledge transformation refers to developing, acquiring, transforming and sharing knowledge across firm boundaries
- It resembles 'Western' style networking: i.e. about technical and business knowledge
- However, also a response to limitations in factors markets – liability of newness – i.e. China-specific
- There is variation in: the type of knowledge (content), governance mode (mobilization/coordination), level of formality

  • Business knowledge (8% of total): coordination of knowledge in an informal way
  • Technical knowledge (28% of total): coordination of resources; via informal or formal collaborations (20% of total); mobilezation of resources; via more formal ways (16% of total).

In total 36% of all antecedents are related to access to external knowledge, making it the most crucial factor. These results are altogether not surprising and follow other research on Chinese ventures (e.g. Krug, 2004; Peng & Luo, 2000; Tsang, 1996; Van de Ven, 2004). However, what is surprising is that the government as an actor is 'left out'. It appears that networking for knowledge follows 'Western' style networking in the sense that it is about technical and business knowledge. On the other hand it is also clearly a response to limitations in factors markets, e.g. liability of newness, which is rather China-specific (Krug & Polos, 2004).

The findings suggest that this competence is crucial for all sectors, but there are considerable differences in the type of knowledge (content), governance mode (mobilization/coordination) and level of formality. With respect to content, access to external knowledge can refer to both business knowledge (8%) and technological knowledge (28%). In terms of *business knowledge*, this competence utilizes the personal network of the CEO to share business information. Business information here refers mostly to information about new opportunities, market knowledge and sharing of solutions to managerial problems. This competence allows coordination of resources – knowledge – and this is done in an informal way. Coordination via informal connections is based on complementary interests and contributions (cf. Riis, 2008). Furthermore, it also allows for coordination of work – customer projects – between local firms within the industry. This is another form of sharing resources, but also in an informal way.

Access to *technological knowledge* is another activity that this competence allows for. There is a variety of activities: cooperation with customers for developing new ideas, coordination of technological development within the industry, commercialization of university research, recruitment of new talents, research cooperation with university to develop new technologies and communication and collaboration with external experts. The first two activities refer to *coordination* of resources, be it via informal or formal collaborations (20% of network antecedents). The latter four activities refer to the *mobilization* of resources, mostly in more formal ways (16% of network antecedents).

These different activities, in terms of governance, content and formality of sharing of resources, are used for different innovative activities. Our findings suggest that standard software development – radical, stand-alone innovation – requires a balanced use of variety of external sources, related to technical knowledge development and governed in both formal and informal ways. Middleware development – radical, modular innovation – on the other hand requires those activities that result in sharing of business knowledge, which is in line with the strategic flexibility competence that allows these firms to search for the right business model. Governance of such networked assets is predominantly informal. Enterprise software development – incremental, systemic innovation – focuses on activities that enhance cooperation with customers, commercialization of university research and accumulation of technical knowledge. Governance of the cooperation is usually formalized in contracts.

Reputation development refers to the ability that enables firms to pursue innovative goals by developing and subsequently employing 'reputational assets' in the market, i.e. creating visibility and credibility as a successful innovator (cf. Tylecote & Visintin, 2008). A firm's reputation often summarizes a lot of information and shapes the ideas of customers, suppliers, partners and competitors. The results show that:

– A founder's entrepreneurial experience important for risky, radically innovative ventures
– The collective reputation of the firm is more important for less risky, incrementally innovative ventures
– This competence is strongly connected to the other competences
– Developing reputation enables firms to overcome liabilities of newness: easier to convince customers and suppliers/business partners of the enterprise's innovative abilities.

In total 17% of all antecedents are related to reputation, but more important for middleware firms (22%) and standard software firms (18%) than for enterprise software (12%). Standing in the business or technical community and having 'reputational assets' enables firms to achieve various goals, such as innovation, in the market (Henderson & Cockburn, 1994; Teece et al., 1997), by identification of the value of the firm's previous efforts by external constituencies (Podolny & Philips, 1996) and via accumulated human – and social capital in career histories (Burton, Sorenson, & Beckman, 2002). A founder's entrepreneurial experience plays a larger role in risky, radically innovative ventures – such as the middleware sector – than in moderately risky ventures, such as the enterprise software sector. In the latter, the collective reputation of the firm is more important.

This competence is strongly related to the other competences, as it for instance, enhances the chances to get access to (government and personal) finance and increases the likelihood of being a desired business partner. Moreover, it is a way to overcome liabilities of newness in two ways because it is easier to convince customers and suppliers/business partners of the enterprise's innovative abilities. Having a reputation for being innovative thus reinforces the other innovative competences.

Organizational integration refers to the ability to commit employees to the firm and contribute their resources to engage in firm-specific learning (cf. Penrose, 1995; Whitley, 2003). Firm-specific learning is collective and tacit on the basis of mutual interplay between partners (cf. Riis, 2008). The results show that:

– Organizational integration commits employees to the firm and contribute their resources to engage in firm-specific learning
– Collective coordination and learning helps to
  • internalize externally accessed knowledge
  • collectivize the various individual personal knowledge sources
– Organizational integration is a *coordination mechanism*
  • for more risky innovative activities it refers to 'absorptive capacity'
  • for less risky innovative activities it refers to employee commitment.

In our study, the organizational integration competence is related to collective coordination and learning. Over 14% of all antecedents are related to organizational integration. However they are especially important for the enterprise software sector: 22% of all antecedents mentioned in that sector, compared to 6% and 9% for standard – and middleware sector respectively. This competence is particularly important for developing incremental, systemic innovations, such as in the enterprise software sector (cf Casper & Whitley, 2004). The more risky and innovative standard software and middleware sectors appear to have less organizational integration and more flexible and fluid human resource systems.

However, the importance of organizational integration as a competence for innovation directly flows from the need for internalizing externally accessed knowledge and/or collectivizing the various individual personal knowledge sources. In short, organizational integration as an innovative competence mostly functions as a *coordination mechanism* (cf Whitley, 2002; Lazonick, 2004; Nooteboom, 2004). For the more risky ventures this is mostly necessary to absorb new technical and business knowledge, or refers to what Cohen and Levinthal (1990) named 'absorptive capacity'. For the less risky, incrementally innovative ventures it is mostly necessary to socialize and commit employees to invest in collective knowledge and learning.

At first sight organizational integration and strategic flexibility appear to be contradictory. However, enterprises exactly need both competences: On the one hand, strategic flexibility refers to the ability that allows firms to change strategic directions quickly to adapt to changing economic and institutional changes; i.e. to quickly 'drop' existing ways of doing business – and knowledge – to adapt to new circumstances and newly available knowledge. On the other hand, given their inexperience, limited resources and lack of legitimation, these enterprises need to internalize and collectivize this new knowledge and experience; i.e. need to invest in long-term routines and stable ways of doing business. This competence functions as an internal coordination mechanism. Therefore, there is a subtle balance and trade-off between flexibility and stability. Perhaps the best analogy is March's distinction between explorative and exploitative activities. Following Nooteboom's (2004) cycle of exploitation and exploration, enterprises need to explore first, searching for new knowledge, then consolidate this and generalize it within the enterprise boundaries to be able to exploit the new knowledge. All in all, this suggests a strong coherence among the various innovative competences.

Discussion and Conclusion

The findings suggest that private software enterprises in Hangzhou developed five innovative competences: financial commitment, strategic flexibility, external knowledge transformation, reputation development and organizational integration. External knowledge transformation appears to be the most crucial competence. The analysis allows to propose two implications:

(1) *Configuration of innovative competences.* The findings suggest that there are various interconnections between the competences: such as between reputation development, strategic flexibility and external knowledge transformation; and between organizational integration and networking external knowledge transformation. The five competencies do not represent different components, but form a 'configuration' or coherent set of competences in this particular institutional setting. Each innovative competence reinforces while simultaneously depending on the support of the others, as was nicely illustrated by the connection between strategic flexibility and organizational integration. Another example is how reputation, external partners and employee commitment are interrelated via the firm's position in the industry's social structure (Podolny & Philips, 1996). A firm's position in this social structure and its external partners influences its reputation. In turn, the firm's position in the social structure is to a large extent determined by the position of its employees in that social structure. Then, the extent to which employees are committed to the firm – level of organizational integration – will have significant effects on the firm's reputation and hence on access to external partners and knowledge. Clearly, these five competences are interrelated and by no means mutually exclusive.

(2) *Institutional – and technological regimes.* All five competences are important for developing innovations across sectors to the effect that first, these specific five competences are credibly developed within this local institutional regime. Second, the institutional regime appears to shape innovative competence development to a large extent because *even across sectors where technological and market characteristics are substantially different* – and the requirements for innovative activities

are distinct – we find the same five innovative competences. However, it is worthwhile to point out that the extent to which these competences play a role varies across sectors. Moreover, these differences in level are directly related to the technical and market characteristics and innovative patterns in the distinct sectors, as discussed in the previous part. Combined these findings support the significant but diverse roles of technological and institutional regimes.

References

Amit, R., & Schoemaker, P.J.H. (1993). Strategic assets and organizational rent. *Strategic Management Journal, 14*, 33–46.

Aoki, M. (2001). *Toward a Comparative Institutional Analysis*, Cambridge, MA: The MIT Press.

Asian Development Bank (2003). *The development of private enterprise in the People's Republic of China*. Manila, Philippines: Asian Development Bank.

Batjargal, B. (2007) Internet entrepreneurship: Social capital, human capital, and performance of Internet ventures in China, *Research Policy, 36*(5), 605–618.

Breschi, S., Malerba, F., & Orsenigo, L. (2000) Technological regimes and Schumpeterian patterns of innovation. *The Economic Journal, 110*, 388–410.

Buenstorf, G., & Murmann, J.P. (2005). Ernst Abbe's scientific management: theoretical insights from a nineteenth-century dynamic capabilities approach. *Industrial and Corporate Change, 14*(4), 543–578.

Burton, M.D., Sorensen, J.B., & Beckman, C.M. (2002). Coming from good stock: Career histories and new venture formation. *Social structure and organizations revisited, 19*, 229–262.

Carlsson, B., & Stankiewicz, R. (1991). On the nature, function and composition of technological systems. *Journal of Evolutionary Economics, 1*, 93–118.

Casper, S., & Whitley, R.D. (2004). Managing competences in entrepreneurial technology firms: A comparative institutional analysis of Germany, Sweden and the UK. *Research Policy, 33*, 89–106.

Casper, S., & Soskice, D. (2004). Sectoral systems of innovation and varieties of capitalism: explaining the development of high-technology entrepreneurship in Europe. In F. Malerba (Ed.), *Sectoral systems of innovation: Concepts, issues and analysis of six major sectors in Europe*. Cambridge University Press: Cambridge.

Cohen, W., & Levinthal, D. (1990). Absorptive Capacity: A new perspective on learning and innovation. *Administrative Science Quarterly*, 35, 128–152.

Coriat, B., & Weinstein, O. (2002). Organizations, firms and institutions in the generation of innovation. *Research Policy, 31*, 273–290.

Dosi, G. (1988). Sources, procedures, and microeconomic effects of innovation. *Journal of Economic Literature, 26*(3): 1120–1171.

Edquist, C. (Ed.) (1997). *Systems of innovation: Technologies, institutions and organizations*. London: Frances Pinter.

Eisenhardt, K.M. (1989). Building theories from case study research. *Academy of Management Review, 14*, 532–550.

Fagerberg, J. (Ed.) (2007). *The Oxford handbook of innovation*. Oxford University Press: Oxford.

Fagerberg, J., & Godinho, M.M. (2007) Innovation and catching-up. In: Fagerberg, J., Mowery, D.C., & Nelson, R.R. (eds) (2007), *The Oxford handbook of innovation*, Oxford University Press: Oxford

Fiol, C.M. & Lyles, M.A. (1985) Organizational learning, *Academy of Management Review*, *10*(4): 803–813.

Hage, J.T., & Hollingsworth, J.R. (2000). A strategy for the analysis of idea innovation networks and institutions. *Organization Studies*, *21*(5), 971–1004.

Hall, P., & Soskice, D. (Eds.) (2001). *Varieties of capitalism: The institutional foundations of comparative advantage.* Oxford: Oxford University Press.

Hangzhou Government Online. (2007). http://english.hangzhou.gov.cn/english/. Accessed 28 February 2007.

Hangzhou Statistics Online. (2007). http://www.hzstats.gov.cn/english/. Accessed 28 February 2007.

Henderson, R., & Cockburn, I. (1994). Measuring competence? Exploring firm effects in pharmaceutical research. *Strategic Management Journal, 15*, 63–84.

Hollingsworth, J.R. & Boyer, R. (1997). *Contemporary capitalism: The embeddedness of institutions.* Cambridge: Cambridge University Press.

Krug, B. (Ed.) (2004). *China's Rational Entrepreneurs: The development of the new private business sector*, London: RoutledgeCurzon

Krug, B., & Polos, L. (2004). Emerging markets, entrepreneurship and uncertainty. In B. Krug (Ed.), *China's Rational Entrepreneurs: The development of the new private business sector* (pp. 72–96). London: RoutledgeCurzon.

Krug, B., & Hendrischke, H. (Eds.) (2007). *China's Economy in the 21st century: Enterprise and business behaviour.* London: Edward Elgar.

Lavie, D. (2006). Capability reconfiguration: An analysis of incumbent responses technological change. *Academy of Management Review, 31*(1), 153–174.

Lazonick, W. (2004). The innovative firm. In J. Fagerberg, D.C. Mowery, & R.R. Nelson (Eds.), *The Oxford Handbook of Innovation* (pp. 29–55). Oxford: Oxford University Press.

Lu, Q. 2000. *China's leap into the information age.* Oxford: Oxford University Press.

Malerba, F., & Orsenigo, L. (1993). Technological regimes and firm behaviour. *Industrial and Corporate Change, 2*, 45–71.

Malerba, F., & Orsenigo, L. (2000). Knowledge, innovative activities and industrial evolution, *Industrial and Corporate Change, 9*(2), 289–314.

Malerba, F. (2004). *Sectoral systems of innovation: Concepts, issues and analysis of six major sectors in Europe.* Cambridge: Cambridge University Press.

Meuer, J., (2008). Smart business network in non-modular industries: Analyzing China's biopharmaceutical R&D business with the viable systems model. In P.H.M. Vervest, D.W. van Liere, & L. Zheng (Eds.), *The Network Experience – New Value from Smart Business Networks*. Berlin, Germany: Springer.

Nooteboom, B. (2004). *Inter-Firm Collaboration, Learning & Networks. An Integrated Approach*. New York, London: Routledge.

Parker, R., & Tamaschke, L. (2005). Explaining regional departures form national patterns of industry specialization: regional institutions, policies and state coordination. *Organization Studies, 26*(12), 1787–1807.

Peng, M.W. (2003). Institutional transitions and strategic choices. *Academy of Management Review, 28*(2), 275–296.

Peng, M.W., & Luo. Y. (2000) Managerial ties and firm performance in a transition economy: the nature of a micro-macro link. *Academy of Management Journal, 43*(3), 486–501.

Penrose, E. (1995). *The theory of the growth of the firm*, 3rd Edn. Oxford: Oxford University Press [first published 1959]

Podolny, J.M., & Phillips, D.J. (1996). The dynamics of organizational status. *Industrial and Corporate Change, 5*, 453–472.

Priem, R.L., & Butler, J.E. (2001). Is the resource-based "view" a useful perspective for strategic management research? *Academy of Management Review, 26*(1), 22–40.

Riis, J.O. (2008). Shared visions in smart business networks: A stakeholder and an Organizational learning approach. In P.H.M. Vervest, D.W. van Liere, & L. Zheng (Eds.), *The network experience – New value from smart business networks*. Berlin. Germany: Springer.

Qian, Y. (2000). The process of China's market transition (1978–98): The evolutionary, historical, and comparative perspectives. *Journal of Institutional and Theoretical Economics, 156*(1), 151–171.

Tan, J. (2005). Venturing in turbulent water: a historical perspective of economic reform and entrepreneurial transformation. *Journal of Business Venturing, 20*, 689–704.

Teece, D.J., Pisano, G., & Shuen, A. (1997). Dynamic capabilities and strategic management. *Strategic Management Journal, 18*, 509–533.

Tsui, A.S., Bian, Y., & Cheng, L. 2006. *China's domestic private firms: Multidisciplinary perspectives on management and performance*, London: M.E. Sharpe.

Tylecote, A., & Visintin, F. (2008). *Corporate governance, finance and the technological advantage of nations*. London: Routledge.

Van de Ven, A.H. (2004) The context-specific nature of competence and corporate development. *Asia Pacific Journal of Management, 21*, 123–147.

Wernerfelt, B. (1984). A resource-based view of the firm. *Strategic Management Journal, 5*, 795–815.

Whitely, R. (1999). Divergent capitalisms. Oxford: Oxford University Press.

Whitley, R. (2000). The institutional structuring of innovation strategies: Business systems, firm types and patterns of technical change in different market economies. *Organization Studies, 21*(5), 855–886.

Whitley, R. (2002). Developing innovative competences: The role of institutional frameworks. *Industrial and Corporate Change, 11*(3), 497–528.

Whitley, R. (2003). The institutional structuring of organizational capabilities: The role of authority sharing and organizational careers. *Organization Studies, 24*(5), 667–695.

Whitley, R. (2007). *Business systems and organizational capabilities*. Oxford: Oxford University Press.

Xin, K., & Pearce, J.L. (1996). Guanxi: Connections as substitutes for formal institutional support. *Academy of Management Journal, 39*(6), 1641–1658.

Zhu, Z., & Krug, B. (2007) China's emerging tax regime: Local tax farming and central tax bureaucracy. In: Krug, B., & Hendrischke, H. (Eds.) (2007). *China's Economy in the 21st century: Enterprise and business behaviour*. London: Edward Elgar.

14. Smart Business Network in Non-Modular Industries

China's Biopharmaceutical R&D and the Viable Systems Model

Johannes Meuer

Rotterdam School of Management, Erasmus University Rotterdam, The Netherlands,
jmeuer@rsm.nl

Abstract

Research on SBNs has so far overwhelmingly focused on business processes highly modular by nature. The chapter challenges the applicability of SBN concepts for the improvement of networks functioning by using the Viable Systems Model (VSM) – a model closely resembling an SBN – for the analysis of a business process characterized by a high degree of integrality. Due to the complexity of the products and the large range of separate scientific disciplines required for identifying, defining, and solving problems, the process of biopharmaceutical drug design here is identified as a suitable research field. Based on an organization-population analysis of a biopharmaceutical High Tech Park, four conditions for the application of SBN concepts are being carved out. First, network elements need clearly identifiable objectives and functions to avoid interference with other system elements. Second, the presence of single coordination devices enhances the functional capability of the network, as does a unified logic underlying its technology, norms, and language. At last, a sufficient degree of system inherent viability in the form of independence from external shocks is required. In the absence of these conditions the applicability of SBN concepts for the design improvement of networks seems rather limited.

Introduction

Smart Business Networks (SBN) started off with the idea that the technological revolution in Information and Computer Technology (ICT) would enable actors to gain benefits from designing networks by improving the coordination and integration of information and resource flows (van Hillegersberg, Boeke, & van den Heuvel,

2004; Vervest, Preiss, van Heck, & Pau, 2004a; Vervest, van Heck, Preiss, & Pau, 2004b). A network designed in such a way would then be considered 'smart'. Other researchers have moved away from this strong embedding of SBNs in ICT networks and have advanced the concept to fit strategic approaches by emphasizing the role of network orchestrators smartly coordinating and integrating different tasks (Shaw, Snowdon, Holland, Kawalek, & Warboys, 2004). The literature on SBN so far has somewhat struggled to clearly define what exactly constitutes 'smart'. Researchers have mentioned a number of characteristics to approximate the intentional application of ICT to coordinate modules designing a network to achieve 'better than usual' results (Holland, Shaw, Westwood, & Harris, 2004; van Liere, Hagdorn, Hoogeweegen, & Vervest, 2004).

This chapter asks whether SBN concepts are generally applicable to the study, analysis, and design of systems. More explicitly it will focus on the dependence of SBNs on the conditions of modularity and coordination as so far literature in this field has mainly addressed highly modular systems with clearly identifiable network coordinators (Busquets, 2008; van Liere et al., 2004). Consequently, the chapter focuses on the concept's ability to deal with systems in the absence of a modular nature and a definable coordinator. For doing this, a highly integral business system is exemplarily analysed with the help of a SBN concept. Integrality is opposite to modularity in that standardization is rather difficult, interfaces hard to define, and coordination among actors significantly rests in the tacit knowledge of individuals.

The Viable Systems Model (VSM) is identified as a more strategic form of an SBN enabling an analytical approach to the study of complex systems. The empirical system here is identified as the business of biopharmaceutical R&D. The development of drugs is a long, risky, highly uncertain, and remarkably integral process involving a large diversity of technological disciplines and organizational constellations. Moreover, the biopharmaceutical industry can hardly be considered economically viable, i.e. self-sustaining and capable of dealing with changes in its immediate and future environment (Pisano, 2006b). It still by and large depends on support of governments, risk in-averse investors and philanthropists to fund its activities. The VSM is applied to one of China's largest biopharmaceutical High Technology Parks as a micro-cosmos of the Chinese biopharmaceutical industry.

The chapter is structured as follows. First, highlighting previous research it describes the link between SBN, modularity vs. integrality and coordination, and introduces the VSM as a strategic model of a SBN. The review is followed by an introduction into the drug discovery process and its integral nature. The description of a number of scientific disciplines developed during the last three decades serves to show how this diversity exacerbates the organizational challenges by hindering the integration of technological perspectives into a unified technological regime. In section "The Variable Systems Model for Biopharmaceutical Innovation," the organizational population of the biopharmaceutical Hightech Park is being analyzed as a SBN, the results of which are reported in section "Results: Consequences of Integrality." The findings are discussed in the last section. Based on the results four conditions are carved out that support the design and development of SBNs.

Smart Business Networks and the Viable Systems Model

Smart vs. 'Dumb'

The idea of SBNs has basically added the attribute 'smart' to the concept of networks or more specifically business networks. Literature on SBNs has identified organizations (electronics factories (Busquets, 2008)), inter-organizational linkages (insurance company (van Liere et al., 2004)), large scale networks (product development (Braha & Yaneer, 2004)), or industrial areas (Rotterdam port (Vervest et al., 2004a)) as objects of analysis. The few contributions in literature that have focused on SBNs have identified a number of features to distinguish 'smart' from 'dumb' networks. They are considered smart in that they are viable themselves and decomposable. This quality is either attributed to a number of actors in that it is considered a distributed element existing in the form of shared behavioural process standards, or a single-actor attribute represented as a loosely coupled distributed coordination facility which is characterized by functionality in assembling, storing, modifying, and distributing information (Busquets, 2008). Most research ex- or implicitly considers smartness to be a relative concept which is time- and situation-bound and therefore allows the measurement of levels of smartness (Holland et al., 2004; Van Heck & Vervest, 2007; Vervest et al., 2004a). It is assumed that smartness can be achieved by better coordinating and integrating network tasks. Participation in network tasks or networking thereby forms the basic activity. Other approaches to achieve smartness are the generation of architectures from complex system, the development of guidelines to cope with complexity, or the creation of business operating systems. Being smart comprises the ability to manage coordination tasks, stabilize networks (which supposedly are otherwise instable), mitigate unforeseeable events, or successfully reduce complexity of a system.

Modularity vs. Integrality and the Coordination Task

For the structuring of systems whether business processes, models, or organizations the concept of modularity has been crucial. It refers to the possibility of breaking up a system into sub-systems and to clearly define interfaces by specifying points where subsystems can be combined (Nooteboom, 2004; Pisano, 2006a). Modularity has significant implications. Being able to reduce the complexity of an entire system into a number of less complex (sub-) systems enables an in-depth focus on individual problems, facilitates learning, and supports innovation in (parallel) subsystems. It therefore enables autonomous innovation (Pisano, 2006b), reducing the degree to which sub-systematic innovation is required to be systematically compatible with other elements. This fosters the development of technological regimes, affecting the emergence of a set of shared rules and norms as actors in the field use similar theories to identify and solve problems (Marsili, 1999). The emergence and deepening of technological regimes fosters standardization. The reduction in overall complexity goes hand-in-hand with a reduction of coordination efforts and costs. Strategically, modularity enables firms to outsource specific activities and thereby to develop core competencies. Modularity therefore is a highly valuable feature of business activities in that it clearly defines subsystems and their interfaces and increases the ability to coordinate their activities within and between them.

In contrast, integrality refers to systems in which interfaces are difficult or impossible to define because subsystems are highly interdependent and require integration in order to increase the systems functionality. Subsystems need to be highly compatible. Unlike in the case of modular systems where autonomous innovation is beneficial, it adds coordination complexity in the case of integral systems by fostering the development of separate technological regimes. Standardization both between and within subsystems is difficult, hindering learning and transfer of knowledge, and emphasizing the tacit knowledge and experience of actors. The development of a unified technological regime is less likely yet more significant in integral systems. Strategically, it rather suggests up- or downstream integration of businesses instead of outsourcing. Integrality therefore significantly increases complexity of a system and challenges the coordination task by adding costs and efforts.

Whether modular or integral, systems need to be coordinated. The literature on SBNs has pointed out that one can benefit from the advantages of modularity by assigning this task either to many actors in the form of a distributed coordination facility or to a single actor, identified as a network orchestrator or an essentially central actor with a specific function in terms of authority and information distribution (Busquets, 2008; Nooteboom, 2004; van Liere et al., 2004). However, as the previous paragraphs have shown, modular systems are much easier to coordinate as subsystems can be developed and managed separately. This suggests that the higher the degree of integrality and the higher the complexity in the coordination task is, the less applicable are SBN concepts.

Viable Systems Model as a SBN

One model identified as a SBN is the VSM which was introduced by Stafford Beer in 1979 (Beer, 1979). Beer applied several insights from organic concepts of "…systems into a coherent framework" in order to devise a model that could help to analyze highly complex systems regarding their among-subsystems' distributed viability (Brocklesby & Cummings, 1996; Devine, 2005; Shaw et al., 2004). He defined five subsystems and included an element acknowledging the effects of a system's immediate environment. Figure 14.1 graphs a standard VSM as can be found in numerous sources in literature (Beer, 1979; Brocklesby & Cummings, 1996; Devine, 2005; Shaw et al., 2004).

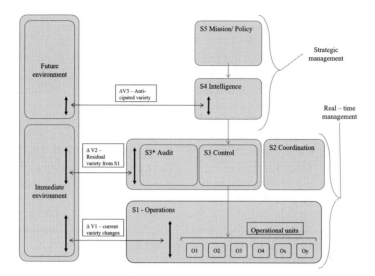

Fig. 14.1 The Viable Systems Model (VSM)

The first subsystem (S1 – Operations) contains all operational units of a system be it a company, business process, or industry. The second subsystem (S2 – Coordination) is responsible for coordinating the activities of the operating units in S1 by representing a regulatory centre intending to restrict deviating behaviour of operational units by providing constant feedback slopes. The third subsystem (S3 – Control/Audit) implements policies by using monitoring indicators to allocate resources and correcting deviations from the systems overall objectives. Subsystem S2 and S3 are considered the core elements of the real-time management structure. Subsystems S1 to S3 are responsible for the internal activities of the system. The fourth subsystem (S4 – Intelligence) is responsible for gathering information about the immediate and future environment surrounding the system. It requires a thorough understanding of both the systems environment and the functioning of the subsystems S1 to S3 to gather the relevant information for devising new strategies. The fifth subsystem (S5 – Policy/Mission) designs policies and sets the long-term mission of the system; it furthermore maintains a balance between its current and future management (Beer, 1979; Devine, 2005). Three forms of variety are being dealt with in the analysis of the system. Changes in the current variety (ΔV_1) are directly managed by the operational units in subsystem S1. The residual variety (ΔV_2) which exceeds the capabilities of S1 is mainly being managed on subsystem S3 (Control/Audit) which exercises control over the operat`i`onal units via the coordinating subsystem S2. The anticipated variety (ΔV_3) originating from the system's future environment is dealt with by subsystem S4 (Intelligence) (Devine, 2005). Conceptually, four central features of the VSM have been pointed out in earlier literature. First, a VSM inhibits a certain degree of adaptability to environmental changes. It secondly integrates sufficient variability to cope with environmental challenges. Third, several levels can be analyzed due to their organization as a nested hierarchy. At last, the feedback mechanism enables the system to remain in a stable regime condition (Devine, 2005).

The VSM is a generic approach to the analysis of complex systems and especially facilitates the analysis of interactions of a system with its environment. The VSM model strongly emphasizes the orchestration task yet extends this element by allowing functions for audit and control, mission and policy, and coordination. Apart from considering system-inherent elements, the VSM includes the immediate and future environment. The VSM has been applied earlier to topics such as knowledge management, organizational agility, and other more traditional business systems (Bititci, Turner, & Ball, 1999; Devine, 2005; Leonard, 2000).

VSM's have been identified as SBNs as these systems are 'smarter' than others in that they increase a systems' viability. It was first linked to the idea of SBNs by Shaw and his colleagues in 2004 where they applied the system to the UK electricity market (Shaw et al., 2004). They claim that properties of network smartness can be summarized in two crucial factors, 'distributedness' and functional locality without which not the network but a single entity such as a business would be considered 'smart'. Devine introduced the VSM to the development and design of National Systems of Innovation (NSI) (Devine, 2005). The policy approaches to fostering innovative industries have become more and more prominent among nations, especially in Asia. He marked that research on innovation policies so far has not sufficiently "…tab[ed] into the system literature or capture[d] concepts recognized by system practitioners" (Devine, 2005). In his analysis he applied the VSM to the NSI of a small economy and devises strategies on how to overcome potential shortcomings. The paper shows a more analytical approach to NSI's and other models aiming at taking into account the complex nature of an industry's external environment. However, Devine does not consider differences in underlying technologies of different innovative activities. In fact, most of the NSI literature and recommendation regarding its implementation still follow a 'one-size-fits-all' approach by acknowledging technological complexity merely to the degree that allows a generalization of policy designs across all innovative activities. These approaches fail to recognize that technological differences require different organizational structures (Greeven, 2008). Therefore, the following section introduces the technological features and properties of the biopharmaceutical industry.

Biopharmaceutical R&D

With the discovery of recombinant DNA (rDNA) the first biopharmaceutical company, Genentech, was found in 1976. From an organizational perspective this was novel in that for the first time a company intended to combine business with basic science, a field formerly reserved for universities and research institutes. It was also novel in that most of the business did not take place within a single entity but in the form of a variety of collaborative arrangements.

In most countries, the activities of the industry are strongly influenced by the initiative of provincial, national, or supra-national governments in the form of NSI programs and frameworks (Europe Innova – Innovation and Clusters, 2007; Lakhan, 2006). In some countries, this influence in terms of funding and research directions exceeds impulses from the business community (Zhao, 2006). This strong dependency on outside support also gives an indication about its economic performance. Undisputedly, the most economically successful biopharmaceutical industry can be found in the United States; yet even in this case, the industry has in economic terms been underperforming (Pisano, 2006b).

One of the reasons why expectations regarding profitability have not been met lies among others in the fact that technological complexity has been underestimated. Many thought that with the means of improved technology, the complex and uncertain process of drug design would be revolutionized, creating fundamentally novel diagnostics and therapeutics, and ultimately substantially increase the quantity of commercializable compounds (Hamilton, 1993). This would take place by reducing development times and thereby uncertainty involved. Consequently, a large number of drugs could be created and sold. However, the new biological mechanism not only proofed to be more complex than anticipated. They also led to an entire series of 'technological revolutions', significantly extending the range of instruments given to researchers for the development of new drugs. Whereas 'classical' drug design – already complex and uncertain – was mainly based on medicinal chemistry, modern biotechnology opened several, somehow independent approaches to the drug development process. The complexity of the drug development process is described in the following sections.

The Complexity of Drug Design

Despite the fact that medicinal drugs, whether in the form of pills, anoints, powders, or liquids, might seem to be relatively simple products, they are in fact more sophisticated and complex items than other technology-intensive articles (Pisano, 2006b). The process of developing a new drug is more expensive and time-consuming, contains higher risks due to its potential negative impact on human biology, and is subject to extensive regulations. It can broadly be separated into five phases. The discovery phase aims at identifying and validating a probable target for instance to interfere with a biological mechanism that causes a disease. This requires a thorough understanding of the chemical, biological, and physical mechanisms involved. After having identified such a target, researchers search for a molecule to inhibit the enzyme. Compounds are being synthesized and optimized against the target. Proceeding to pre-clinical trials with the selected molecules, they undergo testing regarding their safety and efficacy. Research is being conducted in the form of in-vitro and in-vivo animal testing. The active compound and the inactive ingredient are highly interdependent in their formulation so that successful research often depends on the scientist's tacit knowledge and experience with the compound. With satisfactory results, an Investigational New Drug application will be filed in order to proceed to clinical trials. These serve to test and guarantee the safety and efficiency of the designed drug in the human biological system and help to make first estimations about its market potential. With satisfying results during the last clinical trial phase, the company can file a New Drug Application. After approval, a manufacturing base has to be set up according to Good Manufacturing and Laboratory Practices (GMP/GLP). During commercialization, the company will try to increase the acceptance of the drug, prepare for the time when the patent protection runs out and fight against generic copies.

Throughout the process – which may take up to 20 years – the costs and regulations involved are substantial. Depending on the research results and the field of application, clinical trials may include 10,000 of patients in various trial sites. It remains uncertain whether a compound will actually succeed through all development phases. From 10,000 to 12,000 compounds initially being screened, only one will eventually be brought to market. Its economic success is similarly uncertain as the acceptance of the drug by patients and doctors is difficult to estimate. Intellectual Property (IP) concerns are regularly more complex and obscure in biopharmaceutical R&D than in other industries because the most relevant knowledge lies in tacit knowledge, experience, or processes (Pisano & Teece, 2007). The large number of new technologies has moreover added to the challenges of scientists in this field.

Technological Revolutions

The emergence of modern biotechnologies marked the divide between classical and modern drug development. When earlier medicinal chemistry was the sole approach now radically new technologies are available to scientists. Contrary to early opinion however, the variety of technological regimes have rather added to the challenges of developing drugs. In order to approach this large technological diversity one would try to categorize different technologies for instance according to similar features or functions. This proofs to be more difficult than anticipated as the large differences in categorizations from EU, OECD, or Ernst and Young show (Center for Integrated Biotechnology, 2008; Ernst & Young, 2006; OECD, 2008). The following categorization by Pisano however distinguishes the function of technologies and the technological approach chosen (Pisano, 2006b).

Table 14.1 Technological regimes according to application

Synthesis	Biological processes	Design and screening
rDNA	Structural genomics	Rational drug design
Monoclonal Antibodies	Proteomics	High throughput screening
Combinatorial Chemistry	RNAi	Random drug design
*Multiple approaches	System biology	*Multiple approaches
	*Multiple approaches	

As is shown in Table 14.1 it defines three functional groups, i.e. approaches to synthesis, to the analysis of biological processes, and to screening technologies, and names the most significant technological approaches in each group. Their emergence has led to a number of organizational challenges for this industry.

Organizational Challenges

Modern biopharmaceutical drug R&D is a highly complex, uncertain and integral process. Each scientific discipline helps to shed some light on a given problem, but neither by itself can give a comprehensive answer. Contrary to the opinion that the emergence of biotechnology would improve the process of drug development by reducing uncertainty, the large number of new technologies added to the uncertainty involved. Problem-solving in this field requires the integration of a large number of different technological approaches. Drug R&D requires the knowledge and experience of various scientists that – on a continuous basis – exchange large amounts of information. As each choice taken in one scientific discipline has significant effects on other biological features of a molecule, it is impossible to design a drug by separately solving isolated problems. The requirement to integrate a large number of technological regimes, exacerbate the challenges of drug R&D. These technological regimes differ in the logics and languages used for problem identification, formulation, and solving and are responsible for communicative difficulties between scientists (Marsili, 1999).

The Viable Systems Model for Biopharmaceutical Innovation

In order to test the dependence of SBNs on the conditions of modularity and facilitated coordination, the organizational population of a biopharmaceutical base was analyzed with the help of the VSM. Shanghai's Zhangjiang Hi-Tech Park was found in 1992 in order to provide a unified site for the biomedical industry. It is the largest and leading biopharmaceutical sites in China. Due to the presence of not only purely biotechnology firms, but also pharmaceuticals, industry associations, regulatory authorities and other affiliated organizations, the park can be considered a microcosmos of the biopharmaceutical industry in China.

The Zhangjiang Biopharma Base Development Co. publishes every two years a directory of resident companies related to the industry. It includes information about an organizations' main field of operation, the prevailing technologies, and the state of its product development. The empirical data shown in this chapter is based on a text analysis of these descriptions in the base directory of 2005. Each organization was – according to its primary function – assigned to one of the five sub-systems of the VSM. The various technological disciplines, the activities, and the technological approaches of the companies were researched so that an allocation according to the technological categorization described above was made possible. The allocation of each firm to one of the subsystems and technological regimes was discussed with researchers with a medical background in order to avoid false assignment. Despite the difficulties in specifying the technologies applied by organizations, the description in the directory served the purpose of this analysis as it represents an account of the underlying logic and language, i.e. technological regime that prevails within the firm. The analysis is supported with information gathered during 34 in-depth interviews with managers, scientists, and politicians related to the Chinese biopharmaceutical industry in Shanghai and Beijing between November 2007 and May 2008.

The Population Affiliated to VSM Subsystems

As Fig. 14.2 shows, the relatively small share of biopharmaceutical firms in the population (37.5%) indicates how diverse the organizational environment needs to be in order to sustain the activities of this industry. Subsequently, biotechnology service companies represent another 20.0% (32 units) providing medical engineering equipment and electronics, technical and managerial consulting, and international technology transfer services. The pharmaceutical companies (17.5%) support the downstream integration of the activities in biopharmaceutical organizations. Two industry associations complement the industrial landscape.

The various organizational types were assigned to one of the five subsystems or the immediate environment. Organizations that provide human or financial resources were hereby considered entities of the immediate environment. Some organizations provide functions on various subsystems. Universities for instance educate future employees and are therefore affiliated to the industry's immediate environment, but also conduct basic research and can therefore be considered units on the operational level. The number of actors assigned to subsystems therefore exceeds the number of organizations in the population.

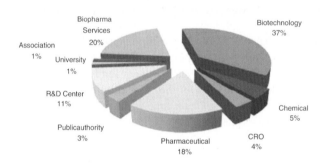

Fig. 14.2 Types of organizations in the biopharmaceutical base

Table 14.2 The VSM population affiliated to subsystems

	No. of firms	% share	Overlaps (No. of firms/% share of x in y)						
			S1	S2	S3	S4	S5	HR	F
S1 – Operation	142	66.0		1	7	9	0	16	0
S2 – Coordination	15	7.0	6.7%		2	7	5	1	4
S3 – Control	13	6.0	53.8%	15.4%		10	0	3	1
S4 – Intelligence	19	8.8	47.4%	36.8%	52.6%		2	5	1
S5 – Policy/Mission	5	2.3	0.0%	100.0%	0.0%	40.0%		0	3
IE: Human resource	17	7.9	94.1%	5.9%	17.6%	29.4%	0.0%		0
IE: Finance	4	1.9	0.0%	100.0%	25.0%	25.0%	75.0%	0.0%	
– sum	215	100.0							

Table 14.2 gives an overview of the population analysis. As can be seen, S1 the operational is the most populous subsystems (66%). The coordinating subsystems (S2 – 16 units, 7%) and the controlling and auditing subsystem (S3 – 13 units, 6%) are similar in size. The NSI Intelligence subsystem (S4) contains a surprisingly large number of organizations (19 units, 8.8%). The diversity within this subsystem is remarkable. It comprises intelligence tanks for various aspects of biopharmaceutical business, such as international technology transfer and business collaboration offices, organizations collecting basic technical information on drug screening, safety and engineering, and consulting firms. The policy and mission subsystem seems adequately small (S5 5 units, 2.3%). However, the S5 level is composed out of multiple players, among them central, provincial and municipal governments.

The VSM model theoretically implies separate identities and functions of the subsystems. As mentioned earlier, some organizations function on a number of subsystems within the VSM. The degree to which the organizational populations of subsystems overlap indicates to what extent subsystems can actually exert their designated function independently.

While on the real-time management level (S2, S3) only little overlap exists (with only 2 S2 firms in S3), the overlap on the strategic management system (S4, S5) is more substantial (40% of S5 firms in S4). Between the real-time and strategic management system, substantial overlaps exists among the levels S3 and S4 (52.6%) and S2 and S5 (100% of S5 in S2). This implies that subsystems do not exist as separate entities in this case. Whether or not they are capable of exercising their function to some extent lies within the realms of individual organization and the cooperative and coordinative structure between organizations affiliated to one subsystem.

In this regard, two aspects gathered during interviews seem noteworthy. First, independent associations take significantly different roles in China than anticipated in theory. While they would be expected to serve as important communication tools for firms to voice their opinion (Greenwood, Suddaby, & Hinings, 2002), they rather function (and are perceived as such) as top-down communication tools for the government to announce new rules and regulations. Second, while competition between government levels is not at all unknown to the Chinese economic system and in fact often benefits the economic development (Krug & Hendrischke, 2008), it represents in this case a major obstacle to the development of a coherent and efficient NSI for the country's biopharmaceutical industry.

The immediate environment consists out are those organizations that provide financial or human resources. The number of institutions educating and developing human resources is relatively large (17 units, 7.9%) including next to universities also Institutes of the Chinese Academy of Science, other public research institutes, and international pharmaceutical firms. The number of institutions providing financial support seems negligible (4 units, 1.9%). The large overlap of financial institutions with the coordinating and the policy-setting subsystems indicates the significance of public finance in the Chinese biopharmaceutical industry. The overlap of human resource organizations with the operational subsystem S1 (94.1% of HR-environment organizations are in S1) shows that substantial HR development takes place within operating firms.

Again, the interviews reveal a number of additional aspects. Regarding the HR base in China biopharmaceutical industry, three elements seem noteworthy. First, the VSM does not show those universities outside the park where most of the firms recruit young talents. Second, the model does not allow for integrating the large number of returning Chinese scientists from the US and Europe. Both influences however have a substantial impact on the human resource base (Frew et al., 2008; Xin & Normile, 2008). At last, the low degree of social acceptance of running a business – especially among more experienced senior scientists – represents a substantial barrier for spurring the entrepreneurial activities in China's biopharmaceutical industry. Regarding the financial environment, the absence of private Venture Capital (VC) firms fittingly points out one of the main problems this industry is facing – globally anyways, yet exacerbated in China. As interviews have shown, VC firms that fund activities in China are either based in Hong Kong or in Europe and the US. Public investment still represents the dominate source for funding small and medium sized biopharmaceutical firms in China (Zhao, 2006).

Technological Regimes on the Operational Level

Taking into account the technological regimes among the companies in the operating subsystem, they were categorized regarding the type of technology they emphasized in their company presentation. The categorization described in the previous chapter on the biopharmaceutical technological revolutions has been used as guidance.

Of the 142 companies on the operational subsystem, only 115 (80.99%) pursue some sort of R&D activity. Other activities on this level are apart from R&D for instance, trade, consulting, or clinical research services. Of those with R&D business activities more than 90% use one or more of the new approaches, either to biological systems, to synthesis, or to drug design and screening. Those companies that combine traditional and modern approaches to drug development make up for 38.3% of these firms. The various technological approaches developed during the last two to three decades have been differentiated into their field of application. They all represent own technological regimes, making it difficult to integrate the various approaches into one common technological logic (Pisano, 2006b).

In the operational population of the biopharmaceutical base, 60 firms (52.2%) are using new approaches to investigate biological processes (see Fig. 14.3). Structural genomics and proteomics account for 35.8 and 34.6% of the approaches used in this group respectively, while RNAi represents 17.3% and systems biology merely takes a share of 12.4%. Only about a fifth of the firms are pursuing research in this area using multiple approaches (19.8%).

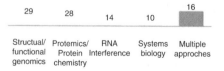

Fig. 14.3 New approaches to biological processes

As the following figure shows (Fig. 14.4), of those firms using modern appro-aches to the synthesis of molecules more than two fifth use an rDNA approach (41.9%), while about a third work with monoclonal Antibodies (34.9%). Only one out of five companies uses combinatorial chemistry for the synthesis (23.2%). In this field, the share of firms using multiple approaches is – with only 16.3% – even lower than in the previous group.

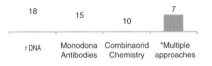

Fig. 14.4 New approaches to synthesis

In the last category, new approaches to the design of drugs and screening, only six firms seem to use computational methods ('rational' drug design) representing 7.7% of the firms, while about one fifth engage in high-throughput screening (19.2% or 15 firms). The combination of modern approaches is similarly low with 8.9% of the companies with R&D activities. In this group 73.1% of the firms are still employing rather traditional methods to the design and screening of drugs.

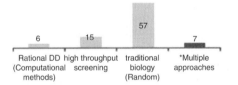

Fig. 14.5 New approaches to drug design and screening

Figure 14.5 summarizes the number of companies in the operational subsystem (S1) of the biopharmaceutical base according to their technological approaches regarding biological processes, synthesis, and design and screening.

Results: Consequences of Integrality

The analysis points out a number of remarkable aspects for the system at hand. First, an internal diversity can be observed on subsystem S1 (Operation), where the various organizational types and the different technological regimes point out a highly heterogeneous population. A similar diversity can be found on subsystem S4 (Intelligence) as research in a variety of different (information-intensive) fields leads to the development of a number of organizations that collect and process information. The breadth of available sub-units in the intelligence level is remarkable. Not only are most of the technological approaches in the form of research, standardization, and data collection and dissemination centres represented, there are also a large number of business consulting, and international technology transfer offices. This diversity significantly hinders the functioning in S4. In the form existing, it is not clear how the subsystem is able to collect relevant information both regarding the systems-functioning and its environment, nor does it seem possible for the intelligence system to give valuable advice to policy makers on subsystem S5. While the diversity observed on the two subsystems (S1, S4) effect the functioning of the entire system in different ways, their origin can be traced back to the large number of technological regimes is characteristic for the biopharmaceutical industry.

Second, similarly diverse are subsystems S5 (Policy/Mission) and S2 (Coordination). Here, it is caused by the competitive situation between national, provincial, and local governments, let alone the competition between different national institutions influencing for instance support programs in the industry. The various coordinating activities on S2 substantially affect organizational units in the operational subsystem (S1), adding to the uncertainty scientists and managers are already dealing with due to the technological challenges. The competitive situation on S5 on the other side substantially hinders the development of a coherent NSI. While similar competitive constellations have been identified in other business related fields in China, this aspect in the biopharmaceutical industry is not necessarily specific to the Chinese environment. In many European countries, similar competitive constellations can be observed, forcing local clusters to compete on a national level, while forcing them at the same time to cooperate on a supra-national level (Europe Innova, 2007; Krug & Hendrischke, 2008).

Third, significant functional overlapping exists between subsystems. This is especially the case between subsystems audit (S3) and intelligence (S4), and between coordination (S2) and policy and mission (S5). The consequences for the viability of the system are significant. Whether and how these functions are exercised, how independent decision-making and how effective information flows are being managed essentially lies within the realms of single organizations. Taking into account not only the diversity among subsystems (overlaps) but also the diversity within subsystems deriving from a competitive constellation, which mainly exists between and within the coordinating and the policy subsystems, it seems that China's NSI approaches to the biopharmaceutical industry exists in the form of three parallel, separate, yet competing (un-)viable systems models.

At last, the analysis points to a number of significant influences on the industry as a model that originate in the immediate environment, namely those related to the availability and quality of human and financial resources. The lack of sufficiently educated and trained employees, the inexistence of functioning capital markets, the substantial regulatory requirements that govern the activities of this industry, and the difficulties in protecting IP represent barriers to the development of a viable biopharmaceutical industry that seem hard to overcome by re-configuring the industry as a system.

Discussion

The analysis indicates difficulties the industry as a system is facing and helps to devise strategies to improve its situation. However, it also shows that some of the severest challenges lie outside the realms of the systems; itself it is not capable to deal with these problems. It thereby suggests a number of conditions to applicability of SBN concepts to systems.

The two biggest challenges certainly exist in the form of a large number of technological regimes and a competitive situation between the governmental layers. Integration of technologies could be fostered for instance by interdisciplinary and translational approaches, by facilitating vertical integration of organizations, or by extending support periods of programs granted by public administrations. As regulatory authorities in other countries tab the pool of experts of industry associations to process drug applications, the efficacy and transparency of the Chinese authorities could be substantially improved by assigning professional associations a more crucial role. An option for companies to develop the quality of human resources is to support and engage in more HR development programs. Alternatives for dissolving the competition between the three governmental layers seem somewhat limited. One option eliminating the redundancy lies in streamlining and consolidating conflicting responsibilities. In fact, this is one of the strategies currently pursued by the central government for instance by re-integrating the State Food and Drug Administration (SFDA) into the Ministry of Health (Li, 2002). However, overcoming the competition between the three political layers seems rather difficult. As the central government transfers more and more decision-making power to provincial and municipal governments, it loses its ability to design a coherent NSI, severely hindering the coordination function of the system (Krug & Hendrischke, 2008).

While the above mentioned system-inherent options seem more or less feasible, a number of challenges exceed the internal capabilities of the industry. Dealing for instance with the absence of a functioning financial market in China in general but also of a biopharmaceutical VC market in specific, seems rather difficult. Similarly, it will be difficult to rapidly reform the educational system in China to meet the demands of the industry. The structural rigidities in China's universities and research tanks, the lack of interdisciplinary research approaches, and the little scientific autonomy these institutions enjoy, significantly affect the quality of human resources available to organizations in the biopharmaceutical industry (Xin & Normile, 2008). Especially the fierce intervention of governments when setting research agenda's seems to be a point that urgently needs reform (Wong, 2005; Zhenzhen et al., 2004). The fact that most of the challenges the biopharmaceutical industry in China faces lie outside suggests that the immediate, residual, and anticipated variety in the immediate environment is too large to be dealt with by the different subsystems. Based on these results a number of conditions for the applicability of SBN can be carved out:

- The various elements required for the design of a SBN, in the given case exemplified by the subsystems such as control, audit, intelligence, etc., need to be clearly identified as system elements in order to guarantee an efficient exercise of assigned tasks. Their internal structure as well as their relation to other system elements has to be coherently aligned to ensure an overall functioning of the network.
- While the diversity identified within subsystems could be considered a local coordination capability as claimed by Shaw et al. (2004), the analysis shows that it significantly obstructs the coordination function of the VSM. This suggests that while subsystems might entail local coordination capabilities to a certain extent, the presence of a single coordinating device such as a network orchestrator is significant for ensuring the functioning of a SBN.
- The presence of a unified logic underlying the entire system (network) in regards to technology, norms, and language, significantly facilitates the design of SBNs. As networking, i.e. the interaction of different system elements, is based upon communication slopes, its functioning significantly rests in the degree to which actors actually understand each other. In the case analyzed, the presence of such a large number of technological regimes hinders the development of standards, interfaces, and consequently modules that could be smartly coordinated.
- At last, SBNs need so possess sufficient viability in the form of system inherent capabilities to independently deal with varieties originating outside its realms. This requires a sufficiently stable institutional environment which is given in other industries but still needs significant development in the biopharmaceutical industry (Greeven, 2008).

As the chapter shows, using a SBN approach to the analysis of this industry identifies a number of conflicts that are regularly unknown, ignored, or underestimated. This seems especially true for the competitive situation between the political layers that add to the uncertainty within the industry and the diversity in technological approaches that hinder the development of a unified technological regime. The fact that both types of diversity are being replicated on various subsystems points out previously unknown interdependencies between subsystems. While the conclusions drawn can be helpful in understanding China's NSI for this industry, the VSM model clearly has difficulties in depicting and subsequently dealing with the integrality that is so characteristic for the drug development process. The homogeneity of subsystems implied by the VSM reduces the industry's complexity and seems to 'force' it into taking a modular format. Increasing the depth and complexity of the VSM might add significant insights into the study of integral industries and strategic SBNs alike. Conceptualizing the internal diversity within subsystems should help to understand their local coordination capabilities. Similarly, a thorough analysis of the existing and missing feedback slopes especially of those within organizations should point out and dissolve conflicts of interest between subsystems. At last, a further conceptualization of the immediate and especially the future environment seems useful to introduce a more dynamic perspective to the study and analysis of SBNs.

References

Beer, S. (1979). *The Heart of Enterprise*. Chichester: Wiley.

Bititci, U. S., Turner, T. J., & Ball P. D. (1999). The viable business structure of managing agility. *International Journal of Agile Management Systems, 1*, 190.

Braha, D, & Yaneer, B. -Y. (2004). Information flow structure in large-scale product development organizational networks. *Journal of Information Technology, 19*(4), 244–253.

Brocklesby, J., & Cummings, S. (1996). Designing a viable organization structure. *Long Range Planning, 29*(1), 49–57.

Busquets, J. (2008). Orchestrating smart business networks. In P. H. M. Vervest, D. W. Van Liere, L. Zheng (Eds.), *The Network Experience – New Value from Smart Business Networks*. Germany, Berlin: Springer.

Center for Integrated Biotechnology (2008). Research areas. Center for Integrated Biotechnology at Washington State University.

Devine, S. (2005). The viable systems model applied to a national system of innovation to inform policy development. *Systemic Practice and Action Research, 18*(5), 491.

Ernst & Young (2006). Beyond Borders – Global Biotechnology Report 2006.

Europe Innova (2007). NetBioClue – The study of the dynamics of bio-cluster evolution. In CoE Management (Ed.), *Graduate school of management and policy*. Scotland UK: University of Dundee.

Frew, S. E., Sammut, S. M., Shore, A. F., Ramjist, J. K., Al-Bader, S., Rezaie, R. et al., (2008). Chinese health biotech and the billion-patient market. *Nature Biotechnology, 26*(1). 37–53.

Greenwood, R., Suddaby, R., & Hinings, C. R. (2002). Theorizing change: the role of professional associations in the transformation of institutionalized fields. *Academy of Management Journal, 45*(1), 58–80.

Greeven, M. (2008). Innovation, competences and the role of knowledge networks in Hangzhou's software industry. In P. H. M. Vervest, D. W. Van Liere, & L. Zheng (Eds.), *The Network Experience – New Value from Smart Business Networks*. Germany, Berlin: Springer.

Hamilton, W. (1993). Strategic choices in technology management: lessons from biotechnology. *Review of Business, 14*(3), 14.

Holland, C. P., Shaw, D. R., Westwood, J. B., & Harris, I. (2004). Marketing translation services internationally: exploiting IT to achieve a smart network. *Journal of Information Technology, 19*(4), 254–260.

Krug, B., & Hendrischke, H. (2008). Framing China: transformation and institutional change through co-evolution. *Management and Organization Review, 4*(1), 81–108.

Lakhan, S. E. (2006). The emergence of modern biotechnology in china. *Issues in Informing Science and Information Technology, 3*, 333–353.

Leonard A. (2000). The viable system model and knowledge management. *Kybernetes, 29*(5/6), 710–715.

Li, C. L. (2002). New developments in China's pharmaceutical regulatory regime. *Journal of Commercial Biotechnology, 8*(3), 241.

Marsili, O. (1999). Technological regimes: theory and evidence: Eindhoven – ECIS – University of Technology.

Nooteboom, B. (2004). *Inter-Firm Collaboration, Learning and Networks. An Integrated Approach*. London, New York: Routledge.

OECD (2008). Glossary of Statistical Terms – Biotechnology. Organization For Economic Co-operation and Development.

Pisano, G. P. (2006a). Can science be a business? Lessons from Biotech. *Harvard Business Review, 84*(10), 114–125.

Pisano, G. P. (2006b). *Science business*. Boston, Massachusetts: Harvard Business School.

Pisano, G. P., & Teece, D. J. (2007). How to capture value from innovation: shaping intellectual pro-perty and industry architecture. *California Management Review, 50*(1), 278–296.

Shaw, D. R., Snowdon, B., Holland, C. P., Kawalek, P., & Warboys, B. (2004). The viable systems model applied to a smart network: the case of the UK electricity market. *Journal of Information Technology, 19*(4), 270–280.

Van Heck, E., & Vervest, P. (2007). Smart business networks: how the network wins. *Communications of the ACM, 50*(6), 29–37.

Van Hillegersberg, J., Boeke, R., & van den Heuvel, W & -J. (2004). Potential of Webservices to enable smart business networks. *Journal of Information Technology, 19*(4), 281–287.

Van Liere, D. W., Hagdorn, L., Hoogeweegen, M. R., Vervest, P. (2004). Embedded coordination in a business network. *Journal of Information Technology, 19*, 261–269.

Vervest, P., Preiss, K., van Heck, E., & Pau, L.-F. (2004a). The emergence of smart business networks. *Journal of Information Technology, 19*(4), 228–233.

Vervest, P., van Heck, E., Preiss, K., & Pau, L. (2004b). Introduction to smart business networks. *Journal of Information Technology, 19*(4), 225–227.

Wong, G. H. W. (2005). Chinese biotech: the need for innovation and higher standards. *Nature Biotechnology, 24*(2), 221–222.

Xin, H., & Normile, D. (2008). Gunning for the ivy league. *Science, 319*(11 January), 148–151.

Zhao, Y. (2006). *Biotechnology development in China, China National Centre for Biotechnology Development (CNCBD)*. Beijing: Ministery of Science and Technology (MOST).

Zhenzhen, L., Zhang, J., Ke, W., Thorsteinsdóttir, H., Quach, U., Singer, P. A. et al. (2004). Health biotechnology in China – reawakening of a giant. *Nature Biotechnology, 22*(Supplement), DC13–DC18.

Network Enablers

Network Enablers

We have discussed essential vocabulary, introduced network theory and introduced models to describe and analyze smart business networks. We included a number of cases to demonstrate smart business networks in action. However, organizations need a solid ICT infrastructure to operate within these networked environments. In this section, we address the technological challenges associated with operating in smart business networks. *Network Enablers* are a set of technologies that particularly allow for quickly connecting and disconnecting within interfirm networks, managing business processes from end-to-end across organizational boundaries and supporting decision-making that optimizes both firm-level and network-level outcomes.

John Collins, Wolf Ketter and Maria Gini focus on how intelligent agents can support organizational decision-makers in making multi-attribute decisions in environments that are characterized by a high velocity of change. Their study is innovative as they present an architecture that offers a unique way of automatically connecting, disconnecting and communicating with the appropriate actors in the network. They offer a technological solution for companies to create the highly-needed quick-connect capabilities allowing companies to change its position in the network more swiftly. Furthermore, they show how organizational decision-makers can be supported by the development of network performance dashboards.

The quick-connect capability receives more attention by Otto Koppius and Arnoud van de Laak. Their survey study in the publishing industry demonstrates that communication standards and business process standards are important requirements for organizations to build a quick-connect capability. An implication of this study for practitioners is that developing a quick-connect capability is greatly facilitated by industry wide communication standards, based on XML for example, and industry wide business process standards.

Once a particular technology has been developed it needs to be implemented. Jan Stentoft Arlbjørn, Torben Damgaard and Anders Haug focus on the obstacles that small and medium sized enterprises are encountering when they implement software applications that touch the core of an organization: their business processes. In their study, they look at ERP implementation projects and identify critical success factors.

Networks in Action section emphasized that organizational preparedness is key to be able to quickly connect and disconnect (see also Koppius and van de Laak (2008)). Marcel van Oosterhout, Ellen Koenen and Eric van Heck offer a possible technological solution to increase organizational preparedness to unforeseen circumstances. They introduce grid technology and demonstrate how it improves organizational agility to respond to rapidly changing circumstances, in particular to disasters.

References

Koppius, O. R., & van de Laak, A. (2008). The quick-connect capability and its antecedents. In P. H. M. Vervest, D. W. van Liere, & L. Zheng (Eds.), *The network experience — New value from smart business networks*. Berlin: Springer.

15. Flexible Decision Support in a DynamicBusiness Network

John Collins[1], Wolfgang Ketter[2] and Maria Gini[3]

[1]Computer Science and Engineering, University of Minnesota, United States of America, jcollins@cs.umn.edu

[2]Decision and Information Sciences, RSM Erasmus University, The Netherlands, wketter@rsm.nl

[3]Computer Science and Engineering, University of Minnesota, United States of America, gini@cs.umn.edu

Abstract

We present the design of a service oriented architecture which facilitates flexible managerial decision making in dynamic business networks. We have implemented and tested this architecture in the MinneTAC trading agent, which is designed to compete in the Supply Chain Trading Agent Competition (Collins et al., 1998). Our design enables managers to break out decision behaviors into separate, configurable components, and allows dynamic construction of analysis and modeling tools from small, single-purpose "evaluator" services. The result of our design is that the network can easily be configured to test a new theory and analyze the impact of various approaches to different aspects of the agent's decision processes, such as procurement, sales, production, and inventory management. Additionally we describe visualizers that allow managers to see and manipulate the configuration of the network, and to construct economic dashboards that can display the current and historical state of any node in the network.

Introduction

Organizations in business networks have a growing need for intelligent software that can assist managers by gathering and analyzing information, making recommendations, and supporting business decisions. Advanced decision support systems and autonomous software agents promise to address this need by acting rationally on behalf of humans in numerous application domains. Examples include procurement (Sandholm, 2007; CombineNet, 2006), scheduling and resource management (I2, 2006; Collins, Bilot, Gini, & Mobasher, 2001), and personal information management (Berry et al., 2006). The recent advent of *Smart Business Networks* (SBN) (Vervest, Preiss, Heck, Pau, 2004; Vervest, van Heck, Preiss, & Pau, 2005; van Heck, & Vervest, 2007) extends the area of traditional business processes and gives rise to new challenges, especially in the area of dynamic and modular business process management, by enabling integration of legacy systems and by providing advanced tools to facilitate human managerial decision making.

We make four major contributions to the SBN literature. One of the major theoretical tenets of SBNs is the ability of actors to quickly connect to other actors to achieve specific business objectives and then disconnect when a task is finished. Our first contribution in this paper extends the SBN literature through the design and implementation of a highly configurable and flexible decision support system that dynamically connects to different nodes of a business network and disconnects them when no longer needed. Our second contribution is the vision of goal directed service composition. This allows business services with formal semantic descriptions to be composed and validated. Thirdly, we are developing a tool to enable managers to visualize, understand, and validate the theoretically designed decision chain with a graphical representation of the actual network chain. Finally, we have developed a flexible economic dashboard architecture that can be dynamically connected to selected nodes to visualize their real-time status, current parts and finished goods inventory positions, risk and reward management, and the like. This architecture can greatly empower business network managers in their understanding of the overall business network structure and facilitate real-time managerial decision making. Currently, we are working on an even more interactive version of this dash-board which allows the human decision maker to interact with the business network to make structural changes.

Since operating on real world business networks has high risks, and might cause serious business problems when not done properly, we tested our architecture and algorithms on a supply-chain testbed, the Trading Agent Competition for Supply Chain Management (Collins et al., 2005) (TAC SCM). We describe the implementation of our flexible decision support system and demonstrate its value using as an example MinneTAC (Collins, Ketter, & Gini, 2008), an autonomous agent that performs coordinated buying, selling, production scheduling, and inventory management in the context of TAC SCM. In addition, we present results of our network visualizer toolbox, where a manager is able to see the current configuration of the network as well as the state of the different nodes. We review the relevant related literature, and finish with conclusions and future work. In the future work section we describe the Dutch flower auction network as an example of a complex, strategic, and uncertain business network on which we are currently working to integrate our architecture and algorithms.

A Business Network Testbed: The Trading Agent Competition for Supply Chain Management

Traditionally, supply chains have been created and maintained through the interactions of human representatives of the various enterprises (component suppliers, manufactures, wholesalers/distributors, retailer, and customers) involved. However, the recent advent of autonomous trading agents opens new possibilities for automating and coordinating the decision making processes between the various parties involved. The Trading Agent Competition for Supply Chain Management (TAC SCM) is an abstract model of a highly dynamic direct sales (Chopra & Meindl, 2004) environment, as exemplified by Dell Inc.,[1] for procurement, inventory management, production, and sales.

TAC SCM simulates a product life-cycle for a manufacturing organization. In the simulation scenario, each of six competing agents plays the part of a manufacturer of personal computers. Agents compete with each other in a procurement market for computer components, and in an auction-based sales market to sell computers to customers, as shown in Fig. 15.1. The scenario models a market situation where products have limited market life, and the major components used to manufacture those products have little or no residual value at the end of that market life. A typical simulation runs for 220 simulated days over about an hour of real time. Each agent starts with no inventory, an empty bank account, and a finite-capacity production facility. Agents must borrow (and pay interest) to build up inventory of computer components before they can begin assembling and shipping computers.

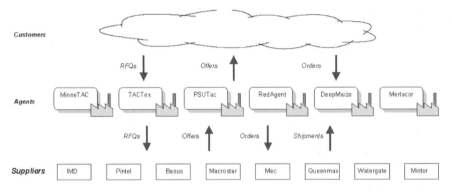

Fig. 15.1 Schematic overview of a typical TAC SCM game scenario. Agents submit daily Request for Quotes (RFQ) to suppliers to buy component parts, and customers request finished computers

Agents have very limited visibility of the actions of other agents, and must deal with significant variability in customer demand, supplier capacities, and other factors. The primary performance criterion is profitability, so the agent with the largest bank account at the end of the simulated year is the winner.

Organized competitions can be an effective way to drive research and improve understanding in complex domains, free of the complexities and risk of operating in open, real-world environments. Artificial economic environments typically abstract certain interesting features of the real world, such as markets, competitors, demand-based prices, and cost of capital, and omit others, such as personalities, taxes, and seasonal demand. Examples related to electronic commerce, besides TAC SCM, include the Penn-Lehman Automated Trading Project (Kearns & Ortiz, 2003), the TAC travel competition (Wellman et al., 2001), and the CAT competition (Niu et al., 2008).

---

[1] http://www.dell.com

Designing an Intelligent Trading Agent for Dynamic Business Networks

Since the inception of TAC SCM in 2002, more than 50 teams have built agents to play in the competition. These agents represent a variety of approaches to solving the various modeling and decision problems presented by the simulation scenario. We wanted our agent to be a flexible research tool, to enable easy testing of hypotheses and comparison of approaches. We intend to use MinneTAC as a teaching tool, to teach concepts in supply-chain management, economic decision making, machine learning, and software design. To address the twin challenges of simulating a business organization and supporting a research agenda, the design of MinneTAC (Collins et al., 2008) models a flexible organization using a service-oriented approach. There are a few top-level decision elements (Procurement, Manufacturing, Sales) and a large number of services that act as analysis modules, supported by a common database. We call these modules *evaluators*. A high-level schematic representation of this design is shown in Fig.15.2.

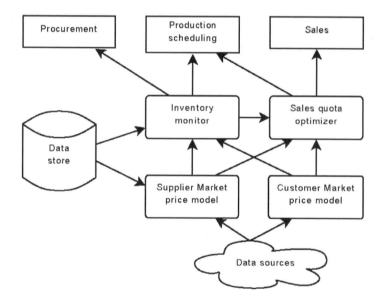

Fig. 15.2 MinneTAC trading agent architecture. Arrows show data flow, not dependencies

Decision components operate by retrieving data from the database, and using evaluation results from evaluators. Evaluators share a common service-oriented design, and they may be composed into chains and feedback loops to perform arbitrarily complex analyses. They may request inputs from other evaluators, from the database, and from external sources. They transform that data in various ways, for example by updating price models, estimating demand trends, or running optimization algorithms to produce sales quotas or procurement recommendations. Results are provided in a common, self-describing format so they can be used by other evaluators or decision components. Connections among decision components and evaluators are entirely configurable and modifiable at runtime; the only real dependency in this design is on the database, and on external data sources such as market data and user inputs. This allows individual researchers to encapsulate modeling and decision problems within the bounds of components and services that have minimal, well-defined interactions among themselves.

In Fig. 15.2, the primary decision components are shown across the top. The Procurement component deals with suppliers, attempting to buy the parts needed by Manufacturing at the lowest possible cost. Manufacturing schedules the production facility with assembly tasks that maximize the expected value of its available inventory and production capacity. Sales sets prices and makes customer offers that are expected to maximize profit, given its available resources. These three decision components are in turn supported by a common data store, and by a large set of evaluators that perform various modeling, analysis, and prediction tasks. These are represented schematically here as the interconnected blocks in the center of the diagram, the "Sales Quota Optimizer," the "Customer Market Price Model," etc. The evaluators, in turn, have access to each other and to various internal and external data sources, primarily in the form of periodic market reports that are issued by the simulation, and a large body of historical data that has been "digested" by machine learning models, such as the "economic regime" model described by Ketter, Collins, Gini, Gupta, & Schrater (2007, 2008).

The radical separation of the MinneTAC agent design into separate decision processes and evaluator services addresses the needs of researchers, who need short learning curves and low risk of interfering with each other. Does it serve the needs of the agent itself, which must effectively coordinate its decisions? The most obvious coordination methods are the "push" approach, in which Procurement tries to keep the factory busy and Sales works to maximize profits on the resulting finished goods, and the "pull" approach, in which Manufacturing and Procurement work to maintain target inventory levels at minimum cost as Sales finds profitable opportunities to sell the available inventory. Another possible approach to the coordination problem is the one used by the RedAgent team at McGill University (Keller, Duguay, & Precup, 2004), in which the primary decision components communicate through internal auction-based markets. The DeepMaize team at Michigan (Kiekintveld, Miller, Jordan, & Wellman, 2006) uses a projected production schedule as the primary coordination structure. Slots in the schedule are filled with products that are expected to return the highest marginal profit at some point in the future. Procurement then works to provide sufficient inventory to run the projected schedule, and sales works to sell what is produced.

In MinneTAC, the database holds a record of all transactions made in the past, as well as inventory data, current customer requests, and supplier offers. The evaluators use this data, along with their own data sources, to produce analyses and recommendations that drive decisions. The version of MinneTAC that ran in the 2007 Trading Agent Competition used a modified "pull" method to coordinate its decisions. It was configured to use current and projected sales quotas over an extended time horizon as the primary coordination mechanism, to drive not only sales, but also production and short-term procurement. Long-term procurement was based on estimates of future customer demand, which is produced by another evaluator, and also used as an input for generating sales quotas.

Evaluators can be composed into arbitrarily complex structures, through a back-chaining process. They do this by requesting the outputs of other Evaluator services in the process of producing their results. Such Evaluation requests are made by name rather than by direct reference, and these names are configurable, either through XML configuration files, or through a user interface. This approach preserves independence among Evaluator services, and makes visible the high-level structure of the agent's decision processes. The result is that complex chains and feedback loops can be constructed from relatively simple services using metadata.

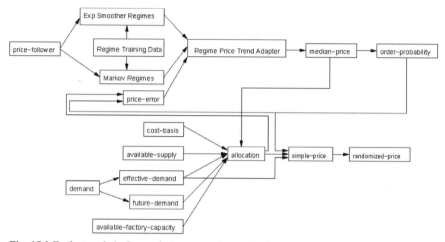

Fig. 15.3 Evaluator chain for a sales manager that uses sales quota and information provided by regimes to determine prices, price trends, and order probability

To illustrate the power of evaluators, in Fig.15.3 we show the evaluation chain that is used to produce sales quotas and set prices in the MinneTAC configuration that ran in the 2007 competition. Each of the cells in this diagram is an Evaluator. Across the top of the diagram is a set of evaluators that estimate current market prices, future price trends, and the shape of the customer order-probability function, based on the method of "economic regimes" developed by Ketter (2001).

We have implemented three different economic regime identification and prediction methods, namely Markov prediction (MP), Markov correction-prediction (MCP), and an exponential smoother lookup (ExpS) process, with the help of evaluators. We also designed a training data evaluator, which is shared by the individual regime evaluators. The training data evaluator uses an external data source that contains an analysis of a large number of past simulations. The analysis was developed using machine learning methods, as described in (Ketter, 2007). These evaluators can dynamically select the most appropriate portions of the training data for a given market situation. In a real business network setting we would train the system on historical transaction data, and update it in regular intervals, e.g. after closing of a set of Dutch flower auctions.

The Sales component used with the evaluator chain shown in Fig.15.3 is conceptually simple – it places bids on each customer RFQ for which the randomized-price evaluator returns a non-zero value. The core of this chain is the allocation evaluator, which composes and solves a linear program each day of the simulation. The problem represents a combined product-mix and resource-allocation problem that computes daily sales quotas that maximize expected profit. The objective function is

$$\Phi = \sum_{d=0}^{h} \sum_{g \in \mathscr{G}} \Phi_{d,g} A_{d,g} \tag{15.1}$$

where Φ is the total profit over a time horizon h, $\mathscr{G}$ is the set of goods or products that can be produced by the agent, $\Phi_{d,g}$ is the (projected) profit for good g on day d, and $A_{d,g}$ is the allocation or "sales quota" for good g on day d. The constraints are given by the evaluators *available-factory-capacity*, the current day's *effective-demand*, projected *future-demand*, and by Repository data, such as existing and projected inventories of parts and finished products, and outstanding customer and supplier orders. Predicted profit per unit for each product type is the difference between *median-price* and *cost-basis* for those products.

Managers need not only to understand and control their decision processes, but also to visualize the data that are being used and produced by the elements of that process. This is very easy to do when decision processes are broken up into a set of discrete, single-purpose services. Figure 15.4 is a screen shot of an early prototype of the user interface.

Figure 15.5 displays the history of daily demand (the output of the "demand" evaluator) along with daily sales quotas (the output of the "allocation" evaluator). This information can be displayed for the overall market, or for individual products or market segments.

Figure 15.6 shows current sales commitments that have not yet been scheduled for production. The MinneTAC design allows a user to dynamically compose such "dashboard" displays by connecting a variety of graphing and plotting widgets to the outputs of the various evaluators. This can be done "on the fly", while the system is running, because the composition of services (Sinn, Hendler, & Parsia, 2002; Wu, Parsia, Sirin, Hendler, & Nau, 2003) and visualizations is entirely dynamic.

Related Literature

This work draws from several fields. In Computer Science, it is related to Software Engineering, Artificial Intelligence, autonomous agents, and multi-agent systems, especially agent architectures, machine learning, and reasoning under uncertainty. In Economics and Information Decision Sciences, it draws from the framework of

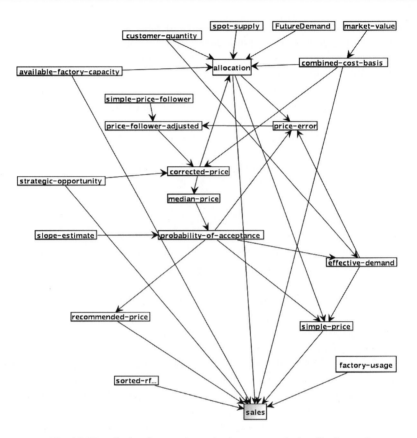

Fig. 15.4 Detail view from evaluator business network visualization tool

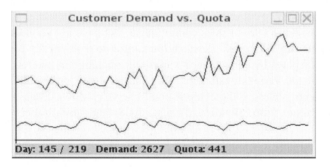

Fig. 15.5 Dynamic network status visualization: daily demand and sales quotas

smart business networks and decision theory. From Operations Research, it draws from work in combinatorial optimization and supply-chain management.

Fig. 15.6 Dynamic network status visualization: outstanding customer orders

Multi-Agent Systems

Most agent design efforts have focused on either the autonomous behavior aspects of agency, or on interactions among agents. Norman, Jennings, Faratin, and Mamdani (1997) describe *agent societies* that model organizational structures and automate business processes. These ADEPT agents negotiate over service agreements that can involve many parties and many dimensions. JADE (Moraitis, Petraki, & Spanoudakis, 2003) is an agent framework that has been used to build trading agents. Its primary emphasis is on building multi-agent systems that comply with FIPA specifications for inter-agent communications, and with flexible deployment in a network environment. These features are not necessary for the TAC SCM domain.

Vetsikas and Selman (2003) describe a method for studying design tradeoffs in a trading agent. This approach could be used effectively in MinneTAC, but the issues addressed by their method are orthogonal to the component/evaluator scheme underlying MinneTAC. Vytelingam, Dash, He, and Jennings (2006) describe the IKB approach to the design of trading agents, consisting of an Information layer, a Knowledge layer, and a Behavioral layer. Podobnik, Petric, and Jezic (2006) have applied this approach to the TAC SCM scenario in CrocodileAgent. The MinneTAC design could be roughly mapped to this scheme, with the database as the Information layer, the set of evaluators as the Knowledge layer, and the decision components as the Behavioral layer.

He, Rogers, Luo, & Jennings (2006) have adopted a design consisting of three internal "agents" to handle Sales, Procurement, and Production/Shipping. Sales decisions use a fuzzy logic module. Some algorithmic aspects are given, but there is little further detail on the architecture of the agent. TacTex05, the winner of the 2005 competition (Pardoe & Stone, 2006) is based on two major modules, a Supply

Manager that handles procurement, and a Demand Manager that handles sales, production, and shipping. These modules are supported by a supplier model, a customer demand model, and a pricing model that estimates sales order probability.

Smart Business Networks

During the mid-nineties Goldman, Nagel, and Preiss (1995) and Sanchez (1995) stressed that in highly dynamic business networks the capability of a quick connect of network actors (businesses) is essential to enable fast response times and greater variety when presented with new product opportunities. The concept of "quick connect" includes a search and select behavior by the different businesses. Goldman et al. (1995) further argue the need for a "quick disconnect" when the business transaction is over, otherwise open network connections can create unwanted information flows that make create unwanted side effects. At the time those articles were published no such network existed. Our architecture offers a unique way of automatically connecting, disconnecting and communicating with the appropriate actors in the network.

One has to pay special attention to the interfaces of the different network actors. Establishing a temporary connection between actors needs to be grounded on a good and matching interface design. This interoperability can be facilitated by modularity. Garud, Kumaraswamy, & Langlois (2002) define modularity as decomposability of a system by grouping elements into a smaller number of subsystems. Modularity is further a very well known concept in the software engineering field, which refers to the extent to which software is divided into components, called modules, which have high internal cohesion,[2] low coupling[3] between each other, and simple interfaces. Our architecture exhibits high cohesion and low coupling.

Hoogeweegen, van Liere, Vervest, van der Meijden, & de Lepper (2006) and van Liere (2007) argue that knowledge of the network structure empowers the decision maker, and leads to better business decisions. With our approach we are able to visualize the network structure, and even drill down on particular network actors to get a detailed picture of specific decision chains. Kambil & Short (1994) already argued in 1994 that there is a strong need to construct software tools for business network representation, visualization, and analysis. These tools can help researchers and managers to visualize the different network actors, or roles, and linkage-based strategies of different organizations enabling the systematic repre-sentation and analysis of changes in emerging organizational forms. Our architecture offers unique capabilities for network visualization, role-and linkage analysis.

Creating performance and information dashboards (Eckerson, 2005) is part of the new emerging field of Business Intelligence (BI) (Shmueli, Patel, & Bruce,

---

[2] A measure of the extent to which related aspects of a system are kept together in the same module, and unrelated aspects are kept out. High cohesion is better than low cohesion.

[3] A measure of the extent to which interdependencies exist between software modules. Low coupling is better than high coupling.

2006). BI is a very powerful tool, as it provides functionalities such as real-time monitoring, performance reporting, support for exploring solution space with normative models, statistical techniques, and visualization. Business intelligence softwarecan crawl the web, mine data, and come back with a report customized to user preferences. Our architecture fully supports BI and our dashboards are customizable for individual managers. According to Adam and Pomerol (2002) the layout of an economic dashboard has a direct impact on the understanding derived by managers. We believe that our customizable design will facilitate managerial decision making. They argue that a graphical user interface (GUI) of a dashboard should be leveraged to maximize the visual impact of the dashboard.

Furthermore dashboards (a) provide users with functions to find more detailed information of a certain metric or indicator (drill-down capabilities), (b) provide users an interactive way of communicating with different actors (agents) in the network, (c) allow customizing the appearance of how information is delivered and its granularity (days vs. weeks vs. months views), and (d) provide search queries which help agents to learn from a user. A complete and extensive work on the visual design of dashboards has been presented by Few (2006). According to Few many software companies have developed and sold dashboard applications since 2001. That year was characterized by the Enron scandal which increased awareness throughout companies of the importance of monitoring closely their most important business processes. Software companies from all kinds of sizes, such as Microsoft and Oracle, have developed dashboards.[4]

Conclusions and Future Work

Experimental work with multi-agent systems in business networks requires an implementation. Often, the design qualities that best support experimental work are different from those normally considered "ideal" in industry. In complex economic scenarios such as TAC SCM, the desired design qualities include clean separation of infrastructure from decision processes, ease of implementation of multiple decision processes, clean separation of different decision processes from each other, and controllable generation of experimental data. The ability to compose agents with different combinations of decision processes enables testing the effectiveness of the competing decision models.

We have presented one way to construct such an agent, using a readily-available component framework[5] and a facility that allows metadata-driven composition of analysis and modeling tools using evaluators. Additionally we presented tools to visualize the network structure, and economic dashboards to present the current state of each business unit.

There are many possible extensions to the basic design we presented here. One that we are currently pursuing is to add an "executive" component to allocate "resources" to competing implementations of basic decision processes within a

---

[4] http://www.enterprise-dashboard.com

[5] We used the Apache Excalibur component framework, see http://excalibur.apache.org/.

single agent. This would allow a high degree of adaptability in the game environment, where the level of demand can fluctuate greatly, and where the actions of other agents can have a significant impact on the markets.

As implementation of business intelligence requires a lot of time, money and effort, managers need to know when to consider business intelligence and when not. We implemented our approach in TAC SCM, an abstraction of a real world supply-chain scenario. The next step is to create a web service wrapper around the evaluators, and integrate it in a real business network, such as the Dutch Flower auction (Kambil & van Heck, 1998; Kambil & van Heck, 2002).

We plan to implement automated web services (Sirin et al., 2002; Wu et al., 2003) to better connect to unknown network actors. This will guarantee a smooth run of the network as suggested by (van Hillegersberg, Boeke, & van den Heuvel, 2004).

Acknowledgements

Partial support for Maria Gini is gratefully acknowledged from the National Science Foundation under award NSF/IIS-0414466.

References

Adam, F., and Pomerol, J. Critical Factors in the Development of Executive Systems – Leveraging the Dashboard Approach. *Decision making support Systems: Achievements and challenges for the new decade* (pp. 305–330). PA, USA: IGI Publishing

Berry, P., Conley, K., Gervasio, M., Peintner, B., Uribe, T., Yorke-Smith, N.: Deploying a personalized time management agent. *In Proceedings of the Fifth international conference on autonomous agents and multi-agent systems*. Hakodate, Japan (2006)

Chopra, S., Meindl, P. *Supply Chain Management*. NJ, USA: Pearon Prentice Hall, (2004)

Collins, J., Arunachalam, R., Sadeh, N., Ericsson, J., Finne, N., Janson, S.: *The Supply Chain Management Game for the 2006 Trading Agent Competition* (Tech. Rep. No. CMU-ISRI-05-132) Carnegie Mellon University, Pittsburgh, PA, USA (2005)

Collins, J., Bilot, C., Gini, M., Mobasher, B. Decision processes in agent-based automated contracting. *IEEE Internet Computing*, 5(2), 61–72 (2001)

Collins, J., Ketter, W., Gini, M. Architectures for Agents in TAC SCM. In AAAI Spring Symposium on Architectures for Intelligent Theory-Based Agents (pp. 7–12). Stanford University, Palo Alto, CA, USA (2008)

CombineNet: *Sourcing solutions*. Retrieved from http://www.combinenet.com/sourcing solutions/ (2006)

Eckerson, W.W. *Performance Dashboards: Measuring, Monitoring, and Managing Your Business*. NY, USA: Wiley (2005)

Few, S. *Information Dashboard Design: The Effective Visual Communication of Data*. O'Reilly Media (2006)

Garud, R., Kumaraswamy, A., Langlois, R. *Managing in the Modular Age: Archi-tectures, Networks, and Organizations*. Oxford, England: Blackwell (2002)

Goldman, S., Nagel, R., Preiss, K. *Agile competitors and virtual organizations*. Van Nostrand Reinhold, NY, USA (1995)

He, M., Rogers, A., Luo, X., Jennings, N. R. Designing a successful trading agent for supply chain management. In Proceedings of the fifth international conference on autonomous agents and multi-agent systems (pp. 159–1166) Hakodate, Japan (2006)

van Heck, E., Vervest, P. Smart business networks: How the network wins. Communications of the ACM, *50*(6), 28–37 (2007). DOI http://doi.acm.org/10.1145/1247001.1247002

van Hillegersberg, J., Boeke, R., van den Heuvel, W. Potential of Webservices to enable smart business networks. Journal of Information Technology, *19*(4), 281–287 (2004)

Hoogeweegen, M., van Liere, D., Vervest, P., van der Meijden, L., de Lepper, I. Strategizing for mass customization by playing the business networking game. Decision Support Systems *42*(3), 1402–1412 (2006)

I2 *Next-generation planning*. Retrieved from http://i2.com/solution library/ng planning.cfm (2006)

Kambil, A., van Heck, E. Reengineering the Dutch Flower Auctions: A Framework for Analyzing Exchange Organizations. *Information Systems Research, 9*(1), 1–19 (1998)

Kambil, A., van Heck, *E. Making markets: How firms can design and profit from online auctions and exchanges*. Boston, MA, USA: Harvard Business School Press (2002)

Kambil, A., Short, J. Electronic integration and business network redesign: A roles-linkage perspective. *Journal of Management Information Systems, 10*(4), 59–83 (1994)

Kearns, M., Ortiz, L. The Penn-Lehman Automated Trading Project. IEEE Intelligent Systems *18*(6) 22–31 (2003)

Keller, P.W., Duguay, F.O., Precup, D. Redagent – winner of the TAC SCM 2003. SIGecom Exchanges, *4*(3), 1–8 (2004)

Ketter, W. *Identification and prediction of economic regimes to guide decision making in multi-agent marketplaces* (Ph.D. thesis, University of Minnesota, Twin-Cities, USA). (2007)

Ketter, W., Collins, J., Gini, M., Gupta, A., Schrater, P.: A predictive empirical model for pricing and resource allocation decisions. In Proceedings of Ninth international conference on Electronic Commerce (pp. 449–458). Minneapolis, MN, USA (2007)

Ketter, W., Collins, J., Gini, M., Gupta, A., Schrater, P.: Detecting and Forecasting Economic Regimes in Multi-Agent Automated Exchanges. Decision Support Systems (2008). In publication

Kiekintveld, C., Miller, J., Jordan, P.R., Wellman, M.P. Controlling a Supply Chain Agent Using Value-Based Decomposition. In Proceedings of Seventh ACM conference on Electronic Commerce (pp. 208–217). Ann Arbor, USA (2006)

Liere, D. *Network Horizon and the Dynamics of Network Positions: A Multi-Method Multi-Level Longitudinal Study of Interfirm Networks*, Ph.d. thesis RSM Erasmus University, Rotterdam, Netherlands) (2007)

Moraitis, P., Petraki, E., Spanoudakis, N.: Engineering JADE agents with the Gaia methodology. In R. Kowalszyk, J. Miller, H. Tianfield, and R. Unland (Eds.), *Lecture Notes in Computer Science*: Vol. 2592, Agent-Mediated Electronic Commerce: Designing Trading Agents and Mechanisms (pp. 77–91). Berlin: Springer (2003)

Niu, J., Cai, K., Parsons, S., Gerding, E., McBurney, P., Moyaux, T., et al. JCAT: A Platform for the TAC Market Design Competition. In Proceedings of the Seventh International Conference on autonomous agents and multi-agent systems (AAMAS 2008). Estoril, Portugal (2008)

Norman, T.J., Jennings, N.R., Faratin, P., Mamdani, E.H.: Designing and implementing a multi-agent architecture for business process management. In M.J. Wooldridge, J.P. Müller, and N.R. Jennings (eds.), *Lecture Notes in Artificial Intelligence.* Vol. 1193. Intelligent agents III (pp. 261–275). Berlin: Springer, (1997)

Pardoe, D., Stone, P.: Tactex-05: A champion supply chain management agent. In Proceedings of the Twenty-First National Conference on Artificial Intelligence (pp. 1389–1394). AAAI, Boston, MA, USA (2006)

Podobnik, V., Petric, A., Jezic, G. The crocodileagent: Research for efficient agent-based cross-enterprise processes. In R. Meersman, Z. Tari, and P. Herrero (Eds.), *On the Move to Meaningful Internet Systems 2006: OTM 2006 Workshops*: Vol. 4277 (pp. 752–762). Berlin: Springer (2006)

Sanchez, R. Strategic Flexibility in Product Competition. Strategic Management Journal, 16, 135–159 (1995)

Sandholm, T. Expressive commerce and its application to sourcing: How we conducted $35 billion of generalized combinatorial auctions. AI Magazine, *28*(3), 45–58 (2007)

Shmueli, G., Patel, N., Bruce, P. Data Mining for Business Intelligence: Concepts, Techniques, and Applications in Microsoft Office Excel with XLMiner. NY, USA: Wiley-Interscience (2006)

Sirin, E., Hendler, J., Parsia, B. Semi-automatic composition of web services using semantic descriptions. In Web Services: Modeling, Architecture and Infrastructure workshop in conjunction with 5th International Conference of Enterprise Information System 2003

Vervest, P., van Heck, E., Preiss, K., Pau, L.F. *Smart Business Networks*. Berlin: Springer, (2005)

Vervest, P., Preiss, K., Heck, E., Pau, L. The emergence of smart business networks. *Journal of Information Technology,* 19(4), 228–233 (2004)

Vetsikas, I.A., Selman, B. A principled study of the design tradeoffs for autonomous trading agents. In Proceedings of the Second international Conference on autonomous agents and multi-agent systems. Melbourne, Australia. (2003)

Vytelingam, P., Dash, R.K., He, M., Jennings, N.R.: Trading strategies for markets: A design framework and its application. In H.L. Poutr´e, N.M. Sadeh, and S. Janson (Eds.), *Lecture Noted in Artificial Intelligence*, Vol. 3937 (pp. 171–186) Agent-Mediated Electronic Commerce: Designing Trading Agents and Mechanisms. Berlin: Springer (2006)

Wellman, M.P., Wurman, P.R., O'Malley, K., Bangera, R., Lin, S., Reeves, D., et al. Designing the market game for a trading agent competition. IEEE Internet Computing, *5*(2), 43–51 (2001)

Wu, D., Parsia, B., Sirin, E., Hendler, J., Nau, D.: Automating DAML-S web services composition using SHOP2. In Proceedings of Second International Semantic Web Conference (ISWC2003), Sanibel Island, FL, USA.

Review of "Flexible Decision Support in a Dynamic Business Network"

Don't Forget the Bounded Rationality of the Agent Designer

Kul Bhushan C. Saxena

Management Development Institute, Gurgaon, India, bsaxena@mdi.ac.in

This paper (Collins, Ketter, & Gini, 2008) addresses the managerial needs for intelligent decision support in a Smart Business Network (SBN) environment and recommends autonomous software agent technology to build such systems. Furthermore, it demonstrates this with an example of a business network test-bed of Trading Agent Competition for Supply Chain Management and an example architecture for such a decision support system (DSS) (called Minne TAC trading agent), which can be used both as a flexible research tool and a teaching tool. The flexibility of this tool is demonstrated by its capability of dynamically connecting and disconnecting various nodes of a SBN, comprising of 'decision elements' nodes and 'evaluator' (decision modelling services) nodes.

Flexibility as a design criteria has been at the heart of the concept of a DSS right from the days of traditional architectures proposed for a DSS (Saxena & Kaul, 1986; Sprague & Carlson, 1982). These architectures provided decision support flexibility through a model-base comprising of a number of models and the choice of a model was made by the decision-maker by actuating a model management subsystem. Intelligent agent technology embeds intelligence to automatically invoke the required model as deemed fit for the decision environment, and thus frees the system from the bounded rationality constraints of the decision maker. However, the intelligence embedded in most agents is generally limited to structured routine decisions which are largely deterministic rather than judgemental or experiential tacit-knowledge based. From a practical real-world perspective, this may limit the application of this technology to relatively simple and narrow rule-based decision situations, which may not be the case in the contemporary complex business environments where SBN applications may be more appropriate.

Another type of flexibility required in a DSS is in its user interface which needs to be designed differently for a novice versus an expert DSS user as well as for a frequent versus an infrequent user (Saxena & Kaul, 1986). However, the paper does not address this issue.

As for the autonomous nature of software agents, it frees the decision making process from the bounded rationality of decision-maker, but the autonomy of the software also constrains the decision-making process by the bounded rationality of the software agent designer(s)! This can be handled through exception-handling routines providing a 'manual override' disabling the automated decision process. The more complex the decision situation, the more may be the need for such exception handling procedures, unless the software agent has an experiential learning capability.

In spite of these limitations, the proposed architecture demonstrates a goal-oriented service composition in a SBN environment, provides a visualisation tool which may help decision-makers in understanding the active network architecture at any time, and supports building a dashboard to facilitate monitoring of critical business performance parameters. Thus, the proposed DSS tool can be used as a powerful teaching tool supporting action learning, and provides a valuable contribution to software engineering and multi-agent systems technology.

References

Collins, J., Ketter, W., & Gini, M. (2008). Flexible decision support in a dynamic business network. In P. H. M. Vervest, D. W. van Liere, & L. Zheng (Eds.), *The Network Experience – New value from smart business network*. Berlin: Springer.

Saxena, K. B. C., & Kaul, M. (1986). A conceptual architecture for DSS generators. *Information & Management, 10*(3), 149–157.

Sprague, R. H., & Carlson, E. D. (1982). Building effective decision support systems. Englewood Cliffs, NJ: Prentice-Hall

16. Key Success Factors for ICT-System Implementation in SME's

Jan Stentoft Arlbjørn[1], Torben Damgaard[2] and Anders Haug[3]

[1]University of Southern Denmark, Denmark, jar@sam.sdu.dk

[2]University of Southern Denmark, Denmark, torben@sam.sdu.dk

[3]University of Southern Denmark, Denmark, adg@sam.sdu.dk

Abstract

These years, small and medium-sized enterprises (SME's) are facing management challenges related to secure competitiveness in global production networks and smart business networks. Specialized sub-suppliers are able to compete in a global market, e.g. due to high quality and reliability. However, research also indicates that SMEs when compared with larger companies are less likely to create organizational changes when new systems are being implemented and that they have too much focus on day-to-day operations in the absence of strategic considerations on information communication technology (ICT)-systems. The paper reports on a study on explorative case studies and a quantitative-survey on ICT-implementation in SMEs. Based on this, hypotheses and the research methodology are outlined for further research in the use of ICT in SMEs.

Introduction

These years, companies are facing a number of challenges to maintain competitiveness in the markets, in which they operate. The globalization of the economy with free trade and exchange of goods and the removal of duty barriers are fostering true global supply chains. This puts pressure on wage intensive manufacturing companies, and some companies experience that normal effectiveness and efficiency improvements are no longer sufficient in the global race against competitors from Eastern Europe, India, and China. Thus, several companies initiate outsourcing and/or off shoring activities in order to remain competitive. Companies in general and SMEs in global supply chains and networks in particular meet several challenges:

1. Shorter product life-cycles which, among other things, require increased capabilities to synchronize product phase-ins with product phase-outs,
2. Increased customer requirements for documentation of the product (e.g. FDA approval report, batch numbers, certificates, production reports) which enforce companies to build and maintain documentation systems,
3. Increased customer requirements for traceability of products, components and raw material in the supply chain (e.g. customer access to some parts of a company's ERP-system),
4. Increased requirements to fast time-to-market (stressing the importance of business processes across the company, e.g. from marketing, R&D, purchasing, production, warehousing, and distribution),
5. Companies integrate with customers, suppliers and competitors in chains and networks,
6. New technology provides opportunities to create transparency between different companies in supply chains and networks (e.g. stock levels, sales forecasts, and production plans),
7. Make or buy (outsourcing and off shoring), and
8. Corporate social responsibility.

However, there are also other ways to improve competitiveness, such as looking internally and optimizing systems and business processes. Such initiatives are important in order to become an attractive business partner in global production networks and smart business networks. Global production networks can be defined as globally organized nexus of interconnected functions and operations by firms and non-firm institutions through which goods and services are produced and distributed. Such networks not only integrate firms (and parts of firms) into structures which blur traditional organizational boundaries through the development of diverse forms of equity and non-equity relationships, but also integrate regional and national economies in ways that have enormous implications for their developmental outcomes (Coe, Hess, Yeung, Ficken, & Henderson, 2004). According to Dicken (2007: 15) especially three dimensions of production network are important: (1) their governance structure, (2) their spatiality and their territorial embeddedness. According to Vervest, Preiss, van Heck, & Pau (2004) a smart business network (SBN) is a group of participating businesses (organizational entities or actors that form nodes which are linked together via one pr more communication networks that form the links, or lines between the nodes. They operate with compatible goals, and interact in novel ways. An SBN is perceived by each participant as increasing its own value which is sustainable over time. An SBN is resilient if one or more businesses, nodes in the network, mal-functions. Small and medium-sized enterprises (SMEs) are major players in such networks. However, their competitiveness is threatened by companies from new industrialized countries, and large Western companies undergo technological and organizational innovations that make them competitive against the SMEs (Cagliano, Spina, Verganti, & Zotteri, 1998). In order to survive the competition from low wage-countries in Eastern Europe, Asia and India, SMEs need to be flexible (agile) and provide good quality and fast and reliable deliveries. Furthermore, the SMEs are pressed on profit margins for which reason they have to look to an increasing degree internally for better resource utilization in order to maintain the same overall profit levels. The flexibility is necessary when SMEs participate in global supply chains or global production networks, but, at the same time their internal processes need to have global quality. Both are necessary to act as "connective nodes in supply networks" (Andersen & Christensen, 2004).

Enterprise Resource Planning (ERP) systems, one type of information communication technology (ICT), can be seen as one of the most innovative developments of the 1990s within information technology (Al-Mashari, 2003 and Buonanno, Faverio, Ravarini, Sciuto, & Tagliavini, 2005). Implementing an ERP system in an organization is often a complex and time consuming task that requires several people to work together in regard to changed business processes and system dentition, development and implementation, often with limited economic and human resources. In practice, several enterprises engage in Business Process Reengineering (BPR) and IT projects to achieve integration. However, the impact is often not successful. Doherty, King, & Al-Mushayt (2003) reported that up to 90% of all BPR or IT projects fail to meet their goals. Among these projects, 80% were overdue and over budget, and 40% were abandoned. They attributed this failure primarily to the inadequacies in the treatment of organizational issues, rather than a technology problem. This reminds us that the application of information technology is not easily automated. The real value of information technology depends on its use to redesign the business processes and organizations (Hammer, 1990, Doherty, King, & Al-Mushayt, 2003).

Much research has been done into ERP implementations and BPR projects in large companies regarding topics as key success factors, project management, return on investment (Al-Mashari, 2003). System implementation in small and medium-sized enterprises (SME) seems to be less researched. SMEs differ in several aspects compared with large companies, such as resource pools, CEO involvement in operational decisions, and a production mode focus at the expense of strategic planning (Huin, 2004). Furthermore, there is no general agreement on the effectiveness of such systems, and the ERP system's adoption in SMEs is still low (Buonanno, Faverio, Ravarini, Sciuto, & Tagliavini, 2005). Is it really necessary to develop new ERP solutions dedicated for SMEs, or do the currently available systems cover the needs? If so, the problem may be found in other parts such as managing and organizing ICT implementation projects in SMEs. Also, how should SMEs organize such systems in order that they can be integrated in global production networks and smart business networks? Why do we see so few system solutions and implementations for SMEs when they are prevalent for large companies? Are there certain characteristics that make them function differently? Why do SMEs not implement ERP-systems? What are the enablers and barriers?

To address such questions this paper describes two explorative case studies and a quantitative-survey on ICT-implementation in SMEs. With this basis, the paper outlines hypotheses and a research methodology for further research in the use of ICT in SMEs.

The remainder of the paper is structured as follows. In the next section, a review of relevant literature is presented. Then the applied methodology is described. Hereafter follows a section that presents and discusses data from the qualitative and quantitative analyses. The paper ends with a conclusion in last section.

Literature Review

The focus on reengineering business processes was introduced in the beginning of the 1990s (Hammer & Champy, 1993) as Business Process Re-engineering (BPR). The approach has a radical view of changes and focuses on eliminating non-value added activities in cross-functional business processes. Companies primarily decide to implement BPR projects in order to improve customer service, reduce cycle time, reduce production and service costs, and to improve quality (Carr & Johansson, 1995). However, in spite of popularity, several BPR projects failed. Burgess (1998) summarized reasons for such failures to: (1) A lack of identification of the competitive advantages that the new business process should support, (2) A too narrowly scoped change project with little impact on the overall company performance (Hall, Rosenthal, & Wade, 1993), (3) A not sufficiently deep change that leads staff to fall back into old habits, (4) A lack of top management commitment, (5) A hazard use of consultants (a prince who is not himself wise cannot be wisely advised), and (6) A lack of readiness to handle unexpected events during the change process.

If an organization strives to install a system without establishing a clear vision and understanding of the business propositions, the integration efforts can quickly turn into a disaster, no matter how competent the software package selected (Davenport, 1998). Contributions of ERP systems together with BPR can be significant in terms of scope, configurability and integrativeness (Huq, Huq, & Cutright, 2006). The inability to realize the value of IT systems implementations may be found in the lack of alignment between business and IT strategies (Henderson & Venktraman, 1999). This is also the case for the ability to provide effective change management (Yarberry, 2007). Although it might be difficult to optimize internal business processes due to cross-functional alignment, it is even harder between companies (Hammer, 2001) which cover the domain of supply chain management (Min & Mentzer, 2004).

According to Carr (2003) it is wrong thinking to believe that IT's potency and ubiquity have increased. The same applies for its strategic value. Today, chief executives routinely talk about the strategic value of information technology, how they can use IT to gain competitive edge, and about the digitization of their business models. Previously, an executive would seldom let his fingers touch a keyboard. Carr (2003) defines new rules of IT investments as: (1) Spend less (studies show that the companies with the biggest IT investments rarely post the best financial results), (2) Follow, don't lead (the longer you wait to make an IT purchase, the more you will get for your money) and (3) Focus on vulnerability, not opportunities, what are the weak spots of the software? He concludes that a company can only gain an edge over rivals by having or doing something that they cannot have or do, and that today core functions of IT (i.e. data storage, data processing, and data transport) have become available and affordable to all. In other words, today's technology is developed to an extent, in which the true competitiveness does not come from the available technological features, but merely from the way it is implemented and how business processes are being developed and maintained.

Success of ERP implementations is traditionally measured in technical, economical and strategic terms, how well and smoothly the business fits the implementation, ERP adopting of employees and managers and ERP adopting of customers and suppliers (Marcus, Axline, Petrie, & Tanis, 2000).

Systems in this paper span from automatic systems for which companies pay a license to use over a diversity of systems developed in Access and Excel and other software programs to manual systems with pen, paper and binders. In many companies, an unknown number of systems exist. Often there is no overview of the actual number of systems. Arlbjørn, Wong, & Seerup (2007) reports from a system development project with a large Danish manufacturer in which they found more than 117 different systems (or "kingdoms") more or less connected. Instead of using core functionally in the previous ERP system, new systems were coded in the top of the system. The system structure was characterized by many such buddings. About 30% of the identified systems were local files mainly developed in Excel and Access by staff primarily because they did not succeed in requiring new software or modifications to the existing systems. Therefore, they developed their own solutions making the company vulnerable especially in the case of such employees leaving the company. The company experienced a huge change process that combined business process reengineering and ERP implementation.

Mabert, Soni, & Venkataraman (2000) carried out a similar study of 193 US companies that had implemented ERP-system or were in the process of doing so. The study by Mabert, Soni, & Venkataraman (2000) shows that about 70% of the small firms used a big-bang or mini-big-bang implementation strategy, about 66% of the medium sized and only about 23% of the large companies.

Olhager & Selldin (2003) present a study of ERP-implementation in Swedish manufacturing firms, including 190 answered questionnaires. About 85 of these firms have less than 250 employees, i.e. SMEs according to, e.g. the definition by the European Commission from 2003. Their findings are among other things that: 83,6% of Swedish manufacturing firms have or is in the process of implementing ERP-systems; the cost for implementing ERP-systems range from an average of 0.5% of annual revenues for large enterprises and 3.5% for smaller enterprises;

and that the most common improvements are related to information access and intra-organizational interaction. The study also shows that in general several benefits have been achieved, in particular relating to having more information available within a short time. Of the studied companies (85% SMEs) 62.5% used a big-bang or small big-bang implementation strategy.

Buonanno, Faverio, Ravarini, Sciuto, & Tagliavini, 2005 have completed a study of ERP implementations in SMEs and large companies. The study leads to several interesting findings. First, the empirical questionnaire-survey data show that there is a strong correlation between company size and ERP adoption, i.e. the larger the company, the higher probability for ERP implementation. Secondly, SMEs always scheduled a limited organizational change in the case of ERP adoption, thus they seem not to consider ERP systems as a keystone for organizational innovation. Thirdly, SMEs seem to be less inclined to radical change and less aware of the organizational impact caused by the implementation of an ERP system. Fourthly, SMEs' traditional focus on operations and day-by-day management, coupled with a lack of strategic view on ICT, could be partially accountable for these findings. Fifthly, SMEs disregard financial constraints as the main cause for non-adoption of ERP systems, suggesting structural and organizational reasons as major ones. Thus, SMEs have other conditions for such ERP implementations. SMEs differ from large companies in important ways affecting their information seeking practices (Buonanno, Faverio, Ravarini, Sciuto, & Tagliavini, 2005): (1) Lack of information system management, (2) Frequent concentration of information-gathering responsibilities into one or two individuals, rather than the specialization of scanning activities among top executives, (3) Lower level of resources available for information gathering and (4) Quantity and quality of available environmental information. Many SMEs do not have sufficient resources or will not commit resources to long implementations. SMEs are often unaware of the potential benefits of BPR (Cagliano, Spina, Verganti, & Zotteri, 1998). Larger companies usually have a board and a professional staff for managing the operation. In SMEs the founder is typically part of the daily operations with his or her own agenda. Levy & Powell (2000) argue that ISS recommendations in small firms need to take account of organizational change issues as much as information system implementation. SMEs generally suffer from a widespread lack of culture as to the concept of business processes (Buonanno, Faverio, Ravarini, Sciuto, & Tagliavini, 2005).

Some ERP vendors have developed light versions of their software targeted for SMEs in order to reduce software and implementation costs. In spite of such initiatives, there is no general agreement on the effectiveness of such systems, and the ERP systems adoption in SMEs is still low (Buonanno, Faverio, Ravarini, Sciuto, & Tagliavini, 2005). Crucial success factors in ERP implementations are change and project management competences which, according to Buonanno, Faverio, Ravarini, Sciuto, & Tagliavini (2005), challenge SMEs with a potential lack of preparation. Factors that have strong impact, positive as well as negative, on ERP adoption in SMEs are scarcity of resources, lack of strategic planning, limited IT expertise, and limited opportunity to adopt a process-oriented view of the business (Buonanno,

Faverio, Ravarini, Sciuto & Tagliavini, 2005). Huin (2004) has outlined what he calls strategic and operational requirements (SOR) of SMEs that need to be considered when implementing ERP systems in SMEs. He identified nine SORs that also function as key-characteristics of SMEs: (1) Low levels of organizational hierarchy, (2) CEO involvement in operational decisions, (3) "Blurred" departmental walls, (4) Production modes in SMEs, (5) Planned forecasts vs. real forecasts, (6) Rate of changes in orders, (7) Short lead-time in manufacturing, (8) High staff turnover and (9) Customers' special demands.

Methodology

The applied methodology in this paper is based on two primary sources: An explorative field study and a questionnaire survey on ERP implementation in Danish SMEs.

Explorative Case Studies

The authors have followed two SME's over a period of six months beginning with an overview of existing systems – manual systems as well as software systems. During the period of six months, this process created AS-IS overviews of the system infrastructure on which the two SMEs' business activities are founded. Furthermore, the process also identified to which extent the existing systems are being applied and receive input to consider to what degree these systems sustain the SMEs' strategic objectives. The AS-IS process has been developed by the companies themselves but with advice from the author group. Three meetings were held to create this view. Based on this AS-IS overview, one of the companies decided to implement a customer relationship management module (CRM) to their existing ERP-package. Therefore, we have followed this case company a bit further than the other.

A Questionnaire Survey

The second source for empirical data is a questionnaire survey carried out in the spring 2008. The sample is randomly picked from databases on five industries in the region of Southern Denmark' production industry, which is dominated by two clusters in the food industry and the stainless steel industry. The sample included companies from the steel industry, the machinery construction industry, the wood industry, the plastics industry, and the food industry. The total sample contacted was 182 and so far 95 of these have completed this. Of these 28 uses or are in the process of implementing ERP-systems or related IT-systems (planning systems, order systems, etc.). Research assistants who interviewed the companies by phone completed the questionnaires. Based on a structured and primarily quantitative survey, the telephone interviewer contacted all the companies directly. The interviewee either answered the survey on the phone (84 respondents), filled out an electronic version sent out from the interviewer (11 respondents), refused to participate or the contact failed because the company did not exist any more or similar reasons (87 respondents).

- The survey has a total sample of: 182 respondents
- Total reply was: 95 respondents (52% of the population and 15% of the total sample size of companies in the industry in the region).

The sample is perceived to represent a broad range of manufacturing companies from companies with small and almost no use of ERP, to companies with professional and heavy use of ERP systems. The survey is focused on the relationship between the way each company is prepared and the effects of this on the implementation of ERP system. From the sample size and dimensions, the survey can contribute with significant answers.

Data Analysis and Discussion

Explorative Case Studies

Case alfa. Case company *alfa* has been working extensively with stainless steel sheets for use in tankers and food and processing plants since 1964. The company's client base consists of a wide range of Danish and foreign companies, who primarily require the assistance of the case company's production know-how. Furthermore, customers are also companies who purchase complete tank and processing plants, designed by the case company and supplied to their client-specific requirements.

The case company has highly qualified employees. The foundation is based on a highly-qualified workforce, employing approximately 25 sheet metal workers specializing in stainless steel. The products offered by case company alfa are: Tanks, pressure vessels, pressure vessels with agitator, special vessels in stainless steel, processing equipment for spray drying, industrial fume filter systems, unit construction, transportation tanks for the food industry, and processing equipment for the treatment of foodstuff. Often the customers have to comply with the American health agency Food and Drug administration (FDA) which demand huge documentation requirement at case company alfa.

This company tried to implement new ERP facilities to handle the planning and the purchasing operations. They see the need to use this soft ware, e.g. to meet the increasing demands on traceability and documented processes from customers. They are light users of ERP-system in the beginning of the process and they develop only a little in the studied period. This is mainly due to missing human resources. A key person quit in the beginning of the process, therefore, the project came to a halt. This shows the vulnerability for such an initiative. In the company there is very much focus on operations and to win the next order, and no other person in the company could take over, when the key person quit. They almost do not use external advisors and the existing IT systems are more than 10 years old.

Case beta. The *beta* company is a contract manufacturer specialized in the field of stainless steel production, primarily for industries producing foodstuffs, medicine and chemistry. The Company has 22 well educated industrial tinsmiths, who all make products of high level craftsmanship. They have acquired the requested welding certificates and they are used to producing tanks and equipment that are approved by the authorities and meet the most strictly hygienic requirements. Quality is in focus and has always been at beta. Quality is the brand of the company and its products. All employees take pride in ensuring that the manufactured products are maintained at a high quality level through the complete manufacturing process. No compromise is ever accepted as to the quality, and the employees are comfortable with this. The employees are proud of their company and the products being manufactured.

A new employee was engaged, administratively, to whom the owner had held out prospects of being co-owner and a possible owner take over. Existing work flows have been analyzed such as processes from receipt of customer orders to supply of the final products. A great amount of manual work was found, including manual work in Excel and Word. A weak knowledge sharing was evident and much time spent on starting from scratch again (no systematical reuse). Documentation was organized in manual binders and the company decided to use ERP-system to support the planning, purchasing and customer handling. ERP-system have existed in the company soft ware for years, only a CRM-system was bought and planned to be implemented in the company. The strengthened use of the ERP-system improved the order making process and exchange working was implemented in the ERP-system from the former Excel files. The key resource person was sacked the day before the expiry of the 6-month test period. The owner did not agree to the changes proposed by the new employee, but the effect was a move backward to a focus on operations. The new use of the ERP-system partly failed.

Case study discussion. This explorative piece of research has identified three important change management areas which we find important to address early when SMEs want to implement ICT-systems. Table 16.1 summarizes the main findings from the two explorative case studies. The change management areas are concerned with an explicit focus on: (1) Capabilities to understand and handle the change process that the ICT-system implementation fosters, (2) Capabilities to understand the use of existing systems and tools for implementation, and (3) Existing implementation skills.

Table 16.1 Summary of two explorative case studies

Case Alfa	Case Beta
Orders give focus on operations and daily routines	The most important resource person for development of business procedures is sacked
High needs of supplement to existing ERP-system	Owner cannot see the value of his work – perceives to give no direct effect on earnings
One person implementation process	One person implementation process
Weak use of ERP-systems	The resource person very important for implementing the ERP-system. His disappearance weakens the implementation process a lot
The most important resource person quits and development comes to a stop	No resource person means back to focus on operations and daily routines

Capabilities to Understand and Handle the Change Process of the ICT-System Implementation

During this reported study of system analysis and implementation in SMEs there seems to be at least two important change management issues related to enabling the staff of the SMEs to understand and handle the change process. First, it is important to involve the staff in an in-depth AS-IS mapping of systems being applied (from manual systems to different software packages). This process of visualizing workflows and information flows often provides chocking results (e.g. showing a lot of non-value added loops of work, waiting time or decision making based knowledge embedded in the head of specific staff (tacit knowledge). Secondly, this knowledge should be coupled with strategic considerations about the future. What kind of role should the specific SME actually play in global production networks? Due to the previously mentioned challenges for SMEs and the differences compared with larger firms, it is important to set up activities that maintain a strategic development focus during the process of ICT-system implementation.

Capabilities to Understand the use of Existing or New Systems and Tools for Implementation

The second major change management area is related to the competency to understand how systems can be exploited to gain competitiveness. To which degree are the existing systems actually utilized? During this research, e.g. we have identified a planning system in one of the companies that was bought several years ago but has never been used. Reasons for a non-use are reported as lack of understanding the workflow that this system should sustain and lack of training to use the software. This stresses the importance of anchoring such system implementation at some specific persons in the company, who, over time, can secure understanding and appliance of the system as intended. There are a great number of ERP-software packages available on the market and several of these explicitly focus on customizing the software to SME segments. However, this paper argues that the question of software house is secondary to the question of an indepth business understanding of the current situation and actual implementation skills. As a related perspective it might be considered whether the software should actually be a standard version or developed by the firm. Recent research argues for in-house development of proprietary software since it will increase the control of core IT functions (Olsen & Sætre, 2007). Change management capabilities may also be related to looking beyond the existing systems in the company and thus searching for new systems. The process should not be constrained by a focus merely on the existing pool of systems. It is important to think out of the box. Lastly, it can be considered whether systems should be operated by a third party operated or even operated by a customer or a supplier?

Implementation Skills

This change management area is considered as the most crucial element by the case companies. The main characteristic of SMEs as being day-to-day focused and thus lacking a strategic focus, their lack of resources and competences in different functions (fewer people should know more), and a lack of a process view of the firms' activities in order to be competitive in global production networks are major road blocks for ICT-system implementations.

Questionnaire Survey

The analysis of the data of the questionnaire–survey is divided into three sub-sections. First, analyses of questions related to the preparation phase of the system implementation are presented. Secondly, implementation issues are being analyzed. The last sub-section contains analyses of answers to operation of the system and evaluation of the implementation.

The preparation phase. The motivations of the 28 selected companies for initiating an ICT project are shown in Table 16.2.

As seen, about 60% found an increase of efficiency as one of the most important motivations for starting the projects. Such an efficiency improvement is

Table 16.2 Motivation for initiating the ICT Project

Motivation	Percent
Reduce costs	20.7
Increase efficiency	58.6
Development of the company	37.9
Free resources of employees	34.5
Free management/administration resources	24.1
Other	51.7

Table 16.3 Readiness for the ICT-system

Readiness factors	1	2	3	4	5	Not sure
It was clear which advantages the systems could provide	7.1	3.6	21.4	35.7	32.1	0.0
System requirements were clearly defined at project start	3.6	7.1	17.9	35.7	25.0	10.7
The organization had adequate expertise to define system requirements	10.7	0.0	25.0	50.0	14.3	0.0
The company had a clear picture of the competitive advantage the system could provide	7.1	14.3	35.7	25.0	10.7	7.1

Scale 1-5, "strongly disagree" to "strongly agree"

Table 16.4 Implementation issues (1)

Implementation issues	1	2	3	4	5	Not sure
Relevant employees were well-informed and adequately involved in the project	7.1	7.1	28.6	42.9	14.3	0.0
Adequate resources were available during implementation	3.6	7.1	35.7	25.0	25.0	3.6

Scale 1–5, "strongly disagree" to "strongly agree"

related to the often very significant effects of the better possibilities of sharing, accessing and administering business information. In this light, it may be surprising that only about 60% saw this aspect as a major motivation factor. In Table 16.3 is described how the selected companies evaluated factors related to their readiness for implementing the ICT-system.

As seen in Table 16.3, a slight majority of the companies found that they were well-prepared for initiating the project. However, about 40% did either disagree or thought that they were neither well-prepared or not. The implementation phase. Tables 16.4 and 16.5 show different issues relevant for the implementation phase.

The far most common reason given for not having adequate resources during the implementation phase was that the company was too busy with daily operations. The problems during the project that were mentioned were primarily different technical issues. The unexpected events that emerged during the project were mainly related to technical and organizational issues.

Table 16.5 Implementation issues (2)

Implementation issues	Yes	No	Not sure
Adequate resources have been available to handle change processes related to the systems	60.7	39.3	0.0
There have been problems during the course of the project	71.4	28.6	0.0
Unexpected events occurred during the implementation process	57.1	39.3	3.6

As seen about 90% found that adequate resources for technical issues were present, but, on the other hand, resources to handle change processes were inadequate in about 40% of the cases. Furthermore, as seen, most companies experienced problems during the project. In Table 16.6, the course of the implementation phase is evaluated.

Table 16.6 Evaluation of the implementation phase

Implementation evaluation	Yes	No	Not sure
Employees were more concerned with daily operations than the implementation process	57.1	39.3	3.6
Management was deeply involved in the implementation process	67.9	28.6	3.6
The ICT project was linked to the company strategy	78.6	17.9	3.6
Employees were lacking understanding of the relevance of the project	14.3	82.1	3.6

The evaluation of the implementation phase shows that in many companies (about 40%) daily operations were given higher priority than the project. This indicates that the project has not been given adequate resources or priority.

The operation and evaluation phases. Table 16.7 shows how the ICT projects are evaluated by the companies. The ones not completing the implementation at the right time gave reasons such as inadequate human resources, technical problems and poor time plans. The companies not completing the project according to budgets mainly gave reasons related to planning. The mentioned requirements that the system places on the employees are mostly related to training in the use of and understanding the system.

Table 16.7 Evaluation of the ICT project

Project evaluation	Yes	No	Not sure
Was the implementation completed at the right time?	60.7	32.1	7.1
Was the implementation carried out according to budgets?	57.1	28.6	14.3
Have the planned advantages been achieved?	82.1	7.1	10.7
Does the system work as planned?	92.9	3.6	3.6
Do the systems place new requirements for employee competencies?	60.7	39.3	0.0

As seen in Table 16.7, about one third of the companies did not carry out the project according to the time plans. Also almost one third did not complete the project according to the budgets. Such issues may reflect that many companies give ICT projects too little resources or priority. Table 16.8 shows future ICT plans of the company.

Table 16.8 Future ICT plans

ICT plans	Yes	No	Not sure
Does the company have concrete plans of implementing additional ICT systems?	28.6	71.4	0.0
Is there a desire for new systems, but not adequate resources to start a project?	10.7	89.3	0.0

Discussion

Only about 60% of the companies found that they were well-prepared for their IT-projects, in the sense that most of the companies knew what they could expect from the system and had produced clear definitions of the requirements for the IT-system. The remainder only felt partly prepared or not prepared at all. This could be an indication that the methods needed or process models for carrying out an ICT project are not present or the companies are not aware of their existence. In connection to the lack of preparation for many companies, the discovery that the most common reason given for not having adequate resources during the imple-mentation phase is that the company was too busy with daily operations, is not surprising. As described in literature, underestimation of the resources required for completing an ICT project is common.

An interesting finding is that about 90% found that adequate resources for technical issues were present, but, the resources to handle change processes were inadequate in about 40% of the cases. This also corresponds with the literature where it is often pointed out that ICT projects are often seen as technical projects, implying that organizational issues are neglected.

Compared to earlier studies, a surprisingly high number of companies completed the project according to time plans and budgets, both about 60%. Whether this has actually been the case, or that the explanation is that time plans and budgets have been modified underway is something that needs to be investigated later. However, the fact that about one third did not meet their time plans and about one third did not meet their budgets still illustrates that there is a problem in many ICT projects, and therefore a need for more research in this area.

Finally, most of the companies find that their system lives up to their expectations, and that the expected benefits have been achieved. The companies that did not believe to have obtained the expected benefits, all gave the reason that this was because their project was still in the implementation phase, and that they believe to achieve the expected benefits later. Therefore, the results of our study seems to be somewhat consistent with the study by Olhager & Selldin (2003), who found that Swedish SMEs to a great extent experience benefits from implementing an ERP system, rather than failures.

Conclusion and Implications

The study presented in this paper does not provide detailed explanation of why many of the individual projects have been able to meet their time plans and budgets, while others did not; but only rather superficial explanations, i.e. lack of human resources, technical problems, and poor time plans. There are several factors that can have been decisive for the success of some of the investigated SMEs, for instance:

- The implemented ERP-systems are simple
- Little ERP-system functionality is used
- Relatively large budgets have been given to the projects
- The projects have not been very ambitious
- Budgets and time-plans have been loosely defined.

To get in depth with such questions, the next step is to carry out qualitative studies of selected companies of the study. A planned multiple case study survey will involve 25–30 companies. The process of implementation will be monitored and the researchers will also be involved in the design and the actual implementation process. E.g. resources will be used to involve relevant advisors in the process. This investigation could provide insights concerning the investment in customization of the standard ERP software, and how the radical changes of existing business processes are because of the ERP system. Also it should be investigated in what sense the studied SMEs believe that they have been well-prepared for engaging in their ERP project. Finally, it would be interesting to learn more about how the SMEs studied have dealt with issues such as: training of users, daily support, integration with other information systems, etc.

But also, the he discussion of the research data in previous section raises a range of questions we need to approach, when the purpose is to explore implementation of ICT-systems in SMEs. The aim is to follow implementation processes in SMEs in a processual way, because the discussion has revealed the implementation process (in itself) as the critical barrier for successful use of ICT-systems in SMEs. In this implementation process, we need to cope with at least the following issues:

1 Lack of knowledge about which ICT-systems are needed
1a   Does the SME need to extend its existing systems?
1b   If not present, how will the ICT expert knowledge be provided?
2 Lack of business understanding
2a   Not only the manager/management, but also the users and other related persons need an understanding of the advantages and disadvantages of ICT-systems.
2b   If not present, how can they achieve this understanding during the process?
3 Lack of understanding of business processes
3a   Identification of critical points in the business process must be handled through the implementation process.
3b   If not present, how can identification of critical points take place?
4 Lack of organizational anchoring
4a   If the SME does not have an organizing plan, how it can be provided?
5 Lack of ICT implementation experiences and skills
5a   How can SME representatives obtain the capabilities needed to implement and use new systems?
5b   To what extent can the capabilities be bought? If a thorough understanding of business processes is needed to adapt new ICT, it can be a barrier towards buying ICT-systems.

In order to investigate various implementation processes, this piece of research suggests that future research can proceed with a quantitative survey of at least about 200 SMEs in order to identify a number of about 30–40 case firms engaged in implementing ICT-systems. There is a need for variance in firm type, the ICT-systems they are trying to implement, and their capabilities to work with the implementation process. When 30–40 case firms have been identified, the following case study is suggested:

- Firstly, a pre-analysis is needed to identify the need for information systems. The perception and diagnosis of existing processes will be described. As will the organization, key persons, and the need for change.
- Secondly, we proceed to the Core analysis. The core analysis is a diagnosis of the ICT supported systems. The need for and exclusion of an ICT supported system will be discussed and selected according to the future processes which the firm aims to fulfill and participate in.

- Thirdly, we follow the focal Implementing process. Different implementation processes with different complexity are followed during a period of six months.
- Fourthly, a Follow-up Sequential analysis of the implementation processes at least every six months in a two to three year period to analyze improvements and document the pros and cons of activities and processes.

The managerial implications of this study are expected to be considerable. The study will be a major step towards a process model for SMEs to develop and implement ICT-systems relevant for their persistent participation on the globalized scene.

References

Al-Mashari, M. (2003). Enterprise resource planning (ERP) systems: a research agenda? *Industrial Management & Data Systems, 103*(1), 165–170.

Andersen, P. H., & Christensen, P. R. (2004). Bridges over troubled water: suppliers as connective nodes in global supply networks. *Journal of Business Research, 58*(9), 1261–1273.

Arlbjørn, J. S., Wong, C. Y. & Seerup, S. (2007). Achieving competitiveness through supply chain integration. *International Journal of Integrated Supply Management, 3*(1), 4–24.

Buonanno, G., Faverio, P., Ravarini, A., Sciuto, D., & Tagliavini, M. (2005). Factors affecting ERP system adoption: A comparative analysis between SMEs and large companies. *Journal of Enterprise Information Management, 18*(4), 384–426.

Burgess, R. (1998). Avoiding supply chain management failure: Lesson from business process re-engineering. *The International Journal of Logistics Management, 9*(1), 15–23.

Cagliano, R., Spina, G., Verganti, R., & Zotteri, G. (1998). Designing BPR support services for small firms. *International Journal of Operations & Production Management, 18*(9/10), 865–885.

Carr, N. G. (2003). IT doesn't matter. *Harvard Business Review, 81*(5), 41–49.

Carr, D. K. & Johansson, H. J. (1995). Best practices in reengineering: What works and what doesn't in the reengineering process. New York: McGraw-Hill.

Coe, N. M., Hess, M., Yeung, H. W. -C., Ficken, P., & Henderson, J. (2004). 'Globalizing' regional development: a global production networks perspective. *Transactions of the Institute of British Geographers, 29*(4), 468–484.

Davenport, T. H. (1998). Putting the enterprise into the enterprise system. *Harvard Business Review, 76*(4), 121–131.

Dicken, P. (2007). Global shift: Mapping the changing contours of the world economy. London: Sage Publications.

Doherty, N. F., King, M. & Al-Mushayt, O. (2003). The impact of inadequacies in the treatment of organizational issues on information systems development projects. *Information & Management, 41*(1), 49–62.

Hall, G. J., Rosenthal, J., & Wade, J. (1993). How to make re-engineering really work. *Harvard Business Review, 71*(6), 119–131.

Hammer, M. and Champy, J. (1993) *Reengineering the Corporation – a Manifesto for Business Revolution*, Nicholas Brealey Publishing, London.

Hammer, M. (2001). The superefficient company. *Harvard Business Review, 79*(8), 82–91.

Henderson, J. C., & Venkatraman, N. (1999). Strategic alignment: Leveraging information technology for transforming organizations. *IBM Systems Journal, 32*(1), 472–484.

Huin, S. F. (2004). Managing deployment of ERP systems in SMEs using multi-agents. *International Journal of Project Management, 22*(6), 511–517.

Huq, Z., Huq, F., & Cutright, K. (2006). BPR through ERP: Avoiding change management pit-falls. *Journal of Change Management, 6*(1), 67–85.

Levy, M., & Powell, P. (2000). Information systems strategy for small and medium sized enterprises: an organisational perspective. *Journal of Strategic Information Systems, 9*(1), 63–84.

Mabert, V. A., Soni, A., & Venkataraman, V. A. (2000). Enterprise resource planning survey of US manufacturing firms. *Production and Inventory Management Journal, 41*(2), 52–58.

Markus, M. L., Axline, S., Petrie, D., & Tanis, C. (2000). Learning from adopters' experience with ERP-problems encountered and success achieved. *Journal of Information Technology, 15*(4), 245–265.

Min, S., & Mentzer, J. T. (2004). Developing and measuring supply chain management concepts. *Journal of Business Logistics, 25*(1), 63–99.

Olhager, J. & Selldin, E. (2003). Enterprise resource planning survey of Swedish manufacturing firms. *European Journal of Operational Research, 146* (2): 365–373.

Olsen, K.A., & Sætre, P. (2007). ERP for SMEs – is proprietary software an alternative? *Business Process Management Journal, 13* (3): 379-389.

Soliman F. (1998). Optimum level of process mapping and least cost business process re-engineering. *International Journal of Operations & Production Management, 18*(9/10), 810–816.

Vervest, P., Preiss, K., van Heck, E., & Pau, L. -F. (2004). The emergence of smart business networks. *Journal of Information Technology, 19*(4), 228–233.

Yarberry Jr., W. A. (2007). Effective change management: Ensuring alignment of IT and business functions. *Information Systems Security, 16*(2), 80–89.

17. The Quick-Connect Capability and Its Antecedents

Otto R. Koppius[1] and Arnoud J. van de Laak [2]

[1]Rotterdam School of Management, Erasmus University Rotterdam, The Netherlands, okoppius@rsm.nl

[2]Greenwich Consulting Benelux, The Netherlands, arnoud@vandelaak.eu

Abstract

The last few years have seen the rise of a new breed of interorganizational systems, built around web services and business process standards that allows for new and efficient ways of cooperation with new business partners in the network. This quick-connect capability in turn may affect how organizations in a business network structure their own network of relationships. In this paper, using a survey among organizations in the Dutch Graphimedia industry, we develop and validate a measure of the quick connect capability as consisting of four subcomponents: quick connect, quick complexity, quick disconnect and low switching costs, and we show that this quick connect capability can exist on both the supplier side as well as the customer side. We furthermore show that investing in interorganizational systems that enable the usage of communication standards and business process standards leads organizations to develop such a quick connect capability, particularly on the supplier side. These results suggest that it is valuable for organizations to invest in the quick connect capability in order to achieve the flexibility that is necessary to compete in a dynamic business network.

Introduction

The last few years have seen the rise of a new breed of interorganizational systems, built around web services and business process standards that allows for new and efficient ways of cooperation with new business partners in the network. This quick-connect capability in turn may affect how organizations in a business network structure their own network of relationships. While such observations are not new (e.g. Sanchez, 1995; Butler et al., 1997; Liere Van, Hagdorn, Hoogeweegen, & Vervest, 2004), empirical evidence remains largely based on anecdotal evidence. Therefore, the purpose of this paper is twofold: first, to develop a measurement instrument for the quick-connect capability, second to study the factors that lead organizations to have such a quick-connect capability.

The Quick-Connect Capability

The concept of a quick-connect capability was first introduced in 1995 by Ron Sanchez as 'quick-connect' electronic interfaces and was coined to describe a situation where three or more businesses work together to achieve the development of a new product: "A shared CADD/CIM system can thereby provide a quick-connect electronic interface through which firms can quickly establish communication and coordination links" (Sanchez, 1995: 147). In this paper we define a quick-connect capability as "The capability to quickly establish an inter-organizational tie that facilitates the exchange of information and transactions, facilitates quickly disconnecting and quickly handling complexity with new business partners." This definition of the quick-connect capability (QCC) construct is an adaptation from Liere Van et al. (2004: 267), with the addition of the quick-disconnect and quickly-handling complexity components, to emphasize that the purpose of a QCC is not just to merely connect with low switching costs, but also to quickly achieve the level of complexity necessary for efficient coordination, as well as being to terminate existing business relationships quickly without being locked-in.

Having said that, a quick-connect capability is first and foremost about 'connecting quickly'. An approach to inter-organizational exchange that relates to transaction costs (Williamson, 1981) and switching costs (Shapiro et al., 1999). Organizations that are organized inefficiently may have high transaction costs when they engage in exchanges with other organizations. As transaction costs are often formulated as labor intensive, time consuming we assume that transacting with high transaction costs is not quick-connect (Kumar, Van Dissel, & Bielli, 1998; Liang et al., 1998). Switching costs are a specific form of transaction costs, i.e. the cost of transacting with a new supplier when an organization is already engaged in a similar relationship. Switching costs form a disincentive to investigate new potential suppliers and leaving a current supplier for a new supplier. Buyer switching costs are a result of current relationship-specific investments in tangible assets, organizational procedures, and training of employees. Businesses that have to make these kinds of investments every time they engage in a new relationship are expected to connect and disconnect slowly. (Jackson, 1985; Morgan & Hunt, 1994; Heide & Weiss, 1995)

Thus, to achieve a quick-connect both transaction costs and switching costs need to be low. This could suggest that relationships that are formed using a quick-connect capability are superficial with low impact, as strategically important relationships will most often come with significant relation-specific investments. However, the use of quick-connect capability in principle should allow businesses to both engage in a high impact relationship, while keeping relationship-specific investments moderate. A concept that envisions those same characteristics is interimistic relational exchange: "a short-lived exchange relationship in which companies pool their skills and resources" (Lambe, Spekman, & Hunt, 2000: 213) The concept has been developed in an attempt to show the downside of pure long term relationships and underline the value of short-lived relationships. Interimistic exchange relationships are found to be a distinct category of relationships between pure transactional relationships on one end of the spectrum and pure long-term relationships on the other end of the spectrum that cannot be reduced to either type.

Quickly achieving this complexity of exchange is a challenge for organizations though. Typically, executing complex exchanges happens in of either two situations: (1) extensive contractual agreements or (2) long-term relationships based on inter-organizational trust. Both exchanges require time, the first situation in negotiating all details of the exchange and structuring them in a contract. The second situation will take time as trust-building is required to let two organizations enter into a complex exchange without full understanding of what liability is assigned to the partners in the exchange (Gulati, 1998; Ring & Van de Ven, 1994) A partial answer to this challenge may be found in two concepts from strategy literature, integration capability (Zollo & Singh, 2004) and alliance capability (Kale et al., 2002; & Gulati, 1998). Both of these concepts are framed as capabilities that organizations can build by investing organizational resources in developing such a capability. In particular, knowledge codification of experiences of previous integration processes is found to benefit the chance of success of relationship, which suggests that an important part of the alliance and integration capability is based on the creation of best practices and process standards. While in the alliance literature these capabilities are first developed at the relational level and subsequently transferred to other relations, eventually leading to a generic, network-level capability, we suggest that organizations can also develop a QCC more directly at the network-level by investing in information systems that enable interorganizational standards. These standards will be described in the next section.

Antecedents of the Quick-Connect Capability

To achieve a quick connect with a new organization, an organization should be compatible with its potential partners. Standardization of communication, information and processes is required to prepare collaboration with other, yet unknown, business partners. A standardized approach to inter-organizational relationships can be formulated as a standardized business interface: "The effects of standardized interfaces between firms (…) facilitate the 'mixing and matching' of component developers and other resource providers in configuring product creating resource chains" (Sanchez, 1995: 147). Drawing on the conditions that are required for modularization, namely (1) standardization of coordination and (2) standardization of information (Jacobides, 2005), we divide a standardized business interface is divided in communication standards (standardization of information) and business process standards (standardization of coordination).

Communication standards are the first layer on top of the physical infrastructure (Hagel & Seely Brown, 2001) The clearest example of the difference between infrastructure and communication standards would be a telephone line as infrastructure and a traditional phone on one end, and a VoIP telephone on the other end. The infrastructure is in place, but both communication devices use different communication standards that make it impossible to establish a connection.

Examples of generic technical communication standards are FTP, EDI and e-mail standards. More relevant to the idea of information standardization are business communication standards such as barcodes and industry specific XMLs. The latter ones are also known as specifications: standard templates for product or process definitions. To allow market procurement of assets that are important to the production process, the standardization of information is essential as it forms one common language that replaces each organizations dialect (Jacobides, 2005; Baldwin & Clark, 2003). Hence we have:

Hypothesis 1: The Adoption of Communication Standards Leads to a Quick-connect Capability.

Communication standards by themselves are not sufficient, since these are not by themselves related to the task that the communication it supposed to coordinate. For this we need business process standards. Business process standards are technical specifications for organizational tasks, activities and business documents that are shared among at least two or more organizations. These technical specifications are both shared by partners and open to others. (Bala, & Venkatesh, 2007; Gosain, Malhotra, El Sawy, & Chehade, 2003) These technical specifications are in fact the standardization of coordination, the process specifications explain to business partners how to guide and direct each other to achieve a shared end result. The goals of business process standards can be summarized as (1) automation, (2) integration, and (3) facilitation of value chain activities such as supply chain management, collaborative forecasting, product development, and inventory management (Markus, Steinfield, Wigand, & Minton, 2006; Wigand, Steinfield, & Markus, 2005; Bala, & Venkatesh, 2007) The operationalization of a set of business process standards in practice will require an interorganizational system (Barrett & Konsysnki, 1982) that embodies those standards and that other organizations can tap into in order to quickly connect with other organizations, leading to:

Hypothesis 2: The Adoption of Business Process Standards Leads to a Quick-connect Capability.

Industry Context: The Dutch Graphimedia Industry

The Dutch Graphimedia Industry comprises of 46.416 employees working in 2.991 industry-related companies. 81% of all companies in the industry can be profiled as printers, while 11% are specialized preparing companies (i.e. lay out studios) and 8% are specialized finishing companies (e.g. bookbinders) Most printers are also active in the field of preparing and finishing products. The overall turnover of the Graphimedia industry was 7.4 billion euro in 2005. The firms with a large number of employees (>100) are in two-third of the cases working in continuous shifts also at night. The same can be stated for half of the finishing companies. Most probably, since in these companies the large investments in machinery and equipment requires high use of available capacity. The research in this paper focuses on printers and layout studios that make up 80% of the Graphimedia industry. Printers get their orders directly from customers who they service with their internal layout department, via independent layout studios or advertisement agencies. In Fig. 17.1 a typical production chain is given for the production of a book. In this case the customer, for instance a publisher, selects a layout studio. The layout studio has offered a quotation to the customer, containing price, quality and the specifics of the order. To be able to offer a customer a complex quotation, the layout studio has contacted the printer, the finisher and the bookbinder. The layout studio coordinates the production process with the network parties. The layout studio and the printer are in contact about the quality and the specifics of the design. The layout studio and the finishing companies generally have a less intensive relationship.

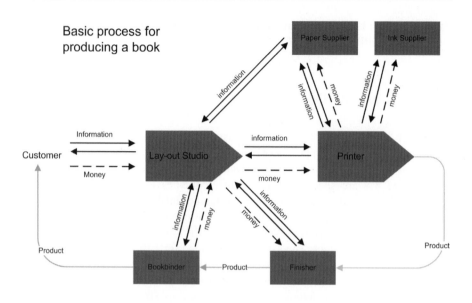

Fig. 17.1 Example of the basic process in the Graphimedia industry

This production chain can be interpreted as a network. In this particular network the layout studio functions as coordinator, but different configurations are often seen. Large printers have the capability to function as coordinator. A common configuration is where the printer has vertically integrated the layout activities into its business, replacing the coordination role of the layout studio in Fig. 17.1. Experienced customers such as book publishers and advertisement agencies can eliminate the layout studio and the layout department of the printer from the supply chain, taking on the role of coordinator.

So in principle, each printer is surrounded by a network of companies that provide it with orders. A typical small layout studio will have one preferred printer. Larger layout studios and professional buyers will have ties to more than one printer and bookbinder to avoid dependence on any specific company in the network. Figure 17.2 is made after the example of a business network in Anderson, Hakansson, and Johanson et al. (1994). These companies are regularly layout studios, advertising agencies and publishers. A complete finished product often requires the cooperation of 3 or more parties in the network.

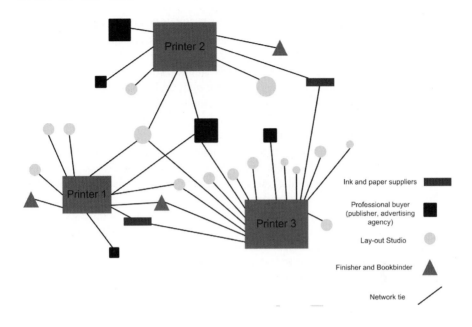

Fig. 17.2 Typical Graphimedia network around three printers

For coordination between the different parties, organizations in the Graphimedia industry have traditionally relied heavily on standards. Communication standards were originally centered around ISDN and Iomega Zipdrives, currently all Internet-based, with FTP being most commonly used as well as newer web services like yousendit.com. Business process standards exist through the use of common industry applications such as Adobe InDesign and QuarkXpress and the PDF document format. The existence of these standards combined with the idea that the industry functions like a network suggest that the Graphimedia industry is a suitable place for a study into quick-connect capability in business networks. The exploratory interviews corroborate this position, for instance one of the printers interviewed said: "The ease of getting information from and to our customers has increased incredibly. When I started my first job, everything was on paper and until a few years ago, customers walked in with piles of CD-ROMs. Now I get an email when one of our regular customers starts uploading a document to our FTP server".

Survey Methodology

To test our hypotheses, as well as our conceptualization of the QCC (described in more detail in the instrument development section), we sent out an online survey to executives, managers and account managers in the Dutch printing industry. For this study 1900 e-mail invitations were sent to members of the Dutch National

Association for Businesses in the Graphimedia Industry (KVGO). As the available e-mail addresses were mostly 'info@company' addresses, the invitation may not reach management-level employees or directors in the larger organizations of the sample and hence bias our sample towards smaller companies. To reduce the effect of this bias, 95 additional personalized e-mail invitations were sent directly to managers in large printing companies with email addresses obtained from company websites and through existing industry contacts. A total of 67 e-mails bounced, which brings the net number of sent out invitations to 1928. The respondents were rewarded with a chance of winning one of the available six gift vouchers: 2 vouchers of 50 Euro for those responding the first day, and 4 vouchers of 25 Euro for all participants. Additionally, although the survey was anonymous, the respondents could leave their e-mail address if they were interested in a two page report with the outcomes of the study. A total number of 463 people started the survey, of which 155 respondents finished the online survey. After excluding 5 respondents that were insufficiently knowledgeable about the industry, the final sample size for our analysis was 150, representing a 7.8% response rate. This low response rate is likely to be due to the generic nature of the info@company... addresses, which often requires the receiver to forward it to the appropriate person, thus substantially lowering response.

Instrument Development

All constructs were measured on a 1-7 Likert scale. To minimize the cognitive effort of the respondents all questions except one used similar scale anchors, 'strongly disagree' and 'strongly agree'. Also, an effort was made to avoid generic definitions and present the respondents with printing industry specific terminology.

Quick-Connect Capability

Developing the new measurement instrument for quick-connect capability was done in a six step process that is described in Table 17.1. The development of the scale was grounded in the approaches to instrument development of Straub (1989; IS research) and Churchill (1979; Marketing research) Both methods work from qualitative to quantitative and incorporate testing for reliability and validity in at least two places in the development process. This study attempts to follow those guidelines.

The first step of the development process is best described as divergent and explorative. Open questions were used in discussions with fellow researchers to develop a more detailed understanding of 'what is quick-connect capability?' and

'how does quick-connect capability work?' as well as relying on the literature in related areas. At the end of this first phase, and in line with the theoretical conceptualization presented earlier, quick-connect capability was split up in four subcomponents:
1. Quickly establish inter-organizational relationships
2. Quickly abandon inter-organizational relationships
3. Low switching costs
4. Newly established relationship is quickly able to handle complexity.

Table 17.1 Measurement process for the QCC instrument

Step	Description	Goal	Outcome
1	Creation of categories/ subscales	Achieve complete overview of construct, avoid overlap	Four QCC categories
2	Collect and select Relevant survey items from Marketing, Strategy and IS were collected and divided in the four categories	Create a set of survey items that measures QCC and is mutually exclusive and collectively exhaustive	A set of 12 survey items divided in 4 categories
3	Two judges assessed the four subscales	Test the new scale for inter-rater reliability	Overlap was found between two subscales, scale was divided in QCC-Customer and QCC-Supplier
4	Initial testing: the questionnaire was shown to the director of a mid-sized printing company	Test the survey for understandability, errors and omissions	Satisfactory test of updated QCC instrument, with 22 items in 6 categories; tester feedback resulted in more Grafimedia specific questions
5	Final testing: the online and final version of the questionnaire was filled out by the owner of a mid-sized layout studio	Test the survey for final errors, test the online survey system	Release date was delayed with one day, due to a technical error
6	Reliability analysis and Factor analysis	Test the data that is produced by the survey for internal reliability and correct loading of the factors	Following the reliability analysis 4 items were deleted; One QCC scale was deleted due to overlap

The second step was convergent in nature. In a literature study the categories were studied more extensively. With a solid literature study as foundation a battery of potential survey items was created by screening journal articles that had used a survey methodology. For the four categories combined the battery contained a total number of 41 items. Finally 12 items were selected with 3 items per category.

The third step involved improving the instrument with feedback from knowledgeable experts that are not influenced by the design discussions. To acquire that feedback and test for inter-rater reliability the instrument was assessed by two judges (DeSarbo et al., 2005) Two junior IT consultants were presented with a list of the twelve QCC items in random order. They were asked to put each item in the right category. This test resulted in adaptation of items for the quickly abandon inter-organizational relationships category to more clearly distinguish it from low switching costs. Second, both judges reported that combining items with categories was hindered severely by the mix of questions in the original instrument for 'business partners' and 'customers'. The solution for the second problem was more complex. Discussion and contemplation on the issue resulted in the idea that a QCC differs on the supplier side compared to the customer side. More specifically, since the decision to abandon/switch relationships on the customer side is made by the customer and not by the printer (it seems unlikely that a printer would voluntarily drop a customer), for customers only the items relating to the 'quickly establish an inter-organizational relationship' and 'quickly able to handle complexity' categories are theoretically meaningful, whereas all four categories are applicable for relationships with an organization's suppliers. The instrument was changed accordingly, and two new categories were created that were focused specifically on customer relationships. The categories 'quickly establish an inter-organizational relationship' and 'quickly able to handle complexity' form the construct QCC-Customer. The existing four categories were adapted to focus on supplier relationships only. These four categories together form the construct QCC-Supplier. After this adaptation the total number of items for the QCC instrument has increased from 12 to 22. The new QCC instrument was again presented to the two judges. They confirmed that the changes had contributed to a clearer relation between item and category, despite the substantial increase in number of items. The final instrument is displayed in Table 17.2 and we will describe the constructs now in more detail.

Table 17.2 QCC survey instrument

Construct	Survey item	Source
QCC-Customer (Connect1)	When we cooperate for the first time with a customer, normally we need only a short time to fine tune the cooperation	New
QCC-Customer (Connect2)	If we sign a longterm contract (1year or longer) with a new customer, normally it takes only little trouble to negotiate the details of the contract	New
QCC-Customer (Connect3)	When we sign a longterm contract with a new customer, the process of cooperation is already a subject during the contract negotiations	New
QCC-Customer (Connect4)	When we first get an order from a new customer, it usually takes a lot of time to understand the details of the order (reverse scored)	Kim et al. (2006)
QCC-Customer (Complexity1)	When we execute an order for a new customer, we immediately share information intensively	Malhotra et al. (2005)
QCC-Customer (Complexity2)	When we sign a contract with a new customer, we directly involve the customer in initiatives to improve the quality of products	Patnayakuni et al. (2006)
QCC-Customer (Complexity3)	When a new customer orders a complex end-product with us, it usually takes time to optimize the quality of that product (reverse scored)	new
QCC-Customer (Complexity4)	When we sign a contract with a new customer, we directly share best practice examples to fine tune the cooperation	Patnayakuni et al. (2006)
QCC-Supplier	When we cooperate for the first time with a business partner it	new

(Connect1)	usually takes a long time to set up our cooperation	
QCC-Supplier (Connect2)	When we place an order to a supplier for the first time, it requires very little effort for us to explain the attributes of the product to the supplier	new
QCC-Supplier (Connect3)	When we sign a contract with a supplier, the process of cooperation is already a subject of discussion during the contract negotiations	new
QCC-Supplier (Connect4)	When we place an order with a supplier for the first time, it takes a lot of time to communicate and explain the details of our order (reverse scored)	Kim et al. (2006)
QCC-Supplier (Complexity1)	When we execute an order with a new supplier, we immediately share information intensively	Malhotra et al. (2005)
QCC-Supplier (Complexity2)	When we select a new supplier for a complex product/semi-finished product/service, the end-product will be optimal	new
QCC-Supplier (Complexity3)	When we sign a contract with a new supplier, we directly involve the supplier in initiatives to increase the quality of products	Patnayakuni et al. (2006)
QCC-Supplier (Complexity4)	When we sign a contract with a new supplier, we directly share best practice examples to fine tune the cooperation	Patnayakuni et al., 2006
QCC-Supplier (Disconnect1)	When we want to stop the cooperation with a supplier, we can switch very fast to a new supplier without implications for the quality of our products	new
QCC-Supplier (Disconnect2)	When we want to stop the cooperation with a supplier, we can switch very fast to a new supplier and our customers will never know of the change	new
QCC-Supplier (Disconnect3)	Your organization is capable of switching to a new supplier and discontinue the relationship with an existing supplier, without any delays in the production or workprocess	new
QCC-Supplier (Switch1)	Purchasing from a new supplier requires training for a number of our employees	Heide and Weiss (1995)
QCC-Supplier (Switch2)	Developing procedures to deal effectively with a new supplier will take a lot of time and effort	Heide and Weiss (1995)
QCC-Supplier (Switch3)	Developing working relationships with new suppliers is a time-consuming process	Heide and Weiss (1995)
CommStd1	When we exchange large files with customers and suppliers, we always do that digitally	new
CommStd2	The way we exchange large files with once-only customers does not differ from the way we exchange large files with regular customers	Malhotra et al. 2005
BusProcStd1	Files from customers or suppliers always need to be transferred/edited before we can process it	Malhotra et al. 2005
BusProcStd2	Files from regular customers is processed in the same way as files from once-only customers.	Malhotra et al. 2005
BusProcStd3	With large customers we use framework contracts	new
BusProcStd4	With important suppliers we use framework contracts	new

QCC-Customer: Quickly Establish Relationships with Customer

Organizations that have a quick-connect capability are supposed to be able to quickly set up relationships with new partners. The first three items are new and created for this study. The fourth item was originally developed by Kim et al. (2006) to measure complexity in buyer-supplier transactions.

QCC-Customer: Quickly Handling Complexity with a Customer

A characteristic of QCC is that relationships are set-up quickly. Typical development of an inter-organizational relationship goes slow and building trust among the partners is an important, but slow process. A relationship between two partners that have a QCC will be able to handle complexity right after initiating the relationship. Item 1 is taken from an article on information integration by Malhotra, Gosain and El Sawy (2005) Again the original item was created to measure the ability of the partners to handle complexity. For this study the item was specified to new business partners only. Item 2 and item 4 are adapted from a study on relational routines (Patnayakuni et al., 2006). The routines are instituted to handle complex issues in a standardized process. For this study the notion of quickly handling complexity was added by focusing the question on new business partners only.

QCC-Supplier: Quickly Establish Relationships with Suppliers

We now turn to the development of the measure for the supplier-side QCC. Organizations that have a Quick-connect Capability are supposed to be able to quickly set up relationships with new partners. The items are similar to the ones used for the QCC-Customer, except now specified to the supplier side.

QCC-Supplier: Quickly Handling Complexity with a Supplier

A characteristic of QCC is that relationships are set-up quickly. Typical development of an inter-organizational relationship goes slow and building trust among the partners is an important, but slow process. Similar to the customer-side, a relationship between two partners that have a QCC will be able to handle complexity right after initiating the relationship. The items are similar to the ones used for the QCC-Customer, except now specified to the supplier side.

QCC-Supplier: Quickly Abandon Inter-organization Relationships

Organizations that have a QCC can not indefinitely keep on adding more relationships. From time to time they will also need to discontinue a relationship with a partner, for instance to free up capacity to enter into a relationship with a new partner. No previous scale was found that functioned as an example or guide. The items in the table are based on the consequences of discontinuing a relationship with a business partner for product quality, production lead times and whether customers would notice a switch in business partners.

QCC-Supplier: Low Switching Costs

Organizations that have a quick-connect capability have invested in a capability that allows them to quickly connect with partners. These organizations have made an investment in many potential relationships, instead of a relation specific investment in one relationship. Organizations that have a quick-connect capability are supposed to have low switching costs. Here we used the scale that Heide and Weiss (1995) developed for measuring switching costs. Their 3-item scale is based on the source of switching costs, which is mostly commitments to (1) a technology or (2) a particular network partner (Jackson, 1985; Heide & Weiss, 1995). This is also what distinguishes this scale from the quickly-disconnect scale, that focuses on the consequences of the switch.

Testing the QCC Instrument

We now return to the development process of the QCC instrument as described in Table 17.1. In the fourth and fifth step the instrument was presented to potential respondents. In step four, an MSWord version of the questionnaire was shown to a director of a mid-size printing company and an account manager of a layout studio. Primary focus was on improving the questionnaire where items were unclear or ambiguous. Extra feedback was used to make the questions more printing industry specific. A first example is the practice in the Graphimedia industry to use 1 year, 2 year and sometimes longer framework contracts. This was incorporated in both the QCC-Customer scales. A second example is the use of industry specific formulations like 'print proofing' for confirming an order, and 'prepress' to indicate layout studios. Whereas we used the industry-specific formulations in the actual survey, Table 17.2 presents the decontextualized version of the instrument to enable other researchers replicating it in other industries (although we do recommend tailoring the instrument to that particular industry context).

The fifth step was the final test of the questionnaire in the online survey system. A third potential respondent, the owner of a layout studio, filled out the online survey. The feedback contained no remarks concerning the content of the survey.

Analyzing the Cronbach's alpha scores is part of step six of the QCC development process. All multi-item measurement scales in this study were assessed on internal consistency by calculating Cronbach's alpha and tested for construct validity, i.e. convergent and divergent validity, through a factor analysis[3]. These tests resulted in the removal of a few items from the final analysis, but all in all, the conclusion is that the revised instrument used here, provides a theoretically consistent and statistically satisfactory way of measuring the quick-connect capability.

Communication Standards and Business Process Standards

The bottom 6 rows of Table 17.2 list the items that were used to operationalize communication standards and business process standards respectively. Both measures are based partly on Malhotra et al. (2005) work on standards and partly on measuring industry-specific practices (such as transferring large files and the use of framework contracts) that came out of the exploratory interviews that were deemed related to interorganizational standards.

Control Variables

Three control variables were added to the questionnaire. Firm size was mea-sured as number of employees to control for variations in the size of the businesses. Firm age was measured to control for variations that are caused by very young organizations. Finally the core business was measured as a set of dummy variables to control for variations that result from the difference in business characteristics. Respondents were presented with four options (printing, prepress, finishing and other) of which more than one option could be selected.

---

[3] Space limitations prevent a detailed presentation of these analyses here, but they can be obtained from the authors.

Analysis

Before moving to the results of the regression analysis we used to test our hypotheses, we will first assess the representativeness of our sample compared to industry averages. The annual report by the Graphimedia Industry Organization KVGO indicates that the average number of employees in Graphimedia businesses is 15.16. For this study an average number of employees was reported to be 25.96. Contrary to expectations the sample has a tendency towards somewhat larger-than-average organizations, although overall organizational size remains very small both in the sample as in the population.

Regarding the nature of the business of the respondent, compared to the overall averages in the Graphimedia Industry, numbers from the KVGO annual report indicate that 81% of businesses have printing as its primary activity, for this study that number is 79.9% of respondents. Equally 11% of Graphimedia businesses are pure prepress businesses, which is 9.4% for this study. The remainder of respondents in this study is 12.8% which consists of finishing organizations, brokers in Graphimedia products and printers of specialty products.

All in all, we conclude that our sample constitutes a fair representation of the overall Graphimedia industry. As our dependent variables QCC-supplier and QCC-customer were both normally distributed, as well as uncorrelated (which supports the interpretation of these two as separate constructs, as described in the instrument development section based on the initial field testing), we employed two standard OLS regression to test our hypotheses. As none of the variance inflation factor values (VIF) exceeded 2.0 the possibility of multicollinearity is negligible, making OLS suitable. Table 17.3 reports the results.

Table 17.3 Regression analysis results

	QCCCustomer		QCCSupplier	
	Model 1a	Model 1b	Model 2a	Model 2b
Firm age	.095 (n.s.)	.084 (n.s.)	−.152	−.164 (0.85)
Number of employees	−.053 (n.s.)	−.068 (n.s.)	−.041	−.029 (n.s.)
Dummy printers	−.121 (n.s.)	−.094 (n.s.)	−.161 (.091)	−.146 (n.s.)
Communication standards		.161 (.076)		.245 (.005)
Business process standards		.160 (.075)		−.221 (.010)
R^2adj	−.008	.031	.038	.128
ΔR^2		.039		.090

Communication standards were found to have a significant positive effect on the quick-connect capability on both the customer and the supplier side, hence hypothesis 1 is retained. The results for hypothesis 2 are somewhat mixed, since business process standards have a positive effect on the quick-connect capability on the customer side, yet a negative effect on the quick-connect capability on the supplier side. A possible explanation for this could be that organizations actually have a suite of business process standards at their disposal, with different business process standards to be used for different customer. This could explain them scoring low on the business process measures, since that is not uniform across customers, yet still scoring high on the QCC measures.

Our focus in these models was on the IT-enabled antecedents of a QCC in the form of communication and business process standards. However, as the explanatory power of particularly the customer model is on the low side, it is clear that these are not the only causes of a QCC. For instance, internal sharing of best practices regarding new customers or suppliers, either formally through organizational routines or a knowledge management system, or informally through an advice network of knowledgeable employees, may very well contribute also to organizations developing a QCC. Such aspects were not investigated here, but are a promising area for future research.

Conclusion

In this paper, we developed and validated a measure of the quick connect capability as consisting of four subcomponents: quick connect, quick complexity, quick disconnect and low switching costs, that can exist on both the supplier side as well as the customer side. We furthermore showed that investing in interorganizational systems that enable the usage of communication standards and business process standards leads organizations to develop such a quick connect capability, particularly on the supplier side, although the role of business process standards is more complicated than initially assumed. Standards allow a firm to quickly integrate a new customer or supplier into its network or switch relationships when necessary. Note that this does not imply that a firm should switch suppliers frequently or spend more time finding new customers instead of retaining existing ones, it merely says that should that need arise, then the firm is capable of doing so quickly. This does raise the question of what the consequences are of having a quick connect capability for a firm's relationships with suppliers and customers. Do relationship become less embedded and more arm's length, or does a QCC enable organizations to achieve (most of) the benefits of long-term relationships in a much shorter timespan, as the research on interimistic exchange (Lambe, Spekman, & Hunt, 2000) might suggest? While we leave this question, as well as QCC's effect on firm performance for future research, these results do suggest that it is valuable for organizations to invest in the quick connect capability in order to achieve the flexibility that may be necessary to compete in a dynamic business network.

References

Anderson, J. C., Hakansson, H., Johanson, L. (1994). Dyadic business Relationships within a business network context. *Journal of Marketing, 58*(4), 1–15.

Bala H., & Venkatesh, V. (2007). Assimilation of interorganizational business process standards 362. *Information Systems Research, 18*(3), 340–362.

Butler, P., Hall, T.W., Hanna, A.M., Mendonca, L. and Auguste, B. (1997) A Revolution in Interaction. *The McKinsey Quarterly*, 1: 4–23.

Churchill, G. A. (1979). A paradigm for developing better measures of marketing constructs. *Journal of Marketing Research, 16*(1), 64–73.

DeSarbo, W.S., Di Benedetto, C.A., Song, M. and Sinha, I. (2005) Revisiting the Miles and Snow strategic framework: uncovering interrelationships between strategic types, capabilities, environmental uncertainty, and firm performance. *Strategic Management Journal, 26*(1), 47–74.

Gosain, S., Malhotra, A., El Sawy, O. A., & Chehade, F. (2003). Towards frictionless e-Business: The impact of common electronic business interfaces. *Communications of the ACM 12,* 186–195.

Gulati, R. (1998). Alliances and networks strategic. *Management Journal, 19*(4), 293–317.

Jackson, B. B. (1985). Winning and keeping industrial customers. Lexington, MA: Lexington Books.

Jacobides, M. G. (2005). Industry change through vertical disintegration: how and why markets emerged in mortgage banking. *Academy of Management Journal, 48*(3), 465–498.

Kale, P., Dyer, J.H. and Singh, H. (2002). Alliance capability, stock market response, and long-term alliance success: the role of the alliance function. *Strategic Management Journal, 23*(8), 747–767.

Kim, K.K., Umanath, N.S., Kim, B. (2006). An Assessment of Electronic Information Transfer in B2B Supply-Channel Relationships *Journal of Management Information Systems, 22*(3), 294–230.

Kumar, K., Van Dissel, H. G., & Bielli, P. (1998). The merchant of Prato- revisited: Toward a third rationality of information systems. *MIS Quarterly, 22,* 199–226.

Lambe, C. J., Spekman, R. E., & Hunt, S. D. (2000). Interimistic relational exchange: Conceptualization and propositional development. *Journal of the Academy of Marketing Science, 28*(2), 212–225.

Liang, T-P., Huang, J-S. (1998). An empirical study on consumer acceptance of products in electronic markets: a transaction cost model. *Decision Support Systems, 24*(1), 29–43.

Liere Van, D. W., Hagdorn, L., Hoogeweegen, M. R., & Vervest, P. H. M. (2004). Embedded coordination in a business network. *Journal of Information Technology. 19*(4) 261–269.

Malhotra, A., Gosain, S., El Sawy, O.A. (2005). Absorptive capacity configurations in supply chains: gearing for partner-enabled market knowledge creation. *MIS Quarterly 29*(1), 145–187.

Markus, M. L., Steinfield, C. W., Wigand, R. T., & Minton, G. (2006). Industry-wide information systems standardization as collective action: The case of the U.S. residential mortgage industry. *MIS Quarterly, 30,* 439–465.

Morgan, R. M. & Hunt, S. B. (1994). The commitment-trust theory of relationship marketing. *Journal of Marketing, 58*(3), 20–38.

Patnayakuni, R., Rai, A., Seth, N. (2006). Relational Antecedents of Information Flow Integration for Supply Chain Coordination. *Journal of Management Information Systems 23*(1), 13–49.

Sanchez, R. (1995). Strategic flexibility in product competition strategic. *Management Journal, 16*, 135–159.

Shapiro, C., Varian, H.R. (1999). Information Rules, Boston: Harvard Business School Press.

Straub, D. W. (1989). Validating instruments in MIS research. *MIS Quarterly, 2*, 147–169.

Wigand, R. T., Steinfield, C. W., & Markus, M. L. (2005). Information technology standards choices and industry structure outcomes. *Journal of Management Information Systems, 22*(2), 165–192.

Williamson, O. E. (1981). The economics of organization: The transaction cost approach. *The American Journal of Sociology, 87*(2): 233.

18. The Adoption of Grid Technology and Its Perceived Impact on Agility

Empirical Evidence from a Business Experiment with Small and Medium Enterprises in the Netherlands

Marcel van Oosterhout[1], Ellen Koenen[2] and Eric van Heck[3]

[1] Rotterdam School of Management, Erasmus University Rotterdam, The Netherlands, moosterhout@rsm.nl

[2] Deloitte Consulting, The Netherlands

[3] Rotterdam School of Management, Erasmus University Rotterdam, The Netherlands, evanheck@rsm.nl

Abstract

This paper discusses the role and impact of grid technology on the performance of small and medium enterprises (SMEs). Its focus is on an application that uses grid technology among a community of SMEs for data backup and recovery. Based on literature from technology adoption theory this paper identifies several adoption profiles of SMEs. Each profile has its own characteristics in terms of perceptions of the grid technology, organizational readiness, external pressure to use the technology, and perception on how the application will improve the firm's agility. The research was carried out in one of the business experiments of a large European research project on business use of grid technology. The results indicate that seven profiles could be identified and that two profiles (ready adopters and initiators) are eager to adopt the grid enabled application. The results show how early adopters can be identified and how difficult it is to develop applications with small and medium sized enterprises successfully. Conclusions and recommendations for future research are provided.

P.H.M. Vervest et al. (eds.) *The Network Experience*
© Springer-Verlag Berlin Heidelberg 2009

Introduction

Firms face a variety of unexpected disruptions and incidents that can have serious effects on the performance of the company. Recently, calamities (e.g. terrorist attacks, severe weather conditions, explosions, power grid failures) have received a lot of attention, but also more local incidents such as fire and/or theft can seriously effect a company's operations. Most of these incidents result in a lack of access to the firm's data or even a loss of company critical data. This could potentially lead to a standstill of business operations. Small and Medium Enterprises (SMEs) are often more vulnerable due to their lack of resources and capabilities to handle these disruptions or incidents.

Dealing with environmental uncertainty has received a lot of attention in literature. One of the latest streams of literature focuses on the concept of agility – that is the timely and adequate (re)actions of a firm to the unexpected (Verstraete, 2004). The concept originated in the manufacturing area in the early nineties (Goldman, Preiss, Nagel, & Dove, 1991; Goldman, Nagel, & Preiss, 1995). Later, the concept of agility has been broadened to organizational agility (Kidd, 1994; Dove, 2001) and supply chain and business network agility (Van Hoek, Harrison, & Christopher, 2001; Yusuf, Gunasekaran, Adeleye, & Sivayoganathan, 2004). Information technology is one of the important enablers for enhancing agility (Desouza, 2006). Based on the connectivity provided via the Internet, small companies can come together and deliver the quality, scope and scale of products and services, which they were not able to provide individually (Van Heck & Vervest, 2007). Customer agility goes one step further. It entails the co-option of customers in the exploration and exploitation of opportunities for innovation and competitive action (Sambamurthy, Bharadwaj, & Grover, 2003).

However, it is not clear how advanced technologies such as grid technologies enable companies to react faster and better. This research provides empirical evidence on how SMEs adopt grid technologies and how they perceive these technologies in improving their agility. The objective of this study is to empirically validate factors affecting the adoption and integration of grid technology in SMEs and to assess the impact of these technology types on the agility level of firms. This research builds on technology adoption theory work of Rogers (1995), Iacovou, Benbasat, and Dexter (1995), van Heck and Ribbers (1999), and Dove (2001) and combines it with insights from the agility and information technology stream of research (Goldman et al. (1991, 1995), Desouza (2006), and Overby, Bharadwaj, and Sambamurthy (2006)). The two central research questions in our study are:

1. What are the factors responsible for the adoption and integration of grid technology in SMEs?
2. What is the impact of grid technology in SMEs on backup and recovery agility?

Research was carried out in one of the business experiments in the EU-funded research project BEinGRID (www.beingrid.eu). GRID is a technology for

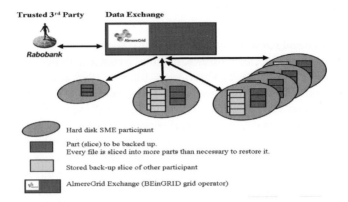

Fig. 18.1 Data backup and recovery service based on Grid concept

resource sharing by sharing of computing power, data storage or services. In the business experiment an application was developed as a solution for backup and recovery of data. This solution is based on the sharing of hardware for data storage by users in a grid. Fig. 18.1 provides an overview of the DBRG concept.

Users of this Data Backup and Recovery service based on Grid, in short (DBRG) offered part of their local hard disk space to store encrypted slices of backup data from other users of the service. The grid infrastructure provider coordinated the distribution and recovery of the data slices from the different users. Furthermore, the DBRG concept includes a trusted third party that arranges the contractual and financial settlement. DBRG is a hybrid form that can be placed within the data and the service GRID. Adapted from the definition of Foster & Kesselman (1999) we define DBRG as *"a hardware and software infrastructure that provides dependable, consistent, pervasive, and inexpensive access to secure & enormous-sized data storage space."* The DBRG application standardizes the backup processes, the backup process becomes simplified, the system (and business critical data) is re-usable and scalable and the integration of the backup & recover process and its information flow can be executed across the firm.

This chapter is structured as follows. First, in section "Research Method and Data" we provide a short literature review on adoption and diffusion of innovations and discusses the conceptual model for the adoption of DBRG adapted from the innovation and technology adoption model of Rogers (1995) and Iacovou et al. (1995). We discuss the research methodology, which is based on a combination of quantitative (surveys) and qualitative (interview) research methods. Section "Empirical Results" discusses the findings of our research. These include the findings of a pre-study among 2,485 Dutch SMEs and the findings of a field experiment among 12 SMEs in the region of Almera. Finally, section "Effects on Agility" discusses conclusions and limitations.

Adoption of Innovations

There is a wide body of literature available on the adoption and diffusion of techno-logical innovations (Spector & Brown, (1976); Gatignon & Robertson, 1989; Iaco-vou et al., 1995; Rogers, 1995; Van Heck & Ribbers, 1999; Moreau, Lehmann, & Markman, 2001; Waarts, Everdingen, & Hilligersberg, 2002; Levin, Levin, & Meisel, 1987) and acceptance and use of IT, i.e. TAM model (Davis, 1989). We distinguish research on categorization of adopters over time and research of indi-vidual adoption factors for technological innovations in general and information systems (IS) in particular. Categorization of adopters over time is interesting for segmentation purposes and focusing marketing efforts to speed up adoption of technologies in time. The specific characteristics that lead to adoption are impor-tant to recognize innovators and early adopters. We used field study data to cate-gorize different types of DBRG adopters and analyzed specific characteristics and differences in adoption factors among the different adopter groups.

Rogers (1995) states that individuals, or in our case SMEs, do not all adopt an in-novation at the same time. The difference in time makes it possible to classify the individuals into adopter categories and to draw diffusion curves. The S-curve is a cumulative representation of the number of adopters over time. A reason for this recurrent phenomenon is the role of information and uncertainty reduction across the diffusion process (Rogers, 2005). Five adopter categories can be distinguished (Kotler & Keller, 1994): innovators, early adopters, early majority, late majority, and laggards.

Most of the studies that analyze how attributes of the innovation influence its adoption build on the pioneering work of Rogers (1995). Rogers (1995) ana-lyzed the factors that affect the rate at which innovations diffuse and are adopted. Rogers distinguished five factors: perceived attributes of the innovation, the type of innovation-decision, communication channels used, the nature of the social system, and the extent of change agent's promotional efforts. Inspired by the work of Rogers, Iacovou et al. (1995) developed a model specifically focused on the adoption of Electronic Data Interchange (EDI) by SMEs. They used expected benefits, organizational readiness, and external pressure as the three factors influ-encing the EDI adoption and integration decision. Van Heck & Ribbers empiri-cally demonstrated this model by measuring these factors in 137 small businesses in the Netherlands. Furthermore, they extended the model with the availability of an EDI standard as a fourth factor. Until now there is, to our knowledge, hardly any research nor empirical validations of the adoption of grid technology. Previ-ous research on the adoption of grid technologies mentions a lack of standards (interfaces, processes) and data management as barriers in the adoption of data-GRID applications (Thibodeau, 2004; Stong-Michas, 2005). Our conceptual model for the adoption of DBRG is adapted from Rogers (1995) and the EDI adoption model of Iacovou et al. (1995). We will now shortly discuss the various cons-tructs and propositions of our conceptual model.

Agility Impact

Impact relates to the actual benefits adopters receive from utilizing DBRG. We analyze these benefits in terms of (perceived) effects on the agility of the backup and recovery process of data by SMEs, in short backup and recovery (B&R) agility. We define this as *"the level of agility that can be achieved with the use of a Data Backup and Recovery System to pro-actively prepare for disruptive change that could have an impact on the firms' data."* B&R agility is indeed part of and contributes to the wider concept of IT agility. We expect that B&R agility positively influences IT agility. However, this is out of the scope of this research. In order to measure the level of B&R-Agility, we use six agility change proficiency metrics defined by Rick Dove (2001): time, cost, scope/range, ease, quality, and robustness of backup and recovery of data. Using these metrics we study Proposition 1:

Proposition 1 (P₁): A higher willingness to adopt grid technology will lead to a positive impact on the perceived level of B&R agility.

Perceived Attributes

Perceived attributes of the innovation consist of five constructs (Rogers, 1995). Relative advantage or perceived benefits refer to the level of recognition of the relative advantage that grid technology can provide the organization (adapted from Iacovou et al., 1995). The degree of relative advantage towards the current use of a data backup and recovery system or using no system at all is relevant. Negative experiences with data loss in the past can be an important reason for potential adopters to adopt a system, when they do not have a data recovery system yet. Alternatively, they can choose for a system, if they are not satisfied with their current solution. This construct can be further divided into perceived direct benefits and perceived indirect benefits. Compatibility is the degree to which the system is perceived as consistent with existing values, past experiences, and the needs of the potential adopter. Three other attributes of innovation are complexity, triability and observeability. These attributes are excluded in the pre-measurement of our field study, since these attributes only can be measured after potential adopters actually have experienced usage of grid technology. It is expected that SMEs with management that recognize the benefits are more likely to adopt and enjoy higher impacts compared with firms with management that do not recognize the benefits. Resulting in Proposition 2:

Proposition 2 (P₂): Higher perceived benefits of grid technology will lead to a greater intent to adopt and integrate grid technology.

Organizational Readiness

Organizational readiness refers to the availability of the needed financial and technical resources of the organization required for adoption and integration of DBRG (Iacovou et al., 1995). The grid technology is a technological innovation, so there will be need for technological resources and expertise within the SME. Technical readiness deals with the level of sophistication of IT usage and IT management in a firm (Van Heck & Ribbers, 1999). Since the usage of grid application is based on a simple web based tool, technical readiness is assumed not to be a barrier for adoption. Financial resources are necessary to make use of the application. Van Heck & Ribbers (1999) describe financial readiness as the financial resources available for EDI to pay for the development, implementation and usage of the EDI system. In this case only the usage of the grid application requires payment. Willingness to change is another important factor which influences organizational readiness. Waarts et al. (2002) define willingness to change as the attitude towards IT innovations. According to them, a positive attitude to change has a positive effect on early adoption. In this study we examine how corporate information can be spread through a network of SMEs. This is business critical information and in most cases it is strictly necessary that nobody else can read the files that are shared via the grid application. A new technology can be scary for adopters because they are not familiar with all the risks. Familiarity or acquaintance with grid technology could be a factor that affects the rate of adoption positively. Acquaintance will be defined here as foreknowledge about the technology. Hitherto, there is no research done to this variable in combination with adoption of an innovation. It is expected that small firms with higher organizational readiness will be more likely to be adopters compared to lower levels of readiness. Resulting in Proposition 3:

Proposition 3 (P_3): Higher organizational readiness will lead to greater intent to adopt and integrate grid technology.

External Pressure

Influences from the SMEs environment can be determinants for the adoption. Competitors, customers, suppliers, partners and governments are actors in the environment of the potential adopters. A study of Waarts et al. (2002), analyzed the influence of competition on the adoption decision of an ERP (Enterprise Resources Planning) system. They noticed that this applies for competitors within the same industry. Van Heck & Ribbers (1999) also found the comparable result, but they include in their research towards external pressure also imposition of the trading partner. This last issue is very important in their study to EDI (Electronic

Data Interchange), since EDI couples trading partners via a shared infrastructure. The grid technology as part of the service also couples companies via a shared infrastructure. In addition to competitors, customers can also be an important external pressure. This is important in a situation wherein companies can no longer profit from their customers if business critical data gets lost. In this case they can not accept new customers, but even worse they can not help existing customers. Customers will switch to a competitor that is able to fulfill their needs. Recent regulations have increased the need for preservation of data. The Dutch Law and Dutch Tax-service have instantiated regulations regarding the storage of corporate documents for a certain period of time. This type of external pressure can stimulate adoption of a service. We expect that SMEs that encounter more pressure from their environment, will adopt grid technology more frequently than those that do not encounter such pressure. Resulting in Proposition 4:

Proposition 4 (P_4): Higher external pressure will lead to greater intent to adopt and integrate grid technology.

We also expect that a combination of factors would lead to greater intent to adopt and integrate, resulting in Proposition 5:

Proposition 5 (P_5): The combination of higher perceived benefits, higher organizational readiness and higher external pressure will lead to greater intent to adopt and integrate grid technology.

Adoption and Integration

DBRG adoption is the process during which a firm becomes capable of backing up and restoring data via a grid based data backup and recovery service. After the adoption decision a DBRG integration process takes place, during which a firm alters its business practices and applications to make optimal usage of the DBRG. Based on Iacovou et al. (1995) we distinguish an adoption/impact typology for SMEs with six profiles: unprepared adopter, ready adopter, coerced adopter, unmotivated adopter, initiator, and non-adopter.

Unprepared Adopters can be described as firms that experience external pressure as a reason for adopting, but who lack financial or technical resources (i.e. organizational readiness) to integrate grid technology in their operations. Ready Adopters are SMEs that are prepared to adopt and have the necessary resources. Coerced Adopters are pressured to adopt. However, they have not recognized the need for it and their organization is not ready to integrate grid technology. Unmotivated Adopters feel external pressure and possess necessary resources for adoption; however, perceived benefits are relatively low, for example firms that already have a well-working data backup and recovery solution. DBRG initiators are the true innovators among the innovators. Although there is relatively low external pressure, they recognize the need for a grid application and they possess the required resources for adoption and integration. Finally, Non-adopters are firms that do not intend to adopt. They experience no external pressure and they either lack organizational readiness and/or have a low perception of the benefits grid technology can bring. The four propositions representing the important relations in our conceptual model were defined and transferred into a survey instrument. The next section discussed the research method and data.

Research Method and Data

To investigate the grid adoption and effect model, an empirical study of SMEs was conducted in the period between April and December 2007. In this study, we define a SME to be a firm with less than 100 employees. We started our research with a pre-study among Dutch SMEs. For this we used a survey, which focused on current usage of IT in general and backup and recovery solutions in specific. The survey was followed by a field experiment among 12 SMEs in the region of Almere. In this field experiment we used a structured questionnaire to assess adoption readiness and perceived effects. We conducted a pre-measurement (before usage of DBRG) and a post-measurement (after usage of DBRG). This paper reports on the results of the survey and the pre-measurement as part of the field study.

The population for the survey was a representative database of contacts of a Dutch bank in various sectors in the Netherlands. From the total population of 77,000 SMEs in the Netherlands 10,000 SMEs were approached, with a response of 2,485 companies (is a response rate of 24.85%). For the field experiment about 400 local SME customers of the bank in the Dutch region Almere were approached. Twelve SMEs actively took part in the field experiment. Most firms provide professional services. Firm size is relatively small, with four self-employed businesses. Furthermore, ten firms have a certain level of data backup and recovery capability, while two firms have no capability at all (i.e. make no backups of their data).

In the pre-study survey we used a structured questionnaire, which was distributed via e-mail and hosted on a web-site. In the field experiment we used a structured questionnaire to assess adoption readiness for DBRG. This measuring instrument was adapted from the instrument used by van Heck and Ribbers (1999). We used the questions to measure the different independent variables of our conceptual model and we added questions on the dependent variables of our conceptual model and specific questions related to DBRG and different components of a business and exploitation model for a DBRG service. In total, our questionnaire contained 65 questions. The questionnaire included closed format questions and some open format questions. Most variables of our conceptual model were measured via different items on a Likert-scale with a range between from 1 (very unimportant) and 5 (very important). We did a pre-test of the instrument in a small group of 8 respondents. Since we made use of an existing measurement instrument internal validity was sufficient. While the respondents filled out the questionnaire a researcher was present to help them clarify any questions they had about the questions in the questionnaire. A detailed version of the questionnaire can be obtained from the authors upon request.

This was an explorative study and the sample size in our field experiment was relatively small. Therefore, we decided to perform a more qualitative cross-case analysis (like Iacovou et al., 1995) instead of a quantitative regression and factor analysis (like van Heck & Ribbers, 1999). In the analysis phase we rescaled some variables, in order to have a common 5-point scale for comparisons.

Empirical Results

Finding of the Survey Among Dutch SMEs

The survey among Dutch SMEs shows that almost all SMEs have business critical data, mostly financial data, customer data, communication (e-mails and website) and contracts. For about 66% of the survey population this amount is below 10 Gb of data. Almost 50% of all the companies have experienced data loss through a human error and more than 60% lost data as a result of a computer malfunction. SMEs (85%) are severely affected by the loss of crucial data. Although data recovery is already an integral part of daily operations for most of the SMEs, the current method of working is characterized as a rather inefficient manual process. Most SMEs lack the resources (financial and technical) for a full data backup and recovery process. The majority of SMEs (70%) use different forms of manual data backup and recovery, like CD-ROMs. However, these solutions are quite labor intensive and in case of emergencies do not really provide a sufficient recovery solution. So far about 5% of the SMEs make use of an external provider for managing their backup and recovery process via on-line backup software. Most on-line models used in the market are based on client-server computing, where data is stored on an external dedicated server of the service provider. The main driver of online-backup services is the availability of Internet connections. However, even with current ADSL and cable speeds, sophisticated incremental backup schemes are needed to backup large amounts of data. A few providers make use of peer-to-peer computing. Sixty percent of the SME are satisfied with their current backup facilities.

Easy Adopters Vs. Difficult Adopters

The organizations in our field study sample are part of the innovators (based on adoption in time, i.e. Rogers, 1995). They represent 3% of the sample (12 out of 400), which closely matches the 2.5% which characterizes the innovator group stated by Rogers (1995). We can split our sample in two subgroups, the easy adopters and difficult adopters. *'Easy adopters'* have enough financial and technical resources to adopt the DBRG, they have technical expertise, they are willing to change and they see the need for or the benefits of DBRG. In most cases they have had dramatic experiences with their current backup system with data loss in the past. Most of them are acquainted with GRID-technology. They like to use DBRG for better serving their customers. Governmental regulations are important for them to save their data in a secure place. Two categories of Iacovou et al. (1995) are part of the easy adopter group: the ready adopters and the DBRG initiators. *'Difficult Adopters'* can be described as adopters that are willing to adopt, but the implementation of DBRG will not come without hardship. This stems from the fact that they do not have the needed resources, knowledge or they do not recognize the real benefits or needs.

Effects on Agility

Table 18.1 presents an overview of the perceived impact of grid technology on the backup and recovery agility metrics, split out for the different adopter categories in our sample. The highest impact is expected in terms of the ease to backup (3.67) and the ease to recover (3.92) data. Also, perceived effects on quality and robustness score relatively high. Respondents expect a negative effect on time to recover (2.81), which can be explained by the distributed nature of the architecture for data recovery. However, this is considered not to be very important (3.46). When we compare the easy adopters vs. difficult adopters, we find a number of differences. Difficult adopters perceive a more positive effect on quality and robustness of backup agility compared to easy adopters. Also, effects on quality and robustness of recovery agility are perceived higher by the difficult adopter group.

Table 18.1 Scores on the B&R-Agility variables per adopter group

Scores on perceived B&R-Agility level per adopter group. (Firm ->)	Unprepared adopter	Ready adopter	Coerced adopter	Unmotivated adopter	DBRG initiator	Non-adopter	Mean
	D & F	B, G, I & K	H	L	C & E	A & J	
Scores on backup agility Time	3.00	3.75	3.00	3.00	3.50	4.00	3.38
Costs	5.00	3.50	3.00	2.00	3.50	3.00	3.33
Scope	4.00	3.25	3.00	3.00	3.00	3.50	3.29
Ease	5.00	4.00	3.00	2.00	3.50	4.50	3.67
Quality	4.00	3.75	4.00	4.00	2.50	3.00	3.54
Robustness	3.00	4.25	4.00	4.00	2.00	3.50	3.46
Mean	4.00	3.75	3.33	3.00	3.00	3.58	3.44
Scores on recovery agility Times	3.00	3.33	2.00	2.00	3.00	3.50	2.81
Costs	3.00	3.50	3.00	1.00	3.00	3.50	2.83
Scope	4.00	3.50	4.00	4.00	3.00	3.50	3.67
Ease	5.00	4.00	4.00	3.00	3.50	4.00	3.92
Quality	4.50	4.00	4.00	3.00	2.50	3.50	3.58
Robustness	3.50	4.00	4.00	4.00	2.50	3.50	3.58
Mean	3.83	3.72	3.50	2.83	2.92	3.58	3.40
Total mean	3.92	3.74	3.42	2.92	2.96	3.58	3.42
= 'Easy Adopter'				= 'Difficult Adopters'			

The difficult adopter group compared with the easy adopters perceives the effects on time and costs lower. The results indicate that Proposition 1 needs to be rejected. Perceived impact on B&R agility differs per adopter group and per agility metric. We also analyzed the importance of the different metrics (on a scale from 1 to 5). For backup agility, scope (4.67) and quality (4.67) are perceived as most important. For recovery agility, quality (4.58) and robustness (4.58) are perceived as most important. The time to recover (3.46) is considered least important. Within backup agility, time (4.25) also has a low importance, but it is still higher than within the recovery agility. All average scores are above 3.00, this means that all variables are perceived as important.

Factors Influencing DBRG Adoption

Overall, the perceived attributes of innovation is the strongest determining factor for the DBRG adoption decision, followed by organizational readiness and the weakest determining factor is external pressure (which, however, affects the adoption decision positively). It shows that we find support for Proposition 2 among 91% of the respondents, we find support for Proposition 3 among 75% of the respondents and we find support for Proposition 4 among 67% of the respondents. In conclusion, we can state that all three factors separately do have a considerably strong effect on the DBRG adoption process (Proposition 2, 3 & 4). The adoption decision of 50% of the SMEs is based on all three factors together. It is not a very strong effect. Therefore we reject Proposition 5.

We also analyzed the average scores of the independent variables for the different adopter groups. When we compare the easy adopters vs. difficult adopters, we find a number of differences. Perceived attributes of the innovation are comparable with the exception of compatibility, which exhibits a higher score in the easy adopter group. On the organizational readiness dimension, financial resources and acquaintance score considerably higher in the easy adopter group. Finally, with regards to external pressure, difficult adopters feel more external pressure for adoption, especially from the government.

Conclusions and Limitations

In this chapter, we discussed two central questions. The first question is: What are the factors responsible for the adoption and integration of grid technology in small businesses? The empirical investigation suggests that adoption of grid technology is most influenced by the perceived (in)direct benefits, followed by organizational readiness. External pressure by clients and legal compliance has a lower influence in our sample. The adopter groups that will adopt are the profiles of the ready adopters and the DBRG initiators (Easy Adopters). They experience the perceived attributes of the innovation and their organization is ready for adopting. The Ready Adopters also feel external pressure, unlike the DBRG Initiators. Fifty percent of the adopters that we found in our sample were 'Easy Adopters'. The other fifty percent are 'Difficult Adopters'. They have an intention to adopt, but their organization is not ready yet, or they do not see the perceived benefits of the innovation. The 'Easy and Difficult Adopters' together form three percent of the sample of the SMEs that were invited to participate in BEinGRID. We found two factors in the non-adopter group (97%) that could explain non-adoption. First, respondents in this group perceived insufficient perceived benefits of DBRG compared with their existing data backup and recovery solution. Second, many respondents in this group felt no external pressure at all, nor an internal need for a DBRG, since they felt that they had no business critical data (for example bakeries, barbershops and florists).

The second research question is: What is the impact of grid technology in SMEs on backup and recovery agility? We found that the perceived impact on B&R agility differs per adopter group and per agility metric. The backup agility metrics that are perceived to be the most important are scope and quality. Within recovery agility, quality and robustness are considered to be the most important. The highest impact is expected in terms of the ease of backup and the ease of re-covering data. Also perceived effects on quality and robustness score relatively highly.

This research makes three contributions to the literature. First, based on the diffu-sion theory of Rogers (1995) and adoption models of previous technologies such as EDI, we have developed and validated a conceptual model that can be used for grid. Second, we have developed different adoption profiles for grid, each with their own characteristics in terms of perceptions of the grid technology, its organ-izational readiness, its external pressure to use the technology, and its perception on how the application will improve the firm's agility. Third, we have discussed conclusions and limitations due to differences in the underlying technology char-acteristics of the innovation.

Our study has a number of limitations. Our field experiment was conducted with a relatively small sample. Furthermore, this sample might be biased. It con-sists of customers of a bank in a specific geographic region in the Netherlands. Recent research has shown that the TAM model does not hold for certain cultural orientations (Mccoy, Galetta, & King, 2007). These aspects need to be taken into account in further research. Furthermore, the sample probably consists of inno-vators who are eager to experience and adopt new innovations. We analyzed one specific type of grid usage (sharing of storage space), while potential adopters were all SMEs. Therefore, generalizability is limited to this specific adopter group, specific grid usage, and geographic region. Since our research can be considered a single snapshot adoption study, our results are not necessary valid in predicting the likelihood of adoption for the next group of potential adopters (Waarts et al., 2002).

A second limitation is the difficulty to assess and separate the grid technology effects on adoption and agility impact from the wider solution or service for backup and recovery of data. Respondents who currently have no or insufficient solution for their data backup and recovery will most probably perceive any solu-tion to have positive effects on B&R agility, independent of the technology the solution is based on. In future research we need to split grid specific aspects and the overall service aspects in the analysis of adoption and impact of DBRG.

Acknowledgments

The authors acknowledge the funding from the EU BEinGRID project. We are grateful for the contributions from the partners in the BEinGRID DBRG business experiment: AlmereGrid, LogicaCMG, and Rabobank. Furthermore, we would like to thank the respondents and student assistants.

References

Davis, F. D. (1989). Perceived usefulness, perceived ease of use and user acceptance of information technology. *MIS Quarterly, 13*(3), 319–340.

Desouza, K. C. (Eds.). (2006). *Agile information systems: Conceptualization, construction and management.* New York: Butterworth-Heinemann.

Dove, R. (2001). *Response ability: The language, structure and culture of the Agile enterprise.* New York: Wiley.

Foster, I., & Kesselman, C. (1999). *The grid: Blueprint for a new computing infrastructure.* San-Francisco, CA: Morgan Kaufmann .

Gatignon, H., & Robertson, T. S. (1989). Technology diffusion: An empirical test of competitive effects. *Journal of Marketing, 53*(1), 25–49.

Goldman, S., Preiss, K., Nagel, R., & Dove, R. (1991). 21st century manufacturing enterprise strategy. Bethlehem, PA: Iacocca Institute, Lehigh University.

Goldman, S., Nagel, R., Preiss, K. (1995). Agile competitors and virtual organizations. New York: van Nostrand Reinhold.

van Heck, E., & Ribbers, P. M. A. (1999). The adoption and impact of EDI in Dutch SMEs. In R. Sprague (Ed.), *Proceedings of the 32nd Hawaii International Conference on System Sciences* (pp. 1–11). Los Alamitos, CA: IEEE,

van Heck, E., & Vervest, P. H. M. (2007), Smart business networks: How the network wins. *Communication of the ACM, 50*(6), 28–37.

Iacovou, C. l., Benbasat, I., & Dexter, A. S. (1995). Electronic data interchange and small organizations: Adoption and impact of technology. *MIS Quarterly*, 465–485.

Kidd, P. T. (1994). Agile manufacturing: Forging new frontiers. Wokingham: Addison-Wesley.

Kotler, P., & Keller, K. L. (2006). Marketing management (12th ed). New Jersey, Pearson Education.

Levin, S. G., Levin, S. L., & Meisel, J. B. (1987). A dynamic analysis of the adoption of new technology: The case of optical scanners. *The Review of Economics and Statistics, 69*(1), 12–17.

Mccoy, S., Galetta, D. F., & King, W. R. (2007). Applying TAM across cultures: the need for caution. *European Journal of Information Systems 16*, 81–90.

Moreau, C. P., Lehmann, Dr., Markman, A. B. (2001). Entrenched knowledge structures and consumer response to new products. *Journal of Marketing Research, 38*(1), 14–29.

Overby, E., Bharadwaj, A., & Sambamurthy, V. (2006). Enterprise agility and the enabling role of information technology. *European Journal of Information Systems, 15*(2), 120–131.

Rogers, E. M. (1962, 1995). Diffusion of innovations. New York, Free Press.

Sambamurthy, V., Bharadwaj, A., & Grover, V. (2003). Shaping agility through digital options: Reconceptualizing the role of information technology in contemporary firms. *MIS Quarterly, 27*(2), 237–263.

Spector, A. N., & Brown, L. A. (1976). Acquaintance circles and communication: An exploration of hypotheses relating to innovation adoption. *The Professional Geographer, 28*(3), 267–277.

Stong-Michas, J. (2005). GRID adoption perks up. Network magazine, Accessed on-line 6/20/05 http://www.networkworld.com/research/2005/062005-grid.html .

Thibodeau, P. (2004). Data finds a place on the GRID. Focus computerworld, Accessed on-line 5/4/2004 http://www.computerworld.com/databasetopics/data/story/0,10801,91828,00.html

Van Hoek R. I., Harrison, A., & Christopher, M. (2001). Measuring agile capabilities in the supply chain. *International Journal of Operations & Production Management, 21*(1/2), 126–147.

Verstraete, C. (2004). Planning for the unexpected. *IEEE Manufacturing Engineer, 83*(3), 18–21.

Waarts, E., Everdingen, V. Y., Hilligersberg, V. J. (2002). The dynamics of factors affecting the adoption of innovations. *The Journal of Product Innovation Management 19*, 412–423.

Yusuf, Y. Y., Gunasekaran, A., Adeleye, E. O., Sivayoganathan, K. (2004). Agile supply chain capabilities: Determinants of competitive objectives. *European Journal of Operational Research, 159*(2), 379–392

Network Orchestration

Network Orchestration

Just as an orchestra needs a conductor, a network needs an orchestrator to coordinate the different actors. A conductor's job while helping each instrumentalist to keep pace is to give a new interpretation of a composers' music piece. The conductor does this by coordinating the transitions during the performance using changes in tempo and volume and by giving particular sections a more prominent role. Network Orchestration is about coordinating the transitions between different actors in a network: an orchestrator does not micro-manage the execution of business processes within another company but rather it makes sure that the hand over of outputs from one actor to another actor take place seamlessly and that the flows of information, resources and other inputs are unhindered.

In the end smart business networks should serve a customer better: more options for a customer to choose from at competitive prices. As technology makes it increasingly simple to combine, or mix-and-match, different capabilities to build customized products, there will be an increasing need for somebody, for example the network orchestrator, or other, for example Advocate Agents (Ketter, Batchu, Berosik, & McCreary, 2008), to assist customers in getting the product or service they need. This is the network orchestrator's task: to configure the network in such a way that each actor is activated when needed to jointly produce a product or service for the customer. The quintessential example of the network orchestrator is Li & Fung (Fung, Fung, & Wind, 2007). Li & Fung acts as the network orchestrator using a network that encompasses many producers and countries. Li & Fung dissects the supply chain in small steps with each step being chosen based on the requirements of the product ordered by their customer. Hence, each route through the network is unique. Their network provides the convenience of a one-stop-shop for customers by offering product design and development, raw material and factory sourcing, production planning and management, quality assurance and export documentation to shipping consolidation.

We present four chapters on network orchestration. Each chapter emphasizes a different aspect of the network orchestration process. Duncan Shaw presents a study on how Manchester United, the football club, orchestrates its network to transform a football club into a customer experience. Duncan Shaw demonstrates how Manchester United is able to reconfigure its network to unlock new markets that are complex and difficult to access and service.

Xavier Busquets details a case study of one successful and one failing network orchestrator. He introduces the concept of network boundary management: who can and cannot join the network and how easily a network partner can join the network. He suggests that firms need to have a Business Operating System (BOS) to facilitate the joining and leaving of a business network. This BOS should support at least the following functions: quick connect and disconnect (see also Koppius & van de Laak, (2008)) resulting in a plug-and-play architecture, a separate control layer to manage business processes within and across organizational boundaries

(Pyke, 2008), standardized business processes and communication standards and network performance dashboards (see also Collins, Ketter, & Gini, (2008)) to increase the transparency of the network operations.

Amit Basu and Steve Muylle present a conceptual model of how business processes can be coordinated and governed within a smart business network. It is crucial for a network orchestrator to align its service offering, business model and the evolutionary context to improve firm performance. Different case studies show the effects of both misalignment and successful alignment.

Jens Riis focuses on the importance of having a shared identity among the network partners to create a shared goal for the smart business network. Having a shared identity and objective brings focus to the collaborative effort and can be used to attract new network partners (Hinterhuber, 2002). Jens Riis's study is in particular important for practitioners as it offers methods to create shared identities and it details what happens when such shared identities are lacking.

References

Collins, J., Ketter, W., & Gini, M. (2008). Flexible decision support in a dynamic business network. In P. H. M. Vervest, D. W. van Liere, & L. Zheng (Eds.), *The network experience – New value from smart business networks*. Berlin, Springer.

Fung, V. K., Fung, W. K., & Wind, Y. (2007). *Competing in a flat World: Enterprises for a borderless World*. Upper Saddle River, NJ: Wharton School Publishing.

Hinterhuber, A. (2002). Value chain orchestration in action and the case of the global agrochemical industry. *Long Range Planning, 35*(6), 615–635.

Ketter, W., Batchu, A., Berosik, G., & McCreary, D. (2008). A semantic web architecture for advocate agents to determine preferences and facilitate decision making, *Tenth International Conference on Electronic Commerce*. Innsbruck, Austria.

Koppius, O. R., & van de Laak, A. (2008). The quick-connect capability and its antecedents. In P. H. M. Vervest, D. W. van Liere, & L. Zheng (Eds.), *The network experience – New value from smart business networks*. Berlin: Springer.

Pyke, J. (2008). The rise of the business operations platform. In P. H. M. Vervest, D. W. van Liere, & L. Zheng (Eds.), *The network experience – New value from smart business networks*. Berlin: Springer.

19. Why Smart Business Networks Continue and Develop: A Structural and Processual Model of Value Flows

Duncan R. Shaw

Nottingham University Business School, United Kingdom, duncan.shaw@nottingham.ac.uk

Abstract

Business networks are multi-level value flow systems and in Smart Business Networks (SBNs) the value flows can be orchestrated by a central actor. This paper integrates recent thinking from the domains of ecological systems management, ecological economics and information dynamics to explain how smartness in network design is a direct enabler of network sustainability and cultivation. Shaw (2007) explains how Manchester United Football Club orchestrates the capabilities of its network of commercial partners to produce much more value than it could do by using its internal capabilities. However, Shaw (ibid) does not explain why this happens. Manchester United orchestrates its partners to promote the flow of financial and informational value from millions of fans. In return there is a complicated mix of services delivered to the fans. This type of inter-organisational network is a 'value flow system'. Value flow systems are open systems that are sustained in far-from-equilibrium states (Checkland, 1999) by the constant flow of materials, energy and information (ibid). This paper explains why value 'flows' through such a network to sustain it in a far-from-equilibrium state, i.e. why it exists, persists and takes certain forms. This paper also develops the definition of the term orchestration as centralised smartness in an SBN in contrast with decentralised network smartness such as a distributed co-ordination of capability (Shaw, Snowdon, Holland, Kawalek, & Warboys, 2004).

Introduction

Business networks are complex collections of firms that have many different material and informational interrelations. The complexity of these networks is caused by these interrelations which are mediated by business processes. The business processes that relate one firm to one or more firms in the network can link many different combinations of firms together, they can link different services (or products) of each firm together, they can link the services in many different configurations, and these configurations can change dynamically. This inter-firm configuration, or network architecture, has recently been the subject of several studies (Ethiraj & Levinthal, 2004; Galunic & Eisenhardt, 2001; Schilling & Steensma, 2001; Richard & Devinney, 2005).

Other studies have focused upon how the inter-firm configuration of networks can be influenced by one central firm (a sample includes Busquets, 2008; Dyer & Nobeoka, 2000; Goerzen, 2005; Hagel III, 2002; Iansiti, & Levien, 2004; Moller, Rajala, & Svahn, 2005; Lorenzoni & Baden-Fuller, 1995; Rodon, Busquets, & Christiaanse, 2005; Dhanaraj & Parkhe, 2006; Hinterhuber, 2002; Shaw, 2007). These studies use terms such as 'orchestrator' to label the central firm and they seek to better define what it is and what its role is (Hinterhuber, 2002). Dhanaraj & Parkhe (2006) note that studies of inter-organisational relationships to date have focused on either dyadic or network relationships. Dyadic studies miss the phenomena of a firm's network context and network studies miss a processual view firm's activities. They observe that "...the next stage of theory development must embrace this player-structure duality by taking into account both the structural inducements and constraints of the network, as well as organizational action that perpetuates the network" (ibid, p.665). They also call for a structure and process theory of network orchestration: "A more complete theory of network orchestration awaits detailed treatment of the entire framework. Indeed, as envisioned by Fombrun (1982), it is possible to simultaneously assess the impact of the advantages that emerge from a central position (structure) and network orchestration (process)" (ibid, p. 666). Shaw (2007) explains how Manchester United Football Club orchestrates the capabilities of its network of commercial partners to produce much more value than it could do by using its internal capabilities. However, Shaw (ibid) does not explain why this happens.

Here I seek to explain a key issue in smart network design, with implications for researchers in network management, business process management and service production: how does smartness in the design of an orchestrator's network support the creation of value, and as such, how can it enable network sustainability and cultivation. First I examine the link between the business processes that interrelate the firms in a business network and value. I do these using recent ideas from ecological economics that integrate the methods and models of the thermodynamics of physical processes with those of economic value. Then I use concepts from Hierarchy Theory to develop an analysis framework to analyse the relationship between the structural and process complexity of a system and the value associated with it in three case studies of orchestrated business networks. Next I discuss my findings in the context of the complexity of the structural and process hierarchies of the three cases. Finally I draw some novel implications for the design of smart networks with the objectives of growth in market share and market value.

Background Literature

Entropy and Energy Flows

Entropy is a thermodynamic concept that is used to describe how physical change processes on the micro level are irreversible. The temperature of a hot cup of tea will gradually reduce until it reaches equilibrium with the temperature of its environment. The tea's temperature will not increase unless more energy is added to it from an external source, e.g. by reheating it in a microwave oven. Entropy is a measure of the unavailability of a system's energy to do work. In the cup example the flow of heat energy from the cup to the environment could conceivably be used to power some process, e.g. 'work' could be a paper fan that is turned by the rising steam. The energy that is available for work is less than the total energy of the system. This applies to any process that transforms matter or energy, a certain proportion of the system's energy is transformed into an unusable form which makes the process impossible to fully reverse. The usable proportion of a system's energy is known as exergy (Baumgärtner, 2004; Tainter, Allen, Little, & Hoekstra, 2003), although this depends upon what you want to use the energy for. Deciding on what to use the energy for is a design choice and an anthropocentric act.

Furthermore, "a system's capacity to perform work depends not only on the state of the system, but also on the state of the system's environment" Baumgärtner (2004). The entropy of the system is a fundamental property of the system but the exergy of the system is related to how you want to use it and what you want to use it for because different means of employing energy, e.g. different engineering solutions to a single design problem, have different mechanical and energy use characteristics. To use the energy of a system you need to link it, via some process, with its environment. This creates an open system that is characterised by a process that spans an energy gradient. This thermodynamic definition of entropy (S) is $dS = dQ/T$ where, using the previous example, dQ is the amount of heat energy that flows from the hot cup of tea to the room and T is the absolute temperature of the process. But this definition is based upon heat and it is only valid for a system in or near equilibrium because temperature is a macro-scale concept that is only relevant for a system in equilibrium, i.e. only near equilibrium it is appropriate to use a concept of 'general temperate'. The immense number of moving micro-scale particles that form the emergent macro-scale concept of temperature, e.g. gas molecules, display kinetic energy not temperature.

However, Boltzmann derived a micro-scale statistical definition which is more useful for a study of processes and open systems. In Boltzmann's definition "entropy may be interpreted as a measure of how orderly or mixed-up a system is" Baumgärtner (2004). High entropy systems are homogenous, i.e. they are uniform/more probable, and low entropy systems are heterogeneous, i.e. patterned/less probable. (This definition is also related to the information theory definition of entropy which is a measure of how much information is in a particular message). For a fuller definition of these concepts in the context of thermodynamics see Sears & Salinger (1975) and in the context of thermodynamics and economics see Baumgärtner (2004).

The Implications of the Entropy and Exergy Concepts for Economic Systems

According to the 2nd Law of Thermodynamics entropy only increases in a closed system. In an open system new useful energy, exergy, is accessed from the environment. In effect, although not literally, entropy is 'exported' out of open systems by processes which then appear to be negentropic. Open systems span energy gradients using processes to maintain their far-from-equilibrium states (Allen, Tainter, & Hoekstra, 2003; Tainter et al., 2003; Salthe, 2003). It is the 2nd Law of Thermodynamics that open systems seem to 'bend' to maintain their far from equilibrium states by exporting entropy to their environment like bad neighbours dumping refuse over their garden fence.

The processes that span open systems access external energy gradients. Three other aspects of far-from-equilibrium states are associated with by entropy production in open systems: (1) there are different 'qualities' of energy gradient, (2) lower quality energy needs more organisation to be accessed and (3) energy gradients are consumed with use (Allen et al., 2003; Tainter et al., 2003). Firstly, the quality of energy sources differ in their concentration, accessibility and ease of use, e.g. heating a home via a wood fire is easier that using electricity produced by a nuclear power plant's uranium. Secondly, the lower the quality of an energy source then the more it will need to be aggregated, the harder it is to access or the harder it is to use. Lower quality energy sources need more complex organisations of systems and process to use them (Allen et al., 2003; Tainter et al., 2003), e.g. the development of horizontal drilling enabled oil companies to access oil fields that were inaccessible with purely vertical drilling technologies and electricity produced by nuclear fission requires a much more sophisticated industrial economy than oil-powered electric generation. Thirdly, when higher quality energy sources are used up the remaining energy sources are of a lower quality, which leads to a need for the development of organisational complexity in order to use them.

This interpretation of the concept of entropy applies to firms not just in terms of their physical energy needs but it also applies in terms of their commercial objectives. A recent special issue on the applications of statistical physics to economic problems strongly justifies the use of the physical science concepts, like entropy, for studying economic systems (Farmer & Lux, 2008). Farmer and Lux use inter-level, i.e. scalar emergence, to justify the use of statistical physical concepts in economics using Adam Smith's "classic idea that economic phenomena are emergent properties of the low-level inter-actions of selfishly motivated agents who may be entirely unaware of the consequences of these actions at a higher level" (ibid, p. 2). They also use Ettore Majorana's conceptualisation of social and economic phenomena as a statistical set of potential microscopic configurations "whose exact realization one cannot determine given our incomplete knowledge of all pertinent factors" (ibid, p. 2). This articulates the many possible pathways a process can follow, i.e. it is processual emergence. Although processes are also subject to the constraints of higher levels and display properties of scalar emergence. The common phenomenon between social, economic and physical systems is emergence and emergence involves some form of abstraction or loss of information when phenomena pass from lower to higher levels. In physics there is a lack of information concerning the details of lower level physical phenomena which is due to the complexity of modelling immense numbers of particles. In economic or social science the lack of information concerning the details of lower level economic or social phenomena is due to the complexity of many actors as well as social science's lack of equivalents to the laws of physics. But in both scientific domains a higher level, more abstract, statistical model can be used for description and prediction. Herbert Simon used this to study patterns in firm sizes and was one of the initiators of Hierarchy Theory (Simon, 1955). Statistical techniques have also been used to analyse the structure of information flows in smart networks (Braha & Bar-Yam, 2004). Baumgärtner also discusses how thermodynamic concepts can be incorporated into economic analyses with some usefulness and some constraints (2004).

Emergence in Economic and Organisational Systems

The concept of processual emergence is the link between Boltzmann's micro-scale statistical definition of entropy and concept of value flows in macro-scale inter-firm business processes. Scalar emergence is a property of hierarchical systems whereby emergent phenomena do not exist on levels that are lower than the one that they are produced on (Checkland, 1999; Salthe, 1985). It is only possible to experience the emergent behaviour of elements on level zero from a higher level of the system, level one, and above. The related concept of processual emergence deals with the options that any business process has at each stage of its enaction. For example, if we consider the process enacted by a person walking across a room then at each step, or at each moment, there is a choice of changing direction, speed or any other characteristic of the process. These choices emerge during the enaction of a process instance and are unforcastable, e.g. when firms supply services to customers they can never totally forecast what the services will be actually used for (Shaw, 2007). In business processes these choices are commonly in response to dynamic changes in the environment, customer needs and the information that is held by the process enactor. On a micro-scale the molecules in a gas display processual emergence in that their trajectory cannot be forecast because of the complexity of their environment. On a macro-scale, the choices of firm in a network are just as infinitely complex but practically they are limited by the bounded rationality (Simon, 1997) of the firm's managers and information systems that they are part of. This is why I focus on orchestrated inter-firm networks since orchestrators help the orchestrated firms by giving them better quality choices (Shaw, 2007). Orchestrators give a wider choice of options but also filter out low quality choices. Where 'choice quality' is congruent with the values of both the orchestrated and the orchestrator. On a micro-scale energy gradients are consumed by processes and entropy increases as systems are homogenised and diversity is reduced. On a macro-scale customers' needs are serviced and markets are penetrated and then saturated. On all scales physicals resources are consumed when they are transformed into states that are less useful to the transforming system or firm. The micro-scale is related to the macro-scale in terms described by hierarchy theory, below. But both micro and macro-scale processes dissipate the characteristics of the systems that they span, and are their cause, in a process of consumption that is finite in closed systems. Customers cannot be sold the same service twice for the same instance of service-need. But they can become repeat customers when their environment repeats the events that generate the original service need and their valuation of that service.

The sustainability of Manchester United's Smart Business Network (SBN) of partner firms is based upon the flow of value through its value system which is a processual phenomenon (Shaw, 2007). The equilibrium position of a firm is its asset value, which is much less that its value as a functioning company. A far-from-equilibrium state is a function of behaviour not just constitution. This relates activities and business processes to value. In process philosophical terms a firm is what it does (Rescher, 2000). This is also an example of holism since in general systems terms a network of firms is more than the sum of its parts, it is how they relate to each other.

In economic systems some customers are easier to service than others and some markets are easier to extract value from than others. One problem here comes from the complexity of business processes that are required to produce high specification products and services. Increasingly firms are working together in more complex organisational forms, i.e. networks, to transfer resources and value

(Lyman, Caswell, & Biem, 2008). This enables the production of higher specification, i.e. more specific, products and services through the use of more complex business processes. The main driver of this has been increased inter-firm competition from globalisation and the need to produce a product or service that is a better quality, i.e. a better fit with the customer's specific needs. But the benefit for the end user of the product or service is access to new capabilities or services. For example the modern car is an incredibly complicated set of components that requires many tiers of heavily synchronised firms. Synchronisation techniques such as Just In Time Manufacturing are methods of ensuring inter-process fit and are part of wider lean manufacturing philosophies which seek to mitigate the costs of increasing network and process complexity.

The increasing complexity of business processes at the firm and network level is an effect of closed system commercial competition, and it is driven by firms forming networks to access areas of value that cannot be accessed by single firms or even supply chains that are organised more simply. For example single firms have upper limits to their information processing capabilities because they are boundedly rational (Simon, 1997). Simple supply chains expand the information processing, speed and market access capabilities beyond those of a single firm, but ordinary supply chain members just consume and supply to their adjacent partners. If one firm orchestrates the supply chain then the organisation of the network's business processes can be much more complex. Orchestration adds a level to the organisation of the network so that the network's outputs can be much more specific and so it can access lower quality (i.e. harder to get at) markets. Orchestration is the management of the value flow system of an SBN and orchestrator organisations, like those analysed below, operate on a higher level than ordinary network members (Shaw, 2007).

The increase in the specification of the network-level product is enabled by an increase in the complexity of the sum of the networks' business processes. The successful implementation of this is a measure of the smartness of the design of the network. Next I use General Systems concepts from Hierarchy Theory (Wilby, 1994) to investigate how a managed increase in network complexity can be used to develop new products, services and markets for a SBN. Such markets may currently be unaccessesable or inconceivable.

The sustainability of member firms and the SBN itself is dependent upon the network spanning a large enough value gradient to sustain its activities (Fig. 19.1) The relevance to SBNs is that the size of the value gradient that the network can span depends upon its structural configuration. The value flow through the network depends upon how smartly the network is designed in terms of the structuring of member firms' service contributions to the whole and the processes that compose them into network-level products and services. I will use this division of SBN Smartness into structural design and process design in my analysis together with the latest ecosystem sustainability concepts from Hierarchy Theory to contribute to researchers' and managers' understanding of competition at different network levels. I also develop insights on how to balance complexity and specification/quality in network design since making systems more complex also increases 'frictional' overheads such as tax or coordination costs.

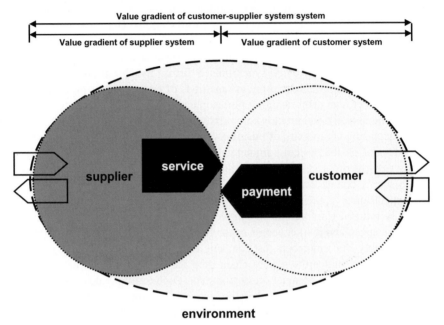

Fig. 19.1 The value gradients of the customer, supplier and joint system interact with their respective environments via business processes

Hierarchy Theory is an approach for modelling complex systems "through a self reflective process of observation and description" (Wilby, 1994, p. 659) and it is "concerned with the fundamental differences between one level of complexity and another" (Checkland, 1999, p. 81). Hierarchy Theory is a protocol for dealing with observed complexity. It relates higher lever constraints to lower lever options and is commonly used for the analysis of complex systems such as in ecology (Allen & Hoekstra, 1992). System levels are hierarchical and are arranged in at least two forms (Salthe, 1991), the scalar hierarchy and the specification hierarchy. In a scalar hierarchy the asymmetry in the differences between levels are that higher levels contain, constrain and are the context of lower levels (Salthe, 1985). Larger scale entities are made up of smaller scale entities. Level separation is based upon degree of aggregation. Alternatively a specification hierarchy is a sequence of development from general to specific. It is a process of refinement. Stage separation is based upon degree of specification. A SBN's configuration of structure and process affects its ability to access and process value and thus to sustain itself. Scale and specification hierarchies are both used here to analyse three cases to investigate how network sustain themselves in far from equilibrium states.

Research Method

This study focuses upon the trade off between the Smart design of what (the scalar architecture of levels of roles in firms and roles of firms in networks) and the Smart design of how (the specification architecture of levels that are more commonly referred to as process stages). I use three examples from my recent research to show how network organisation enables business processes to link the sides of a value gradient so as to liberate value and so sustain the network. This study is a multi-actor as well as a multi-level study so it takes an interpretive stance, because of the subjective nature of human interaction, and iterates around a hermeneutic circle, between network and service level perspectives so as to consider an interdependent whole (Klein & Myers, 1999). The novelty of using scalar and specification architectural concepts from hierarchy theory to describe network smartness points to a qualitative approach because the investigation is concerned with initial questions of 'how' and 'why' rather than of 'how many'. Following Yin's recommendations (2003) my investigation uses a case study approach because it is concerned with contemporary phenomena, which I have no control over, and of business relationships between many different firms from many different sectors. The use of just three case studies has external validity implications, that is, generalisation implications (Lee, 1989), but this is justified at the outset of theory generation (Benbasat, Goldstein, & Mead, 1987)) and although sample size may limit statistical generalisation it does not degrade analytic or theoretical generalisation (Robson, 2002; Lee & Baskerville 2003; Yin, 2003). This use of exemplar cases is consistent with the theory building objectives of this study.

I am concerned with dynamic phenomena so I have used different data collection methods and different sources (Eisenhardt, 1989). Interviews ranged from short informal conversations to semi-structured meetings and interviews. Most interviews were with the organisations' senior managers although lower level staff with more process specific knowledge were also interviewed. Overall, I used triangulation to converge evidence, analysis and synthesis upon the same process and network structure phenomena. A good relationship with each of the cases' participants over a minimum of 6 months per case also helped to reduce validity reactivity and increase trust as well as disclosure. Data sources included meeting notes, telephone conversations, archival data, organisation reports and the website content of the different organisations involved. Preliminary case study findings were validated by senior managers of the case organisations.

Analyses of Three Smart Networks Using Scale and Specification Hierarchy Perspectives

In Tables 19.1 and 19.2 I analyse three case networks to investigate how network structure gives access to processes that in turn produce services. These are then composed into a whole network service to meet an environmental need that is in turn embodied in a specific customer value. This is an analysis of the cases' scalar hierarchies as well as their specification (i.e. process) hierarchies because they are multi-level value flow systems and as such have multiple scalar levels and multi-stage processes that transmit value. Value does not literally flow but the values of the actors are all 'connect up' into a value gradient in the sense that each actor perceives a relationship between the service needs of others, their capacity to meet them and their own values. The y-axes of Table 19.1 and Table 19.2 contain rows for each of the three case networks.

The x-axis of Table 19.1 shows the relationship between scalar organisation, specification organisation and value. The Structural configuration column describes how the networks of different organisational elements are hierarchically configured. The Process configuration column describes how the contributions of the organisational elements are configured into a process which produces a service. The Network-level configuration of services column describes how the different services are configured into a network-level service. The Environmental-level service-need column describes the general requirements of the customer population. The Customer-level value captured column describes how customers use the services they need and what consumption actually does for them.

Table 19.2 shows how these networks can be reorganised or reconfigured from either (or both) scalar and specification perspectives to better meet internal and external needs and access new value in a new ways. Where aspects of the case examples are not reorganised or reconfigured they are labelled 'same'. A structural reconfiguration of network members or a process reconfiguration of the service, or both, enables a change to the overall service of the network via a new mix of sub-services. This may fit a previously unmet service-need which captures previously unmet value from current service customers. Or it may access new segments of the market which also captures previously unmet value.

Discussion

The columns in Tables 19.1 and 19.2 combine scalar hierarchy and specification hierarchy perspectives since they view the structural hierarchy of firms, and in the council's case firm elements, and they also view the process of service composition through a hierarchy of stages. This is required in order to model these three multi-level value flow systems because the service that is the output (i.e. end stage) of a process can be viewed at the whole network level (i.e. the service of the network) or at the level of one member's service contribution. The relations between structural and processual phenomenon are only describable using a combination of scalar hierarchy and specification hierarchy perspectives. The scalar hierarchy perspective enables the study of how the networks' elements relate to each other in terms of how higher levels constrain lower levels. The specification hierarchy perspective enables the study of the how contributions of each network's members are configured into processes that produce services and how these services are designed to meet a general requirement of the customer population which then translates into specific uses for each customer and specific benefits of use (Fig. 19.2). Thus services can exist, from a scalar perspective, at the network level and at the customer level. Also, from a specification perspective, services can meet service-needs which are inputs to later stage processes, which in turn may be scalar sub-processes or specification stages or both.

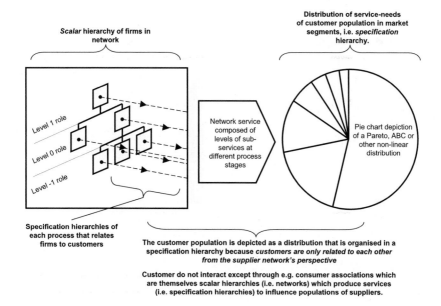

Fig. 19.2 The scalar hierarchy of the supplier network relates to a customer population via specification hierarchical processes which gives, from the supplier perspective, the distribution of the customer population a specification hierarchy

Table 19.1 How network structure gives access to a process that produces a service which is configured into a whole network service to meet an environmental need that is embodied in a specific customer value

	Structural configuration (network-level)	Process configuration (service - level)	Network-level configuration of services	Environmental-level service-need	Customer-level value captured
Manchester United's partner network (global)	MBNA and Barclaycard are two of Manchester United's many commercial partners.	MBNA and Barclaycard provide a credit card service.	A set of services that link fans and United.	Fans need to feel 'in touch' with the team and each game.	A closer association between fans and United in retail transactions with associated United-themed loyalty benefits.
City Council network (larger network) (local)	The council directly employs 30,000 staff in 7 departments which contain several levels of organisational unit. This structure works with many partner organisations such as the police, fire, ambulance and health services.	Different council departments and partners produce services for citizens including garbage disposal, car parking, low income support, education, child services, low cost housing, crime management, illness treatment.	'Infrastructural' services. All the services that enable citizens to live in the city which are not privately produced or too expensive for average citizens.	The mix of different needs generated by a very diverse city population of citizens and citizen businesses.	The many specific inputs that a citizen's life process requires in order to make city living not just pleasurable but even possible, e.g. a hygienic environment, car parking space, unemployment benefit, knowledge, nurseries, a home, crime protection, medical cures.
The 'nextstep' UK county careers guidance networks (smaller network, arguably part of council network) (local) (NS, 2008)	The 'nextstep' service organisation is networked with partner organisations that provide careers guidance as well as diverse training courses to citizen 'clients'.	Training organisations in the network help clients with career barriers, e.g. Basic Skills training helps with literacy and numeracy problems.	A problem highlighting service that is coordinated with various problem solving services.	Clients' 'routes' to employment are a process that produces many needs that require service inputs, i.e. barriers. E.g. Careers guidance is of limited value to a client that cannot read or write.	Coordinating appropriate training services with a Careers Guidance service provides solution capabilities just when problems are highlighted to a client. Clients value progression towards their career objectives.

Table 19.2 How networks can be reorganised or reconfigured from either scalar and specification perspectives (or both) to better meet internal and external needs and access new value in a new ways

	Structural reconfiguration (network-level)	Process re-configuration (service-level)	Network-level service reconfiguration (new mix of sub-services)	Newly met environmental-level service-need	New customer-level value captured
Manchester United's partner network. Structure *addition* and process reconfigurations to meet an unmet environmental (i.e. fan) need.	Vodafone is the sponsor partner that replaced Sharp because it contributes mobile technology capabilities not just sponsorship cash.	Game updates are texted to a fan. All fans that sign up for this service receive real-time football score information, that is not location dependant	Same: a set of links between fans and United.	Same: fans need to feel 'in touch' with the team and each game.	A closer association between fans and United in time and location dimensions.
City Council network. Structure and process *reconfigurations* to better fit environmental (i.e. staff data) need.	Consolidation of separate HR databases and departments. Link to webserver.	Use of a new ERP HR module enables initial process re-engineering. Initially drives no change to departmental structure, i.e. same employee data but now more widely available via browser.	Same: HR services, e.g. pensions, holiday entitlement, assessment, disciplinary etc.	Same: 30, 000 staff need indirect support as well as direct operational support	Staff can access their own data to check and change (where permitted) thus freeing up managers, increasing accuracy and increasing user convenience.
The 'nextstep' UK county careers guidance networks. Process reconfiguration to meet more environmental needs (i.e. more barriers removed for more clients).	Same network members.	Member organisations are developed by the orchestrator's in-house training team and supported by regular network member meetings.	Training helps members to improve their services by improving process that produce them; inter-member meetings enable solution swapping and best practice sharing. Improved overall service quality.	Same: mapping of clients' routes to employment' and pointing to solutions to any obstacles.	More accurate guidance on each client's 'route' to employment and more barriers surmounted faster.

This multi-level processual link between a scalar network and a population of customers is the value flow architecture that spans the value gradient between network members who make contributions and a population of customers who would value the benefits of using the services that those contributions can be used for. This value flow concept is consistent with the aspects of entropy production in open systems spanning energy gradients that I introduced earlier: (1) different 'qualities' of value gradient, e.g. for any given service the customers in each of the three cases are heterogeneous in their service-needs, expectations and ease of satisfaction, (2) lower quality value requires more organisation to be accessed, e.g. United fans with season tickets in the UK and Europe are easier to access than unknown fans in south east Asia (Shaw, 2007) (3) value gradients are consumed with use, e.g. satisfying a service-need enables the consumer to move along their personal life process whether they are a next step client with a developmental barrier, a council employee with a query or a United fan who wants to know the result of a football game. There will be other barriers, queries and matches but once satisfied each instance of a service-need no longer exists. Phenomena such as repeat customers, regular demand or any other seeming repetition of service-needs do not disprove that value gradients get used up. Instead they are just examples of wider system openness and the degradation of wider value gradients. This is an artefact of the observer's scalar and temporal focus and is not true for a wider focus that reaches closed system boundaries, e.g. the limits of global market size.

In entropy terms it is the particular organisation of service-needs that provides an opportunity to sell a service and the satisfaction of these service-needs dissipates the value gradient that represents this opportunity. Networks of firms sustain themselves in far-from-equilibrium states by dissipating value gradients. They satisfy previously unmet service-needs by understanding the values of customers, e.g. the careers paths and developmental goals of nextstep clients, the informational needs of council employees and the ways that fans can feel closer to United.

The orchestrator organisation uses its network to understand the values of the customer population and contrasts these with the potential contributions and values of current and potential firms in the network. The orchestrator uses this knowledge to configure the contributions and values of the firms and customer populations for mutual satisfaction. A network orchestrator's configuration of structural elements and their processual roles can be reconfigured to access lower quality value gradients, i.e. less attractive but new markets, by increasing the organisational complexity of the network. This can be done by adding new scalar levels, e.g. an orchestrator like Manchester United makes no direct contribution to a credit card service but it greatly helps credit card partners to access new international customers. Also, by adding new process stages, e.g. partnering with Vodafone enables football match results information to be reused in a new text service. Processes that can access new value gradients are created by increasing the scalar complexity of network structure that enact these processes, by adding new levels, or by increasing the specification complexity of their processes by adding stages, or both. Value gradients take the form of unmet service-needs of customers which once met are degraded, i.e. their entropy increases because they become used up and 'disorganised'.

The smart design of a network's architecture can be further examined in a discussion of the architecture's effect on effectiveness and efficiency. Increasing the scalar complexity of a network by adding levels, such as the orchestrator level, enables the network to generate more specific process outputs. This is the connection between the scalar (structural) architecture and the specification (processual) architecture. The orchestrators in these three networks give the entities on the level below higher quality choices by filtering lower quality options and suggesting higher quality options. Where option quality is a measure of fitness for purpose, i.e. it is more specific. This enables access to more of the value gradient in the form of harder to satisfy market segments (see Fig. 19.2). Firms that use a Pareto or ABC analysis of their market segments initially target the easier segments, with more general needs. Later they have to produce more a more specific product and service mix to access new parts of the market. Increasing the network's scalar complexity makes it more effective, i.e. more value is captured. Increasing the specification complexity of the network, by adding process stages, would at first sight make it less efficient since extra stages would mean that the speed of value capture may be decreased. Since process speed is a temporal concept it would seem that decreasing specification complexity, i.e. by the common process reengineering practice of removing process stages, efficiency may be increased. However, this depends upon your perspective. Efficiency here is not the efficiency of the football fan, the council employee or the nextstep client. Here efficiency is the efficiency of the orchestrtor's process for finding an efficient process for the fan, employee or client. Increasing the network's specification complexity, in the form of the orchestrator's process makes the level below more effective. The options given to fans, employees and clients are of higher quality, i.e. value is captured faster. Effectiveness and efficiency can linked by introducing the concept of value per second, i.e. more seconds are invested but much more value is accessed. But there is no room for exploring this here.

Conclusions

This paper describes a theory that explains how the configuration of inter-firm networks along structural and processual dimensions sustains them by using the concepts of values flow and value gradient which have foundations in general systems theory and thermodynamics. This provides an explanatory and predictive theory that can be used to design the structural and processual reconfiguration of networks so as to access new markets. The concept of a value flow driven by a value gradient and operationalised as services and processes that link a network of firms with a population of customers provides the theoretical explanation. The dual architecture of a value flow system provides a framework for redesign in response to either environmental change or internal development drivers.

The insight is that smart network design is based upon the design of these two orthogonal architectures with very different types of emergence between their levels. The contribution for managers is that this has implications for how orchestrators cultivate and manage networks in such areas as the configuration of firms' roles and processes (e.g. cross-selling decisions at different levels and stages) and the design of the product/service mix (i.e. choice of where components are produced both across and up the network vs. the external fit with the needs of current and potential customers).

One contribution of this paper for researchers is that it accomplishes the above by theoretically linking network sustainability via the value flow concept to thermodynamics and open systems. This explains why smartness sustains business networks. Network smartness is the organisational complexity of structure and process that enables access to value gradients. The smart structure and process architecture of the network can be reconfigured when the value gradients are used up. Another contribution is an explanation of how and why a network's architecture, the configuration of structural elements and their processual roles, can be reconfigured to access lower quality value gradients by increasing the organisational complexity of the network. The final contribution is to add to the theory of network orchestration with a description of how the orchestrator uses its knowledge of the network's firms and customer populations to smartly configure their contributions and values of for mutual satisfaction.

Further research needs to be done to examine the relations between micro and macro-scale entropy-like phenomena in value systems. This may be aided by incorporating the concept of scale of observation from hierarchy theory. This study does not explicitly include the affects of scale on the observer's perception of phenomena. For an orchestrator observing on a high level the scale of processes on the partner, employee or nextstep sub-contractor level may be relatively small enough that phenomena similar to statistical micro-scale physical entropy are observed. This study could also be furthered by exploring links with entropy in information theory, which has some strong similarities to Boltzmann's micro-scale statistical definition of entropy. The link between effectiveness and efficiency in redesigning network architectures could also be explored by studying the relationship between value and the speed of generating it.

Acknowledgements

I would like to thank the track chair and two reviewers, for their very valuable comments, as well as the managers and staff of the three case networks involved.

References

Allen, T. G. H., & Hoekstra, T. W. (1992). *Toward a unified ecology*. New York: Columbia University Press.

Allen, T. G. H., Tainter, J. A., & Hoekstra, T. W. (2003). *Supply-side sustainability*. New York: Columbia University Press.

Baumgärtner, S. (2004). Thermodynamic models. In J. Proops, P. Safonov (eds.), *Modelling in ecological economics* (pp. 102–129). Cheltenham: Edward Elgar.,

Braha, D., & Bar-Yam, Y. (2004). Information flow structure in large-scale product development organizational networks. *Journal of Information Technology, 19*(4), 244–253.

Benbasat, I., Goldstein, D. K., & Mead, M. (1987). The case research strategy in studies of information systems. *MIS Quarterly, 11*(3), 369–386.

Busquets, X. (2008). Orchestrating smart business networks. In P. H. M. Vervest, & D. W. van Liere, & L. Zheng (eds.), *The Network Experience – New value from smart business networks*. Berlin: Springer.

Checkland, P. (1999). *Systems thinking, systems practice*. Chichester: Wiley.

Dhanaraj, C., & Parkhe, A. (2006). Orchestrating innovation networks. *Academy of Management Review, 31*(3), 659–669.

Dyer, J. H., & Nobeoka, K. (2000). Creating and managing a high-performance knowledge sharing network: The Toyota case. *Strategic Management Journal, 21*, 345–368.

Eisenhardt, K. M. (1989). Building theories from case study research. *Academy of Management Review, 14*(4), 532–550.

Ethiraj, S. K., & Levinthal, D. (2004). Bounded rationality and the search for organizational architecture: An evolutionary perspective on the design of organizations and their evolvability. *Management Science, 49*, 404–437.

Farmer, J. D., & Lux, T. (2008). Introduction to special issue on applications of statistical physics in Economics and Finance. *Journal of Economic Dynamics and Control, 32*, 1–6.

Galunic, D. C., & Eisenhardt, K. M. (2001). Architectural innovation and modular corporate forms. *The Academy of Management Journal, 44*(6), 1229–1249.

Goerzen, A. (2005). Managing alliance networks: Emerging practices of multinational corporations. *The Academy of Management Executive, 9*(2), 94–107.

Hagel, J. (2002). Leveraged growth: Expanding sales without sacrificing profits. *Harvard Business Review, 80*(10), 69–77.

Hinterhuber, A. (2002). Value chain orchestration in action and the case of the global agrochemical industry. *Long Range Planning, 35*, 615–635.

Iansiti, M., & Levien, R. (2004). *The Keystone advantage: What the new dynamics of business ecosystems mean for strategy, innovation, and sustainability*. Cambridege, MA: Harvard Business School Press.Klein, H. K., & Myers, M. D. (1999). A set of principles for conducting and evaluating interpretive field studies in information systems. *MIS Quarterly, 23*(1), 67–93.

Lee, A. S. (1989). A scientific methodology for MIS case studies. MIS Quarterly 13(1), 33–50.

Lee, A. S., & Baskerville, R. L. (2003). Generalizing generalizability. *Information Systems Research* 221–243.

Lorenzoni, G., & Baden-Fuller, C. (1995). Creating a strategic center to manage a web of partners. *California Management Review, 37*(3), 146–163.

Lyman, K., Caswell, N., & Biem, A. (2008). Business value network concepts for the extended enterprise, proceedings of the smart business networks initiative conference in Beijing, May 2008.

NS (2008). nextstep country-level website: Face-to-face learning and careers advice: next step, www.direct.gov.uk/en/EducationAndLearning/AdultLearning/DG_071762, accessed 11 April, 2008.

Moller, Rajala, & Svahn (2005). Strategic business nets—their type and management. *Journal of Business Research, 58*, 1274–1284.

Rescher, N. (2000). Process metaphysics: An introduction to process philosophy. New York: State University of New York Press.

Richard, P., & Devinney, T. M. (2005). Modular strategies: b2b technology and architectural knowledge. *California Management Review, 47*(4), 86–113.

Robson, C. (2002), *Real world research* (2nd ed.). Oxford: Blackwell.

Rodon, J., Busquets, X., & Christiaanse, E. (2005). Orchestration in ICT-enabled Business Networks: A Case in the Repairs Industry, Proceedings of the 18th Bled eConference eIntegration in Action, Bled, Slovenia, June 6–8.

Salthe, S. (1985). Evolving hierarchical systems: Their structure and representation. New York: Columbia University Press.

Salthe, S. N. (2003). Infodynamics, a developmental framework for ecology/economics. *Conservation Ecology, 7*(3), 3.

Salthe, S. (1991). Two forms of hierarchy theory in modern discourses. *International Journal of General Systems, 18*(3), 251–264.

Schilling, M. A., & Steensma, H. K. (2001). The use of modular organizational forms: an industry-level analysis. *The Academy of Management Journal, 44*(6), 1149–1168.

Sears, F. W., & Salinger, G. L. (1975). Thermodynamics, kinetic theory, and statistical thermodynamics. Reading, MA: Addison-Wesley.

Shaw, D. R., Snowdon, R., Holland, C. P., Kawalek, P., & Warboys, B. (2004). The viable systems model applied to a smart network: the case of the uk electricity market. *Journal of Information Technology, 19*(4), 270–280.

Shaw, D. R. (2007). Manchester United football club: developing a network orchestration model. *European Journal of Information Systems, 16*, 628–642.

Simon, H. A. (1997). *Administrative behavior. A Study of Decision-Making Processes in Administrative Organizations* (4th ed.). New York: The Free Press.

Simon, H. A. (1955). On a class of skew distribution functions. *Biometrika 42*(3/4), 425–440.

Tainter, J. A., Allen, T. F. H., Little, A., & Hoekstra, T. W. (2003). Resource transitions and energy gain: contexts of organization. *Conservation Ecology, 7*(3), 4.

Wilby, J. (1994). A critique of hierarchy theory. *Journal of Systems Practice, 7*(6), 653–667.

Yin, R. K. (2003). *Case study research: design and methods* (3rd ed). Applied social research series (Vol. 5). Beverley Hills, CA: Sage Publications.

Review of "Why Smart Business Networks Continue and Develop: A Structural and Processual Model of Value Flows"

The Dangerous Beauty of Metaphors

Otto R. Koppius

Rotterdam School of Management, Erasmus University Rotterdam, The Netherlands,
okoppius@rsm.nl

Introduction

Metaphors are central to understanding the world around us (Lakoff & Johnson, 1980) and as a consequence, to our scientific analysis of it. Metaphors can help us see phenomena in a different light and thus yield new insight. By taking concepts from physical systems such as entropy, exergy and energy gradients and using them as metaphors for a business system like a smart business network, Duncan Shaw provides the reader with an analysis that is challenging, dare I say occasionally even confusing, but ultimately rewarding. After all, confusion is what a new metaphor is designed to generate: taken-for-granted viewpoints are challenged and while parts of the new metaphor may be rejected, other parts may be incorporated into one's thinking about the phenomenon.

One of these viewpoints that Shaw challenges is the either-or distinction between structural approaches and processual approaches to smart business networks. Most of us –usually implicitly- have a preferred approach to looking at a smart business network: the structural analyst may look at the portfolio of relationships that a firm has, for instance in terms of bridging or closure, and perhaps pay less attention to what is actually being exchanged and how in a specific inter-organizational relation. The processual analyst on the other hand, may look at the interorganizational processes as multiple organizations (or more correctly: people in multiple organizations) try to coordinate their actions in practice, and perhaps pay less attention to the broader network setting that both enables and constraints the context in which such processes take place. Neither is sufficient, both are necessary, yet our discussions do not always reflect this and Shaw's analysis of Manchester United and the two council networks reminds us that it is possible and useful to bring the two approaches together in a single framework that does not inherently favor one over the other.

Ultimately though, a good metaphor is only the first step towards scientific understanding as we move from metaphorical insights to analogies based on conceptual models to isomorphisms based on rigorous formulations, to a generalizable scientific model (Beer, 1984; Tsoukas, 1991). As a metaphor by its very definition is not identical to the topic it is applied to, the new metaphor may cause us to see similarities that are not there or miss important aspects of the topic. I will explore these aspects in the remainder of this commentary, in the hope of moving the metaphor a step closer to scientific understanding of smart business networks.

Questioning the Similarities with a Smart Business Network?

As entropy is a measure of the unavailability of a system's energy to do work, efficient physical systems have low entropy. It may thus follow from this metaphor that we want smart business networks to be as low on entropy as possible as this would imply maximally efficient use of resources. While seemingly plausible by itself, it is equally true that every organization needs to change some of the time in order to survive in a competitive environment (Brown & Eisenhardt, 1997). This implies that contrary to a physical system, a social system like a smart business network achieves optimal performance at some intermediate level of entropy. Similarly, while the concept of exergy as the usable proportion of a system's energy focuses attention on the inefficiencies in the system, thus suggesting to minimize those inefficiencies (just like we might initially want to minimize overhead in an organization), the organizational analogy is a bit more nuanced. Inefficiencies in an organization can act as a buffer, thus for instance promoting innovation (Nohria & Gulati, 1996) and bureaucracy, for all the overhead it introduces, can also function as an enabler (Adler & Borys, 1996) that leads to a well-functioning organization. Rather than wanting to remove all inefficiencies, the real question then for managers in a smart business network then becomes: "How much inefficiency in the network should we be willing to tolerate?"

While the conceptualization of smart business networks as open systems in a state far-from-equilibrium certainly has its merits in emphasizing the dynamics of the network caused by organizations' strategic moves and parties entering or leaving the network, it also raises three questions. First, if a system is in a far-from-equilibrium state, what does it move towards? Contrary to physical systems, actors in a social system have strategic intent and organizations in a smart business network will try to move to a state of competitive advantage for their organization and their network. Second, a far-from-equilibrium state is much less predictable than an equilibrium state, yet organizations need foresight to implement their strategies and thus will need to move away from far-from-equilibrium. Third, while all systems are open in principle, the practice of smart business networks is that entry to the network is not free. Network orchestrators like Li & Fung can set standards that organizations must meet in order to join the network (Magretta & Fung, 1998), just like they can act as a judge and exclude organizations from the network that underperform (Hinterhuber, 2002).

Finally, Shaw notes that a network orchestrator operates on a higher level than ordinary network members. While correct from the physical systems analogy, and 'managing' network orchestrators like Li & Fung do function at this level, there are also 'platform' network orchestrators whose goal is to provide an infrastructure on which other organizations in the network come together to create value, with eBay or Alibaba being prominent examples. Somehow the more appropriate metaphor for these platform network orchestrators to me seems to be that they function on a *lower* level than ordinary network members, thus providing a nice example of how a new metaphor can yield new insight and at the same time constrain that insight.

What Aspects of a Smart Business Network Does the Metaphor Miss?

While Shaw focuses in the cases on the actions of the central player in the network, directing value flows for its network members, this is not the only actor creating value flows. Interactions between 'lower-level' actors without intervention of the network orchestrator create value flows as well (for instance in the Manchester United case, Vodafone and Barclay also collaborate in the development of mobile banking solutions outside of the football context) and the metaphor does not really address the impact that these interactions have on value creation in the network. Structural network theories such as those on brokerage and closure in networks (Burt, 2005) are particularly well-equipped to handle such issues and thus would provide a useful addition to the case analysis. This would also allow a clearer distinction between value creation and value capture: the current focus of the metaphor and the paper is on the creation of value flows, but this value then will be captured/divided by the various organizations in the network and as value creation and value capture require different network structures (Burt, 2005), this presents an intriguing tradeoff for the network orchestrator.

The previous point raises the more general issue of the level-of-analysis of the metaphor. The physical systems metaphor is geared towards analyzing the performance of the system as a whole. This is a very useful lens as it forces organizations to think beyond the boundaries of their own organization to analyze how their actions contribute to the performance of the smart business network as a whole. Yet at the same time the metaphor does not take into account that for all the contributions that an organization can make to network performance, ultimately every organization is accountable (and will be judged by) its stakeholders on its individual performance. Developing performance measurement systems that not only measure the performance of the smart business network as a whole, but can also analyze how much each organization has contributed to the overall network performance, is a formidable challenge. However, it forms an essential component of implementing network thinking in business practice and thus will require substantial research effort.

Conclusion

To phrase the contribution of Shaw's paper in its own terminology, his analysis provides a process reconfiguration of thought flows as well as a structural reconfiguration of links between previously unconnected literatures and in this way, conceptual value is created. Although all metaphors are imperfect by definition, and in this commentary I have highlighted some of the dangers in taking the metaphor too literal or too far in the smart business network context, I hope that this will only help the reader in appreciating the usefulness of the out-of-the-box thinking that metaphors can provide.

References

Adler, P. S., & Borys, B. (1996). Two types of bureaucracy: Enabling and coercive. *Administrative Science Quarterly, 41*, 61–89.

Beer, S. (1984). The viable system model: Its provenance, development, methodology and pathology. *Journal of the Operational Research Society, 35*, 7–26.

Brown, S.L., & Eisenhardt, K.M. (1997). The art of continuous change: linking complexity theory and time-paced evolution in relentlessly shifting organizations. *Administrative Science Quarterly, 42*, 1–34.

Burt, R.S. (2005). *Brokerage and closure: An introduction to social capital.* Oxford: Oxford University Press.

Hinterhuber, A. (2002). Value chain orchestration in action and the case of the global agrochemical industry. *Long Range Planning, 35*(6), 615–635.

Lakoff, G., & Johnson, M. (1980). *Metaphors we live by.* Chicago, IL: University of Chicago Press.

Magretta, J., & Fung, V. (1998). Fast, global, and entrepreneurial: Supply chain management, Hong Kong style – An interview with Victor Fung. *Harvard Business Review, 76*(5), 102–110

Nohria, N., & Gulati, R. (1996). Is slack good or bad for innovation? *Academy of Management Journal, 39*(5), 1245–1264.

Tsoukas, H. (1991). The missing link: a transformational view of metaphors in organizational science. *Academy of Management Review, 16*(3), 566–585.

20. Orchestrating Smart Business Networks

Xavier Busquets

ESADE Business School, Spain, xavier.busquets@esade.edu

Abstract

In this paper I propose the concept of Orchestrating Smart Business Networks (SBN) as a process of dynamic equilibrium between centripetal and centrifugal forces defining network boundaries and exploring its implications on controlling spheres of action and architectures of participation. I explore this proposition in the implementation of Business Network Operating System (BNOS) in two cases with different results that highlight key variables to explain the balance of the two forces proposed. With this exercise, I propose an alternative meaning for *smartness* as an embedded capacity in SBN.

Introduction

This paper proposes a concept of Orchestrating in Smart Business Network's (SBN), grounding it on power theories (Morgan, 1997), highlighting the idea of setting direction and providing an integrative force for focusing network activities. Metaphorically speaking, network smartness is the network equivalent of the human ability to "read between the lines", unleash creativity and look forward in a process of creating a new order (Bohm & Peat, 2002) to create novelty and differentiated outcomes (Powell & Grodal, 2007) while showing robustness, mobilize appropriate resources and control the inherent conflicts of interest found in any network (Burke, 2006; Lorenzoni & Baden-Fuller, 1995; Nohria & Ghoshal, 1996). In this context, how can we conceptualize "orchestrating" as a power characteristic of Smart Business Networks? How are process-based approaches better able to cope with the underlying idea of organizational ongoing process of change and innovation as differentiated outcomes?

In order to explore these questions, the strategy I follow in paper is as follows: first, I propose a definition of Orchestrating SBN grounded on network boundaries; second I analyze this concept with two cases based on real companies but for which fictitious names have been chosen to conceal their identities: (1) Services Provider Network (SPN), whose main task is to provide services to a network of banks coordinating a supply chain of providers; and (2) the European Plants of Electronics (EPN), based on three factories producing electronic products. The comparison between the two cases allows an exploration of factual and contrafatual hypotheses (Kilduff & Tsai, 2003) given that one case (PSN) was a success and the other (EPN) was a failure. I explore these two change processes and conclude by providing some insights on Orchestrating as a power process and its influences on SBN development.

Orchestrating Smart Business Networks and the Business Network Operating System (BNOS)

Orchestrating is not a new concept. It has received attention as, according to my interpretation, as a network structural capacity of *centrality* such as bridging structural holes (Burt, 1992); as functional roles such as leader, architect, judge and business generator (Hinterhuber, 2002); or concentrating the capacity for decision making in networks of innovation (Lorenzoni, & Baden-Fuller, 1995). Centrality and network position are key characteristics to understand power dynamics but in a world where there is (1) an increasing need to combine components in different ways to ensure innovative results and (2) the increase of digitalization and information technologies, there are few studies that focuses on network power dynamics as boundary definition incorporating the above elements of discussion. Theories of Power deal with many sources regarding with co-dependencies among actors that form the network (Demers, 2007; Cook, Cheshire, & Gerbasi, 2006; Morgan, 1997). By contrast, theories of organizational change grounded in power changes focus their attention on the idea of actor's emancipation and autonomy in an exercise of self-organization – as the SBN discourse stresses (Demers, 2007; Morgan 1997). In order to make this paper manageable I focus on one major attribute which is boundary management which deals with structural changes, actor autonomy and informational processes working at different levels of analysis as Shaw discuses on his chapter. In order to do so, I focus on the implementation of Business Network Operating System (BNOS). Although this an evolving concept, main characteristics are (1) its capacity to connect firm throughout an easy plug and play to the SBN (Vervest et al., 2008); (2) an embedded logic to implement inter-organizational and intra-organizational processes and control variables; (3) with a standard architecture and integrable component-based architecture that; (4) scope for making network operations transparent and tangible.

The implementation of BNOS highlights some structural power characteristics such the actor willingness to cooperate or compete (Child et al., 2006), the power distribution among network actors, and the generation of co-dependencies regarding structural position and the control over the new resources such as BNOS (Burke, 2006).

Research Method

Given the exploratory nature of the research problem, I have opted for a research method that combines ethnography and case study research (ten Have, 2004) Empirical research was conducted over a three-year data collection (2004–2007) stage as part of a qualitative/ethnographic approach. The aim was to study the change process and the organization evolution of two cases. The following sources of information were used: (1) Internal documentation, internal communications, reports, description of processes and documentation of the ICT developed; (2) Field observation; (3) Interviews with executives, (4) a focus group with executives; and (5) many informal meetings and phone conversations.

Case Description and Analysis

In order to study structural changes in SBN through the exploration of the power mechanism of boundary management, in this section I analyze the two cases of Electronic Production Network (EPN) and Service Provider Network (SPN) respective implementation of a new BNOS. EPN was a three plan production network in Europe producing electronic sets and the "Future Factory" project which was the name for the ambitious BNOS in Europe for its set of Production Plants whose capacity at that time was measured by two key figures: 3,280,000 Equipments sets a year divided into thee production plants, in order to improve efficiencies, coordination among them and obtain more control in supply chain and point of sales delivery.

Founded in 1983, SPN began its service by building up a network of small providers, evolving as service coordinator for over a hundred large corporations including insurance companies, banks, department stores, and other retail chains. In the year 2000, the firm experienced a problem of declining quality as a symptom of a non-scalable operating, primarily due to the fact that all communication with both end customers and trade professionals was through the telephone. The firm in 2000 commenced a major re-engineering effort with the implementation of an ubiquitous BNOS based on different technologies such as Call Center, the Internet, Web Services and Mobile Systems.

In order to analyze and compare both cases, I propose a dynamic three-stage process that is inspired by the social model proposed by Montgomery and Oliver (Montgomery & Oliver, 2007): (1) in the initial conditions; (2) analysis of centrifugal vs. centripetal forces and (3) forces for dynamic boundary control. In the cases chosen, the unit of analysis is the dynamic change process of boundary management where the input is the crisis both networks needed to manage and as outcome the network contraction or expansion (as the case may be).

Initial Conditions and Context

In both cases studied, the change process started by a crisis. In this phase there is a managerial force in order to proceed with change due to a motivation (1) SPN started its BNOS implementation because of a quality and escalation problem and (2) EPN motivation was a joint effort to cope with market decline. This force is mediated by context specificities and existing patterns and processes of collective action (ten Have, 2004). In both the SPN and EPN cases, social factors account for the willingness to co-operate (Granovetter, 1985). The Electronic Production Network (EPN) started its ambitious BNOS implementation project within the three production plants in Europe as a bottom-up process in a context with a different power distribution: the "North" and "South" ones, each providing 40% of total production, and the "East" one, providing the remaining 20%. The three plants need to adapt to a market in which profit margins were under pressure and there was a drop in demand. However, headquarters (HQ) took control – trying to become the orchestrator – in order to co-ordinate efforts and site the steering committee in the North Plant. According to one executive, "We were used to working autonomously and even competing with the other plants during market expansion. However, in a project of this size, the idea of working together with the other European factory teams would allow knowledge integration and, in the long run, collaborative linking of production processes and practices". The "Future Factory" was in that sense a power shift towards a more co-operative context, but run from the North Plant.

The Process Service Network (PSN) was very successful in managing a large network of end customers, banks and insurers and providers. However, PSN suffered from declining service quality as a result of: (1) the lack of an operating models and an appropriate ICT for supporting all communication within the network and (2) lack of commitment and opportunistic behavior, as one manager claimed, "We had a model of relations with our providers in which we offered work and they took it, if they wanted to, and if they didn't want to, they didn't take it (PSN work represented only 20% of the work providers gave). Then, we thought that it was much better to reach a level of greater commitment, that is we undertook to give a much higher volume of work, and they undertook to accept it and to carry it out within certain parameters". Power distribution in PSN was also asymmetric. Banks depend on the service provided by the focal firm and its capacity to perform while focal firm depended on business provided by banks. Focal firm "openness" with providers produced a situation where it was highly dependent on the willingness of providers to work or not for the focal firm, creating a situation that was very hard to manage.

The first stage is proposed to be the willingness to cooperate dependent on the specific motivation to change, that is what are the expectations vs. the investment and costs needed understanding the co-dependencies among actors of the network. All units engage in transactions (Pfeffer & Salancik, 1978) in a specific context. Information is not neutral and neither is implementation of information systems. In PSN, the focal firm and all actors recognized co-dependencies and focused BNOS implementation on trying to rebalance power structures both with customers and providers. In the EPN case, the tradition – under favorable market conditions – of "independence" conditioned the view of reality and thus the information needed to support BNOS and the attitude towards other existing or potential network actors. In other words, according to my interpretation and consistent with resource dependency theory (Pfeffer & Salancik, 1978), part of EPN behavior was conditioned by its way to enact other plants as only competitors in the network and reproduce past relational patterns into a (potentially) new situation by emphasizing the competitiveness among plants. In short, recognizing the existing relationship co-dependencies is the first step towards building a network change.

Centrifugal vs. Centripetal Forces

This second stage balance centripetal and centrifugal forces. Centripetal forces foster network "centrality" since networks cannot handle "unlimited" number of resources to keep business focus. Identity is the beginning of coordination to organise around certain objectives, defining a domain of action. Centrifugal forces open the network to new opportunities, relationships and actors, such as fostering actor autonomy by creating new ways of managing relationships, redefining power structures and co-dependencies and building a shared vision as Riis describe on his chapter, changing the way reality is perceived or changing managerial mental models to grasp any complementarities there may be (Morgan, 1997; Pfeffer & Salancik, 1978).

In EPN's case, the company failed to define a common sphere of action: during the first year of BNOS, North and South plants came up with so many differences in the implementation strategy that South plant decided to distance itself from the corporate initiative. Attempts to exert autonomy or find new ways of managing enjoyed either limited success or proved counterproductive results. After two years,

South plant's implementation project was successful while the North plant's failed. The latter plant was closed five years later after several plans to axe jobs. HQ had also decided also to move East plant to another location, putting systems implementation on the back burner. The project was successfully finished in just one plant: South's. It became a world-class flexible plant, integrating providers in a Network and willing to disseminate their systems and knowledge to other plants. For example, they reduce lead times from months to days and cut production cost by 20%. Nobody seemed interested in their successful system at HQ level since its success was at expenses of HQ plans. According to one manager "that success was unacceptable given the firm's corporate mindset".

In contrast, SPN management engaged in active communication and transparency with network actors in order to understand different perspectives and gain awareness of other needs. They defined a vision of what was going to happen, asked for participation, drew up rules of action and built a new network resource: the BNOS in collaboration with them. That helped to share this vision among network actors as Riis suggests in his chapter. SPN led network change by exerting more autonomy in network actors. Changes affected (1) the provider's relationship model shifting away from low commitment and towards a market based to higher economic value and formalization, adding SLA and fostering greater autonomy through a pull system in which jobs were published and actors were made responsible for them; (2) the corporate relationship model, which shifted towards more collaboration and searching for opportunities to innovate with its banking customers; and (3) reengineering the network processes, increasing the level of control with the strategy to automate full network processes and managing exceptions in a Control Centre. These changes would be enhanced by the introduction of a new, simpler, and more powerful Business Network Operating System (BNOS) which was accessible to all the players in the company's network and which provided more information and transparency.

Forces for Dynamic Control of Boundaries

Forces at this stage present a certain level of stability where centripetal and centrifugal forces coalesce in an ongoing process at different levels. First, the cost efficiency is one criteria that defines the boundary between economic activity that can be carried out in free markets or that within formal agreements and corporate or contracts (Kilduff & Tsai, 2003; Nohria & Ghoshal, 1997; Williamson, 1994). In this respect, in PSN economic boundaries may shape both costs and incentives and pricing mechanisms – especially in peer-to-peer production of new services. For knowledge assets, how do economic incentives facilitate peer-to-peer production mechanisms? How is peer-to-peer production affected by price sensitivity? How do prices influence the creation of intellectual property at the network level?

Second, at the psycho-social level, business habits create boundaries concerning identity and "familiar" relationships (Granovetter, 1985). However, orchestration deals with new opportunities to avoid the "overembeddedness" that may prevent change (Pfeffer & Salancik, 1978). Interestingly, EPN, and recognizing that context matters, could not "change" any relationship, if fact EPN could not establish any relationship at all, since its view of their context did not change highlighting the existing competitiveness among plants. SPN did the opposite, changing its world view, change power relationships, and, in some case, dropping some relationships and opening up others in the process.

Third, at the technological level, boundaries can be assimilated as information system interfaces among different systems, software modules and service-oriented applications supporting the platform concept of BNOS already proposed whilst also ensuring the appropriate level of distributed control. At the aggregate level, networks recognize as boundaries the centrifugal forces to open up the network to new opportunities and also the cost of access to the network. Centripetal forces are the lock-in effects, or costs of disconnecting (Child, Faulkner, & Tallman, 2006). The increasing scale of PSN and its effect on the reduction of unitary costs and network externalities have an ambivalent effect: on the one hand, they allow networks to expand to embrace new actors and relationships. On the other, they facilitate different views, new knowledge and avoid "overembeddedness". Finally, as argued, context matters. For EPN, market decline, shrinking margins, and perhaps even cultural issues and managerial spite may explain the lack of effective communication and information sharing needed to truly engage and to calculate benefits, costs and risks. It might be argued that the critical variable in EPN was how the contextual variables correlated with the willingness to compete instead of cooperate. This could have been the product of changing incentives as market conditions shifted changes or other contextual aspects that polarized agents, causing power shifts (Cook, Cheshire, & Gerbasi, 2006; Pedersen & Larsen, 2006). Figure 20.1 depicts the above discussion.

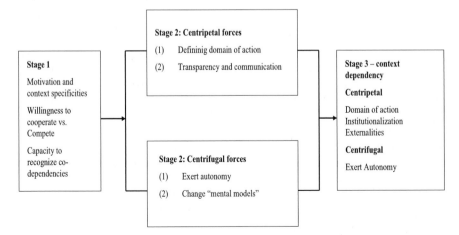

Fig. 20.1 Orchestrating as a boundary management process

Conclusion

In this paper I propose the concept Orchestrating SBN as the process of regulating network boundaries for opening network to new opportunities by centrifugal force such as exerting autonomy among the network actors, changing co-dependencies in relationships and changing view of reality. The centripetal forces observed are defining domains of action by controlling and commanding valued resources, manage transparency and consequently in a more stable situation, the creation of network externalities, institutionalization of behavior. In SBN, I propose specific BNOS deployment and use in order to automatically regulate boundaries and ensuring legitimacy through deterrent-based control systems and to increase efficiency through information tangibility and transparency. The management of BNOS through exerting autonomy and controlling spheres of action allows "innovation in assembly" and co-production in the innovation process, fostering participation frameworks through which network actors can operate. The traditional economics-based approach has viewed information scarcity as a source of power. With SBN there seems to have been a shift in mindset, since information is no longer a scarce resource. A new source of power in SBN may therefore lie in the ability to manage the managerial talent in deploying the specific features of an SBN, opening opportunities and organizing forward in the process.

References

Ahuja, G. (2000). Collaboration networks, structural holes, and innovation: A longitudinal study. *Administrative Science Quarterly, 45*(3), 425–455.

Bohm, D., & Peat, D. (2002). *Science, order and creativity* (2nd ed.). London: Routledge.

Burke, P.J. (2006). *Contemporary social psychology theories*. Palo Alto, CA: Stanford University Press.

Burt, R. S. (1992). *Structural holes: The social structure of competition*. Cambridge, MA: Harvard University Press.

Child, J., Faulkner, D., & Tallman, S. (2006). *Cooperative strategy*. Oxford: Oxford.

Cook, K.S., Cheshire, C., & Gerbasi, A. (2006). *Power, dependency and social exchange, in contemporary social psychology theories*. Palo Alto, CA: Stanford Theory Press.

Demers, C. (2007). *Organizational change theories: A synthesis*. Thousand Oaks, CA: SAGE.

Elster, J.(1994). *Lógica y Sociedad. Contradicciones y Mundos Posibles*. Barcelona: Gedisa.

Granovetter, M. (1985). Economic action and social structure: The problem of embeddedness. *American Journal of Sociology, 91*(3), 481–510.

ten Have, P. (2004). *Understanding qualitative research and ethnomethodology*. Thousand Oaks, CA: Sages.

Hinterhuber, A. (2002). Value Chain Orchestration in Action and the Case of Agrochemical Industry. *Long Range Planning, 35*(6), 615–635.

Kilduff, M., & Tsai, W. (2003). *Social networks and organizations*. London: Sage.

Lorenzoni, G., & Baden-Fuller, C. (1995) Creating a strategic center to manage a web of partners. *California Management Review, 37*(3), 146–163.

Montgomery, K., & Oliver, A. (2007). A fresh look at how professions take shape: Sage. Dual-directed networking dynamics and social boundaries. *Organization Studies, Vol. 28*(5).

Morgan, G. (1997). *Images of organization*. Thousand Oaks, CA: SAGE.

Nohria, N., & Ghoshal, S. (1997). The differentiated network: Organizing multinationals for value creation. San Francisco: Jossey Bass.

Pedersen, M.K., & Larsen, M.H. (2006). Innocuous knowledge: Models of distributed knowledge networks. In K.C. Desouza (Ed.), *New frontiers in knowledge management*, Palgrave.

Pfeffer, J., & Salancik, G. (1978). *The external control of organizations*: A resource dependence perspective. New York: Harper & Row.

Powell, W., & Grodal, S. (2007). *Networks of Innovation in the Oxford Handbook of Innovation*, Oxford.

Vervest, P. H. M., Van Heck, E., Preiss, K., & Pau, L. (2008). Smart business networks. The Netherlands: ERIM.

Williamson, O.E. (1994). Transaction cost economics and organizational theory. In N. J. Smelser, & R. Swedberg (eds.), *The handbook of economic-sociology* (pp. 77–107).

21. Electronic Intermediaries in Smart Business Networks

Amit Basu[1] and Steve Muylle[2]

[1] Cox School of Business, Southern Methodist University, United States of America, abasu@cox.smu.edu

[2] Vlerick Leuven Gent Management School, Belgium, steve.muylle@vlerick.be

Abstract

This paper examines the role of an Electronic Intermediary (EIM) in coordinating business processes in a Smart Business Network (SBN). A conceptual model is presented that links EIM business model, EIM evolutionary context, and EIM service scope to business performance, and generates insight into the coordination role of the EIM. The model is illustrated through its application to a set of EIMs in various geographies, across a two-year time frame. Also, the coordination role of an EIM is considered within its broader governance context.

Introduction

Electronic intermediaries (EIM) are organizations that provide online services that enable other organizations to interact with each other in business processes. EIMs are increasingly challenging traditional value chains. By connecting multiple organizations into networks in which members link and interact to achieve highly efficient and effective service delivery, EIMs are becoming a common and valuable part of many smart business networks (SBNs) (Vervest, van Heck, Preiss, & Pau, 2005), that leverage capabilities of members for competitive advantage.

Much of the existing research in the area of electronic intermediation has focused on electronic marketplaces (Malone, Yates, & Benjamin, 1987). However, EIMs can offer a variety of services other than market making. It can be argued that EIMs stimulate new roles in which participants transact, collaborate, and integrate, coordinated by an "electronic hand" (as opposed to Adam Smith's (1776) notion of an "invisible hand" guiding the process of buyer-seller matching though price discovery). However, academic research in this area has been very sparse to date, and has often taken a very narrow perspective on such mechanisms. In particular, the notion of an EIM assuming roles other than that of market maker and/or online exchange has not received much attention in the literature.

The objective of this paper is to examine how an EIM can coordinate business processes within an SBN. Toward that end, we present a conceptual model that ties together three dimensions of EIMs: the business model adopted by the EIM, the evolutionary context of the EIM, and the scope of the EIM in terms of its online service and process support. By identifying a suitable business model and choosing online services that are consistent with its business model and its evolutionary context, the EIM can coordinate business processes in the SBN and enhance its business performance. We illustrate the conceptual model with some specific patterns of activity and support that it would imply, and then examine the extent to which these patterns are observed in practice, based on data from a small set of EIMs. We also consider the implications of the role an EIM can play in the governance of an SBN.

The paper is organized in five sections. In section "Literature Review," we review the relevant literature on EIMs and business networks. In section "Conceptual Model," we present our conceptual model. In section "Case Study Insights," we illustrate the model with data from a set of case studies of actual EIMs, and finally, in section "Implications for SBN Governance," we discuss the implications of our model for co-ordination and governance of activities within SBNs, and identify further research opportunities.

Literature Review

Three streams of literature on the design of EIMs are related to the approach presented in this paper. The first is the literature on electronic business models, the second includes research on electronic business services provided by EIMs, and the third examines the evolutionary context of an EIM.

Electronic Business Models and Services

A business model is defined as the set of services and processes a firm offers to its customers while electronic business services are defined as a set of logically related activities performed to achieve an intangible business outcome through the adoption of Internet technology. A typology of e-business services is presented in Muylle and Basu (2008). This integrative typology is grounded in the e-business model literature (e.g., (Alt & Zimmermann, 2001)), the electronic intermediary literature (e.g., (Dai & Kauffman, 2002; Segev, Gebauer, & Farber, (1999)), and conceptual research on electronic business architectures (e.g., Basu & Muylle, 1999; Kambil & van Heck, 1998, Tenenbaum et al., 1997). Transaction, decision support, and integration services are distinguished as potential services a firm can offer to its customers as part of its electronic business model, and a comprehensive typology of electronic business models is presented (see Table 21.1). The concurrent consideration of business model and service support allows a firm to plan its online services and a fit between the firm's business model and service scope can be predicted to positively impact business performance.

Table 21.1 Business models and service support (from Muylle & Basu, 2008)

Business model	Transaction	Decision support	Integration
Exchange	X	–	–
Collaboration hub	–	X	–
System integrator	–	–	X
Value-added exchange	X	X	–
Business process integrator	–	X	X
Integrated exchange	X	–	X
Full service provider	X	X	X

While the business model literature largely concerns "principals," namely firms that themselves want to trade through the online entity, other units of analysis can be adopted. In this paper, we focus on intermediaries (EIMs) rather than principals, employing the business models and service sets identified by Muylle and Basu (2008). In additon, we consider the dimension of evolutionary context.

The Evolutionary Context of an EIM

Given the short history of EIMs, very few studies have studied the impact of evolutionary factors such as the origin, ownership and reach (in terms of firms that can participate in the EIM), on the business model and services that the EIM offers. One such study is by Kambil et al. (1999), who argue that the emergence of different types of online market structures (as oppo-sed to hierarchical coordination mechanisms) is influenced by structural characteristics of the industry and the needs of buyers and sellers. Another approach is presented in Kambil and van Heck (2001), where the EIM's ownership structure is used to categorize the significance of different types of services. Other studies do not explicitly factor in business models or the EIM's operating context when defining the level of support it should provide for various service sets.

To be brief, while each of the streams of literature reviewed in this section augments our understanding of EIMs, there is no comprehensive and intuitive framework that combines consideration of business models, service scope, and evolutionary context in planning and coordinating an EIM. The approach presented in this paper addresses this problem.

Conceptual Model

Our model of EIMs consists of three dimensions, linked to business performance, as shown in Fig. 21.1. Each of the dimensions is described next, followed by a discussion of business performance.

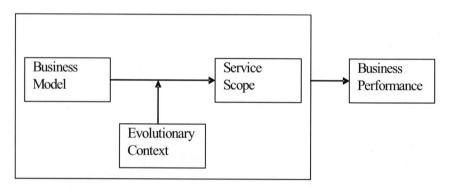

Fig. 21.1 EIM conceptual model

Service Scope

In keeping with the electronic business services typology proposed by Muylle and Basu (2008), the functional scope of an EIM can be characterized in terms of three categories of services.

1. *Transaction services.* Transaction services comprise the process of buying and selling online. Specific transaction services are:

    - *Search.* Finding relevant entities and objects for any business transaction, and enabling sellers and buyers to locate each other to exchange goods and services.
    - *Authentication.* Ensuring the authenticity of the parties involved, as well as the quality of the products and services being transacted.
    - *Valuation.* Price discovery, which can be of two types: (1) fixed pricing; and (2) dynamic pricing.
    - *Payment.* Paying for online purchases, with electronic payment instruments at the transaction services level.
    - *Logistics.* Moving products and resources within the participating firms, including shipment and delivery of purchased products from the seller to the buyer.

2. *Decision support services.* Decision support services enable participant firms that interact with the EIM to obtain information and use analytical models that enhance their ability to make effective business decisions. These services can be supported at two levels. The first level is where the EIM enables each

participant firm to better monitor and plan its own operations, independent of other firms (regardless of whether these other firms are also participants in the EIM or not). The second level is where the EIM enables multiple participant firms to interact with each other in ways that helps each of them make better decisions. Specific decision support services are:

- *Configuration.* Helping buyers define needs, including facilitating interactions between buyers and sellers to develop a product that can meet those needs.
- *Collaboration.* Facilitating interactions between participant firms that support joint or collaborative work between multiple people in one or more organizations, using Web-based computer and communication technologies.
- *Business Intelligence.* Providing information about market conditions and trends, at the unit, firm, industry and overall market levels.

3. *Integration services.* Integration services help firms that participate in the EIM to integrate their information, computing and communication systems, on either an intra-firm or an inter-firm basis. Through these services the EIM enables automation of business processes across the boundaries of different component information systems. Although intra-firm integration can sometimes be facilitated by an EIM, the most likely utilization of the integration services of an EIM is across participant firms. Specific integration services include:

- *Data Integration.* Enabling a firm's software applications to access its partners' databases regardless of the specific database structures, soft-ware and systems that each entity employs.
- *Application integration.* Using mechanisms such as Web services and eXtensible Markup Language (XML) to integrate the computer applications of different participating firms.

Business Model

A comprehensive typology of EIM business models based on the set of services offered to customers is presented in Table 21.1 (Muylle & Basu, 2008). Each of the business models is characterized by the specific service or combination of services offered by the EIM. While an EIM pursuing an exchange business model only offers transaction services, an EIM adopting a value-added exchange business model also offers decision support services. Likewise, an EIM taking on a business process integrator business model offers both decision support and integration services. The most elaborate business model is the full service provider, which offers transaction, decision support, and integration services. It is important to note here that the business model dimension is separated from the service categories as the scope of an intermediary that uses each business model does not necessarily correspond to be the union of the scope associated with the component roles (Muylle & Basu, 2008).

Evolutionary Context

Many EIM's are pure-play intermediaries, namely firms that are independent entities with only online operations. However, it is also possible for a set of firms that have offline business relationships to set up an EIM for specific business processes spanning one or more of the major service categories discussed above. Our categorization of EIM ownership and contexts is as follows:

1. *Pure-play.* An EIM created by a firm that is a pure intermediary, with no ownership interests in any firm participating in the EIM (e.g., eBay).
2. *Closed Online Extension.* An EIM owned by one or more principals (i.e., firms that are participants in the EIM). The owners may have pre-existing relationships with each other through traditional offline interactions (e.g., CoViSint), a subsidiary of compuware corporation.
3. *Open Online Extension.* A hybrid of the two earlier types, set up by an initial consortium of firms, but the set of participant firms changes quite frequently (e.g., FreeMarkets), acquired by Ariba.

This classification is related to that of Kambil and van Heck (2001), where three categories of online exchange are considered, namely private exchanges, consortia exchanges and independent exchanges. In that approach, the primary discriminator between the alternatives was the ownership of the exchange. Our classification extends the classification to two dimensions, ownership and openness (where openness refers to support for online admittance and authentication of new participants). One category from Kambil and van Heck (2001) that we do not distinguish is the private exchange, since it is essentially a closed extension with a single owner.

The context dimension is orthogonal to the business model and service dimensions. For instance, the integration of product catalogs is important for integrated exchanges and full service providers, but more so in the context of an online extension than a pure-play intermediary.

Business performance

While business performance can be defined in financial terms (i.e., EIM profits, revenues, transaction volume), and/or organizational growth (expansion of the EIM in terms of offices, customers, employees, partners, geo-graphy, and industry), these perspective are not always appropriate in an SBN setting. Indeed, an EIM can also be evaluated in terms of value added for the participant firms that invest in the EIM. This value-add may entail member revenue increases, cost savings, and better decision making. The latter is in line with the coordination science literature (e.g., (Malone & Crowston, 1994)) in which decision rights and their distribution are linked to firm performance. Anand and Mendelson (1997), for instance, state that information technology reallocates information among decision makers and find that a fully distributed coordination structure, in which the branches make their own decisions based on local knowledge and aggregate data provided by the center, offers better absolute performance than either a centralized or decentralized coordination structure. Nault (1998), however, warns that the collocation of information and decision rights, his so-called mixed mode, suffers from coordination problems that are not present in case of fully centralized or decentralized decision rights. Clearly, business performance is closely linked to coordination advantages and costs, bolstering the importance of effective coordination by EIMs in SBNs.

In keeping with Muylle and Basu (2008), an EIM that clearly identifies a suitable business model and chooses services that are consistent with the business model can be expected to enhance business performance (and bring about coordination advantages). In an EIM setting, however, evolutionary context is expected to moderate the business model – service scope – business performance relationship, as shown in Fig 21.1. More specifically, an EIM that is pursuing a specific business model needs to consider its evolutionary context in planning and coordinating it service scope for enhanced business performance.

Case Study Insights

In order to illustrate the conceptual model and examine the role of an EIM in coordinating business processes within an SBN a multiple case study research was conducted over a two-year time-frame, 2003–2005, across different geographical regions. Through a key informant approach (Campbell, 1955), ten EIMs have been analyzed, with particular focus on identifying the e-business services they support, the business models adopted by them, and their evolutionary context. Also, business performance and the form and nexus of the coordination of the operations of the network within which they operate were considered.

The results highlight that the coordination role of the EIM not only depends on the business model it adopts and the business services it supports, but also on its evolutionary context. Given the central role of an EIM in interconnecting its various participants, it is intuitively reasonable to expect that the EIM can and should play a significant role in the creation of an orderly and robust business network, and in the formulation and implementation of appropriate governance mechanisms for the collaborative enterprise. However, the coordination role of an online extension intermediary may be different from that of a pure-play intermediary. For instance, a pure-play intermediary that uses the exchange business model has to provide extensive authentication services for both products and parties (traders). On the other hand, a closed online extension exchange may have to provide only product identity authentication, and may not have to provide any participant authentication, and little or no product quality authentication (Basu & Muylle, 2003). This interplay between the service scope of an EIM and the role it can play in the governance of the SBN is an important consideration for the design of effective and successful SBNs.

As proposed in Muylle and Basu (2008), we find that EIMs which reconcile their business models with business service support perform well, and consistently so (as validated over the two-year time-frame in our case study set). A case in point is TradCom, an integrated exchange in the MRO market in Belgium, the Netherlands, and Luxembourg, which has reinforced its position through significant enhancements in logistics and integration. It has stayed away from decision support services, and has been very successful. Yearly transaction volume has increased from EUR2m to EUR8m with 2,100 customers, and suppliers have grown from 5 to 18 firms. In addition, suppliers enjoy revenue increases as new customers of other participant, complementary, suppliers enter the network. Likewise, Inter-Sources, a Western European value-added exchange operating across multiple industries, made major enhancements in the area of decision support, thereby enjoying significant growth in volumes from EUR50m to over EUR2b and from 2 to 15 participants, while sustaining operating profitability since Q4 2003.

Also, evolutionary context is found to be an important moderator. Rubber-Network, for instance, positioned itself as an open extension integrated exchange in the global tire and rubber industry, but its activities more reflect a closed extension (no new partners are sought or invited). Also, this EIM is enhancing its decision support services because of owner demands in view of its "community benefits" charter; in effect it is functioning as a full service provider. However, its owners are mutual competitors so information sharing has to be limited to non-strategic items. The number of customers has stayed at nine, and the number of employees is down from 60 to 54. Its most significant performance benefit has been in transaction volume and cost savings in purchasing. It is questionable if this EIM would survive if it would be operating in a pure-play setting. Another case is i-Faber, an EIM which has reinforced its position as a pure-play exchange in Italy and Eastern Europe through the adding of an online scouting service which was quickly adopted by all participants. i-Faber is profitable since the second semester of 2004 with EUR1.1b in transaction volume for the year. Also, the number of buyers and sup-pliers shot up from, respectively, 75 and 1,200, to 200 and 5,400. A small confound, however, is that i-Faber has added integration services and has launched supply chain integration (to establish the entire procure-to-invoice cycle online) due to pressure from some large customers. It is of interest to note that, in line with Nault (1998), coordination costs are incurred by both RubberNetwork and iFaber, as they collocate decision rights and information outside their evolutionary context.

Implications for SBN Governance

The consideration of each of these factors (business model, service scope, evolutionary context, and business performance) is important in the design of governance mechanisms for any SBN that is organized around an EIM. Indeed, consider the service scope dimension. The key responsibility of an EIM focusing on transaction services is to establish and communicate the business rules for setting up and executing transactions through its online marketplace. Each participant acts in its own self interest, and therefore there is little need for the EIM operator/owner to gain visibility into the operations and processes of individual participant firms. In the case of an EIM that provides decision support services, there is a greater need for the EIM to work with the participant firms to obtain the relevant information about their operations that enable the EIM to provide meaningful and valuable business intelligence, collaboration and configuration services. Finally, an EIM that provides integration services has to gain visibility and has to coordinate not only the information flows from participants, but also their information systems and business processes, so that the appropriate end-to-end integration among participants can be achieved.

The impact of evolutionary context is also significant. For instance, the relationship between a pure-play EIM and its participants is largely an arm's length peer relationship. On the other hand, the prime movers in an online extension (both closed and open) are often the founding participants, who establish the goals and scope of the EIM and thus set the business rules of the SBN. This includes the financial and operating goals of the EIM, and the scope of the collaborative processes within the network.

The framework presented in this paper provides valuable insights for managers of firms in SBNs that contain EIMs, whether these are participant firms or the EIMs themselves. In particular, it can help identify key questions that need to be addressed in the development of appropriate governance and evaluative mechanisms. In particular, the framework helps determine what type of governance role is consistent with its scope and role within the business network. As to the latter, an important avenue for further research is to go beyond the coordination role of EIMs and explicitly consider evaluation and control as key issues in the effective governance of an SBN. Established research on the design of control mechanisms that distinguishes between formal and informal governance mechanisms such as outcome control, process control, and clan control, can serve as focus and offer valuable insights (Eisenhardt, 1985; Kirsch, 1996 & Ouchi, 1979).

References

Alt, R., & Zimmermann, H. (2001). Introduction to special section – Business models. *Electronic Markets, 11*(1), 3–9.

Anand, K.S., & Mendelson, H. (1997). Information and organization for – Horizontal multi-market coordination. *Management Science, 43*(12), 1609–1627.

Basu, A., & Muylle, S. (1999). Customization in online trade processes. *IEEE Computer Society Proceedings* of the International Workshop on Advanced Issues of Electronic Commerce and Web-based Information Systems. Santa Clara, California, April 8–9, 1999.

Basu, A., & Muylle, S. (2003). Authentication in electronic commerce. *Communications of the ACM 2003, 46*(12), 159–166.

Campbell, D. T. (1955). The informant in quantitative research. *American Journal of Sociology, 60,* 339–342.

Dai, Q., & Kauffman, R. J. (2002). Business Models for Internet-based Electronic Markets, *International Journal of Electronic Commerce* 6(4), 41–72.

Eisenhardt, K. M. (1985) "Control: organizational and economic approaches. *Management Science, 31*(2), 134–149.

Kambil, A., & van Heck, E. (1998) Reengineering the Dutch flower auctions: a framework for analyzing exchange organizations. *Information Systems Research, 9*(1), 1–19.

Kambil, A., & van Heck, E. (2001). *Making markets.* Boston, MA: Harvard Business School Press, 2002.

Kambil, A., Nunes P.F., & D. Wilson. (1999) Transforming the marketspace with all-in-one markets. *International Journal of Electronic Commerce, 3*(4), 11–28.

Kirsch, L. J. (1996) The Management of Complex Tasks in Organizations: Controlling the Systems Development Process, *Organization Science, 7*(1), 1–21.

Malone, T. W., & K.G. Crowston. (1994). The interdisciplinary study of coordination. *ACM Computing Surveys, 26*(1), 87–119.

Malone, T. W., Yates, J., & Benjamin, R. I. (1987) Electronic markets and electronic hierarchies. *Communications of the ACM, 30*(6), 484–497

Muylle, S., & Basu, A. (2008). Online Support for Business Processes by Electronic Intermediaries forthcoming in Decision Support Systems.

Nault, B. (1998). Information technology and organization design: locating decisions and Information," *Management Science, 44*(10), 1321–1335.

Ouchi, W.G. (1979). A conceptual framework for the design of organizational control mechanisms. *Management Science, 25*(9), 833–848.

Segev, A., Gebauer, J., & Farber, F. (1999) Internet-based electronic markets. *Electronic Markets, 9*(3), 138–146

Smith, A. *An Inquiry into the Nature and Causes of the Wealth of Nations.* Library of Economics and Liberty, 1776. http://www.econlib.org/library/Smith/smWN0.html

Tenenbaum, Jay M., Tripatinder S. Chowdhry, and Kevin Hughes, *eCo system: Commerce Net's Architectural Framework for Internet Commerce*, White Paper and Prospectus, Version 1.0, 1997.

Vervest, P.E., van Heck, E., Preiss, K., & Pau, L.F. (2005) *Smart business networks.* Berlin: Springer.

22. Shared Visions in Smart Business Networks

A Stakeholder and an Organizational Learning Approach

Jens Ove Riis

Center for Industrial Production, Aalborg University, Denmark, riis@production.aau.dk

Abstract

A business network rests on contributions from different and complementary disciplines and interests. A stakeholder model provides a basis for assessing the cohesion of the network. The paper will propose that a shared vision be developed to serve as a platform for cooperation among actors, based on experience from industrial enterprises. As a business network develops over time, a complex interplay among actors develops. An organizational learning approach will be used to develop an overall picture of this interplay. Case examples will support discussions and implications.

Complementary Contributions

Any business endeavor, product or service is realized through a concerted effort of several actors with different background and belonging to different organizational units. As a traditional example, the construction of an apartment house will involve architects various kinds of engineers, financial specialists construction people, a leasing company, and a maintenance organization. A newer example is the development and marketing of a multi-media educational program that involves pedagogical specialists, software and multi-media specialists in addition to professionals in the subject areas covered.

New business development may take place within the organizational context of a company, or as an inter-company effort in a network of companies. In both situations it is important to establish cooperation between actors representing complementary disciplines and interests. In the first case an organizational structure, systems and norms already exist to support this cooperation. In the latter case, however, an organizational structure and systems should be established to nurture the development of a cooperative culture.

In this paper we shall make an attempt to provide an understanding of the foundation for a business network by studying how expectations of each actor (individuals and companies) involved in a business network can be met, and if mutual interplay in a business network is supportive or counterproductive to the business model of the network. Several contributions have been made to understand the mechanisms of a network. For example, Williamson (1979) focuses on the transaction costs between nodes (actors) of a network. A resource approach focuses on the specific competences of individual actors, e.g. Prahalad & Hamel (1990).

We shall draw on the coalition model proposed by Simon & March (1958), because it includes a broader view of the interrelationships between actors in a network than just transaction costs and competencies. Having to combine complementary contributions and expectations (success criteria), a major challenge exists to make each stakeholder comprehend the potential of business network to realize individual goals of stakeholders. For this reason we have worked with the development of a vision of the outcome and of the way in which the business idea will be realized. This connects well with the original definition of a smart business network.

When a network has been formed and has functioned for some time, a complex interplay develops. Individual actors may apply local rationality which however is not always productive for the network as a whole. In many cases, the development of an understanding of the current interplay among partners can provide important insights into the actual operation of a network and point to ways of improving the performance. This part of the paper will draw on organizational learning theories.

While the stakeholder model provides a snapshot picture of the extent of common support for the goals and plans of a business network, the organizational learning models will look at the mutual interplay between actors as it develops over time. Thus, the two approaches supplement one another.

The paper aims to contribute to

1. Establishing a new business in such a way that each contributing actor can see the potential benefit, on the one hand, and on the other, can understand his/her expected contribution (role), through the development of a shared vision
2. Operating a new business effort in such a way that the mutual interplay between contributing actors create a positive synergy.

We shall first discuss the methodology applied dominated by action research. Then the development of a shared vision among stakeholders will be discussed, and case examples from company development projects will demonstrate how a shared vision can be established. Experience from practice will form a basis for discussing critical issues. The following section adopts a dynamic perspective by studying the mutual interplay among actors (stakeholders) from an organizational learning point of view. Case examples will illustrate various means for developing a shared picture of this interplay. Finally, implications will be discussed and conclusions drawn.

An Action Research Methodology

The empirical data supporting this paper has been provided over a period of more than a decade mostly as action research studies in industrial companies. In two PhD dissertations, the vision development in three companies has been studied (Rytter, 2004; Dukovska-Popovska, 2006). The studies include a thorough analysis of the situation in the company prior to interventions, description of a series of workshops organized by the research team and follow-up documentations.

In addition, the author and colleagues have carried out a number of action research studies in industrial companies aimed to create a common understanding of the present strategic situation and mutual interplay among stakeholders, e.g. Riis (1990), Riis & Johansen (2003).

Case examples will illustrate and demonstrate the points and will be selected from the empirical database. The nature of the research methods applied is to combine theoretical concepts and models and empirical data from action research to develop conceptual frameworks, models and methods for helping companies in dealing with the issues addressed.

Development of a Shared Vision: A Stakeholder Approach

The coalition model provides an understanding of the underlying interests of stakeholders (actors) participating in the organization. The model identifies a number of stakeholders around a business, a firm or a network, each of which will make a needed contribution for its realization. For this effort the stakeholder will be rewarded. Freeman (1984) has used a stakeholder approach for strategic management.

To ensure the survival and success of the business idea it is necessary to find a coalition of actors who want to support realization of the business idea. It is not a democratic model with equal amount of influence. Rather, the power of a stakeholder will depend on the need for his/her contribution compared with the compensation. It is difficult, if meaningful at all, to transform either the various contributions or rewards on to a single scale of measurement.

An implication of the coalition model is that a business idea is only seen as a means for a stakeholder to achieving an aim. It is still important to define goals and strategies of a business, firm, network or project, and to position its products and services on the market, e.g. Fry & Killing, (2000). But such goals will indicate to stakeholders what the expected outcome of the endeavor will be. Each stakeholder will compare his/her own goals with the overall stated objectives to decide whether to join or not. Each stakeholder will define, implicitly or explicitly, a set of success criteria for the project, to be measured on individual scales. A stakeholder who is supposed to make a contribution that otherwise is difficult to find, often, in fact can impede the progress of the project. Hence, it is essential during the initial phase and also during operations to ensure that each stakeholder finds that there is an appropriate balance between contribution and reward.

A stakeholder analysis can provide an understanding of the mindset, motives of stakeholders and expected reaction, and it may include identification of important stakeholders, assessment of their desired contribution and perceived reward, an estimation of their reaction and behavior, e.g. Mikkelsen & Riis (2007). On the basis of their experience with large private and public projects, D'Herbemont & Cesar (1998) proposes a mapping of the expected reaction of stakeholders on the basis of the extent of their antagonism and synergy, respectively.

Thus, the stakeholder model addresses the question of where do goals of an organization or network come from, and how robust these goals are with respect to achieving the necessary support. Since expectations of stakeholders may point in different directions, it is important to develop a common platform, against which each stakeholder can mirror his/her own situation (interests, expectations, conditions, etc.). The introduction of a shared vision aims to provide such a platform.

A Shared Vision

Many authors have proposed the development of a vision. For example, Kotter (1996) includes vision development as one of his eight steps of company development, and Womack & Jones (1996) also argues for the use of visions. However, they do not offer much information about the roles that a vision may play and how a vision may be developed.

The Role of a Vision. We see a vision as a bridge between the mission, goals, and strategies of an enterprise or a business network, on the one hand, and the detailed development of roles of actors as well as systems for their interplay on the other. Such a bridge may ensure that the enterprise or network is able to position the business idea strategically and, internally, may serve as a lodestar for each actor to define his/her contribution. We have detailed the role of a vision:

- Enable a strategic positioning of the business idea and its implied services on a competitive market
- Reconcile conflicting objectives and viewpoints held by stakeholders (actors) whose contributions are important for realizing the business idea
- Engage and motivate people from the organization to participate by pointing out what they are supposed to do, i.e. their own role, and the benefit and reward they may expect to receive
- Provide a basis for the detailed design of the various subsystems and functions of a business network, such as product development, sales & marketing, manufacturing, supply chain, and finance.

A vision is a story told by many actors. A vision cannot be expressed by means of the specific vocabulary used by any of the disciplines and functions involved in a business network. Other means of expressions have be to used, for example an image or a picture of how the business idea will function. Emphasis should be on showing what will happen, i.e. illustrating future processes. Another way of indicating how a vision looks is to describe it as a story of a future situation. Since a vision is concerned with the future, it should take outset in wishful thinking, e.g. guided by statements like "What if …" "Imagine that …" and "It would be interesting to explore the idea of …". In this way the story becomes more like a fairy tale. A vision thus may explore radical ideas and encourage participants to dare to sail on the Blue Ocean (Kim & Mauborgne, 2005). In the following we shall illustrate different ways of expressing a shared vision.

Case Example: A Three-Minute Video of a New Product

In a company developing and producing consumer electronics, management some years ago was about to give up to be able to market a new generation of their products offering a large screen and new functionalities, such as internet access and e-mail communication. However, a small group of development managers adopted an approach known from agile software project management. Instead of spending much time on preparing a detailed set of requirement specifications, they produced a three-minute video. It first showed an image of the new product and then demonstrated the features of the new product by showing how a user would look for e-mails, check information on the company private web site, and read and listen to messages received while it was on stand-by.

Top management agreed to let the product development team go ahead under the condition that the development time was extremely short. The team agreed and showed the video to all sections managers, each representing a functional specialization needed. The video enabled these managers to define what was required from their side and to identify critical interfaces with other sections.

Several versions of the video were produced as the development process came along and as the various technical solutions emerged.

The case example illustrates how a story of a new product told on a video was able to persuade top management to initiate the product development project, and the video was also instrumental for managing the requirement specification process by providing a dialogue between the various specialist groups.

Case Example: A New Business Model

An industrial company developing and manufacturing marine components world-wide also offers systems solutions by configuring to individual customers a group of components controlled by a control unit and software. The company has decided to strengthen the systems side in order to achieve a better competitive position. Management realized that their major customers, shipyards, were now situated in the Far East countries. This called for a novel business model to approach potential customers and to provide technical support in the bidding phase, product delivery and after sales service. The traditional mode of technical sales staff visiting the shipyards had worked well for customers located in Europe.

Although a rather small company, it has gained a significant market position worldwide in its specific market niche. For some time the management had realized that much effort was spent on developing and engineering systems solutions in close contact with customers, especially because the market had shifted from predominately being in Europe to Far East countries. Management felt a need to develop a new business model for systems solutions.

An idea came up to upgrade selected agents to dealers capable of negotiating with customers, systems design and even organize suppliers for peripheral parts. The dealers should be supported by the main office in Denmark. As part of the new business model three elements were specified in terms of an idealized vision, including:

- An idealized phase model of a customer order project. This would identify expected patterns of cooperation with customers, dealer, systems design and production
- An idealized dealer. Compared to the traditional agent, new roles and tasks were to be defined for the dealer, e.g. market research, preparation of bids, contract contract negotiations with customers, systems configuration and engineering, as well as after sales service.
- An idealized intelligent systems support. As a new organizational unit, a center of excellence for systems design was proposed at the main office to be able to offer technical support to dealers and the company's own sales department.

An integration model in the shape of a circle was developed showing the size of all potential markets as sectors of the circle and the current market share. For each market the model indicated which sales organization should be used, either a dealer, an agent supported from sales department and systems design, or directly serviced by the sales department. The new business model (vision) was detailed and tested in discussions with a potential dealer, sales department, top management, systems engineering, purchase and production. And everybody was interested in finding out what was in the new business model for them, e.g. their expected contribution and reward. Some of the implications of having developed the new business model were:

- During discussions, top management realized that the company was not present in the country with the largest market. As a consequence they initiated negotiations with a local company to cooperate.
- With the new business model the engineering manager was able to point out, who should be asked to help establish the center of excellence, and who should should continue specifying systems in cooperation with the sales department servicing most of the European countries.

Thus, the new business model with its elements and integrating model was able to indicate to stakeholders (partners inside and outside the company) their individual role.

Case Example: Discussing a New Manufacturing Vision Through a Serious Game

The production management of an industrial company was under pressure to improve quality, delivery and productivity. Top management had showed keen interest in a new manufacturing philosophy, called Continuous Flow Manufacturing (CFM). Although in sympathy with the idea, production management was uncertain about how to sell it internally. At a meeting with consultants, a proposal was discussed to develop a company-specific game to demonstrate to key managers and employees in production what CFM would imply and to solicit suggestions for its detailed design and implementation. The proposal was accepted. The game was run in an afternoon and involved more than 20 managers, foremen and key operators. They were to accept and produce customer orders of a selected part of the company's product program. The production processes were simplified in the game, each workshop was determining the processing time by throwing a dice to induce stochastic variation. The game was advanced day by day when all participants had done their job, e.g. accepting new customer orders, ordering raw materials and components, and producing and assembling in the workshops.

After 1½ h of gaming during which the incoming customer orders had gradually increased, the managers from sales, production, and purchase were asked to sit down and discuss which production rate would be appropriate for the next game period. Having always called for precise sales forecasts, the purchasing manager for the first time in his career experienced the uncertainties of predicting sales.

And with the rather long lead times for supplies, he realized the impact of his own decisions on the overall performance of the company.

Also the other participants in the game experienced the mechanisms of CFM and the requirements to each actor. Several suggestions related to its implementation were proposed. The case example illustrates what we have experienced in several other games how powerful an emulation of the interplay of the daily operation is for obtaining a comprehensive understanding of the functioning of production and for empowering actors to propose new specific solutions within the overall vision. In particular, it was an eye opener for the purchasing manager.

Case Example: Development of Regional Tourism

A small group of businessmen and local politicians was eager to stimulate tourism in their region. They decided to hold a one-day workshop for an extended group in which key potential players were invited. An external consultant served as a facilitator. After a brief introduction to the background and the original, sketchy idea, participants were asked to freely come up with loose ideas. During lunch the ideas were used to form three distinctly different directions for stimulating tourism. The participants spent the afternoon in groups to develop each of the three directions, e.g. to propose new organizational units and systems, and to spell out how the network of public institutions and private firms would functions. At the end of the day, the three groups presented their results, and it turned out that despite different outsets some of the proposals were similar. A taskforce group was formed to further develop the proposals. After three months it presented two alternative visions to the workshop participants who were asked to evaluate what was in it for them. The visions implied establishing new organizations and systems, as well as changed roles of existing firms and institutions.

The Process of Developing a Manufacturing Vision

When a coach for a sport team calls for a time-out, he wants all players to stop for a while and to jointly evaluate the current situation and agree on how to proceed. Development of a vision may also be considered as a series of 'Time-outs' in which actors retract from the daily operations and reflect on the current mode of working and interacting, and speculating on the future, often in a dreaming and playfulness mood. A series of three to five, one-day Time-outs will normally take place in the course of three to five months.

An essential underlying idea is that managers and employees in a company or partners in a business network have ideas and capabilities to develop new solutions. However, they are rarely voiced explicitly, discussed jointly or brought into a unified context. Accordingly, a framework grounded on a collaborative dialogue is designed to capture actors' innovative ideas and knowledge about the present situation in their company. Placed in the right strategic perspective, such ideas and knowledge, in our experience, often have great innovative potential and therefore may contribute significantly to the survival of the company. A framework for development of a manufacturing vision has been developed and tested in several companies (Riis & Johansen, 2003). It consists of the following five phases:

1. *Initiation.* Staging and organizing the process, plus clarifying the starting point as well as the ambitions and scope of the process
2. *External trends and strategic challenges.* Creating a shared picture of the need to change, external trends and future strategic challenges of the enterprise
3. *Development of a manufacturing vision.* A collaborative dialogue-based process designed to capture managers' and employees' innovative ideas and knowledge
4. *Evaluation of the manufacturing vision.* Evaluation of ideas and elements of a manufacturing vision with respect to the strategic challenges defined, and an examination of the risks and resources associated with implementing the developed manufacturing vision
5. *Application and planning of the next steps.* Planning how to proceed by making use of the organizational momentum created, the potential strategic contribution of the manufacturing vision, and critical areas for designing a production system.

We have organized the development process as a mixture of intensive, one-day seminars and taskforce work. Up to 20 actors representing various stakeholders participate in the seminars directed towards divergent thinking to getting ideas of new directions and new solutions voiced and discussed in a constructive dialogue. No decisions are made at a seminar, but it may serve as a soundboard for assessing a detailed proposal presented by a taskforce. In contrast, a taskforce composed of a number of specialists is supposed to develop and combine the ideas and proposals from the seminars and to prepare one or two visions that are feasible from the point of view of the various disciplines and functions.

The process can be characterized as a gradual refinement process where resources in a continuous assessment process are canalized to clarify critical points in the strategy.

Two or three contrasting vision ideas. We have observed that participants in the development process experience a barrier lying in front of them when they are to develop the final vision. This is a creative, imaginative, explorative process that is very much different from the preceding analytical, systematic process. To overcome this barrier, we have proposed and experimented with the idea of pursuing a number of contrasting ideas that may eventually lead to two or three proposals of a vision. In this way, the decision point is postponed, and the contrasting vision ideas may give rise to a constructive discussion of pros and cons of each proposal.

This idea is very much in line with dialectic planning, proposed by Churchman (1970).

Switching between levels of abstraction. A vision represents an idea at a higher level of abstraction than the specific solution elements needed for actors to implement the vision. It is necessary to work with these two levels of abstraction, and we propose that the development process is formed as a switching back and forth between these levels. A vision idea may be evaluated at the abstract level; but only to a certain extent. Each actor needs to transform the overall ideas of the vision onto his/her own world in order to assess what it implies in terms of its technical feasibility and with respect to evaluating "what is in it for me".

A manufacturing vision ties in with other functional areas, such as product development, sales and marketing, and supply chain. It is our experience that the process of developing a manufacturing vision often challenges other areas to develop a vision for their function that may lead to an overall business vision. Also, a business vision may be initiated as a top-down process, and through involvement of functional areas this may lead to a coherent, substantiated set of visions.

Discussion

The process of developing a shared vision for a network may differ from that of a manufacturing vision in an industrial company. The five-step process presented above may still apply, but the organizational setting is different. In a network there is no hierarchical organizational structure, and the partners are tied together in a number of win-win relationships.

Inside-Out. We believe that neither a top-down nor a bottom-up approach may apply. Rather, an inside-out process may be more appropriate, to be understood as a circular and iterative process starting among one or a few kernel members of a network. By gradually involving more partners in for a discussion, a shared vision of the business idea of the network may emerge. The initiator or a kernel group may serve an orchestrator role (Shaw, 2008). Especially, when a new network is formed, the initial phases are often started with vague and lofty ideas that need coherence and substantiation.

The notion of a shared vision for a business network rests on the assumption that active participation of actors (nodes in the network) is a pre-requisite for obtaining their commitment and support. However, it does not imply that all actors should be involved from the very beginning. Several factors influence the decision of who should be involved, how and when, for example the question of mutual trust and confidentiality.

The development of a shared vision may be seen as a parallel process of dealing with business and technical matters, on the one hand, and addressing and developing personal relationships.

The ability to visualize the business idea plays an important role for actors to comprehend and evaluate the strength of the overall concept and the opportunity and demands on part of the individual actor. Development of a shared vision thus is a learning process in which loose ideas and wishful thinking gradually are transformed into business plans and detailed specification of individual roles. In this process actors should be given time to become familiar with their expected contributions and rewards.

Understanding the Mutual Interplay of Actors: Organizational Learning

As a business network is formed and start to function, a complex interaction between actors in the network and outside will evolve, partly guided by formal coordination processes. But actors will also react individually to incidents and behavior of other actors, which in turn may lead to new reactions from other actors; thus causing a chain reaction to emerge. Experience shows that very few actors, if any at all, have a comprehensive picture of this dynamic interplay.

This mutual interplay among actors (stakeholders) may be seen as a result of collective, tacit learning processes. Senge (1990) has adopted a systems dynamic approach to capture these dynamic processes, and Argyris (1993) has offered several examples of such self-exciting chains of behavior in organizations. Usually, organizational learning has a positive connotation and is used to discuss development of individual and collective knowledge and competencies, e.g. Nonaka & Takeuchi's model of learning as shifts between tacit and explicit knowledge (1995), and Kolb's identification of the key roles of reflection and experimentation (1984). But the informal, mutual adaptations that take place when individuals and organizational units interact support the position that organizational learning will take place whether they are intended or not. As the following case examples will illustrate, the mutual interplay often leads to undesired behavioral results, partly because each person or section does not know the consequences of their own action.

Observations in industrial companies indicate that managers and employees seldom have an overall picture of the mutual interaction between sections and departments. To find an explanation, we have used the Indian legend of the blind men and the elephant. Each man is holding on to a part of the elephant and is asked to explain what he believes this is. For good reasons they come up with different explanations; for instance the man touching the leg of the elephant may think that he is holding on to the trunk of a tree. Similarly, individuals in an industrial company develop their own set of experiences, and little effort is taken to explain that each of them is holding on to part of 'an elephant'.

Case Example: Different Experiences Lead to Different Learning

In an industrial company producing engineered equipment the sales department usually had to spend much time negotiation with a potential customer. However, most often the delivery date was not changed during the negotiations. So, when engineering design took over upon completion of a sales contract, the project was in a hurry. An internal delivery plan was prepared for engineering design, production, purchase, assembly and on-site assembly. However, engineering design took the time they felt was needed. First, when production and purchase had reminded them of the lateness of delivery, they speeded up their work. As a consequence, production and purchase, being late, had to improvise in order to meet the final delivery date, for example to outsource operations that would normally have been carried out in-house, moving assembly operations from in-house to being carried out on site, all of which resulted in extra costs. What had engineering design learned from this practice? They would tell that they do a pretty good job, and that production and assembly, even if they receive the data behind schedule, are capable of meeting the final delivery date. Engineering design had not been informed of the extra costs incurred; so viewed from their perspective it is possible to understand their "learning". As an outsider it is easy to point to the idea of providing engineering design with feed-back about the extra costs for each customer order as a means for stimulating their learning in another direction. The case example illustrates how sections and departments interact in such a way that nobody comprehends the overall interplay, often with consequences that are unintended.

Case Example: Two Customer Order Processes

A small engineering company developed in close cooperation with customers automated production cells. In view of future challenges, management wanted to involve key employees in improving the competitiveness. A Time-out workshop was organized during which the process of handling customer orders was discussed. For each step in the process, participants were asked to explain what they were doing, what was difficult, and how they related to the other functions.

For the first time participants in the workshop experienced an exposition of how the functions played together in carrying through a customer order. During the workshop, one participant noted that there were actually two types of customer orders, one requiring a great development effort and much interplay with customers, as the project truly had many development elements; the other type represented customer orders with structure and elements rather well known. Consequently, they would call for two different processes. For development orders many interactions between the various functions in the company should be organized, e.g. between sales, engineering design, purchase, production, and maintenance. The development of a novel conceptual solution was an order-winning criterion. With respect to the other type, a one-way street was envisioned for the customer order process, relying on many years of experience in specifying and developing engineered solutions.

The idea of having two customer order processes was further developed and made it easy for each participant in the processes to judge the necessary and timely effort needed. However, it took almost a year to fully implement the two processes, and another six months before a desired effect was achieved.

Methods for Capturing the Mutual Interplay

Several methods exist for giving people an understanding of how individual actions produce overall results. For example, the fishbone-diagram method has successfully been used at meetings for production units to identify cause-and-effect relationships for a given problem. It is simple to use and effective in drawing a map of potential causes structured in a number factors (men, machines, methods, management, etc.). However, it does not capture the interdependencies among the factors.

A problem matrix is another, rather simple method, but geared to disclose the mutual interplay between organizational units that have developed over time as a result of mutual adaptations (learning) processes (Riis, 1990). It often leads to identification of problem chains with self-exciting mechanisms (vicious circles). A problem matrix may be established at a half-day seminar with participants from all relevant organizational units. Each person, or group of persons, is asked to write down on poster cards the problems that he or she experiences in his (her) section. The cards are then placed on a wall or black board under each section and grouped according to the type of problem. Ordinarily we distinguish between problems imposed by other sections, internal problems, and problems exported to other sections.

Figure 22.1 shows a rather simple example of a problem matrix. It may be seen that the uncertain market causes sales to export uncertain forecasts to planning, which, in turn, make planning unable to meet delivery dates. Furthermore, planning cannot provide long term forecasts for purchase, resulting in an even poorer basis for making planning decisions. This leads to self-exciting problem chains. By adding arrows connecting corresponding exported and imposed problems, several problem chains may be identified, each of which provides a picture of the way in which problems experienced in the various sections are interacting. Following the seminar, further analysis should be carried out and may result in additional problem statements and the drawing of more arrows, cf. Johansen & Mitens (1986).

Types of problems	Sales	Design	Planning	Purchase
Imposed problems	Uncertain market		Poor basis for making decisions	Long lead times from suppliers
Internal problems	Insufficient knowledge of products		Deficient knowledge of products	
Exported problems	Uncertain forecasts	Unsystematic documentation	Unable to meet delivery dates	Unable to deliver raw materials

Fig. 22.1 An example of a problem matrix

Although very simple, the development of a problem matrix at a seminar has proven to be a powerful instrument for the creation of a common awareness and understanding of the often intricate mutual interaction. Most often individuals have come to realize that alone they are not able to solve essential problems disclosed in industrial enterprises, because of the complex nature. Our experience indicates that individuals appreciate the development of a problem matrix, because it provides a better understanding of the current pattern of interaction and a basis for a concerted effort to improve the overall performance.

Another way of creating an understanding of the current mutual interplay is to develop and apply a company-specific role playing game, cf. Riis, Smeds, and Nicholson (2003).

Discussion

As the case examples demonstrate, it is important to establish a transparent picture of the mutual interaction between partners in a business network in order that they can interpret the behavior of other partners in the light of the overall vision of the network, and subsequently can act accordingly. Without a widely accepted vision, adaptation processes between partners may lead to local optimization that in turn may result in self-exciting chain reactions that are counter-productive to the overall performance of the business network. Hence, the shared vision plays a key role for guiding the mutual adaptation (learning) processes.

On the other hand, any network will undergo changes and adjustments over time that may warrant adjustments in the shared vision. New employees may not be introduced to the history of the network and its original shared vision, and hence are left alone to interpret the interplay taking place between partners. External changes, for example in markets and technology, may lead to local adaptation processes that point in new directions and encourage a change in the overall vision. Hence, the development of a share vision and the mutual interplay between actors in a business network are interlinked and may support each other.

Implications and Conclusions

The paper has addressed two issues related to, respectively, the forming of a business network and its development. The first issue touched on the question of how to establish and maintain involvement of each partner in a business network, when partners are making complementary contributions that do not lend them to comparison on a single measurement scale. A coalition model from organization theory has been used in the area of industrial company development and project management to form a basis for stakeholder analysis and for developing a shared vision of the future of a company or network. The nature of stakeholder analysis and shared vision has been discussed, as well as means for working with these two topics.

As a contribution, the paper has provided an understanding of the organizational foundation of a business network, being formed on the basis of complementary interests and contributions. In addition, practical means were presented and discussed, drawing on a number of case studies. This insight may be used when a business network is formed and also later on during the life of the network, when external changes warrant an altered structure of actors' individual role.

The second issue focused on organizational learning taking place among partners of a business network. Special attention was given to collective, tacit learning stemming from the mutual interplay between partners. By way of two case studies it was shown that often unintended consequences emerge. Means for uncovering this mutual interplay between partners were discussed.

As a contribution to the second issue, the paper has provided insight into the mutual interplay of partners in a business network by drawing on organizational learning theories. Practical methods for dealing with the issue were discussed. As an implication, the paper has pointed out that it is not sufficient to develop a business idea of a new venture; partners (stakeholders) should also be brought on board, and their engagement should be maintained.

References

Argyris, C. (1993). *On organizational learning*. Cambridge, MA: Blackwell.

Churchman, C. W. (1970). *The design of inquiring systems*. New York: Basic Books.

D'Herbemont, O., & César, B. (1998). *Managing sensitive project*. London: MacMillan Press.

Dukovska-Popovska, I. (2006). *Development of manufacturing vision – Process and dialogue*. PhD dissertation. Aalborg: Aalborg University.

Freeman, E.R. (1984). *Strategic management – A stakeholder approach*. Boston, MA: Pitman Publishing Inc.

Fry, J.N., & Killing, J. P. (2000). *Strategic analysis and Action*. Scarborough, ON: Prentice Hall.

Johansen, J., & Mitens, L. (1986). *Methods for analysis and diagnosis of production management* (in Danish). Aalborg: Aalborg University.

Kim, W.C., & Mauborgne, R. (2005). *Blue ocean strategy*. Boston, MA: Harvard Business School Press.

Kolb, D. A. (1984). *Experimental learning*. London: Prentice-Hall.

Kotter, J. P. (1996). *Leading change*. Boston, MA: Harvard Business School Press.

Mikkelsen, H., & Riis, J. O. (2007). *Fundamentals of project management* (in Danish). Rungsted: Prodevo.

Nonaka, I., & Takeuchi, H. (1995). *The knowledge creating company – How Japanese companies create the dynamics of innovation*. New York: Oxford University Press.

Prahalad, C.K., & Hamel, G. (1990). The core competence of the corporation. *Harvard Business Review, 12*, 295–336.

Riis, J. O. (1990). The use of production management concepts in the design of production management systems. *Production Planning and Control, 1*(1), 45–52.

Riis, J. O., & Johansen, J. (2003). Developing a manufacturing vision. *Production Planning and Control, 14*(4), 327–337.

Riis, J. O., Smeds, R., & Nicholson, A. (Editors) (2003). *Interactive Learning in Production Management*. Proceedings of the 7th International Workshop on Experimental. Aalborg: Aalborg University.

Rytter, N. G. (2004). *Strategic development of production by concept development* (in Danish). PhD. Dissertation. Aalborg: Aalborg University.

Senge, P. (1990). *The fifth discipline*. London: Random House.

Simon, H. A., & March, J. G. (1958). *Organizations*. New York: Wiley.

Shaw, D. R. (2008). Why smart business networks continue and develop: a structural and processual model of 'value flows'. In P. H. M. Vervest, D. W. van Liere, & L. Zheng (Eds.) *The network experience – New value from smart business networks*. Berlin, Germany: Springer.

Williamson, O. (1979). Transaction cost economics: the governance of contractual relations. *Journal of Law and Economics, 22*(2), 233–261.

Womack, J. P., & Jones, D. T. (1996). *Learn Thinking*. New York: Simon & Schuster.

Index